Young People, Crime and Justice

In the minds of the general public, young people and crime are intrinsically linked; widespread belief persists that such activities are a result of the 'permissive 1960s' and the changing face of the traditional nuclear family. Roger Hopkins Burke challenges these preconceptions and offers a detailed and comprehensive introduction to youth crime and the subsequent response from the criminal justice system. This extended and fully updated new edition explores:

- the development of young people and attempts to educate, discipline, control and construct them;
- criminological explanations and empirical evidence of why young people become involved in criminality;
- the system established by the Youth Justice Board, its theoretical foundations, and the extent of its success;
- alternative approaches to youth justice around the globe and the apparent homogenisation throughout the neoliberal world.

The second edition also includes new chapters looking at youth justice in the wider context of social policy and comparative youth justice.

Young People, Crime and Justice is the perfect undergraduate critical introduction to the youth justice system, following a unique left-realist perspective while providing a balanced account of the critical criminology agenda, locating the practical working of the system in the critical socio-economic context. It is essential reading for students taking modules on youth crime, youth justice and contemporary social and criminal justice policy. Text features include chapter summaries, review questions and lists of further reading.

Roger Hopkins Burke is Principal Lecturer in Criminology in the Division of Sociology at Nottingham Trent University.

"An accessible, comprehensive text providing an up-to-date account of key issues in youth crime. A key strength is the reflective nature of the book which will engage the reader in understanding the complex study of young people, crime and justice."

Daniel Marshall, *Lecturer in Criminology,*
Anglia Ruskin University, UK

"This extended second edition of *Young People, Crime and Justice* brings the well-received first edition right up to date contextually, procedurally, politically and theoretically. Through his logical and comprehensive approach Roger Hopkins Burke brings clarity to the messy and contested areas of youth crime and justice without sacrificing detail. The author's logical approach, practical summaries and review questions ensures it will become standard issue to students of youth justice."

Jo Deakin, *Lecturer in Criminal Justice,*
University of Manchester, UK

Young People, Crime and Justice

Second edition

Roger Hopkins Burke

Routledge
Taylor & Francis Group

LONDON AND NEW YORK

First published 2016
by Routledge
2 Park Square, Milton Park, Abingdon, Oxon OX14 4RN

and by Routledge
711 Third Avenue, New York, NY 10017

Routledge is an imprint of the Taylor & Francis Group, an informa business

British Library Cataloguing-in-Publication Data
A catalogue record for this book is available from the British Library

Library of Congress Cataloging-in-Publication Data
Names: Burke, Roger Hopkins, author.
Title: Young people, crime and justice / by Roger Hopkins-Burke.
Description: 2nd edition. | Abingdon, Oxon ; New York, NY : Routledge,
    2016. | Includes bibliographical references and index.
Identifiers: LCCN 2015039170| ISBN 9781138776616 (hardback) |
    ISBN 9781138776623 (pbk.) | ISBN 9781315773100 (ebook)
Subjects: LCSH: Juvenile delinquency—Great Britain. | Juvenile justice,
    Administration of—Great Britain.
Classification: LCC HV9145.A5 B87 2016 | DDC 364.360941—dc23
LC record available at http://lccn.loc.gov/2015039170

ISBN: 978-1-138-77661-6 (hbk)
ISBN: 978-1-138-77662-3 (pbk)
ISBN: 978-1-315-77310-0 (ebk)

Typeset in Times New Roman
by Swales & Willis Ltd, Exeter, Devon, UK

Printed and bound in Great Britain by
TJ International Ltd, Padstow, Cornwall

For Tom and Oliver

Contents

Tables

Acknowledgements

I would like to thank those colleagues who have been supportive in rather difficult times for me. You know who you are. A special thanks to my boss Jason Pandya-Wood whose dynamism is remarkably inspirational. A very special thank you to my extremely talented sons, Tom and Oliver, who have helped keep me sane (well, 'ish') in the past few months and equally my two cats, Miles and Hendrix. Finally, thanks to the staff and production team at Routledge. You make these things possible.

1 Introduction

The problem of youth crime

Key issues

1 Measuring youth offending
2 The extent and nature of youth offending
3 Children, risk and crime: the On Track Youth Lifestyles Surveys
4 Structure of the book

Young people and crime have always been linked in the minds of the general public. Moreover, there are widely held common-sense notions that such activities are a relatively recent phenomenon and invariably an outcome of the 'permissive 1960s' and the breakdown of the traditional nuclear family that has occurred in the intervening years. It is also widely believed that in the past young people were orderly, disciplined, well behaved and law-abiding (Pearson 1983). Indeed, this has been a commonly held and extremely influential viewpoint which has had a considerable impact on political thinking and policy agendas.

The criminal behaviour of children and young people was to become a significant political issue in both the USA and the UK at the end of the twentieth century, with demands that if young people are prepared to break the law, they should also be prepared to take responsibility for their actions and this might well mean incarceration in the same institutions as adults. This is contrary to the dominant orthodoxy in both societies – and increasingly in the world beyond – throughout that century, that young people should be dealt with differently from their elders (Pitts 2003a).

These concerns about young people and their offending behaviour are, nevertheless, nothing new and they have reoccurred throughout history with a parallel erroneous assumption on the part of the public that things were always better in the past (Pearson 1983). Thus, for some, youth offending is little more than a recurring 'moral panic' – a notion which implies that the social reaction to a certain phenomenon is out of proportion to the scale of the problem (Young 1971; Cohen 1973) and is thus a relatively minor social problem where many, if not most children and young people, commit criminal offences, or acts of deviancy, which are part of a normal transition to adulthood. Left to their own devices they will simply grow out of such behaviour and become responsible, law-abiding citizens. For others, young people who offend are at risk of becoming persistent and serious offenders starting out on criminal careers which, without an appropriate and timely intervention in their lives, is likely to lead to them becoming the next generation of adult offenders readily equipped to inhabit the increasingly expanding prison estate. Interestingly, the number of young people entering the youth justice system as first-time offenders has decreased quite considerably during the past few years as we will see below. This finding suggests that either far fewer young people are indulging in illicit behaviour than was the case only a few years ago or something more ambiguous is happening. Calculating the extent of offending by children and young people is seriously problematic and crime statistics need to be considered with extreme caution.

Measuring youth offending

Statistical data about the prevalence of crime committed by children and young people are obtained from two main sources. First, there are the official crime statistics which consist of data compiled by the police and the courts and are routinely published by the Home Office as indices of the extent of crime; and second, there are self-reports which are a means of assessing the extent of crime by asking – in this case, children and young people – directly whether they are perpetrators. Each of these sources has their strengths but they also have significant shortcomings.

The most fundamental observation to be made about the official statistics is that they are both partial and socially constructed. Thus, for a criminal statistic to exist, a crime event has to be reported to the police by the public and this clearly does not happen in all cases for a variety of reasons (see Bottomley and Pease 1986). Moreover, even when an incident is reported to the police, it will not count as a crime unless it is recorded as such and again, there are a multitude of reasons why this might not happen (see Walker 1983). Changes in patterns of law enforcement – and thus what is to be regarded as criminal and recordable as such – make it very difficult to compare levels of youth criminality during different time periods. Muncie (1999a: 17–18) observes that:

> Self-evidently, changes in legislation and in the number of arrests and sentences do not represent actual changes in the amount of crime, but changes in the capacity of the criminal justice system to process individual cases. More police and prisons coupled with the political will and resources to support law enforcement have an infinite ability to increase the amount of recorded crime.

The converse could also be true, less police and cutbacks in the criminal justice system alongside a political will (or perhaps a lack of it) not to pursue crime could lead to a reduction in recorded crime and could help explain the reduction in first-time entrants into the youth justice system that we consider below.

Self-report studies have been widely used for over half a century to gain a more accurate picture of both the prevalence of criminality and exactly why people become involved. They also have significant shortcomings. First, they depend on the willingness of those being interviewed to admit their 'criminality' to researchers. Second, they are invariably administered through the use of questionnaires which have a notoriously low completion rate, in particular, among ethnic minority groups (Coleman and Moynihan 1996). Third, they tend to ignore some significant hidden crimes such as domestic violence which includes crimes against children.

Self-report studies have tended to confirm the notion that a great many young people have committed a crime at some point in their lives and that involvement in criminality is in some way part of a normal transition to adulthood. Belson (1975) found in his earlier study of London schoolboys that 98 per cent admitted offences of some kind, with 70 per cent having stolen from a shop. Rutter and Giller (1983), in a large-scale review of self-report studies, produced similar findings. A decade later Anderson et al. (1994) found – in a study of young people conducted in Edinburgh – that two-thirds admitted to having committed a crime during the previous nine months.

Three influential reports during the mid-1990s found offending by children and young people to be extremely widespread and expensive to society. First, a study conducted for the Home Office supported the evidence of previous research and showed that one in two males and one in three females aged between 14 and 25 years admitted to having committed a criminal offence, with a similar ratio admitting the use of illegal drugs (Graham and Bowling 1995). Second, the Audit Commission Report *Misspent Youth: Young People and Crime* (Audit Commission 1996) estimated that people under 18 years of age committed seven million offences a year against individuals, retailers and manufacturers, with public services spending over £1 billion a year in response to offending by this age. Third, NACRO (1998) estimated the average response cost in dealing with one individual to be around £52,000 (made up of prosecution, incarceration and supervision costs as well as family intervention and care). The direct cost of offending to the community was found to average around £22,700 per young offender. In short, these three influential reports found that many young people commit criminal offences at a great cost to society and this recognition was considered indicative of a significant social problem worthy of rigorous government intervention.

The costs of youth offending to the economy should nevertheless be put into some context. For example, it has been estimated that in the USA the economic losses from various white-collar crimes are about ten times those from 'ordinary' economic crime (Conklin 1977), with corporate crime killing and maiming more than any violence committed by the poor or the young (Liazos 1972). Corporate crime has received little publicity in the mass media – in contrast to often low-level offences committed by young people – unless there has been fraud on a massive scale. Examples in the UK include the collapse of the investment managers Barlow Clowes in 1998, which left 17,000 small investors owed a total of

£200 million; the Guinness-Distillers Affair of 1990; the disclosure in 1991 that the late Robert Maxwell had appropriated £500 million from his employee's pension fund; and the collapse of Asdil Nadir's 'Polly Peck' empire in 1993 with the disappearance of £450 million. The latter subsequently jumped bail and fled the country (S. Jones 2001). Croall (1992, 2001) observes that the activities of the corporate criminal are not only greater in impact than those of the ordinary offender, but also longer-lasting in effect. The view taken in this book is that offending behaviour by children and young people is still a highly significant issue which requires a rigorous and appropriate intervention where this is deemed both *necessary* and *appropriate*.

It is very important to recognise that young offenders are not a homogenous group and this is a key theme in this book. The great majority of young people who commit offences do so infrequently and are predominantly responsible for less serious property crimes. It is this group that tends to grow out of their offending behaviour at a relatively young age, which can be diverted from their activities by a warning from the authorities while they are extremely unlikely to become regular drug users. It is also very likely that many grow out of both offending and drug-taking activities without any criminal justice intervention at all, although this is very hard to quantify. The influential Audit Commission report (1996) readily acknowledged that the great majority of young people who offend do so infrequently, but at the same time, noted the existence of a substantially more problematic, small hard core of persistent offenders who apparently fail to respond to attempts to divert them from their activities and who are responsible for a disproportionate amount of crime. Research conducted by the Home Office found that about 3 per cent of young offenders aged 14–25 commit 22 per cent of youth crime (Flood-Page et al. 2000) with 0.2 per cent of males having made six or more court appearances by age 17 and accounting for 28 per cent of the total for that age group (Home Office 2001). Crimes committed ranged from minor anti-social behaviour to more serious offending.

Defining a persistent young offender

The Home Office (1997) defines a persistent young offender as:

> A young person aged 10–17 years who has been sentenced by any criminal court in the UK on three or more occasions for one or more recordable offences and within three years of the last sentencing occasion is subsequently arrested or has information laid against him for further recordable offence.

The Youth Lifestyles Survey – which was conducted in England and Wales between October 1998 and January 1999 – offers a simpler alternative definition of a persistent young offender 'as someone who, in the last year, had committed three or more offences' (Campbell and Harrington 2000). Among those aged 12–17 who fitted into this category, the survey found that 23 per cent had been sanctioned (cautioned or taken to court) in the previous twelve months (24 per cent of male and 21 per cent of female persistent offenders). Younger persistent offenders – those under the age of 18 – were more likely to have been sanctioned (23 per cent) than those who were older (14 per cent). This finding could be explained because they had committed more offences – the average number of offences committed by persistent offenders under 18 was five compared to four for those aged 18 to 30 – or because younger offenders tend to commit more commonly detected offences (e.g., criminal damage or shoplifting) whereas older persistent offenders are more involved in fraud and theft from the workplace, which are less likely to result in sanction or even detection. With this recognition, the whole notion of 'growing out of crime' is itself suspect.

There are significant methodological issues which make it impossible to both accurately estimate the full extent of current persistent or non-persistent offending behaviour and legitimately compare it with any other time period (Campbell and Harrington 2000). Thus, those who are not caught by the police – or those who receive informal warnings rather than recorded cautions – are not included in the crime figure. Low police clear-up rates suggest that many offences and offenders go undetected and the published figures are thus serious underestimations of the true extent of crime. Moreover, policies that have been introduced at different times to divert young offenders from the criminal justice system – through measures such as informal cautions – will have the effect of reducing the number sanctioned and who are therefore recorded in the crime statistics. These observations need to be borne in mind when we now consider the most recent youth justice statistics for England and Wales (Youth Justice Board/Ministry of Justice, 2015).[1]

The extent and nature of youth offending

The statistics considered in this section are based on the flow of young people through the Youth Justice System (YJS) from 1 April 2013 to 31 March 2014 and are collected from a number of official agencies.

Gateway to the youth justice system

In 2012/13, there were 126,809 arrests of young people (aged 10–17) for notifiable offences, which accounted for 11.8 per cent of the total number arrested. Young people accounted for 10.5 per cent of the offending age population (i.e., those aged 10 and over) which suggests that this group is over-represented in the criminal justice system.

The following year – 2013/14 – there were 25,625 youth cautions given to young people in England and Wales, which was a decrease of 17 per cent on the 30,739 given the previous year, and a decrease of 73 per cent on the 96,381 given ten years previously in 2003/04. There were 400 Penalty Notices for Disorder given to 16–17-year-olds in 2013/14 and in 2013 there were 277 Anti-Social Behaviour Orders (ASBOs) given to young people.

First-time entrants to the youth justice system

In 2013/14, there were 61,053 offences committed by young people (aged 10–17) who had at least one offence that resulted in a youth caution or conviction. Of these 22,393 (37 per cent) were first offences, and the rest were further offences. Ten years previously, in 2003/04, there were 185,478 offences committed by young people, with 48 per cent being first offences. Since 2012/13, the number of first-time entrants has fallen by 20 per cent from 28,059 to 22,393 in 2013/14 – continuing the downward trend that has occurred since the 2006/07 peak. The number of first-time entrants has fallen by 75 per cent since 2003/04 and by 51 per cent since 2010/11. In 2013/14, 76 per cent of first-time entrants had a youth caution, compared with 89 per cent in 2003/04.

Characteristics of those in the youth justice system

A total of 41,569 young people received a substantive outcome in 2013/14 which was a reduction of 16 per cent from 49,222 the previous year. Overall, 81 per cent were male, and 78 per cent aged over 15 years. Most (75 per cent) came from a white ethnic background. There were 42,596 young people who had first or further offences resulting in a caution or conviction in 2013/14, which was a 20 per cent reduction from the 53,337 the previous year.

Proven offences by young people

There were 90,769 offences for which a young person was convicted in 2013/14, down by 8 per cent from the previous year and this figure has reduced by 68 per cent in the ten years since 2003/04. The main offence types for which young people were convicted in 2013/14 were: violence against the person (22 per cent), theft and handling (18 per cent) and criminal damage (11 per cent).

Young people sentenced

In 2013/14 there were 45,891 young people proceeded against at magistrates' courts, a fall of 21 per cent on the number in the previous year and following the downward trend seen since 2002/03. A total of 33,916 young people were found guilty at courts in 2013/14 with 33,902 sentenced, a fall of 23 per cent from the 43,903 the previous year. The number sentenced to immediate custody fell by 21 per cent, from 2,815 in 2012/13 to 2,226 in 2013/14, a fall of 65 per cent in the ten years since 2003/04, when 6,288 young people were sentenced to immediate custody.

Use of remand for young people

There were 20,953 remand episodes given by the courts for young people in 2013/14, which represents a decrease of 8 per cent on the previous year. Remand decisions that involved young people being bailed (conditional or unconditional bail) accounted for

85 per cent of all sentencing occasions where there was a substantive remand episode. There were a further 6 per cent of remand episodes where a young person was remanded in the community, including remand to local authority accommodation. Nine per cent of remand episodes involved young people being remanded to custody (1,930 remand episodes).

The average population in custody on remand in 2013/14 was 260 young people, accounting for 21 per cent of the average custodial population, compared with 26 per cent in 2010/11 when the average population in custody on remand was 528. While the overall number of young people in custody has fallen by 21 per cent between 2012/13 and 2013/14, the number on remand has fallen by 23 per cent. For those young people remanded to custody in 2013/14, 62 per cent were not given a custodial outcome following their remand. Of these, 25 per cent were acquitted and 37 per cent were given other court convictions.

Young people in custody

The average population in custody (under 18) in 2013/14 was 1,216, which represents a decline of 21 per cent from an average of 1,544 the previous year, while the average population in custody (under 18) has fallen by 56 per cent from 2,771 ten years previously in 2003/04. The average population in 2013/14 (including 18 year olds held in custody in the youth secure estate) was 1,318. This is a 23 per cent reduction on the figure the previous year, which was 1,708.

Proven re-offending by young people

In the twelve months ending March 2013, there were 52,648 young people who were given a reprimand or warning, convicted at court (excluding immediate custodial sentences) or released from custody. Of that cohort, 18,998 committed a proven re-offence within a year. This gives a one-year re-offending rate of 36.1 per cent with the young people committing an average of three offences each – 56,779 offences in total. The rate of re-offending by young people rose by 0.6 percentage points compared with the previous year and by 2.7 percentage point compared with 2002. The number of young people in the re-offending cohort has nevertheless gone down every year since 2007/08: with a reduction of 25 per cent compared with 2011/12, and a 61 per cent reduction compared with 2002.

Criminal histories of young people

In 2013/14, 82 per cent of young people sentenced for indictable offences had previous cautions or convictions, with 18 per cent of these being first-time entrants to the youth justice system. The proportion sentenced to custody who were first-time offenders was 8 per cent, a proportion which has fluctuated between 5 and 8 per cent in the ten years since 2003/04. Some 65 per cent of young people cautioned for indictable offences had no previous cautions or convictions.

Comparisons with the adult system

Young people (aged 10–17) accounted for 13 per cent of first-time entrants to the criminal justice system in 2013/14. Adults (18 and over) thus accounted for 87 per cent. Young people sentenced for indictable offences accounted for 7 per cent of the total court sentences, young adults (18–20) for 9 per cent and the remaining 84 per cent were adults (aged 21 and over). Young people in custody accounted for 1 per cent of the total custody population in June 2014. In 2012/13 the proportion of people who re-offended was highest for young people aged 10–17, with a re-offending rate of 36.1 per cent; young adults (18–20) 30.0 per cent, adults (21 and over) had a rate of 24.2 per cent. Young people accounted for 26 per cent (sixty-eight offences) of the total offences involving threatening with a knife or offensive weapon in 2013/14.

The most significant finding from this brief review of the statistics of young people in the youth justice system is the recognition that there has been a significant decline in recent years – in particular over the past decade – in the number of young people entering the system. This should thus be borne in mind when we consider the findings of a significant self-report study published ten years previously (Home Office 2005b) but we should note that many of the children in the cohort would have been of the appropriate age for entry to the youth justice system during the time period we have just considered.

Children, risk and crime: the On Track Youth Lifestyles Surveys

The On Track Youth Lifestyles Surveys were undertaken as part of the National Evaluation of the On Track multiple intervention programme which targeted 4- to 12-year-olds and their families in twenty-four high-deprivation/high-crime areas within England and Wales, with the aim of reducing the risk of children offending and becoming involved in anti-social behaviour as well as enhancing those pro-social factors that counteract the impact of risk.

Problem behaviour

From the responses to the Secondary School Survey, nine main types of problem behaviour were identified which fell into two broad categories: (a) substance use, which includes use of alcohol, tobacco, and drugs; (b) anti-social and offending behaviour, which includes stealing, receiving stolen property, attacking someone, carrying a knife to school, and vandalism. A ninth problem behaviour was identified as truancy. Exclusion from school was not identified in this study as a problem behaviour because it represents an action taken towards the child rather than his or her behaviour.

Substance use

Alcohol use was common among all groups (61 per cent overall) except children of Pakistani background (3 per cent). Smoking was more common among girls

(19 per cent) than boys (12 per cent). Drug use was significantly higher among older children (24 per cent of Year 10/11) and children of mixed black/white background (21 per cent).

Anti-social and offending behaviours

Self-reports of stealing in the previous twelve months dramatically increased with age (19 per cent in Year 7 compared with 34 per cent in Year 10/11). Thirty-nine per cent of the mixed black/white group reported stealing in the last twelve months compared to 12 per cent of the Asian group. The percentage of 'looked after' children (42 per cent) reporting stealing was nearly double that reported by those living with two birth parents (23 per cent). There was only a small difference in the proportion of boys (29 per cent) reporting stealing compared with girls (25 per cent). Self-reports pointed to less likelihood of receiving stolen property than stealing, which may indicate lesser involvement in more generalised criminal activity.

Fourteen per cent of the sample reported attacking someone with the intention of hurting them in the previous twelve months. Boys (19 per cent) were more than twice as likely as girls (8 per cent) to say that they had attacked someone and the likelihood of doing so increased with age. There were also differences between ethnic groups; for example, 10 ten per cent and 13 per cent of Indian and Pakistani children respectively reported an attack on another person compared to 18 per cent of Bangladeshi children. A high proportion of 'looked after' children reported attacking someone (21 per cent). There were considerable differences between boys' (15 per cent) and girls' (4 per cent) self-reports of carrying a knife. The percentage of children carrying a knife to school almost doubles between Year 7 (6 per cent) and Year 10/11 (12 per cent). A much higher proportion of 'looked after' children (21 per cent) reported carrying a knife to school than children in other family types. Girls (32 per cent) were as likely to commit acts of vandalism as boys (33 per cent) and the likelihood of doing so increased considerably with age (from 20 per cent of children in Year 7 to 40 per cent in Year 10/11). Forty per cent of the mixed black/white group reported having vandalised property, double that reported by the Asian group.

Exclusion from school and truancy

Boys (17 per cent) were twice as likely as girls (8 per cent) to have been excluded from secondary school during the previous twelve months with the difference even more pronounced at primary school (boys 12 per cent, girls 1 per cent). Differences in school exclusion by ethnicity were also pronounced with nearly double the proportion of black (20 per cent) and mixed black/white (20 per cent) compared to white children (12 per cent) reporting exclusion from secondary school. Within the white group, white Irish reported the highest level overall for the different ethnic groups (26 per cent). There were also very high reports by 'looked after' children (32 per cent) of exclusion from their secondary schools.

Although some overlap between truancy and school exclusion certainly exists, reports of truancy overwhelmingly exceeded reports of school exclusion, suggesting that only a small proportion of truants were displaying behaviour serious enough to lead to their exclusion from school. There was very little difference between secondary school girls (16 per cent) and boys (18 per cent) reporting truancy during the previous four weeks, although differences between girls (4 per cent) and boys (12 per cent) were much more marked at primary school. At secondary school a much higher proportion of children from the mixed black/white group (23 per cent) had truanted in the previous four weeks than children from other ethnic groups. Although only 13 per cent of the Asian group reported truanting, within this group truancy among Bangladeshi children reached 22 per cent. These figures are likely to be underestimates as a proportion of truants and excluded children will not have been in school at the time of the survey.

The extent of problem behaviour

To identify the extent of the involvement of young people in problem behaviour, combinations of nine problem behaviours were considered: alcohol use, smoking, substance abuse, stealing, receiving stolen property, attacking somebody, carrying a knife, vandalism and truancy from school.

Eighty-one per cent of secondary school children reported involvement in three or fewer problem behaviours. However, higher proportions of children of mixed black/white and white background reported combinations of four or more problem behaviours than did children from other ethnicities. Age was a key factor in the level of problem behaviour with those reporting between four and nine problem behaviours increasing from 10 per cent in Year 7 to 30 per cent in Year 10/11.

Problem behaviour and offending

A general measure of offending (based on responses to the questions on stealing, receiving stolen property, attacking someone, carrying a knife to school and vandalism) together with sub-measures of property crime, attacking someone and vandalism were constructed from responses to the questionnaire. Responses on these measures were compared with self-reports of being found guilty of a crime.

Overall, 52 per cent of secondary school children reported involvement in offending with little difference between boys and girls (55 per cent of boys and 49 per cent of girls) admitting they had committed an offence in the last twelve months. The most frequent types of self-reported offending were vandalism (32 per cent) and stealing (27 per cent) with the gender distributions fairly similar. Boys (26 per cent) were more likely to admit to receiving stolen property than girls (16 per cent) and they were more likely to commit the less commonly reported types of crime. Thus, 19 per cent of boys had attacked someone in the last twelve months compared with 8 per cent of girls and 15 per cent of boys had carried a knife to school in the last twelve months but only 4 per cent of girls had

Risk on the availability of drugs increases over the school years from 13 per cent high risk in Year 7 to 52 per cent in Year 10/11, by which age few children (9 per cent) display no risk. Mixed white/black Caribbean children present highest levels of risk on availability of drugs (44 per cent high risk) followed by white/black African (38 per cent) and black Caribbean (37 per cent).

Individual/peer domain

A high proportion of respondents in secondary school (76 per cent) reported having friends who are involved in problem behaviour, 38 per cent at the high-risk level. Sixty-six per cent of respondents indicated that they held conflictual attitudes towards others, with 14 per cent at the level of high risk.

The majority of children (58 per cent) present some attitudes condoning problem behaviour, 21 per cent at the level of high risk with no difference between boys and girls. Children become more accepting of problem behaviour as they get older: 41 per cent have moderate or high risk in Year 7 rising to 74 per cent in Year 10/11.

Risk, protection and offending behaviours

The detailed analysis of the contribution of risk and protection factors to different types of offending reveals that offending is not a homogenous activity. Protective factors did not emerge from the study as making a significant contribution to less offending but the analysis confirmed the importance of risk factors, highlighting that different risks come into play for different types of offending. Five key results were found that could be used as the basis of a preventive strategy.

First, the most commonly reported types of offending by secondary school pupils were vandalism, stealing and receiving stolen property with the biggest contributory factors to all of these offences being (i) high risk on the involvement of friends in problem behaviour and (ii) high risk on holding conflictual attitudes. High risk on these factors were found to at least double and sometimes quadruple the odds of being involved in those common offences.

Second, although risk factors in the family domain do contribute to the likelihood of children offending, they are nevertheless lower than the risk factors in other domains, which suggests that the domains of community and particularly individual/peer are more important for criminality among secondary school pupils.

Third, most children who admitted some kind of offending have friends who also offend. There is thus a very strong social component too much offending by children that has often not been recognised in traditional crime prevention and reduction programmes, suggesting that it might be more appropriate to work with friendship groups rather than individuals.

Fourth, community disorganisation and neglect had the third highest overall levels of risk (27 per cent assessed as high risk) and made a contribution to several types of offending independently of other community risk factors, which suggests that interventions are extended to include the fabric of the neighbourhoods.

Fifth, offending related to motor vehicles is an activity that particularly appeals to boys, and although admitted by less than 10 per cent of respondents, being a boy was found to be the most important contributory factor to theft of a car and theft from a car. Being male was also a contributory factor in attacking someone, admitted by 14 per cent of respondents, where it more than doubles the odds. There was an even more significant contribution to carrying a knife to school, an activity reported by just 10 per cent of respondents and where boys had odds of almost five times the girls of admitting this.

We will return to all these themes throughout this book, at which point these findings should be reconsidered.

The purpose and structure of this book

This book provides a comprehensive and contemporary discussion of the relationship between young people and crime and the nature of the youth justice response. It is the second significantly updated and expanded edition of a book which was originally published in 2008 and covers the syllabus for the vast majority of contemporary university juvenile justice and young people and crime undergraduate courses (as with the previous edition) while at the same time expanding the parameters of debate in an accessible fashion. Moreover, it does four things that other texts in the area do not necessarily do. First, most undergraduate juvenile texts are underpinned by at least an *implicit* critical criminology 'hey system leave those kids alone and they will grow out it' approach. This text broadly follows a left realist perspective developed elsewhere by the author which recognises the need to deal with the problematic actions of individuals and the conditions which encourage those behaviours not least for the good of the young person involved. The text is thus compatible with contemporary youth justice system orthodoxy but, at the same time, it is far from uncritical; not least because the socio-economic context in which the system has to operate has deteriorated significantly since the heady days in which it was created during the last years of the twentieth century. Interestingly, the resistance of critical criminology to the contemporary youth justice system introduced by New Labour – via the Youth Justice Board and youth offending teams – has now been replaced in some quarters by an enthusiasm for preserving it, albeit in a revised form.

Second, the critical criminology agenda is not simply dismissed by this text, which provides a balanced account and recognises the validity of the observations made from that perspective and indeed its compatibility with other viewpoints. The empirical recognition that most children or young people 'offend' in some way, not least because of the seductions of crime and the pleasures and the normality of participation (e.g., recreational drug use) are readily acknowledged in the author's concept of 'the schizophrenia of crime', which recognises that while involvement in offending behaviour – of some kind – is virtually universal in society, there is at the same time a widespread popular commitment to law and order discourse from the very same people.

Third, it is recognised that involvement in offending behaviour is for many a merely transitional stage in life to a later predominantly law-abiding and materially satisfactory existence. Indeed, as we have seen above, there have been large reductions in the number of young people entering the criminal justice system during the past few years. However, for a small minority of young people (between 3 and 4 per cent), offending remains a real problem that needs a rigorous intervention for their own good, albeit as part of a much wider social policy strategy. Without that intervention, the young person faces a life of social exclusion, offending and raising a further generation in their own image. Indeed, there is no evidence of a significant reduction in this hard-core category during the past few years. While this in itself is not a revolutionary acknowledgement, the observation that the contemporary system might, perhaps suitably adjusted, provide the basis for a radical and successful intervention has been rather unorthodox in academic youth justice circles. Thus, the critique of the system presented in this proposed text does not commence from the orthodox critical criminology standpoint that it could not possibly work. It takes the opposite position that it could work if implemented properly by those with a commitment to its success. In short, this text like the first edition, locates the practical working of the contemporary youth justice system in the critical socio-economic context – no other text does this.

The first part of the book, 'Young people, criminality and criminal justice', traces the development of young people from their social construction as children and adolescents, considers attempts to educate, discipline, control and construct them in the interests of a myriad different interest groups, not least industrial capitalism, and examines their deviance, 'offending behaviour' and the consequential societal response from the beginnings of industrial modernity, via the morally certain modern era at its most confident, to the present-day morally uncertain, fragmented, non-confident modernity or postmodern condition.

Chapter 2, 'Children, young people and modernity', discusses the social construction of childhood and youth, industrialisation, modernity and the essential requirement for the first time in the history of humanity for an abundant fit and healthy population. The process of discipline, industrial schools, reformatories and more generic educative methods that came to construct this population as functional, or essential, for the needs of industrial society.

Chapter 3, 'From justice to welfare and its malcontents', tells the story of juvenile justice from its inception, and its gradual transition from a justice model with unequivocal theoretical foundations in the rational actor model of crime and criminal behaviour, to the triumph of a fatally flawed welfarism with its theoretical foundations in both the predestined and victimised actor models, and epitomised by the Children and Young Persons Act 1969. The chapter concludes by considering the apparent failure of welfarism – or at least its unintended consequences – and the crucial issue of net-widening that brought into the parameters of a newly expanded well-meaning criminal justice system a whole raft of previously non-problematic young people.

Chapter 4, 'Youth justice and the new conservatism', discusses the ambiguous story of juvenile justice during the Conservative administrations 1979–97 with 'short, sharp shocks', bifurcation, diversionary schemes, with significantly (to liberal/left/critical criminologists at the time) substantial reduction in the youth prison population but, at the same time, a parallel growth in social exclusion and poverty for a substantial minority, termed by this author the 'excluded tutelage' model of youth justice.

Chapter 5, 'New Labour and the Youth Justice Board', considers the election of New Labour, its ambitions, the Crime and Disorder Act 1998, the establishment of the Youth Justice Board (YJB), youth offending teams (YOTS) and the foundations of the 'reintegrative tutelage' model of youth justice. The chapter considers the origins, rationale, intended purpose in terms of its left realist origins and the wider context of risk society/analysis and the 'what works' agenda. It considers the extent and limitations of youth justice successes in this period and ends with the election of the Coalition government in 2010.

Chapter 6, 'Theorising the development of youth justice', concludes the first part of the book by discussing four models of criminal justice development introduced briefly in the first edition of the book and developed elsewhere by this author. These models provide four different, apparently competing, but ultimately compatible explanations of the development of the juvenile justice system and in whose interest this all occurred.

The second part of the book, 'Explaining offending behaviour by children and young people', considers the various criminological explanations – and the relevant empirical evidence to support these – of why it is that these groups can get involved in criminality. Chapter 7, 'Youth offending as rational behaviour', considers rational actor model theories which propose that criminal behaviour is very much like any other activity with involvement simply a matter of choice. While it has long been recognised that children and young people are incapable of making the same rational decisions as adults, the rational actor model has, nevertheless, undergone a revival during the past thirty years and it is now recognised that rationality can be 'bounded' or limited and thus young people do make decisions which are rational for them but in the context of the life circumstances in which they find themselves. The contemporary youth justice system has significantly come to incorporate notions from this revised variant of the rational actor model, not least in the proposition that young people should take responsibility for their actions.

The theories discussed in the following three chapters are fundamentally underpinned by the predestined actor model, which proposes that criminal behaviour is to be explained in terms of factors – either internal or external to the human being – that cause or determine them to act in ways over which they have little or no control.

Chapter 8, 'Biological explanations of youth crime', thus considers first those theories that propose that offending by children and young people is simply a product of some physiological defect which has been inherited from their biological predecessors; followed by two contemporary variants, altered biological states which considers alcohol and drug use as being the instigations or accentuations of offending behaviour, and socio-biological theories which propose that biological predispositions are triggered in very different ways in different environmental conditions often dependent on the socialised upbringing of the young person.

Chapter 9, 'Psychological explanations of youth crime', examines those theories which consider youth offending behaviour to be the product of a criminal personality or mind. First, there is the influential psychodynamic approach with its roots in the notion of psychosexual development, which leads us to latent delinquency theory, maternal deprivation theory, child-rearing practices and 'broken family' theories. Second, behavioural learning theories propose that offenders subconsciously learn and develop abnormal, inadequate, or specifically criminal personalities or personality traits that differentiate them from non-offenders and which can be isolated and measured and their offending behaviour predicted. Third, cognitive theories propose that behaviour is learned through watching what happens to other people and then making choices to behave; an approach that moves psychology away from its roots in the predestined actor model to incorporate notions of choice from the rational actor model.

Chapter 10, 'Sociological explanations of youth crime', considers theories where offending is attributed in some way to the social environment in which the young person grows up. Earlier versions clearly have their foundations in the predestined actor model and propose that offending behaviour is transmitted to others – and later generations – by frequent contact with criminal traditions which have developed over time in disorganised urban areas. Subsequent anomie or strain theories propose that most members of society share a common value system that teaches us both the things we should strive for in life and the approved way in which we can achieve them; however, without reasonable access to the socially approved means, people will attempt to find alternative ways, including criminality, to resolve the societal pressure to achieve. Delinquent subculture theories develop anomie theory further by observing that lower-class values serve to create young male behaviours that are delinquent by middle-class standards but which are both normal and useful in the social context in which these young people find themselves. Thus, youth offending is considered a consequence of the efforts of lower-class youth to attain goals and respect valued within their own subcultural social world. From this perspective, offending behaviour by young people in gangs and subcultures is simply 'cool' and enables the individual to gain appropriate respect from their peers. Matza (1964) subsequently provides an influential link with the non-determinist tradition by noting that young people are capable of making rational choices but these are limited by structural constraints, and thus provides an explanation as to why it is that most young offenders 'grow out' of offending not least because most of them had little commitment to deviancy in the first place and they no longer consider involvement to be 'cool'. Social control theories provide a significant explanatory component within the contemporary youth justice system and are based on the fundamental assumption that criminal acts take place when an individual has weakened or broken bonds with society. Later researchers have sought to integrate control theory with other perspectives such as anomie, labelling, social learning, subcultural and control theories.

Later sociological theories can be at least partially located in the victimised actor model, which proposes that offenders are themselves the victims of an unjust and unequal society which targets and criminalises the behaviour and activities of disadvantaged sections of society. Thus, the labelling tradition proposes that no behaviour is inherently deviant or criminal, but only comes to be considered so when others label it as such. Hence, being found out and stigmatised may encourage an individual to become involved in further deviance and seek solace from others so involved. Conflict and radical criminologists have developed the labelling thesis to draw our attention to the capacity for powerful groups to make laws to their advantage and to the disadvantage of the poor; while critical criminologists have more recently revitalised that tradition by observing that it is members of the less powerful social groups who are the most likely to suffer the weight of oppressive social relations.

Left realism is an eclectic perspective with strong sociological theoretical foundations which recognises that many criminological theories have – at least some – validity in the appropriate circumstances. It is recognised that crime is a real problem that seriously impinges on the quality of life of many poor people and that it must be challenged and a comprehensive solution to the crime problem or a 'balance of intervention' is thus proposed. On the one hand, crime must be tackled and offenders are required to take some responsibility for their actions; on the other hand, the social conditions that encourage crime must also be confronted. It is this approach that was very influential with 'New' Labour governments in the UK and is fundamental to the contemporary youth justice system.

The third part of the book, 'The contemporary youth justice system and its critics', will consider the system established by the Youth Justice Board (i.e., the work of youth offending teams), the theoretical foundations, a critique of that system and the extent of its success.

Chapter 11, 'The Coalition, the Big Society and youth justice policy', considers the worldwide economic crash of 2008, the subsequent electoral demise of New Labour and the Coalition between the Conservatives and the Liberal Democrats. There follows a discussion of the debates both in favour and in opposition to the proposed abolition of the Youth Justice Board and its survival in a rather emasculated form in the Ministry of Justice; and an examination of the Big Society, the Conservatives charity-driven version of communitarianism, its wider social policy, criminal justice and, more specifically, youth justice policy. The chapter finishes with the demise of New Labour and the arrival of the Coalition.

Chapter 12, 'The contemporary youth justice system', introduces and examines the parameters of the contemporary youth justice system and the concerns of academics and other commentators at the outset and in the aftermath of its establishment. Thus concerns are identified relating to the speedy establishment of a new system which involved a self-acknowledged rupture with the previous juvenile justice system that was perceived to have failed, with its apparent successes now seemingly ignored. The chapter concludes with a critical and reflective discussion of the large decline in the number of children and young people entering the youth justice system and questions whether this is an accurate reflection of the number currently engaging in offending behaviour

Chapter 13, 'Effective youth justice in practice', considers the operation of the contemporary youth justice system with its foundations in effective and evidence-based practice. There is thus an examination of the role and significance of identified key areas of effective practice in a multi-agency youth justice system with the central aim of reducing youth offending. First, assessment, planning and supervision are all considered essential elements of practice with young people at all stages of the youth justice system and guide and shape all work conducted within the system. Second, the likelihood of individual children and young people becoming involved in offending behaviour has been crucially linked to the number of risk factors present in their lives and the key areas of effective practice for identifying and responding to these risk and protective factors are seen to be parenting, education, training and employment, substance misuse and mental health problems. A third category addresses the lives of apprehended young offenders and thus offender behaviour programmes which have been shown to make a significant contribution to reducing criminality, neighbourhood prevention schemes targeted at young people living in areas of high deprivation and criminal activity, restorative justice interventions which seek the integration of the young person back into mainstream society, intensive supervision and surveillance programmes which target that small minority of offenders who are responsible for a disproportionately large number of offences, remand management and settlement services which exist primarily to divert appropriate young people from unnecessary custodial remands and to manage those awaiting trial or sentence, and resettlement which in an ideal world would include the cessation of – or at least reduced – offending and engagement in employment, education or training activities on release from a custodial sentence.

The fourth part of the book, 'Alternative youth justice systems and the contemporary world', considers alternative approaches to youth justice elsewhere in the world and the apparent convergences and policy transfers that have led to a process of apparent homogenisation throughout the neoliberal world.

Chapter 14, 'Youth justice in wider context', discusses youth justice in a wider socio-economic social policy context and discusses significant contemporary issues affecting children and young people: (1) governance and social control; (2) young people and (un)employment; (3) homelessness and the benefit system; and (4) social exclusion. In doing so, there is a revisiting and reflection on a number of key issues in this book: risk-based contemporary youth justice, social exclusion and reintegrative tutelage and restorative justice. The chapter concludes with a discussion of youth social exclusion in an era of austerity and Loïc Wacquant and the government of insecurity – the criminalisation of a social policy thesis.

Chapter 15, 'Comparative youth justice', considers the globalisation of youth justice and the different approaches/strategies in place in different parts of the world, policy transfers and convergences in strategies utilised in different societies worldwide in neoliberal-dominated developed societies. Crucial relevant issues are discussed such as the complexities of youth justice reform in various societies which demonstrate that neoliberal hegemony is mediated by local conditions and cultures.

Chapter 16, 'Conclusions: the future of youth justice', reflects on some of the key issues introduced in this book and reflects on some of the possible alternative futures available to youth justice both in the UK and internationally before a reconsideration of communitarian political philosophy. The chapter concludes by outlining the theoretical basis of radical moral communitarianism and its policy implications for children and young people who offend.

Summary of main points

1   Young people and crime have always been linked together in the minds of the general public with this becoming a significant political issue at the end of the twentieth century.
2   The number of young people entering the youth justice system as first-time offenders has decreased quite considerably during the past few years, although calculating the extent of offending by this group is seriously problematic.
3   Official statistics are both partial and socially constructed.
4   Self-report studies have been widely used for over half a century to gain a more accurate picture of both the prevalence of criminality and exactly why people become involved.
5   Self-report studies tend to confirm that a great many young people have committed a crime at some point in their lives as part of a normal transition to adulthood.
6   The great majority of young people who commit offences do so infrequently, are predominantly responsible for less serious property crimes and tend to grow out of their offending behaviour at a relatively young age.
7   Research has shown that a small hard core of persistent offenders are responsible for a disproportionate amount of crime.
8   Children and young people are very likely to have been the victims of bullying or crime.
9   This book provides a comprehensive and contemporary discussion of the relationship between young people and crime and the nature of the youth justice response.
10   It locates the practical working of the contemporary youth justice system in a critical socio-economic context.

Discussion questions

1   Are public concerns about offending by children and young people a recent phenomenon?
2   How we know the extent of offending by children and young people?
3   Do you think that there has been a significant decrease in the extent of offending by children and young people in recent years?
4   What are the key characteristics of persistent young offenders?
5   What is the social group most likely to have been a victim of crime?

Note

1 The data come from various sources including the Home Office (HO), Ministry of Justice (MoJ), youth offending teams (YOTs) and youth secure estate providers. The report is produced by the Analysis team and the Information team in the Youth Justice Board (YJB) under the direction of the chief statistician in the MoJ.

Part I

Young people, criminality and criminal justice

2 Children, young people and modernity

Key issues

1 The emergence and consolidation of modern societies
2 The social control of childhood and adolescence
3 Young people, social control and discipline
4 The centrality of parenting
5 Reflections on the century of the child

The first part of this book traces the social construction[1] of young people in the modern era in terms of the concepts of childhood and adolescence and examines the strategies that were introduced to educate, discipline and control this increasingly important section of the population – ultimately in the interests of a capitalist economy and its agents – and it then proceeds to trace the history of what was to become a specialist juvenile justice system designed to deal with those individuals who came to deviate from, and transgress against, the legal and social norms established by the child tutelage strategies of modern society.

This chapter discusses the child tutelage strategies employed by which children and young people came to be constructed as an important and essential element of the population during the period of industrial modernity. For it was with the emergence of the modern era that there came for the first time in history a requirement for an ample, fit, healthy, increasingly educated and skilled but always obedient population. We will start by considering how modern societies differed from their pre-modern societies and how the role, status and behavioural requirements of young people were to be significantly different from those in the previous socio-economic era. This is an important analysis because it helps us to establish the reality that the lives of both the young and the old, what they might expect from life, and what is required from them is always closely linked to the requirements of the economy. This is a significant point to which we will return throughout this book.

The emergence and consolidation of modern societies

In pre-modern societies, the role and the status of children and young people were ambiguous and because of the nature of the pre-industrial capitalist economy, they were of little significance or importance and often a drain on limited material resources. It was a world where a large population was invariably a disadvantage rather than an advantage. It was, nevertheless, a situation that was to be significantly reversed with the emergence of modern industrial societies where for the first time in history an abundant, fit, healthy populace was to become essential.

Pre-modern societies were predominantly rural and agrarian, with the great majority of people living a virtual subsistence existence in the countryside where any significant increase in population would put an enormous pressure on very limited resources, with the outcome being periodic famine and starvation. Thomas Malthus (1959) had famously argued during the nineteenth century that, if unchecked, the population would grow geometrically while, at the same time, agricultural product would increase only arithmetically. Disaster, it was argued, had only been averted by the three periodical population controls of famine, plague and war and, therefore, in such a world children – or more accurately, little people – were of little intrinsic value to society and invariably an economic liability.

Malthus was a political economist and was concerned with what he perceived to be the decline of living conditions in an England which was becoming rapidly industrialised and urbanised with consistently appalling living conditions for the vast majority of poor working people who had emigrated to the new towns and cities from the countryside. Malthus blamed this decline on three elements: first, the now overproduction of children; second, the consequential inability of resources to keep up with the fast-growing human population; and, third, the irresponsibility of the lower classes in producing this unsustainable populace. He therefore proposed that the family size of the lower classes should be regulated so that the poor did not produce more children than they could support.

But modern industrial societies were fundamentally different from their predecessors and required an ever-increasing population and Malthus was unappreciative of this new reality. In this new world, children were now an asset and increasingly they were to be nurtured, pampered and disciplined in the interests of a society that needed them. A discussion of the processes by which children and adolescents were to be constructed as a significant component of society needs thus to be located in the context of the transition from pre-modern, medieval, invariably feudal societies to industrialised modern societies. It will be worthwhile, therefore, to reflect first on the ways in which these societies significantly differed.

'Modernity' or 'modernism' are terms used to describe the development of a secular, scientifically rational, increasingly industrialised and urban tradition with its origins in the seventeenth-century scientific revolution and the eighteenth-century philosophical Enlightenment and which had come to replace the previous feudal and medieval tradition in Western Europe. The principal defining features of subsequent mature modern societies can be identified in the areas of economics, politics and culture (Hopkins Burke 1998b, 2005). Economically, there was the development of a market economy with the growth of production for profit rather than the predominantly immediate local use that had characterised subsistence-existence rural communities. Wage labour now became the principal form of employment with the development of industrial technology and the extension of the division of labour and specialisation, although poor people were significantly to lose their long-term rights to land that they had in feudal societies. Politically, there was to be the growth and consolidation of the centralised nation state with formalised boundaries and frontiers, the growth and extension of state institutions with their bureaucratic forms of administration and myriad officials, ever-increasing systematic forms of surveillance and control and the development of representative democracy and political party systems. Culturally, there was a challenge to the previously dominant local folk traditions in the name of rationality, which stressed the virtues of scientific and technical knowledge as being superior to any other form (see Harvey 1989; Nelken 1994; Morrison 1995; Hopkins Burke 1999a).

Modern societies are mass societies characterised by mass production and consumption, corporate capital, organised labour and, importantly, an extensive large demand for workers (Harvey 1989; Hopkins Burke 1999a, 2001). In such societies, a fast-growing population is essential and crucial to a successful industrial economy and in such changed circumstances, children and young people were now seen as important economic assets because they would grow up to be the next generation of productive workers – or indeed military personnel – on which the economic strength and defence of the modern state was to become heavily dependent. There were to be, nevertheless, frequently reoccurring concerns about the quality of that population with a corresponding increasing demand for state intervention in the rearing and socialisation of young people, not least when their behaviour was problematic, or indeed criminal. The discussion continues by examining the increasing and varied attempts to control and shape that young population and, indeed, to ensure that their parents carried out their duty to socialise a compliant, disciplined, obedient and law-abiding populace which was appropriate to the needs of the economy.

The social control of childhood and adolescence

The way childhood is viewed today in the twenty-first century is very much the product of modern societies and modernist modes of thought. In pre-modern times childhood had not been seen as a distinct period of development in the way it is now (Aries 1962). Young children dressed like adults were viewed in the same way as their elders and participated fully in adult life, including the drinking of alcohol (Aries 1962; Hoyles and Evans 1989). Moreover, in the pre-modern era, the child mortality rate often exceeded 75 per cent during the first five years of life (Hoyles and Evans 1989) and it would have made very little sense to have developed emotional attachments to your children in the way we do today, let alone start making plans for their future.

Our modern conception of childhood began to develop in Western Europe during the sixteenth century with the emergence of a small recognisable middle class and its demand for a formalised education for its sons (Aries 1962). Previously, the apprenticeship system had been the main form of education and preparation for adult life had involved children from all social groups being sent into the homes of other families of equal social status. The idea of education now began to embrace formal schooling, a shift that reflected increasing attachment to the child, with middle-class parents choosing to keep their children close to them (Aries 1962; Hoyles and Evans 1989). Furthermore, during the eighteenth century, the contemporary conception of a house emerged and became established among the wealthier classes with the establishment of separate and specialised rooms (Aries 1962) and it was at this time that the child came to be seen as an irreplaceable and unique individual, the centre of the family and who started to assume great importance in society (Hoyles and Evans 1989). It is important to recognise nevertheless that this evolution in the concept of childhood occurred mainly in the statistically tiny upper and middle classes. The poor – who made up the substantial proportion of the population – continued to live like medieval families into the early nineteenth century (Aries 1962). However, it was these newly emergent middle-class attitudes to childhood that were to provide the dominant template of acceptable – and increasingly enforceable – child socialisation from the nineteenth century onwards.

Muller (1973), a Canadian academic but with an analysis still appropriate to generic Western European society, argues that the development of our modern conception of childhood – and thus the increasingly compulsory introduction of bourgeois childrearing socialisation mores into the lower social classes – can be divided into four phases, each distinguished by trends in birth and death rates. The first identified phase – which had clear foundations in pre-modern socio-economic conditions and values – was to end around 1750 with the beginnings of mass industrialisation and urbanisation. It was a period when birth and death rates were both very high but quite similar, with the outcome being a reasonably stable population size. Thus, with a high rate of childhood mortality and an average life expectancy of only 25 years, children were seen as fragile, easily replaceable, and of little importance (Muller 1973; Hoyles and Evans 1989). Childhood was merely a necessary evil on the way to productive adulthood.

The second phase encompassed the period between 1750 (the beginnings of the Industrial Revolution) and the final triumph of industrial capitalism and urbanisation around 1880, when infant mortality dropped drastically without a corresponding drop in the birth rate, with the outcome being the population boom which was to so concern Malthus.[2] This rise in population combined with rapid industrialisation and urban expansion was largely responsible for the widespread use of child labour. Children were simply a cheap, plentiful and available source of labour and were often small enough to perform jobs that full-grown adults could not, such as crawling under machines to repair them. Societal support for child labour, moreover, spread far beyond the obvious interests of entrepreneurial, capitalist mill and mine owners. As late as 1866, the International Alliance of Workers – an early prototype trade union organisation – proclaimed child labour to be 'a legitimate and logical step forward . . . In a rational society, every child over the age of nine years should be a productive worker' (cited in Muller 1973: 6).

The third phase was the period 1880 to 1930, which saw the birth rate go down and, at that time, children came to assume central importance in the family of all social classes. The French Enlightenment philosopher Jean-Jacques Rousseau had proposed childhood to be a desirable state of innocence and had argued that society needed to protect the child against adult corruption and although this idea had begun to gain in popularity among the upper and middle classes during the late eighteenth century, it was during this third phase that the idea crossed class boundaries and became significant in the socialisation of the mass of working-class children (Muller 1973). Several factors were important in this process of transition and the often-enforced introduction of bourgeois child socialisation mores into a sometimes resistant working class. First, with the arrival of compulsory education and the raising of the minimum age of employment, children began to be financial burdens on their parents rather than sources of income. Second, with increasing urbanisation, the family lost its status as an economic unit that produced food and other necessary commodities and took on the role of a consumer. Third, with the decline in the birth rate, there was a reduction in the size of families. Not only were fewer children being born but extended family households were becoming less common. Children of all social classes now came to assume a central place in the family; they had much more contact with their parents and became increasingly dependent upon them to provide the necessities of life. Increased contact nevertheless meant more discipline and punishment, as the idea that children were innocent but easily corrupted grew in popularity. In general, children were expensive but emotionally invaluable because they were seen as an avenue for upward mobility and a guarantee that their parents would be taken care of later in life. The idea that the family should not only be held responsible for the appropriate socialisation and discipline of their children but also to be considered responsible when the child deviated from enforced social mores and transgressed against the rules of society became increasingly accepted during this period.

The fourth phase is the period from 1930 to the present day and is also child-centred but in a different way from the previous phase. The contemporary goal is care, understanding, and respect for the needs of the child, rather than the needs of the parents but if this all goes wrong and the child socialisation process fails to deliver an acceptable product, then the parents become increasingly responsible and – certainly since the introduction of the contemporary youth justice system post-1998 – accountable for that failure.

We have thus seen that childhood, since its 'discovery' in the seventeenth century, has been increasingly viewed as a time of innocence and dependence, when protection, training and appropriate socialisation are paramount. Youth, in contrast, is expected to be an age of deviance, disruption and wickedness (Brown 1998) and this expectation has been strongly linked to the historical discovery of the pseudo-scientific notion of adolescence. Many researchers (Gillis 1974; Hendrick 1990a, 1990b; Jenks 1996; Brown 1998) follow Aries (1962) and argue that adolescence was 'discovered' during the Victorian era and from that time onwards it became identified as a cause of delinquency (Gillis 1974: 171). Prior to that time, when there was little differentiation between children and adults, the problem of youth or adolescent offending simply could not exist.

It was the rapid growth of industrial modernity in the early nineteenth century – at the same time as the emerging distinction between child and adult – that led eventually to fewer young people in the workplace and, with more spare time on their hands, they took to hanging out together on the streets. The social construction of the notions of adolescence, acceptable youthful behaviour, juvenile delinquency or 'hooliganism' (see Pearson 1983) became increasingly apparent from that time onwards. The social commentators of the time had their own middle-class conceptions of what should constitute acceptable youthful behaviour and the incremental criminalisation of working-class youth began as early as 1815 with the creation of the Society for Investigating the Causes of the Alarming Increase of Juvenile Delinquency in the Metropolis (Pinchbeck and Hewitt 1981; Muncie 1999a).

Hendrick (1990b) discusses the emergence of the social and scientific term 'adolescence' that was constructed by the professional middle classes in accordance with the work of the child study movement and especially the highly influential G. Stanley Hall, who described this stage of development in biologically determinist terms as one of 'storm and stress' in which instability and fluctuation were normal and to be expected (Hall 1905, cited in Hendrick 1990b). Hall ominously based his notion of 'normal adolescent demeanour' on the 'unspontaneous, conformist and confident' white middle-class youths he observed and it was this model that was soon to be prescribed as desirable for young people of all social classes (Griffin 1997). Thus, the marginalisation of whole cross-sections of young people – especially, the working class, girls and ethnic minority groups – became implicit with the social construction of a notion of adolescence acceptable to middle-class sensibilities.[3] Although theories of 'delinquency' were to broaden their approach during the twentieth century, the ways in which adolescence is conceived remain heavily influenced by the 'storm and stress' model (Newburn 2002b).

A historical perspective on youth justice is essential in helping us understand contemporary perceptions of offending by children and young people. Throughout history we can find references to the escalating problems of youth crime (West 1967; Pearson 1983). Moreover, we can trace historical debates and discourses surrounding the nature of youth crime and political solutions which are remarkably similar to contemporary political debates. Historical studies show us that fears about the rising trends in youth crime are repeated throughout British social history with the present continuously compared unfavourably with the halcyon days of the past, thus signalling a moral decline (Humphries 1981; Pearson 1983). While these studies also inform the reader that this golden age, where youth was unproblematic, has never actually existed, it is a conclusion that does not appear to be widely recognised or understood by either the general public or their political representatives.

Young people, social control and discipline

Our discussion to date suggests that the concepts of childhood and adolescence appear to have emerged with the rise of industrial modernity and the capitalist system of production (Thane 1981), although no simple relationship between the two can be identified (Springhall 1986). Within pre-industrial European economies, children were working in the home – or around it – by about the age of 4 or 5 and were thus quickly absorbed into the productive process and would mix with adults in both work and social situations (Pollock 1983). They were thus easily subject to adult control and discipline. As the middle and upper classes came to understand childhood as a time of innocence and preparation for adulthood, the technical demands of the economy produced the need for ever-longer periods of training and apprenticeship. Children and young people, therefore, came increasingly to spend time in their own company and with their peers on the street while decreasingly being under the control and tutelage of their elders. We have here the origins of the contemporary notions of 'peer group' pressure and the formation of the deviant youth subcultures that are so central to legitimate explanations of youth offending in the late twentieth century and beyond and which we explore in detail in the second part of this book. It is, moreover, with the growing concerns about the behaviour of youths on the streets of Victorian England that we see the creation of a range of interventions and legislation aimed at the discipline and tutelage of working-class youth in the image of middle-class sensibilities and ensuring that they are fit for purpose in a capitalist industrial economy. The concept of adolescence was to be central to this process of tutelage.

The development of compulsory schooling and changes in the economy were, therefore, the two interlinked elements crucial to the widespread application of the concept of adolescence to working-class young people (Walvin 1982), the outcome being the creation of a time of delay and discontinuity which could be seen as a peculiar property of youth. Throughout the nineteenth century, schooling expanded – first in voluntary and then, following the 1870 Education Act, in state schools. By 1893 the school leaving age was 11 and by 1899 it had risen to 12. Compulsory schooling combined with efforts to enforce attendance had a considerable impact: first, children were pulled off the streets and the problem of their control was transferred to the classroom (Humphries 1981); second, they had their access to the symbols and material benefits of adult economic life postponed, while their importance to the labour market became marginal.[4]

The outcome was a 'moral panic' prompted by the large numbers of children and young people on the streets (Pearson 1983), a situation that was made worse in the last decade of the nineteenth century by a major economic recession which led to widespread unemployment among all age groups. At the same time, the accuracy of national statistics concerning juvenile crime improved substantially and these changes were mistakenly used as evidence of a massive increase in crime. The outcome was increased action taken against certain types of visible 'crime' on the streets – for example, drunkenness, gambling, malicious mischief, loitering, begging and dangerous play – which criminalised further groups of young people (Muncie 1984: 40).

At the same time, young women were observed to be involved in a street problem of a different kind with prostitution – often involving children – flourishing in the larger cities and towns. There was consequently widespread public demand for the resultant legislative response, the Criminal Law Amendment Act 1885, which increased the age of sexual consent to 16 and this has remained so to this day. A significant motivation for involvement in prostitution was clearly the appalling social and financial position of many working-class families and the limited economic opportunities available to working-class young women themselves.

A number of middle-class women were also worried about the conditions faced by young women in domestic service, the factories and sweated labour shops. Still others were appalled by the experiences of young women in the domestic home where a large number worked hard for many hours a day looking after their families and hidden from the public eye. They did not, however, pose the openly visible problem presented by young men because they had always been controlled and supervised in the home (Nava 1984). Home life was nevertheless undergoing a process of restructuring. The separation of the home from work, the changing rhythms of working life and the demands for different forms of skill all had an impact upon the shape of household life. Some of the changes were consciously promoted by the middle class, who through their economic and political power were able to influence significantly the shape of, and power relations within, the family, and their ideals and beliefs came to dominate nineteenth-century legislation and ideology (Gittins 1985).

Gittins observes that this was not just a family, but a gender ideology, and part of a careful and deliberate attempt to reorganise the relations between the sexes according to bourgeois norms and values. These changes affected both the way in which young men and women experienced these institutions and how young people were perceived by adults, or at least by middle-class adults. The outcome was that young men and women were both now viewed as problematic and they had to be fitted into the new social and industrial order that the reformers wanted. Those who were undisciplined, dangerously independent and precocious were a matter of grave concern (Hendrick 1986). The family was thus to play its part, with women undertaking the major productive role therein and providing the conditions for the activities of men in the world while providing a reserve army of labour, to be called upon as and when the economy required their services.

Central to the changed nature of the experiences of youth were developments in the nature of leisure provision, which by the second half of the nineteenth century had begun to take a form we would recognise today. Cunningham (1980) identified four factors which influenced this development. First, there were the market forces of supply and demand where in response to the growing relative affluence of the working class there developed a considerable commercial sector which included the growth of various forms of variety theatres and 'penny gaffs', public houses, travel opportunities, such as day excursions, popular literature, such as the 'penny dreadfuls', and sports of various kinds. Second, these market forces were modified by the attachment of the working class to forms of leisure created in the first half of the nineteenth century, and before, which included loyalty to various games and sports and to the public house. Third, there was increased provision by government and charity organisations in the name of 'rational recreation', which had led to the spread of public parks, libraries, wash houses and museums. Fourth, there were growing concerns about the dangers of leisure that were expressed in calls to control various activities including some in the home.

The middle class already had a degree of control over the working-class experience of employment, schooling and other forms of incarceration, including hospitals, poor houses and prisons, with considerable effort expended in an attempt to cultivate correct attitudes and behaviour within the churches. What appeared to elude the middle class was any influence over the private world of the working-class home and the 'dangerous' pastimes enjoyed therein. There was widespread abhorrence of 'brutal' sports, cheap entertainments, drinking and gambling, all of which were seen to be ungodly, as posing a threat to social order and as a reflection of the moral failure of the working classes. Leisure was simply that dangerous time between leaving work and going to bed when many of the worst fears of the middle classes about the working-class young were readily apparent and were therefore to be singled out for attention (Hendrick 1986). At the same time, there was considerable growing concern about working-class unrest and political activity.

The growth of working-class political organisation was seen by many in the middle class as heralding a period of intensified class conflict, with socialism perceived as a threat to stability (Simon 1965). Crucially, it can be argued that something akin to a remaking of the working class – based on solidarity and organisational strength – took place in the years between 1870 and 1900 (Stedman Jones 1984) and these developments indicate a transformation in the central forms of working-class activity, and the dangers were not lost upon the middle class, with young people being seen as particularly susceptible to the appeals of extremism (Rosenthal 1986).

There were also concerns about the ability of Britain to maintain the empire and it was argued that this had particular implications for domestic stability and wealth (Ramdin 1987: 63) while the South African war of the 1890s revealed the poor physical condition of young working-class recruits, where over a third of volunteers were not fit for military duty (Springhall 1977: 14). Moreover, there was the emergence of other industrial and trading nations – in particular the USA and Germany – and the possibility of 'economic defeat'. There was, therefore, a demand for state and voluntary welfare measures designed to increase 'national efficiency' among influential social groups who previously had been hostile or indifferent to social issues (Thane 1982: 61).

Middle-class reformers already had access to common-sense explanations of the problems faced by young people but there now appeared scientific justifications to explain why they lacked the potential for intellectual and emotional development. Dyhouse (1981) observes that the concept of adolescence provided a significant means by which a pathological picture of working-class young people could be sustained. Significantly, the way in which a number of behaviours were attributed to a phase of physiological and psychological development helped to shift attention away from material inequality as a way of explaining the position of young people. Juvenile delinquency thus came to be explained as the 'natural attribute of adolescence' and the terms a 'lack of parental guidance' combined with 'troublesome adolescence' were to remain the dominant form of explaining youth offending until at least the 1950s.

It was, nevertheless, working-class adolescents, in particular, who were thought to be the most likely to display delinquent and rebellious characteristics during this 'storm and stress' period in the life cycle because it was widely assumed that their parents exercised inadequate control over their brutal adolescent instincts (Humphries 1981). The new concept of 'adolescence' was, therefore, considerably enhanced by the efforts of psychologists and those who saw it as their duty – or job – to intervene in the lives of young people and who now had a suitable vocabulary of scientific terms with which to carry forward their intentions.

Equipped with the new language of social science – and stimulated by fears of social disruption and imperial decline – significant elements of the expanding newly affluent middle classes devoted time and energy to charitable work (Stedman Jones 1984). Much of this charitable effort was centred in the large cities where there was a significant middle-class presence in close proximity to the forms of deprivation and 'problems' that so alarmed their sensibilities. London, especially the East End, became the site for many forms of philanthropic intervention. The composition of the middle class in London was skewed towards professions such as law, medicine, the church, the military and the civil service, groups which were of considerable importance in determining the formation of characteristic attitudes towards the problem of poverty. The absence of substantial, direct economic links between these particular groupings of the rich and the poor – as, for example, between employer and employee – can be seen as explaining the importance of charitable activity in London, 'both as a mode of interpreting the behaviour of the poor and as a means of attempting to control them' (Stedman Jones 1984: 240).

There does appear to be something of a change of attitude among key groups to the notion of intervention, particularly in the case of the 'casual poor'. The London dock strike of 1889 and the riots three years previously, along with the concerns already outlined earlier, provoked the 'intellectual assault which began to be mounted against laissez faire both from the right and the left in the 1880s' (Stedman Jones 1984: 297). Nevertheless, while the extent of government action concerning perceived social problems undoubtedly increased from 1870 to 1900, it was limited when compared with the demands for action and the nature of the problems themselves. The state, both local and central, was envisaged as providing a 'safety net', a net which operated to a large extent through the Poor Law. Beyond this there were incursions into welfare, such as in education, but by and large such works were to be left to voluntary organisations and it was thus in the 1880s that the first 'youth organisation', the Young Men's Christian Association (YMCA), began to make a mass impact (Simon 1965).

From the mid-nineteenth century, youth work came to assume many guises, although with the passing of the Education Act 1870 and the gradual introduction of other welfare legislation, there was a significant shift in style and emphasis. With schools apparently now offering basic instruction and other agencies material and welfare assistance, many clubs and youth organisations turned overwhelmingly to 'the inculcation of intangible social and spiritual values amongst their clients rather than in improving their material well-being' (Jeffs 1979: 4). Youth work can therefore be understood not as an effort to further the natural intellectual development of the individual but as a means of producing subjectivity (Donald 1985). The problem was how young people were to be attracted by the sponsors and workers to these places of improvement in their 'own' time. The answer to that conundrum was to be recreation, that is, in return for an opportunity for some amusement, young people would have to submit themselves for 'improvement' and if they were to be 'improved', then they would have to be taken out of the home, off the street, or away from any other environment that contributed to that which was offensive to middle-class values. The two apparently antagonistic elements of amusement and improvement were eventually to come together in the notion of 'improving amusement' with, for example, many of the London boys' clubs putting the emphasis on sport (Simon 1965).

The effectiveness of the new youth provision was, however, somewhat limited. For a while clubs sought to exploit the demand for recreation among working-class adolescents and, at the same time, subtly combine the provision of sport with the sponsorship of conservative ideology, they did not necessarily attract large numbers (White 1980). There was simply resistance among many working-class young people to the various attempts to improve them (Dawes 1975; White 1980).

Other more structured forms of intervention with young people were, nevertheless, emerging during the 1880s. The Boys' Brigade was the first to mix drill, athleticism and the wearing of a uniform, and it was later followed by a number of similar organisations during the last decade of the nineteenth century, with the outdoor healthiness and social imperialism of scouting appearing in the following decade. Blanch (1979) proposes three main strands of nationalist attitudes which link these early male organisations and demonstrate their significance for the bourgeois child tutelage project. First, there was the idea of national efficiency in the drive to mental and physical fitness which was rooted in drill and discipline. Second, there was the idea of model authority, for within these organisations we find a highly organised hierarchical system of authority by ranks and levels and it was seen by their proponents as providing a model for social organisation and leadership. Third, there was the 'enemy outside'.

Young people at least knew what they were joining and what was expected of them. There was some resistance to drill, military manoeuvres and uniforms but members were attracted by sport, the band and the annual camp (Humphries 1981). Furthermore, there were significant differences between the Boys' Brigades and the Scouts. From the outset, the latter were independent of any particular religious organisation and they utilised a rather different concept of discipline (seen as an inner quality, rather than something that had to be externally drilled) (Jeffs 1979).

These organisations nevertheless failed to reform the behaviour and attitudes of those who the reformers saw as 'being at risk', namely the working-class young. First, the uniformed organisations were predominantly pre-adolescent. Second, the majority of working-class young people were in effect excluded from such organisations either because of the cost of membership and their uniforms or because it was alien to their culture (Springhall 1977). Third, there was resistance from a significant proportion of those who did join. Nevertheless, to some extent, such youth movements did allow the assimilation of upper-working-class and lower-middle-class boys into the new social order (Springhall 1977).

Those young men who wanted to advance within the existing socio-economic system were therefore provided with a means of preparing themselves in a way which was acceptable to those who presided over entry into desired jobs and social organisations. Those who did not wish to advance on these terms could at least be offered some recreation in the hope of containment. Work with girls and young women nevertheless tended to emphasise a different type of 'getting on', and suggests there were serious limits to this process. It was feared that the involvement of young women in the labour market and, consequently, their acquisition of independent spending power, would tempt girls away from their allotted roles of wife and mother. If young women were 'upwardly aspiring', then what such organisations could provide them with was an experience in the 'womanly arts' so that they might influence their men (Dyhouse 1981).

The middle-class improvers could, however, only offer a limited social mobility between classes for both young men and women. They supported and operated within a capitalist socio-economic system which required a particular division of labour with a predominant need for manual labour and would have considerable difficulties in accommodating large numbers of young people wanting significant advancement. While the rhetoric of individual achievement came easy, it had to be contained within particular class, gender, racial and age structures. The place of a woman was in the home; to be British was to be best, 'betters' were to be honoured and youth had to earn advancement and to wait its turn.

Much early youth work was directed at young people in the same class as the providers but the organisations were themselves controlled by members of the middle class who carried with them specific themes – in particular an attack on working-class cultures – and developed forms recognisable in present-day practice and sought to engage the services of particular 'types' of adult. In this respect they had much in common with the notions of rational recreation that formed the initial development of the working men's clubs (Jeffs and Smith 1988).

The middle class that was so prominent in the above accounts of the subtle – and sometimes not quite so subtle – control, discipline and tutelage of young people was itself the product of a socio-economic system with its own dynamic. Many of the concerns that were expressed by the early sponsors of youth work were reflections of the requirements of the economic system but the relationship between the latter and the nature of intervention is ambiguous (Jeffs and Smith 1988). At one level, many of the efforts of the 'improvers' were directed at the containment and reformation of elements of the system, yet, without doubt, these early workers and philanthropists were sincere in their belief that they were acting in the best interests of the young, and that the values and institutions they saw threatened were there for the good of all rather than the benefit of the few. Their viewpoint was nevertheless formed within a particular social class which in turn was both the creation and the beneficiary of capitalism. Similarly, the organisations they created had to act within that system and inevitably took on the values and ways of operating which made sense within that system. In particular, because youth organisations were, and still are, in the market economy, they have to respond to its dynamics much like commercial operations (Jeffs and Smith 1988). Those advocating rational recreation and improvement were thus in competition for the bodies and minds of the young people with commercial forms of entertainment, in particular, the public house and the music hall.

Youth work could be clearly located as part of the nineteenth-century bourgeois child tutelage project. First, it aimed to assist with the maintenance and development of the social and economic order envisaged by key members of the middle class. Second, it adopted and confirmed distinctively bourgeois forms and values which were often drawn from the experience of public schooling and military service or represented paradigms of middle-class leisure. Indeed, the notion of adolescence as it was articulated – and as we have seen – was largely a bourgeois construction. Third, it acted to alleviate middle-class consciences by enabling them to feel they were doing something about the worst excesses of capitalism. The very fact that they were providing help, and others were defined as not, also allowed them to justify their pre-eminent position. Fraser (1973) argues that it was both a way of confirming superiority and status and of receiving thanks and gratitude. Lastly, this work provided a range of opportunities for 'meaningful' endeavour for those members of the middle class who were denied entry or were unable to enter both the labour market and the representative political arena.

The social control, discipline and tutelage of working-class children and adolescents was, therefore, a significant strategy of middle-class 'moral entrepreneurs' (see Becker 1963) sometimes working consciously in bourgeois or capitalist interests but invariably unaware of the real significance of their work. Increasingly central to much of this work was the surveillance and training of parents to ensure that they carried out the requirements of the tutelage project.

The centrality of parenting

The emphasis on parenting in the contemporary youth justice system that we will encounter in the third part of this book is again nothing new. The notion that 'the family' is in 'crisis', and/or that parents are 'failing', comprises a 'cyclical phenomenon with a very long history' (Day-Sclater and Piper 2000: 135), and the 'parenting theme' (Gelsthorpe 1999) has enjoyed, and continues to enjoy, a certain prominence within debates surrounding youth crime and youth justice. Indeed, the 'improper conduct of parents' was identified as one of the 'principal causes' of 'juvenile delinquency' by the Committee for Investigating the Causes of the Alarming Increase of Juvenile Delinquency in the Metropolis 1816, which was the first public inquiry into youth crime. The committee proposed that 'neglect of parental authority', 'improper conduct', 'disproportionate severity', 'undue indulgence', 'permitting absence from school', 'weakness', 'laxity of morals' and other 'parenting deficits' combined to 'cause delinquency' (Goldson and Jamieson 2002: 83).

This influential discourse was developed and consolidated throughout the nineteenth century and beyond as it accumulated an increasingly 'scientific' support. In the 1850s a Parliamentary Select Committee on 'Criminal and Destitute Juveniles' reported that no parent should be allowed to bring up a child 'in such a way as to almost secure his becoming a criminal' (cited in May 1973: 111). Moreover, Mary Carpenter, an extremely influential moral entrepreneur of the time, defined a threefold classification of 'delinquency' within which the notion of 'inadequate' parenting was unequivocally stated:

> The first class consists of daring, hardened young offenders, who are already outlaws from society. We need hardly ask what has been their previous history; it is certain that they have had an undisciplined childhood, over which no moral or religious influence has been shed. The second class is, if possible, more dangerous to society than the first these are youths who are regularly trained by their parents or others in courses of professional dishonesty. A third class, and perhaps a still more numerous one, consists of children who are not as hardened or daring as the first, or as trained in crime as the second, but who, from the culpable neglect of their parents, and an entire want of all religious and moral influence at home, have gradually acquired, while quite young, habits of petty thieving, which are connived at, rather than punished, by their parents.
>
> (Carpenter 1853: 23, cited in
> Goldson and Jamieson 2002: 83–4)

Goldson and Jamieson (2002: 84) further observe that 'the developing agenda – invariably informed by constructions of (ir)responsibility, (im)morality and (in)discipline – was one in which the legitimacy of state intervention in respect of "malfunctioning" or "dysfunctional" families was increasingly expressed'. Equally, it was not simply the principle of state intervention that emerged, but also the question of sanction and punishment. Thus, during the 1870s and 1880s, various Acts of Parliament were passed that required parents to carry out certain duties, with the threat of a penalty or even the loss of the child if they failed (Morris and Giller 1987).

'The family' was thus a key focus of the Victorian interest in locating the basis of social order (Donajgrodzki 1977) and this legacy was sustained and further developed during early decades of the twentieth century when the 'delinquency' discourse began to claim scientific legitimacy not least from academic psychologists. Although the crime rate had decreased during the war years (1914–18), it had started to rise during the Great Depression period of the 1920s, but despite an almost logical demand for a common-sense link between poverty and crime, the dominant emphasis was placed at the micro-level of parent–child relations and individual personality. Biological-psychological explanations became very influential with the work of Cyril Burt (1945), who characterised the family backgrounds of 'delinquents' in terms of 'defective family relationships' and 'defective discipline', and he argued that parents were primarily responsible for the offending conduct of their children. These arguments influenced key government committees and, in turn, had a major impact on legislation. Perhaps most significantly, a Home Office Departmental Committee on the Treatment of Young Offenders (the Molony Committee) was established in January 1925, and many of its recommendations formed the basis of the Children and Young Persons Act 1933. This legislation was a significant youth justice policy milestone which had the effect of making the courtroom 'a site for adjudicating on matters of family socialisation and parental behaviour' (Muncie 1984: 45).

Reflections on the century of the child

The twentieth century has been considered by many to be the century of the child where the role of an ever-extended childhood has become increasingly important. In this section we will summarise some of the themes considered in this chapter.

First, the history of the past century is underpinned by the increasing professionalisation of the care of children, a development which was to have a significant impact on childrearing within the family. At the same time, this development has meant an incremental questioning of the competence of the family as a unit for the socialisation of children. Moreover, there have obviously been different views not only of childhood but also of the family in different social classes. The interest in social planning and the concept of childhood formed by experts on childhood in the twentieth century further complicated an ambiguous situation with childrearing ending up in the disputed territory between the public and the private sphere

Others have described these developments as the colonisation of the family by the state and public experts (Lasch 1977) and it is clear that at the micro-level the growth of professional groups – institutional experts on childrearing – has changed social relations and in particular those of power between parents/children and institutions, with this process having significant cultural consequences (Oakley 1984). Following the work of Foucault – who we will encounter in more detail in Chapter 6 – scholars have identified the development of a tighter system for surveillance, examination and normalisation of deviance in a modem welfare society (Armstrong 1983). This perspective helps us to identify the two-sided nature of the welfare state – help and support, but with it control and dependence (Hopkins Burke 2004a).

It was in the early nineteenth century that the upper classes began to see childhood through an idealistic lens, as a state of natural, indestructible authenticity and imminence. For the children of these affluent families, childhood was also a time when they were deliberately taught the behaviour and attitudes they needed for their future social status. They were not given responsibility until late in life and unlike the situation among the manual labouring classes, childrearing had no connection with the work of the adults or an early transition to adulthood.

Upper-class voices in the public social debate moreover criticised the free, less controlled childrearing of the working class. Moreover, a connection was identified between working-class childrearing and popular culture from which their social superiors wished to distance themselves (Sandin 1986). Specifically, the rowdy behaviour of urban working-class youth in the streets was seen by the ruling classes as indicative of an autonomous alien subculture and a rejection of the adult world. Among the more affluent classes, children were more strictly controlled by the demands and expectations of the adult world (Sandin 1986), which demonstrates that there is more than one kind of childhood: it is different for boys and girls, in rural and urban communities and between social classes.

By the end of the nineteenth century, the difference between these childhoods was becoming increasingly clear. Children in both town and country helped the family income by looking after the younger brothers and sisters so that the mother could work. They collected coal that had been dropped in the railway shunting yard, gathered fruit and firewood, delivered newspapers or worked as errand boys. The money they earned was handed over to support the family, and it gave status and self-esteem. At the same time, children were the focus of public opinion. Many children appeared idle and drifted around with no adult supervision.

The expansion of school in the towns and cities can be largely explained by the need felt by the upper class to create order in what they perceived to be turbulent urban environments where the control of children through family and work was insufficient. With the new school legislation in the latter half of the nineteenth century, children were compelled to spend a certain part of their growing years in school. Compulsory school and a higher leaving age meant a new reality for children from the lower classes. It meant a whole new childhood where it was no longer possible to stay at home looking after the younger children, or to leave school when the chance of a job arose. New requirements to satisfy the routines of the school were formulated as absolute demands. Breaches of the rules were punished, being seen as a visible expression of an inability or reluctance to meet the demands of society. This was seen as fundamentally a moral problem, which emphasised the importance of new efforts to get children to attend school. At the same time, the children became visible in a new way. Apart from a reluctance to go to school and the conflict between school and home, the other flaws of the children were exposed: illness and deviations of a physical, mental and moral kind.

Childhood was normalised and standardised: it was now important to weed out the 'delinquent' and 'morally depraved' children (Gillis 1974, 1981). For working-class families this development would have had self-evident consequences. The new demands on the children also involved ones on the families. The mothers were expected to be able to send clean, healthy children to school, at the right time. It was important to create a childhood – a long childhood. The men were expected to be able to provide for the whole family, wife and children alike. The higher demands presumably reinforced the trend towards men being paid the wages needed by a sole breadwinner. It is also possible that the new demands had the effect that families became smaller, since the burden of providing for a family had grown with the longer period the children spent as dependants.

The idea of motherhood, which was so strongly emphasised at the turn of the century, corresponds to this development of a new childhood – a non-useful child, dependent on a breadwinning father and a caring mother. The new emotionality in the family – the caring element – is a consequence of this kind of change. The moral demands also increased, now that a new 'normal' childhood of general validity had been established. It was now essential for everyone to benefit from what were considered to be the blessings of childhood. At the same time, a new view of the family was created, with new roles for all members, not least for the children, and a new normality, a new childhood which did not always agree with reality, but which could at least be measured against it (Platt 1969).

Working children and women were now seen as a threat to the living of the adult men and to the view of childhood that had been established among the higher social classes. The place for children and women was in the home. Children had to be saved from being useful. A useful child was by definition a used child. Zelizer (1985) discusses the conflict between the economically useful child and the emotionally valuable child in a number of examples from the USA at the turn of the century. The conflict between the different childhoods was revealed in insurance cases, in questions about adoption, and in the matter of compensation in the event of the death of a child. The valuation of children changed. Initially, the death of a child could be valued in terms of how much it could have been expected to earn for the family before moving away from home. This attitude became controversial after the turn of the century, and in a famous court case a judge ruled that a child had no value in economic terms. The child was worthless – or priceless. It soon became clear, however, that a price could be put on the emotional value of a child, and parents in later cases sued for compensation with reference to the loss of emotional values – translated into economic terms.

A corresponding development occurred in the case of adoption. Child labour was traditionally valued in financial terms, which both determined the price and influenced the gender of the adopted child – boys of working age were preferable to girls. The new view of childhood now opposed this valuation of children. Now children had to be taken care of for their own sake, not for their usefulness. This change in norms did not come about on its own. School was a meeting-place for different childhood worlds, and the differences became all too clear. Other factors can be identified. The years around the turn of the century were characterised by social conflict. The emergence and demands of the labour movement provided the background against which the debate about children was conducted. Attention was drawn to the destitution among the working class, and the bourgeoisie saw that the working class had to be integrated in society and the gulfs bridged to avoid political unrest. Nationalism was held up as a common ideal for the working class and the bourgeoisie.

Children and young people were seen as a potential source of unrest in the streets, and police files were filled with records of delinquent and morally depraved children. The high degree of employment among women, while working-class children were allowed to grow up in the streets of the cities, was regarded as a real threat to fundamental social values. The bourgeoisie complained about the negligence of working-class parents. The family – the very foundation of society – was said to be on the verge of breakdown. The social problems also highlighted the need to counteract new forms of culture. Film and cheap fiction had to be combated. The growing generation should not be lost to values and ideals that were foreign to established society (Douglas 1966).

A struggle for the children was thus waged around the turn of the twentieth century. The church, charity 'organisations', popular movements and private 'child-savers' took an intense interest in children and young people. The interest was shared by a large body of opinion in the bourgeoisie and other established groups, whose concern for the moral and material conditions of poor children was expressed in voluntary actions or through the work of various societies.

In both England and the USA, the child-saving organisations played a major role in moulding public opinion and legislation concerning children (Platt 1969; Donzelot 1980). Various professional groups – kindergarten superintendents, doctors, teachers, clergy, psychologists – declared themselves specially qualified to give parents advice and instruction in childrearing. The professional groups argued among themselves about who was best fitted to the task of saving the children from unwholesome environments such as the home, the street, or the factory. This struggle also had a gender aspect. The question was whether professional men or women should be responsible for childcare, and in what roles. The conflict concerned whether childcare was a professional matter or a field for voluntary charity. Childcare was changed from working for poor and disadvantaged children to include all children. The boundaries between public and private in the matter of child welfare and childrearing were changed in the years around the turn of the century. It increasingly became a public concern, not just a private matter for the parents.

Then as now, there were calls for more institutions for the growing generation, support and advice for families, and the need for school reforms. It is therefore important to reflect why children were singled out – in fact discovered – as a political and social problem. It was not just a matter of children who had real problems or, for that matter, which were a real problem. It is at least as much a matter of the emergence of new professional groups and about changed relations between adults and children, men and women, and different social classes, and about the chances of children obtaining work.

The history of the twentieth century is characterised by the increased professionalisation of childcare which made itself felt in childrearing within the family. The broader social undertakings of the school, family counselling, and parental education are expressions of this process, as are maternity centres and childcare centres. In many respects, this has also meant a questioning of the ability of the family to meet the increased demands of society regarding children and childrearing. The interest in social planning and the view of childhood formed by child experts further complicated the situation with childrearing ending up in a boundary zone between public and private. Some scholars would describe this in terms of the state and the experts colonising the family in the twentieth century (Lasch 1977; Hallden 1988). Regardless of how this development is described, it is obvious that the emergence of new professional groups – professional childcare personnel associated with institutions – has changed social relations and relations of power between parents, children and institutions. The raising of the school leaving age has helped to segregate children from the adult world and working life. One purpose of the school reforms of the 1950s was to create a school for all social classes and the same opportunities for every child. Within the framework of this new school, however, children from different classes continue to follow different educational paths.

A single comprehensive school system has been created for all children (or at least those who do not opt out of the state system), but it contains different childhood worlds and youth cultures. All that they have in common is that their dependence on adults has grown longer, and that schooling has taken on increased importance for their future. There has been a great improvement in the material conditions of children as a result of the general development of welfare and special supportive measures, while in the latter half of the twentieth century, more and more women have once again begun to work outside the home.

This latter development has been made possible in part by new forms of childcare. At the same time, the significance of the home and the family in the lives of children has declined in favour of other forms of care: childminders, nursery schools and leisure centres. For the children it means that the adult behaviour – control of emotions, keeping times, adapting to large groups, and so on – which was previously learned when children started school, is now encountered at an earlier age. This development has other consequences. Childcare and the lower stages of school recruit mainly female personnel. To a greater extent than before, and for more years, children spend their time in a largely female environment, lacking male models outside the home. Yet the increasing importance of public institutions does not mean that children have lost their importance for men and women but it seems as if the leisure centres and leisure associations are organising more and more of the children's time. Leisure time in the sense of truly free time has shrunk. Organised leisure time is mostly planned and defined by adults. Municipal authorities encourage leisure pursuits with an educational content, since they keep children and young people off the streets. Parents use similar reasons to justify sports or club activities: they are seen as preparing children for the future.

The institutionalisation of the lives of younger children is one of the more significant features of childhood in contemporary society. This is accompanied by the growth of new professional groups – pre-schoolteachers, recreation leaders, paediatricians, child and family psychologists and administrators who can supplement and support – and question – the way parents look after their children. These groups have an interest in showing that they are needed so that children will be well looked after. Recreation leaders are experts at organising leisure time. Childcare personnel are experts in childcare. All these professional groups feel a need to define their competence in relation to the way parents look after their children and in relation to other professions. It is in their professional interest to show that they are needed (Dencik 1989).

At the same time, the late twentieth century has seen an increase in what we demand and expect of children. Parents learn from scientific reports and articles in the press that they should let their children listen to music while still in the womb, so as to develop their musical talents. Other psychological experts say that infants have a much greater competence than we think (Schaffer 1991). A new concept – the competent infant – puts all this development in a new scientific framework. Learning can start at a much earlier age. It is important to develop the abilities of the child. Children with innate defects can be diagnosed at the foetal stage and aborted and thus the demand for normality can be set higher and be more narrowly defined with the aid of new science (Oakley 1984).

The twentieth century has also seen a sweeping change in the relation between the different places where children spend their time. Leisure has been given new meanings with the development of organised activities for many children and a decline in the free time available to them. The leisure has not just been organised but also educationalised as a consequence with organisations appealing to new age groups. Very young children are now being encouraged to play sport and music from a very early age. School in recent decades has also assumed greater responsibility for the spare time of children and created forms of closer cooperation with home and parents. School has also been developed in the twentieth century as an important institution for social policy, where medical considerations and preventive healthcare have been crucial for the way of defining children (Sandin 1986).

The start of working life has been increasingly postponed and participation in work is regarded as unsuitable for children. Ironically, this has taken place at the same time as school itself attempts to bridge the gap between school and work through work experience initiatives. The valuation of different kinds of work needs to be considered in the context of debates about children performing in theatres and music-halls, selling things in the street, working as errand boys and youth unemployment. Different classes have had different attitudes to the demands of the school for a monopoly of children's time. The choice between work and school probably differs between families of different social classes, and it is different for girls and boys. The transition from child labour to pocket money is symbolic of the changed role of children.

In the first decades of the twentieth century, a number of institutions were created to look after children who deviated in various ways from the behaviour that was defined as normal. The institutions for delinquent children, for example, which were established in the first half of the nineteenth century, were based on differing principles. The following three chapters take up the story of the changing nature of state intervention in the lives of children and young people who offend, from the beginnings of a particular juvenile justice system to the election of New Labour in 1997 and the creation of the contemporary youth justice system. In Chapter 6 we will reflect back on all these developments and theoretically consider in whose interests they all occurred.

Summary of main points

1 In pre-modern societies the role and status of children and young people were ambiguous and because of the nature of the pre-industrial capitalist economy they were of little significance or importance and often a drain on limited resources.

2 Modern industrial societies required an ever-increasing population. Children were now an asset to be nurtured, pampered and disciplined in the interests of society.

3 'Modernity' or 'modernism' are terms used to describe the development of a secular, scientifically rational, increasingly industrialised and urban tradition. Such societies are mass societies characterised by mass production and consumption, corporate capital, organised labour and importantly an extensive large demand for workers.

4 The way childhood is seen today is very much the product of modern societies and modernist modes of thought.

5 The social and scientific term 'adolescence' was constructed by the professional middle classes in accordance with the work of the child study movement and especially the highly influential G. Stanley Hall.

6 It was working-class adolescents who were thought to be the most likely to display delinquent and rebellious characteristics during this 'storm and stress' period in the life cycle.

7 Much early youth work was directed at young people in the same class as the providers but the organisations were themselves controlled by members of the middle class.

8 The social control, discipline and tutelage of working-class children and adolescents was a significant strategy of middle-class 'moral entrepreneurs'.

9 The emphasis on parenting in the contemporary youth justice system is nothing new with the notion that 'the family' is in 'crisis', and/or that parents are 'failing', comprises a 'cyclical phenomenon with a very long history' (Day-Sclater and Piper 2000: 135).

10 The twentieth century was considered by many to be the century of the child where the role of an ever-extended childhood has become increasingly important.

Discussion questions

1 In what ways are the experiences of childhood different in pre-modern and modern societies?

2 What is a 'social construction'? Explain with reference to notions of 'childhood' and adolescence.

3 What is a 'moral entrepreneur'? Explain with reference to the disciplining and tutelage of working class children in the nineteenth century.

4 Why was there an emphasis on the standards of parenting among the working classes and why do these debates continue to the present day?

5 Why was the twentieth century known by some as the century of the child?

Notes

1 A social construction or social construct is any institutionalised entity or object in a social system 'invented' or 'constructed' by participants in a particular culture or society that exists because people agree to behave as if it exists or follow certain conventional rules. Social status is an example of a social construct (see Clarke and Cochrane 1998).

2 The most likely explanation for this decrease in the infant death rate was the invention of the microscope and the discovery of bacteria (Hoyles and Evans 1989).

3 Hall's interpretation of adolescence was founded on biological notions but problematically no definitive age could be placed upon this transitional phase, or importantly upon the completion of the transition and the onset of adulthood. The various rites of passage that may be seen to constitute a period of adolescence are clearly delineated by societal reaction to the biological individual. Thus, for example, a young person may be sexually mature by the age of 13, but not until 16 can they legally have sexual intercourse with a consenting adult and thus become a parent, yet inexplicably, they cannot drive a motor-car on a public road until they are 17-years-old (Coleman and Warren-Adamson 1992).

4 Changes in technology and in the economy did nevertheless give rise to different types of employment opportunities for young people, particularly in urban areas with large numbers of young men finding employment in the various occupations that emerged with the growing complex of distributive and administrative functions. Frequently these jobs were 'reserved' for those in their teens who in turn were required to leave such employment when they became older and too expensive to employ.

3 From justice to welfare and its malcontents

Key issues

1 The origins of youth justice provision
2 Development of the juvenile justice system
3 Consumer society and criminal youth
4 The triumph of welfarism
5 Conclusions

> Much contemporary academic discourse on the operation of the youth justice system or on the punishment of young offenders reads as if we are now more punitive and less concerned about the welfare of child offenders than at any time in the recent past. We have, however, only to look back a little over a century to see a time when children were not only punished by imprisonment but, on occasion, were subjected to transportation and even the death penalty. In fact, it is really only in the last 150 years that there have been discernible differences in the ways in which adult and child offenders have been treated by the criminal justice system.
>
> (Newburn 1996: 61)

The previous chapter discussed the social construction of childhood and adolescence in the context of the needs of emerging, developing and consolidating mass society modernity and attempts to control the socialisation and discipline of this problematic population, not least in the interests of industrial capitalism. This is a story we will explore further theoretically in Chapter 6. This chapter – and the two that follow – tells the story of the creation of a juvenile justice response to those young people who had transgressed against the law of the land. It is ostensibly the story of a highly ambiguous transition from a criminal justice punishment response, which operated predominantly in accordance with rational actor model criminological principles, to one prescribed by treatment-oriented predestined actor model principles (these models are explored in some depth in the second part of this book). It is an ambiguous story because exactly what can be seen to constitute justice and welfare – or indeed, as we shall discover, punishment and treatment – is both contentious and involves a complex and invariably confused tension between these apparently polar opposites. These three chapters explore that ambiguous transition and the tension between those two models that continues to the present day. It is, nevertheless, a story told in the context of repeated societal concerns and panics about the extent of offending by children and young people and popular demands that something is done to reduce or even eradicate it.

The origins of youth justice provision

Before the nineteenth century there was no special provision for young offenders, who were treated no differently than adults and could be sent to adult prisons, hanged or transported to the colonies. Children were considered to be adult above the age of 7 and were held criminally responsible for their behaviour; thus, for example, on one day alone in 1814, five children between the ages of 8 and 12 were hanged alongside each other for offences of petty theft (Pinchbeck and Hewitt 1973: 352) and this event was by no means exceptional.

The predominantly harsh treatment of juveniles, nevertheless, makes perfect sense in the context of the discussion in the previous chapter where we saw that childhood was not viewed as a particularly important stage of life in the eyes of working-class parents, employers or the law. Throughout the nineteenth century children were, however, gradually singled out from adults as a distinctive category in relation to both criminal behaviour and legal control, and again, there were a multitude of different motivations for implementing these changes. For example, the Society for the Improvement of Prison Discipline and the Reformation of Juvenile Offenders 1817 was convinced of the need to separate the young offender from the hardened adult criminal and avoid the moral contamination of the former; while refinements in prisoner classification brought the particular case of the younger offender to the fore. In 1823 a separate convict hulk (prison ship) was, therefore, introduced for young offenders and fifteen years later the first penal institution solely for juveniles was opened at Parkhurst, although it should be noted that conditions were no less repressive than in an adult prison (Weiner 1990). It was to be the arrival of the first official crime statistics for offences committed by children and younger people during the 1830s that suggested a sizeable and appreciably growing problem and this was to accelerate widespread demands from a whole range of interest groups for a more rigorous intervention.

The need for a distinctive criminal justice process for young offenders was actually first proposed by liberal-minded magistrates who questioned the validity of sending children to prison while awaiting trial for minor offences. Thus, legislation was first introduced into parliament in 1840 that would enable magistrates to deal with children under 12 immediately, act as the moral guardians of destitute and delinquent juveniles and advocate training and discipline in industrial schools rather than imprisonment. The House of Lords nonetheless rejected the legislation because it denied children the right to a jury trial and was deemed contrary to the existing dominant criminal justice orthodoxy. This is a highly significant point and it is a theme that recurs throughout the history of youth justice, for we shall see later in this chapter, a crucial concern of progressive critics of welfarism was the withdrawal of legal rights to children and their parents, which is a cornerstone of the justice/punishment model summarised in Box 3.1.

Box 3.1   The justice/punishment model of youth justice

- Based on rational actor model of criminal behaviour notions that young people have free will and choose to offend.
- Offenders should be held responsible for their actions and punished if they transgress.
- The level of punishment inflicted should be commensurate with the seriousness of the offence committed.
- Offenders should be punished for the offence committed and not on the basis of whom they are or the social conditions in which they live.

Concerns about young offending were nevertheless increasing rapidly with a parallel widespread demand that something be done to reduce the problem. Voluntary reformatories for miscreant young people had been opened by the Philanthropic Society and by private founders in the early nineteenth century, but with increasing concerns about youthful legal violations, a select committee of the House of Lords was established in the 1840s and the outcome was the Youth Offenders Act 1854. This legislation required the Home Office to certify certain recognised institutions and these came to be known as Certified Reformatories and Certified Industrial Schools, and boys and girls aged under 16 who had spent time in adult prisons could be transferred there to complete their sentences. These specifically juvenile institutions came to replace prison terms for many young offenders, and gave boys and girls a basic education plus a trade. There were also several reformatory ship schools or industrial training ships certified in the late 1850s, although they became shore-based in the twentieth century.

The Industrial Schools Act 1857 was aimed at making better provision for the care and education of vagrant, destitute and disorderly children, who, it was thought, were in danger of becoming criminals (Newburn 1995). This Act and the following legislation in 1860–61 enabled magistrates to commit certain young offenders directly to the industrial schools – without a prior spell in prison or a house of correction – and there were thirty such establishments in existence by the end of 1865. The legislation also made provision for the religious persuasion of the child to be taken into account in the choice of a school. Denominational (Non-Church of England) industrial schools also existed after 1866, including some for Catholic children, and these were supported by local taxation. The Education Act 1870 led to the founding of industrial day schools and truant schools, and by the beginning of the First World War in 1914, there were 208 schools for juvenile delinquents, of which 132 were residential industrial schools.

There were widespread motivations for change and in particular pressure from politically powerful religious, philanthropic and penal reform groups concerned with the brutality of conditions in adult prisons and their impact on young offenders was to increase throughout the nineteenth century. Pitts (2003a) notes that towards the end of the century these concerns had spread to the general public, not least because of media campaigns against a perceived 'crisis of control' in the industrial cities, and the apparent inability of the authorities to control problem groups of what can be considered the first modern subcultures (Davis 1990), such as the 'scuttlers' and 'peaky blinders', on the streets (Humphries 1981; Pearson 1983). These developments raised concerns about the apparently declining standards of parenting and the family socialisation process – which are so familiar today – and which were said to be responsible for the social disorganisation epitomised by drunkenness, violence, immorality and criminality that characterised the Victorian urban landscape.

It was the Summary Jurisdiction Act 1879 that substantially reduced the number of children in prison. They were now to be tried by magistrates rather than at higher courts, available penalties were reduced, and those aged under 16 were tried summarily for nearly all indictable offences. Throughout the nineteenth century, destitute and delinquent children were to be treated in the same way while, at the same time, there was little legal recognition given to the differences in cause and kind between adult and juvenile crime.

The Gladstone Committee and the Lushington Committee were established in the mid-1890s and these were to advocate a welfare/treatment model intervention rather than a justice/punishment model intervention with young offenders and the introduction of alternatives to custody. Pitts (2003a: 73) observes that:

> Then, as now, it was a self-proclaimed 'modernising' government that acted on these recommendations, and then, as now, this government argued that the new measures were 'evidence-based', informed by the new sciences of paediatrics, child psychology, criminology and penology and responsibility for this new form of youth justice was placed in the hands of a new legal and administrative reality, the juvenile court.

This focus on the 'welfare' of young offenders and the 'treatment' necessary to reform them is in accordance with the welfare/treatment model of youth justice which summarised in Box 3.2.

Box 3.2 The welfare/treatment model of youth justice

- Based on predestined actor model of criminal behaviour notions that young people are not fully responsible for their actions because of biological, psychological and social factors.
- Treatment and rehabilitation are advocated rather than punishment.

- Cases are to be dealt with by welfare professionals and experts and not the criminal justice system.
- Later variants of the model recommend limited or non-intervention in accordance with the principles of the victimised actor model of criminal behaviour.

By the turn of the twentieth century, young people in the new cities and manufacturing towns were experiencing increasing independence and leisure time with new heightened concerns about delinquency and hooliganism emerging (Newburn 2002), while this close association between 'youth' and 'crime' has remained virtually undisturbed ever since in the minds of the public – a discovery paralleled by continued nostalgic yearnings for a lost 'golden age' of tranquillity and calm that in reality never existed (Pearson 1983).

It was in this socio-economic context that the Children Act 1908 established specialised juvenile courts which were given powers to deal with both the delinquent and the destitute, albeit differently from adults. There was, however, to be a mixture of welfare and punitive strategies and this can be noted in the comment of Herbert Samuel, the minister responsible for introducing the legislation, who stated that 'courts should be the agencies for the rescue as well as the punishment of juveniles' (cited in Gelsthorpe and Morris 1994: 951). Morris et al. (1980) nevertheless note that juvenile courts remained essentially criminal courts while the idea that the child was a wrongdoer was the dominant orthodoxy.

The British legal system had thus introduced different interventions for young offenders from the mid-nineteenth century onwards with the establishment of reformatory and industrial schools. Moreover, in addition to the creation of new punitive measures for dealing with the young, laws were passed removing children from certain areas of industry and restricting their activities in others, while compulsory elementary education was introduced in 1870. In 1889, the 'Children's Charter' introduced legal protections for children from various types of cruelty and enabled the state to intervene in family life. Efforts escalated as campaigners pursued greater legal protection and coverage for children and young people around the turn of the twentieth century. These changes were part of the gradual evolution in the concept of childhood we observed in the previous chapter and the growing interest in how the experiences of youth impacted on adulthood. This new legislation was thus part of – among other things – an effort to ameliorate the condition of young people by providing them with new opportunities and protections, a growing awareness of the developmental importance of childhood and an attempt to impose a middle-class conception of childhood upon the working classes.

These changes in the perception of childhood led to new ideas about the ways in which the delinquent and vulnerable young should be dealt with by the state. From the 1880s onwards, campaigners began to call in particular for the introduction of a special court to handle cases involving children and young people (Behlmer 1998). The establishment of the specialist Juvenile Court by the Children

Act 1908 was one of several reforms of the Liberal Governments of 1906–14, which included the provision of school meals, school medical inspections and pensions for orphans. The new legislation had six parts: infant life protection, the prevention of cruelty, the prohibition of juvenile smoking, the refining of the roles of industrial and reformatory schools, the creation of the juvenile courts and a 'miscellaneous' division which included such provision as the banning of children under 14 from public houses (Hendrick 1994). In short, the legislation further extended the power of the state to determine family matters while formally introducing the juvenile court to the British legal systems.

The British juvenile courts drew upon a diverse range of intellectual influences. They owed much to the development of the social and socio-medical sciences, notably criminology, psychology and psychiatry, which had developed partly as an attempt to discover the causes of and solutions for deviant behaviours and social problems. While some, such as Cesare Lombroso, an Italian criminal anthropologist (Bradley 2009b), looked for biological predispositions towards delinquent behaviours, others looked to the mind. Child psychology and psychiatry – as they are now known – developed at a much slower rate than the study of adults, but had emerged as a distinct discipline by the 1860s. Researchers, from that time onwards, turned their attention to the psychological problems of childhood and how these may differ from those suffered by adults (Parry-Jones 1989). The Child Study Movement was founded in 1893 by James Sully, a British psychologist, and the movement attracted other experts – such as the American psychiatrist G. Stanley Hall introduced in the previous chapter – and also provided a forum for amateur readers alike to explore the psychology and psychiatry of the young. The Movement encouraged the view that all children were individuals and should be treated as such by parents, teachers, and medical and social professionals. This also had resonance with radical changes in the operation of philanthropic welfare activities, notably the development by the Charity Organisation Society (COS) of case work. The COS were concerned with the rational distribution of charitable alms among the needy, which they hoped to achieve through the careful investigation and consideration of the needs of individual families (Lewis 1995).

The Child Study Movement and ideas about the 'scientific' application of welfare had an important influence upon the establishment of the Cook County Juvenile Court founded in Chicago, Illinois in 1899 by female reformers connected with the city's Hull-House Settlement and its Women's Club. The aim of the reformers was to provide individual treatment for troubled children and to neutralise the impact of poor adult influence. They believed that what we now call dysfunctional families were the principal cause of juvenile delinquency and, more specifically, that children from the slums, misbehaved and broke the law because they were not cared for by their parents in 'appropriate' ways. The women attached to the Cook County Court in turn were highly influential in shaping other courts across the USA, although an alternative model was presented by Ben Lindsay, the self-appointed juvenile judge of Denver, Colorado. Lindsay was a firm proponent of developing 'character' among those young men who attended his court and of instilling in them the middle-class values

of duty, courage, independence and self-control (Clapp 1998). These developments had a huge impact among reformists in the UK and inspired the first British
juvenile court, which was established in Birmingham in 1900. The British courts
shared much in common with their US counterparts in terms of a belief that the
delinquent young needed to be saved in order to protect the wider society. As on
the other side of the Atlantic, the causes of juvenile delinquency were located in
the failure of 'character' and of suitable (male) role modelling as well as in the
failure of the family (Logan 2005; Bradley 2008).

Platt (1969) has observed that the arrival of the juvenile court underpinned
with these new psycho-social explanations was to herald the arrival of another
social construction of youthful humanity: the 'juvenile delinquent'. Previously,
there had been simply 'young offenders', to whom varying degrees of responsibility could be ascribed in accordance with the dominant rational actor model
philosophy. Juvenile delinquents – according to the newly emerging predestined
actor model orthodoxy – were significantly perceived to be different from their
non-delinquent peers. Pitts (2003a: 73) observes that:

> It was not simply that they behaved differently: they were different in the way
> they thought, how they felt, in the beliefs and attitudes they held and, indeed,
> in their very biogenetic constitution. Thus, the juvenile court did not simply
> assume powers to sentence children and young people to a new, distinctively
> juvenile, range of penalties and facilities; it also shaped its disposals in accord-
> ance with the relationships the new sciences of human behaviour had proposed
> between the present demeanour of the delinquent and their future needs.

Platt (1969) argues that we need to look beyond the rhetoric of benevolence and
the concerns of the 'child savers' for 'salvation', 'innocence' and 'protection'
that were undoubtedly the motivations of the middle-class women involved. The
ideologies of welfare, nevertheless, enabled constant and pervasive supervision
of children and young people and allowed the state to intervene directly in any
elements of the working class that were considered to be immoral or unruly.
Regardless of the benevolent original intentions of the 'child savers', the outcome
was that troublesome adolescents could now be defined by the new 'professional'
bodies of experts – psychiatrists, social workers and philanthropists – as 'sick'
or 'pathological', with the outcome that young people came to be imprisoned
'for their own good', had very limited legal rights and were subjected to lengthy
periods of incarceration. Morris and Giller (1987: 32) note that most reforms were
either implicitly or explicitly coercive and that in reality 'humanitarianism and
coercion are essentially two sides of the same coin'.

Development of the juvenile justice system

The Probation of Offenders Act 1907 introduced community supervision – based
on the welfarist philosophy of advise, assist and befriend – as an alternative to
custody and by 1920 approximately 8,000 of the 10,000 people being supervised

by probation officers were aged between 8 and 18 years (Pitts 2003a). The following year the use of imprisonment for children under the age of 14 was ended but the Prevention of Crime Act 1908 established specialised detention centres where rigid discipline and work training could be provided in a secure environment. The first of these was at Borstal in Kent, which gave its name to numerous similar establishments.

The borstal system introduced indeterminate sentences of between one and three years for males aged 16–20 and emphasised a mixture of discipline and training with some placing an emphasis on education, being strongly imbued with the values and traditions of English public-school education, and later some even adopted a therapeutic approach (see, for example, Hood 1965). By the early 1920s there was nevertheless some public disquiet following allegations of brutality in a number of these institutions (Humphries 1981; Crimmens and Pitts 2000). The subsequent committee of inquiry (the Molony Committee) investigated the treatment of young offenders under 21 and in particular those who were considered to be in need of 'protection and training'. The focus was on the 'welfare' of young offenders and the 'treatment' necessary to reform them.

Pitts (2003a) observes that the immediate consequences of the 1907/08 reforms were contradictory. Thus, on the one hand, the probation order – a new non-custodial sentence – simply failed to reduce the incarceration of young offenders. From that time onwards, the number of youngsters dispatched to juvenile reformatories and borstals increased significantly with the numbers exceeding 20,000 by the early 1920s. On the other hand – and this was to become very much the case with the establishment of the contemporary youth justice system discussed in detail in the third part of this book – the introduction of a new and apparently more positive secure estate was to persuade some sentencers to take advantage of their supposed benefit. Thus, a system which had been established to create 'alternatives to custody' was in reality imposing greater custodial control on a larger number of less problematic young people. This significant theme of the 'spreading of social control' (Cohen 1980) is another one to which we return later in this chapter and elsewhere in this book.

This twin expansion of institutional and community sanctions occurred, nevertheless, at the same time as a declining crime rate during the first twenty years of the century. Pitts (2003a) observes different explanations for this decline. On the one hand, the political right – epitomised by Charles Murray (1990, 1994) – has, subsequently, pointed to the increased role of incarceration in helping to bring about this decrease in criminality, although we should note that the significant reductions in the prison population in the 1930s occurred at the same time that the UK was experiencing the lowest crime rates of the twentieth century (Pitts 2003a). On the other hand, John Lea (1999) – a left realist – has proposed that these low crime rates were related to the growth of unionised democratic socialism and the development of a 'social contract' which provided rights to health care, housing, education and material security. The outcome was an increasingly reliable workforce, low divorce rates, 'stable' families and 'respectable', law-abiding working-class communities with criminality now consigned to the social margins.

David Garland (2001) has argued that these economic, political and social changes in the early part of the twentieth century were to create the conditions for the emergence of what he has termed 'penal modernism'. The new social demo-cratic politics viewed offenders as socially and economically disadvantaged, or poorly socialised, and thus sought to improve these perceived crime-producing conditions through the judicious use of social and criminal justice policy. Pitts (2003a) notes that these policies attracted cross-party political support because of a widespread belief and confidence in the capacity of social science – and its application by experts and professionals – to solve social problems. He argues that penal modernism found its fullest expression in the 'child-centred' youth justice policies that emerged between 1933 and 1969.

Government commitment to the task of reducing and, if possible, preventing juvenile delinquency thus continued unabated after the First World War, espe-cially as the Home Office became increasingly accepting of the Children Act 1908 (Behlmer 1998). The Children's Branch of the Home Office was established in 1919, which extended their remit beyond the inspection of reformatory and industrial schools to include the management of juvenile courts, probation and places of detention. The Children's Branch was also responsible for monitoring the employment of children, for preventing cruelty to children, as well as for mon-itoring obscene publications and the trafficking of women and children (Lerman 1984). It was through the Children's Branch that subsequent reforms of the 1908 legislation were carried out.

Campaigners and civil servants alike were nevertheless unhappy with the limi-tations of the legislation and sought more proactive measures to reduce offending by children and young people. A report commissioned by the Board of Education in 1920 argued for a link between the high wages earned by boys in 'blind-alley' labour, the paucity of constructive leisure activities in some areas and higher rates of juvenile crime – again picking up on themes expressed by those involved in urban youth work. In January 1925, William Joynson-Hicks, then Conservative home secretary, appointed a committee, chaired by Sir Thomas Molony, to investigate the treatment of 'young offenders'. When the committee reported in 1927, they concluded that 'the welfare of the child or young person should be the primary object of the juvenile court'. They also called for magistrates with experi-ence in dealing with young people, and that younger people should be recruited to these posts. The report reiterated the importance of issues raised by the 1908 Act, notably that juvenile courts should be held at different times and in differ-ent places to adult sittings of courts. It also demanded that court proceedings be made as simple as possible in order that children and young people might better understand what was happening around them. But the report went further, calling for children and young people to remain anonymous and to be in no way identifi-able in media reporting of cases. It was felt that public knowledge of a child's acts could in future unfairly jeopardise their chances of finding employment. The report also demanded that courts be furnished with as much information as pos-sible about the lives of the children brought before them: their school attendance, their health and their home environment. Probation was an important part of the work of the court with young offenders, a method by which the young person could be reclaimed to good citizenship through the firm and wise guidance of an appropriate adult. The Report of the Departmental Committee on the Treatment of Young Offenders, 1927 served as the foundation of the Children and Young Persons Bill which reached enactment in 1933.

The welfare/treatment model was thus further emphasised by the Children and Young Persons Act 1933 with the legislation extending those features of the 1908 legislation that were seen to need adjustment, notably in terms of how the courts operated and by reducing the stigma of going to court. The emphasis was on restoring young offenders to habits of good citizenship and on trying to counteract the impact of poverty on lives of young offenders and hence reduce the levels of criminal behaviour. Although it was acknowledged that middle-class children did come before the courts – often for such offences as travelling on the railway without a valid ticket – working-class children were disproportionately represented in the courts, with boys forming the majority of all cases seen (Henriques 1950; Cox 2003; Bradley 2009a). The boys were seen as suffering from a wide range of disadvantages that arose from their less fortunate backgrounds: parents who could not provide adequate supervision as they were preoccupied with caring for younger children or working; limited access to leisure facilities and supervised play; or parents with high wages but a lack of direction in how to spend and save wisely. Certainly, the legislation and its reformist supporters can be seen as further evidence of attempting to control and shape the working-class family in the image of their working-class peers.

The Children and Young Persons Act 1933 led to an earlier limited practice of having a specially selected panel of magistrates to hear juvenile cases being adopted throughout the whole country, with restrictions placed on the reporting of cases in newspapers, the age of criminal responsibility raised from 7 to 8 and, above all, magistrates were directed to take primary account of the welfare of the child. This latter clause, while heralded as an important victory for the welfare lobby, nevertheless highlighted a fundamental contradiction in youth justice policy that has continued to the present day. The justice/punishment and welfare/ treatment models appear to be inevitably incompatible, with the former emphasising full criminal responsibility and punishment and the latter the needs of the individual child and welfare treatment. The Act also abolished capital punishment for those aged under 18, and the nineteenth-century reformatories and industrial schools were consolidated into a national system of approved schools for the treatment of young offenders aged 10–15.

Some juvenile court magistrates – such as Sir William Clarke Hall, Basil Henriques and Cynthia Colville – keenly embraced new thinking about the causes of juvenile delinquency and the ways in which children and young people could be rehabilitated. Yet not all magistrates were as interested in reclaiming young offenders. Deborah Thom (2003) observes that the pro-corporal punishment lobby remained a powerful one and the Bill which became the Children and Young Persons Act was held up on its way through the Lords so that the provision for beating the child could be restored. Until the Children Act 1948 banned the practice, males could still be sentenced to a birching and – regardless of psychological evidence to the contrary – corporal punishment was seen as an effective means of instilling character into a young man and was widely used in schools, in the armed forces and in families for some years afterwards. In terms of the ever-present ambiguity between the justice/punishment and welfare/treatment models, those of us who were brought up under this regime were always told that it was for our own good with invariable biblical reference to 'spare the rod, spoil the child'.

Most indicators suggest that the levels of juvenile crime rose fairly steadily throughout the 1930s and were to rise sharply – albeit with some variations – during the Second World War (Newburn 2002b). Seismic wartime social conditions were highly significant in the formative years of development in the lives of a generation of young people. The 'black-out' evacuation where children were taken from their families in the city and sent to rural areas, the closure of schools and youth clubs were all blamed for much delinquency (Bailey 1987) and this notion of family disruption or dysfunction remains a dominant approach to explaining criminality among children and young people to the present day.

Corporal punishment on boys aged under 14 increased during the course of the Second World War. In 1938 and 1939 there were forty-eight and fifty-eight cases of whippings respectively in England and Wales; this rose to a high of 531 in 1941, gradually dropping to 165 by the end of 1943 before returning to pre-war levels in 1944 when thirty-seven cases were handled in this way (Cmnd 7227). This rise has been attributed to the need to deal with increasing juvenile crime during the war in combination with retired magistrates being reinstated to cope with the dual pressures of an increasing caseload and younger magistrates serving on war duty. Therefore, attitudes to how children and young people should be treated varied from court to court, region to region, and even among members of the same bench of magistrates. Although the various Children's Acts established the agenda, the magistracy did not always keep up and more authoritarian views continued in many places.

The period between 1945 and the early 1970s was to witness the high point in the confidence of industrial modernity, although for some observers this was built on unstable foundations. There was to be a process of deskilling for many in the industrial working class from the early 1950s (Cohen 1972) while full employment during this period of the long economic boom was closely linked with greatly increased enrolment in higher education institutions and recruitment into the military (Taylor 1997). The period was, moreover, epitomised by an unwritten social contract between the government and their citizens which was fundamentally based on the provision of full employment and the fall-back position of a relatively generous welfare state (including social security benefits, free education, health care and cheap, reasonable quality state-sponsored housing). For the first decade following the end of the war, youth-offending figures were not to return to the expected pre-war levels.

The Criminal Justice Act 1948 was thus introduced in the context of the creation of the welfare state. It placed a number of restrictions on the use of imprisonment but – although it marked the beginning of a trend restricting the use of custody for young offenders (Newburn 2002b) – introduced detention and attendance centres which appeared to reflect a more punitive approach (Morris and Giller 1987). Detention centres were institutions in which young offenders could be sentenced to a short period of custody, in a regime intended to be tough and disciplinary with an emphasis on physical education – the legislative intention being to replace the use of corporal punishment – although there were also elements of education and training. Attendance centre orders required a young person to attend a centre, run mainly by the police, for a number of hours per week, often on a Saturday afternoon. Discipline was a key feature of early attendance centres, which mixed elements of physical education with more practical pursuits. Concern about the 'welfare' of juveniles was also evident with the passing of the Children Act 1948, which sought to end the placement of neglected children in approved schools alongside offenders. Local authority children's departments were also established with their own resources for residential care and trained staff to oversee fostering and adoption (Harris and Webb 1987).

Pitts (2003a) observes that the reforms of 1907/08 had established the right of young offenders to be dealt with differently from adults while the reforms of 1933 and 1948 were concerned with elaborating the nature of that difference. He notes that subsequent policies were infused with ideas about child development with their origins in the Freudian psychoanalytic tradition – which we will encounter in the second part of this book – but also the significant effects of poverty and inequality on the healthy development of the child. The new political consensus favoured the prescriptions of the welfare/ treatment model of intervention, and because the 'welfare' of young offenders was considered paramount, it was proposed that the issue should be dealt with, wherever possible, by experts in the care and protection of children and young people. There was, nonetheless, resistance to this shift in youth justice emphasis from Conservative politicians, senior police officers, magistrates and judges, who wished to retain a strong element of retribution in the youth justice system and who favoured the prescriptions of the justice/ punishment model of intervention.

Bailey (1987) moreover observes the ambiguities of welfarism itself and it is here possible to identify the beginnings of the progressive critique that was to become so significant during the 1970s and which we encounter below. The 'social conception of delinquency' argument which had become so influential during the inter-war period had made good sense to the many administrators and reformers with experience of boys' clubs or settlement work. From this perspective, offending behaviour was seen as a symptom of wider social and personal conditions, in particular, weak parental control, poor character training and lack of opportunity. Furthermore, such explanations suggested practical solutions to the problem – a change of environment, exercises in self-control, occupational training, or the personal influence of suitable adult role models – all of which could be provided through an improved borstal system and probation services. In themselves, they were a series of solutions that were in future years to encourage periodic crackdowns on wayward youth and the introduction of 'short, sharp, shocks' to direct them back to the path of righteousness.

The argument between the proponents of the two apparently different models of intervention was to continue into a post-war period characterised by a continued rise in recorded youth crime and where it was increasingly suggested that the approved school system was unable to cope with some of the hardened young offenders that were appearing before the courts (Newburn 1995). Public confidence in this system was to be seriously damaged in 1959 by rioting at the Carlton Approved School, which involved staff being stoned and mass absconding, with the resulting inquiry recommending the use of more closed facilities for difficult children. Windlesham (1993: 76) observes that from this point onwards 'the twin claws of the pincer that was to hold the development of penal policy in its grip were the remorseless increase in the incidence of crime, and the overcrowding in the prisons'. This seemingly endless increase in the crime rate from 1955 onwards was to become increasingly influential in criminal justice policy formulation and is worthy of further examination.

Consumer society and criminal youth

Those of us born and raised in the UK during the mid- to late- twentieth century were familiar with apocryphal stories of how in the 'good old days' – or 'before the [Second World] War' – people left their doors open and neighbours entered unannounced to borrow a cup of sugar. These accounts of community and working-class solidarity were also a staple of classical sociological texts (see Dennis et al. 1956). But the truth was probably rather different; thus, in all probability, there was little else to borrow. The defining characteristic of the lives of the great majority of people in those days was poverty and that was the case whether in work or not. The extent of ambition for most people was to earn sufficient money to feed, clothe and keep a roof over the heads of their families. There was no television, limited radio, no videos or DVDs, no motor cars for the vast majority of the population and certainly no overseas holidays let alone the social media and computer use that has permeated the lives of all but the poorest and most disadvantaged people in contemporary society. Most people were poor, had limited ambitions and aspirations beyond basic survival and, in reality, were rather unsophisticated in comparison with (in particular young) people in a similar social position today. Significantly, there was a relatively high level of social consensus and group solidarity because people had very similar life experiences.

In the language of the French sociologist Emile Durkheim a century ago, the lives of ordinary working people – regardless of whether they lived in the great mass industrial areas or the rural countryside – were characterised by high levels of mechanical solidarity. They had similar beliefs, understandings and life experiences which encouraged feelings of group solidarity and community that discouraged widespread involvement in criminal activity (Durkheim 1964). Pearson (1983), nevertheless and significantly, warns us against simplistic, popularly held 'common-sense' notions that criminal activity by children and young people is a relatively recent phenomenon but, at the same time, crime was quantitatively and qualitatively different in a society characterised by relative poverty and very limited aspirations. Poor people undoubtedly did steal from each other but the level of economic gain would have been small. Theft from a neighbour would have been relatively unlikely in the areas with the greatest group solidarity and the least money.

We should not really be surprised that crime levels rose so much – and so regularly – from 1955, because the nature of British society was itself to change radically in the intervening years. Wartime rationing finally ended in 1955 and the bright, brash consumer society that was to produce an educated, relatively sophisticated, affluent population of people with diverse knowledge, skills and experiences of life was born. In the language of Durkheim, the lives of people were to become increasingly characterised by high levels of organic solidarity where there is less dependence on the maintenance of uniformity between individuals and more emphasis on the management of the diverse functions of different groups (Durkheim 1964).

Perhaps the most important development in the sixty years following the emergence of the consumer society has been the reality that the UK has become substantially more prosperous than at any time in its history. The annual GDP figures show that the output of the economy has risen by a colossal 377 per cent since 1955, allowing for inflation (The Guardian Online 2015), but significantly this growth in prosperity has not been equally shared, with more inequality in our society than at any time since the 1930s. The skilled industrial worker – largely male – has virtually disappeared and been replaced by casualised, low-paid, temporary, part-time workers ('McJobs')[1] – many of them on 'zero-hours' contracts[2] and a substantial proportion being female. Increased material affluence in the past sixty years was invariably the outcome of a shift towards dual-income families, where both parents work but spend less time with their children, and lone parenthood, with its associated significant social consequences (Joseph Rowntree Foundation 1995). Perhaps, most significantly, the qualitative experience of poverty and unemployment today is rather different than in the past.

Life pre-Second World War was characterised by a generalised, shared working-class experience of poverty, whether in work or not. Today, the level of home ownership is substantially higher than in the past, and car ownership and holidays in increasingly more exotic overseas locations are becoming a widespread norm. The workless and homeless, nevertheless, live alongside, or at least not far from, the relatively affluent. The wonders and delights of the consumer society are aggressively advertised during the low-budget programmes churned out on television twenty-four hours a day to entertain the 'new leisure classes' and, in more recent years, on the World Wide Web. Moreover, the contemporary economically dispossessed have very different aspirations than their predecessors sixty years ago. Many aspire to the products they see widely advertised in television commercials and the social media world beyond and they are not easily distracted from these ambitions. They do not accept long-term unemployment and poverty in the same stoic fashion as their predecessors. They have legitimate aspirations to a share in the 'good life'. It is these socio-economic changes that provided the cultural context for the huge explosion in recorded crime that has occurred since the beginning of consumer society.

Four closely interconnected explanations have been offered from various sources – some more contested than others – to explain this huge increase in crime (Hopkins Burke 1998b). First, relatively non-contentiously, there has been a huge increase in opportunity provided by the growth of the consumer society and it is instructive that 94 per cent of all notifiable offences recorded by the police are against property (Barclay 1995) and of course ownership of consumer durables is very widespread.[3] In contemporary society, most people have something worth stealing even if it is only their welfare benefits. Second, a further more contested explanation points to the 'breakdown in informal social controls' that has occurred in society, with commentators drawing attention to the decline in the traditional nuclear family, the rise of the single-parent family and the 'parenting deficit' (Dennis and Erdos 1992). Third, a less widely voiced explanation observes the disintegration of the traditional collective working-class culture and the triumph of competitiveness and entrepreneurialism.[4] The 'go for it' philosophy of the enterprise culture has penetrated the whole social structure, from the boardrooms of big business to youths carrying out robberies on the street or committing burglaries. Everyone is an entrepreneur now and the boundaries between many legitimate and illegitimate business activities are increasingly blurred (see Hobbs 1988, 1995) and morality is indeed ambiguous (Hopkins Burke 2007). Fourth, the mass working-class culture of modernity was based on the similarity of existence described earlier. In contrast, the increasingly diverse and fragmented consumer society has brought spending power and opportunities, and with it new and diverse groups with subjective and varied interests which have often set them against the traditions of their parent communities. Young people, of course, have been in the vanguard of this change and the development of a group identity through an association with others who share a particular taste in music and clothes has been an important part of the transition to adulthood for many young people since the beginnings of the consumer society. It was against this background that crime levels were to increase substantially over much of the past half sixty years with parallel concerns as to how the authorities should respond to an apparently growing problem, although the official statistics suggest to the more gullible that there has been something of a 'crime drop' in more recent times, a point to which we will return later in this book. We will consider the various explanations as to why young people become involved in offending behaviour in some detail in the second part of this book. We now return to the development of the juvenile justice system and the apparent triumph of welfarism as a mode of intervention during the 1960s.

The triumph of welfarism

The Ingleby Report of 1960 endorsed the structure of the juvenile court and rejected any merger of approved schools with other residential accommodation, or the removal of responsibility for these institutions from the Home Office. The major focus of the report centred on the conflict that it felt existed between the judicial and welfare functions of the juvenile court. Newburn (1995: 165) observes that this resulted in:

A child being charged with a petty theft or other wrongful act for which most people would say that no great penalty should be imposed, and the case apparently ending in a disproportionate sentence. For when the court causes enquiries to be made . . . the court may determine that the welfare of the child requires some very substantial interference which may amount to taking the child away from his home for a prolonged period.

The proposed solution was to be an immediate increase in the age of criminal responsibility from 8 to 12 – with the possibility of a rise to 13 or 14 – and below that age only welfare proceedings to be brought (Morris and Giller 1987). The Children and Young Persons Act 1963, by way of compromise, increased the age of criminal responsibility to 10. The argument that there is little point in punishing children or young people whose offending behaviour may be related to family or other problems was nevertheless to continue to influence policy. Some went as far as to suggest that children and young people should be removed from the criminal justice process altogether, and dealt with by a family council or tribunal which would deal with all children with family or social problems (Cavadino and Dignan 1997).

These debates were central to the introduction of the Children and Young Persons Act 1969, which advocated a rise in the age of criminal responsibility to 14, and sought alternatives to detention by way of treatment via non-criminal proceedings and care orders. The benefits of diversionary policies were stressed and one of its aims was that all offenders under 14 should be dealt with through care and protection proceedings rather than the juvenile court. The police were encouraged to use cautions for juvenile offenders and only refer them to court following consultation with the social services. The expanding role of the social worker was reflected in provision for care orders, which, after being given by magistrates, were to be implemented by social workers. Social workers rather than magistrates would thus make the key decision as to whether the young person would be sent to a residential institution or left at home. Community homes, which were to house all children in care whether or not they had committed an offence, replaced the approved schools which had dealt only with offenders. It was, moreover, intended to phase out borstals and detention centres and to replace them with a sentence of intermediate treatment – again to be run by social services.

The Children and Young Persons Act 1969 was heralded by its pro-welfare treatment model supporters as a decisive instance of 'decriminalising' penal policy but it was never fully implemented. Crucial opposition came from the Conservative government elected in 1970, the magistrates, the police and some sections of the probation service, on the grounds that it undermined 'the due process of law' by relying too heavily on the discretion of social workers. The outcome was that the social welfare philosophy of the legislation was consistently undermined; for example, it had been the intention to keep juveniles out of the criminal justice system but the 1970s were to be characterised by substantial increases in the number of custodial sentences given to young people.

Two central features of twentieth-century youth justice policy were to culminate in the 1969 Act. First, increasing attention was to be given to assessing the suitability of the family situation of the offender when seeking causes of delinquency. Second, the distinction between the delinquent and the neglected child was to become increasingly obscured. The notion of the 'responsible individual' enshrined in the justice/punishment model of intervention was, moreover, replaced by the concept of the 'responsible family' and the juvenile court was empowered to play the part of the responsible parent by establishing child welfare as the primary principle of intervention. There was thus to be an increasing state intervention in family life and socialisation under the guise of protecting children who were considered to be living in 'undesirable' surroundings.

These welfare/treatment model developments appear at first sight to be progressive and humane but came to be criticised from various standpoints right across the political spectrum. Clarke (1975) argued – from a radical criminological perspective – that we were simply witnessing a continuation of dominant nineteenth-century concerns to ensure the stable reproduction of future generations of labour power. The only change was that this process would now be achieved by the reformation of whole families rather than by isolating their 'wayward' children. Morris et al. (1980) and Taylor et al. (1979) criticised the treatment philosophy and the family pathology model of the causes of delinquency inherent in the 1969 Act as justifications for exercising greater coercive intervention in the lives of 'delinquent' children and their families. They argued that a social work understanding of delinquency, given its dominant grounding in psychoanalytical theories, would only reinforce the principle of individual pathology and ignore the material and social inequality inherent in society. Taylor et al. (1979), observing that more children were incarcerated during the 1970s than ever before, argued that the rights of children would be better upheld by returning to the principles of eighteenth-century liberal criminal justice. It is argued from this perspective that the welfare-orientated juvenile justice system based on the discretion of social work and medical experts' erodes the rights of children to natural justice.

In some respects, such arguments mark a return to early nineteenth-century rational actor principles of viewing the juvenile as a young adult and, from this perspective, it is argued that children are the best judges of their own interests and should be free to exercise their own choice from the age of 10 years. Such legalistic arguments for the concept of 'juvenile responsibility for law-breaking' were also ideologically effective in the arguments for order and control promoted by the Conservative government that came to power in 1979 and this is discussed in the following chapter.

Juvenile justice during the 1970s was characterised by dramatic increases in the use of custody and this was in direct contradiction to the intentions of the 1969 legislation. This drift towards custody was primarily an outcome of a combination of three factors. First, there was a popular belief that the 1970s witnessed a rapid growth in youth crime, characterised by a hard core of 'vicious young criminals' (Pearson 1983). Second, there was a tendency on the part of magistrates to give custodial sentences for almost all types of offence. Third, there was the net-widening propensity of welfarism in drawing young people into the juvenile justice process at an increasingly earlier age. These unintended consequences of albeit the partial implementation of the Children and Young Persons Act 1969 thus acted collectively to accelerate the rate at which young people moved through the sentencing tariff. The number of indictable offences recorded for young offenders remained statistically constant throughout the 1970s – with a slight rise in burglaries and a reduction in violent and sexual offences (Pitts 1982: 8) – but the number of custodial orders nevertheless rose dramatically. A Department of Health and Social Security (DHSS) report concluded that the number of juveniles sent to borstal and detention centres had increased fivefold between 1965 and 1980 and this increase in incarceration was believed to reflect a growing tendency on the part of courts to be more punitive (DHSS 1981).

At the same time, social workers were extending their preventive work with the families of the 'pre-delinquent'. Rohrer (1982) observed that this development meant that many more children were under surveillance, the market for the court was extended and more offenders were placed in local authority care for relatively trivial offences. Preventive work thus meant that children were being sent to institutions at a younger age. Thorpe et al. (1980: 8) identify a judicial backlash against the liberalism of the 1969 Act in which popular wisdom about youth justice and its actual practice had become totally estranged:

> The tragedy that has occurred since can best be described as a situation in which the worst of all possible worlds came into existence. People thus have been persistently led to believe that the juvenile criminal justice system had become softer and softer, while the reality was that it had become harder and harder.

Pitts (2003a) observes that the welfare/treatment model thinking during the 1960s was founded on the notion that crime committed by children and young people was an outcome of poverty and the social and psychological damage that arises from this situation. He notes that this proposition is easily dismissed by its critics, who draw our attention to all those socially excluded young people – to use the contemporary terminology – who come from these difficult socio-economic circumstances but do not transgress against the law, and work hard and against the odds to become successful law-abiding citizens. But the proponents of the welfare/treatment model realised that there is a tiny minority of young people – that 3 to 4 per cent we identified in the previous chapter – who do not grow out of crime. Pitts (2003b) notes that it is these seriously problematic young people with deep-seated socio-psychological problems who are the real focus of attention for any youth justice system and who go on to become homeless, teenage prostitutes and serious drug users before graduating to adult prisons and psychiatric institutions.

Conclusions

This chapter has told the story of an apparently gradual transition from a criminal justice/punishment-based model of intervention in the lives of children and young people who offend, towards a more welfare/treatment-based perspective. In reality, from the nineteenth century, when the troubled and troublesome among the youth population was first thought to require a different response to that afforded adults, the history of youth justice has been riddled with confusion, ambiguity and unintended consequences. The transition from a justice/punishment to welfare/ treatment-based model of intervention was never straightforward and a tension between the two models was always there and this continues to be the case until the present day. Moreover, the persistent critique of welfarism is that its rhetoric of benevolence and humanitarianism often blinds us to its denial of legal rights, its discretionary non-accountable procedures and its ability to impose greater intervention than would have been merited on the basis of conduct alone. These issues persist in the next chapter where we resume the story of youth justice from the election of a Conservative government in 1979 with a self-professed agenda of being tough on crime until the subsequent election of New Labour in 1997 and the creation of the contemporary youth justice system.

Summary of main points

1 Before the nineteenth century there was no special provision for young offenders, who were treated no differently than adults and could be sent to adult prisons, hanged or transported to the colonies.
2 There were widespread motivations for change and in particular pressure from politically powerful religious, philanthropic and penal reform groups.
3 The British legal system introduced different interventions for young offenders from the mid-nineteenth century onwards.
4 Moreover, in addition to the creation of new punitive measures for dealing with the young, laws were passed removing children from certain areas of industry and restricting their activities in others, while compulsory elementary education was introduced in 1870.
5 Changes in the perception of childhood led to new ideas about the ways in which the delinquent and vulnerable young should be dealt with by the state.
6 The arrival of the juvenile court from 1908 was to herald the arrival of another social construction of youthful humanity, the 'juvenile delinquent'.
7 The borstal system introduced indeterminate sentences of between one and three years for males aged 16–20 and emphasised a mixture of discipline and training with some placing an emphasis on education.
8 The Criminal Justice Act 1948 was introduced in the context of the creation of the welfare state. It placed a number of restrictions on the use of imprisonment but at the same time introduced detention centres and attendance centres which appeared to reflect a more punitive approach.
9 The Children and Young Persons Act 1969 was heralded by its pro-welfare treatment model supporters as a decisive instance of 'decriminalising' penal policy but it was never fully implemented.
10 Welfare/treatment model developments appeared at first sight to be progressive and humane but came to be criticised from various standpoints right across the political spectrum.

Discussion questions

1   What arguments and discourses led to the emrgemce of a new criminal justice system for dealing with children and young people who had offended?
2   What new interventions were introduced in the nineteenth century for dealing with young offenders?
3   What was the purpose of the borstal system?
4   Why might the Children and Young Persons Act 1969 be considered the highpoint of welfarism in England and Wales?
5   What were the different criticisms of the CYPA 1969 and which groups favoured these?

Notes

1 McJobs: 'A low-pay, low-prestige, low-dignity, low-benefit, no-future job in the service sector. Frequently considered a satisfying career choice by people who have never held one' (Coupland 1992).
2 Zero-hours contracts, or casual contracts, allow employers to hire staff with no guarantee of work. They mean employees work only when needed by employers, often at short notice. Employees' pay depends on how many hours they work.
3 Whereas motor vehicles were in very short supply sixty years ago, they now account for upwards of one-quarter of all recorded crime.
4 This is a process usually associated with the various Conservative governments led by Margaret Thatcher and John Major. However, the trend has been very much in place since the 1950s. Their economic policies and legitimating philosophy merely accelerated the process.

4 Youth justice and the new conservatism

Key issues

1 The socio-political context of the new conservatism
2 Populist conservatism and the moral backlash
3 The retreat from welfarism
4 Populist conservatism and youth justice
5 Postscript: young people and the postmodern condition

The previous chapter told the story of an apparently gradual but highly ambiguous transition from a criminal justice/punishment-based model of intervention in the lives of children and young people who offend, towards a more welfare/treatment-based perspective. This chapter resumes that narrative with the election of a Conservative government in 1979 which presented itself to the electorate as being prepared to take a vigorous stance against crime. Before doing that it will be extremely useful to locate the outcome of that election and its aftermath in the broader socio-political context and in doing so we will return to the end of the Second World War.

The socio-political context of the new conservatism

Britain emerged from the 1939–45 war as militarily victorious but economically exhausted. It was one of the top three post-war superpowers but in reality it was a distant third behind the USA and the Soviet Union. Nonetheless, its political system and the British state had been vindicated by success in war and over the next few years emerged as what many considered to be a model social democracy which combined planning and collectivism with civil liberties (Kavanagh 1987). The Labour government elected in 1945 was largely responsible for what is called the 'post-war consensus', although some of the key elements can trace their origins to the war-time coalition government and the influence of Liberals such as William Beveridge (who devised the welfare state) and the economist John Maynard Keynes (who had a whole school of economics named after him).

Essentially, there was a belief that government could play a positive role in promoting greater equality through social engineering and five major features of domestic politics can be identified as part of this strategy. First, all governments accepted a commitment to maintain full employment by Keynesian techniques of economic management. Ministers would use levers, such as cutting taxes and boosting state spending, to increase the level of economic activity. Second, there was an acceptance and, indeed, some encouragement of the role of the trade unions. In contrast to the pre-war years, governments recognised and consulted them regularly on workplace relations and economic policy. The access of unions to government was increased partly by full employment and partly by governments turning post-1961 to income policies as a way of curbing inflation. Third, there was a mixed economy, with a large role for state ownership of the utilities (such as gas, electricity, coal and rail), some wealth creation (steel and the car industry) and intervention and planning in the economy. Fourth, there was the creation of the welfare state. The object of the national insurance system and the National Health Service (NHS) was to provide an adequate income and free health care when the income of a family was hit by, for example, sickness, old age, unemployment or death of the main breadwinner. The services were provided out of general taxation, or insurance, and were seen as a key component of social citizenship. Fifth, there was a belief that government could play a positive role in promoting greater equality through social engineering; for example, by progressive taxation, redistributive welfare spending, comprehensive schooling and regional policies.

These policies were pursued by both Labour and Conservative governments, the latter because they thought it was necessary to gain working-class support to win general elections and gain the consent of the major interest groups. Consensus is not an ideal term because it may be read as suggesting that there were no differences between the two main political parties. In fact, the above ideas and policies were often challenged by the left wing of the Labour Party and by the free market or right wing of the Conservatives. But much of the political elite – the media, civil service and the leaderships of the parties, particularly when they were in government – shared many of these ideas (Kavanagh 1987).

During the 1960s and 1970s, the two main political parties – Conservative and Labour – competed to reverse the relative economic decline of Britain. There was a growing awareness that the economic league tables showed the country to be at the wrong end for figures regarding industrial strikes, productivity, inflation, economic growth and rising living standards. Virtually all European countries, with the exception of Britain, had so-called post-war 'economic miracles', with the latter often described as the 'sick man of Europe'. The targets for blame included failure to invest in new plant and machinery, restrictive working practices and outdated attitudes on the shop floor ('us and them'), amateurish and incompetent management, incremental loss of overseas markets and the rise of competition increasingly from the developing world with its far lower wage costs. In short, Britain appeared to be the weak link in the international liberal capitalist economic system, plagued by high inflation, low growth and irresponsible trade union power.

It seemed to many that the UK was ungovernable and that no government had an answer to inflation. Consequently, governments of both parties turned their attention to incomes policies as an answer to inflation, seeking to agree a 'norm' for annual wage rises with the unions. This was always difficult for the unions, for their purpose is collective bargaining and while this policy managed to keep prices down for a time, it would collapse when powerful groups broke the 'norm'. Such policies failed dramatically with the Conservative government in 1973–4 (miner's strikes and the 'three-day week') and again with the Labour government in 1979 (the 'Winter of Discontent').

Measures introduced in order to boost economic activity and reduce unemployment tended to have the unintended consequences of pulling in extra imports from overseas, thereby worsening the trade balance, and which again seemed to lead to unacceptable rises in inflation. The consequential loss of confidence of the financial markets meant a sharp slide in the value of sterling, which in turn led to the necessity of a humiliating International Monetary Fund (IMF) 'rescue' package in 1976 where a loan was granted to the British government in return for spending cuts and continued anti-inflation policies. That this happened at a time of high unemployment seemed to signal the end of the era of Keynesian economic policies.

The 'Winter of Discontent' in 1978–9 was a key event. The rash of strikes in crucial public services against the income policies of the Labour government seemed to show that the country was ungovernable and that no government had an answer to inflation. Moreover, it destroyed the reputation of the government for prudent economic management and its ability to gain the cooperation of the unions. Just as the Heath government had fallen following the miners' damaging strike against its incomes policy and subsequently lost the February 1974 general election, so the Labour government lost office in 1979, in very similar circumstances. There were two responses to this failure. From the political right, the new ideas of economists Friedrich Hayek and Milton Friedman – advocating monetarism, a greater scope for markets and limited government – won out over the ideas of the Left for more state ownership and the protection of industry following a withdrawal from the European Community.

The Conservative Party – under the leadership of Margaret Thatcher – won the 1979 election and much of so-called Thatcherism (which along with 'Reaganomics' named after President Ronald Reagan in the USA, provided the origins of what we now call neoliberalism) actually evolved pragmatically as circumstances allowed, but was crucially helped by the failures of the opposition. For example, the privatisation of public-owned utilities, which was to become a flagship policy, was not mentioned in the 1979 manifesto. At the following general election in 1983 and in spite of unemployment doubling to some three million, the government won a landslide victory thanks in large part to divisions in the Labour Party and its left-wing policies. Significantly, the Thatcher government insisted that it could no longer be a universal provider of benefits and the post-war socio-economic political consensus between the main political parties was over, with major changes to the fabric of society arising. First, trade unions would now be required to operate within in a much tighter legal framework, including: the requirement for pre-strike ballots before taking industrial action, the end of the 'closed shop' (union membership as a precondition of employment in a specific industry) and making unions liable for damages incurred in illegal strikes. The unions were hardly consulted by the government during the course of this process and their influence waned in part because of the abandonment of income policies and rising unemployment. Second, the spread of privatisation of the major utilities altered the balance of the mixed economy. Gas, electricity, telecommunications, British Airways and later British Rail were all privatised. There was also a huge sale to tenants of council housing. Third, the government abandoned its commitment to full employment, stating this was the responsibility of employers and employees, and accorded priority instead to keeping inflation low. Fourth, welfare state benefits were increasingly subject to means-testing, with entitlement restricted. Fifth, the government insisted that it could no longer be a universal provider with more left to the market, the voluntary sector and self-help.

There was nevertheless far from universal endorsement of Thatcherism in 1979 (Kavanagh 1987). As late as October 1978, Labour was still ahead in some opinion polls, but the 'Winter of Discontent' turned the public against Labour and the unions. The election was nevertheless more of a rejection of Labour than an endorsement of Thatcherism. It was the recapture of the Falkland Islands from Argentina in 1982 that was important for the success of the Thatcher project, coinciding with an improvement in the public standing of the government and of Thatcher herself. The victory seemed to vindicate her claims in domestic politics that she could provide strong leadership and stand up for the nation. The war rhetoric could now be turned against the perceived enemies within – particularly the trade unions.

There are academic disputes about the extent to which military success boosted Conservative chances in the 1983 election for there were signs of a revival in the polls and greater economic optimism even before the capture. But the big unanswerable question is whether the government would have survived if the Falklands War had not happened. Crucially, Labour could not exploit widespread dissatisfaction in the country, because it was seen as weak and divided (Kavanagh 1987). Thatcher was respected but she was not liked by the British public. For all the talk of sweeping election successes, her government only gained an average of 42 per cent of the vote at general elections but the peculiarities of the British electoral system and the split of the non-Conservative vote between the Labour and Liberal-Alliance parties meant that the government was able to win over 60 per cent of seats in the House of Commons.

Surveys at the time showed limited support for many of Thatcher's values. Crewe (1989) noted the lack of support for her policies on 'tax-and-spend' and replacing the dependency culture with an enterprise culture. Moreover, there was greater approval for a more equal society and for social and collective provision of welfare as against her vision of people looking after themselves. But Labour could not exploit this dissatisfaction, because it was not trusted on the economy or defence and was consigned to the electoral backwoods for eighteen years.

Populist conservatism and the moral backlash

Significantly, there was a strong moralist strand to the new populist conservatism and during the 1970s Conservative intellectuals in both the USA and the UK had mounted a vigorous moral campaign against various forms of 'deviance'. It was in this context that Margaret Thatcher was in 1979 to make crime a major and successful election issue for the first time in post-war Britain. Her general concern was to re-establish what she considered to be 'Victorian values' and to this end targeted the supposed debilitating permissive society of the 1960s and its perceived legitimisation in 'soft' social science. For this political 'new right', the economic, technological and managerial achievements of the modern world should be safeguarded and expanded, but at the same time there should be a comprehensive assault mounted on its cultural and ethical components. Indeed, it was perceived to be this modernist culture with its emphasis on subjective values and individual self-expression that was crucially undermining the motivational requirements of an efficient economy and rational state administration. In short, individuals were seen as increasingly unwilling to achieve and even less prepared to obey (Habermas 1989). Populist Conservatives thus sought a revival in past tradition, in the values of the state, schools, family and, implicitly, in the unquestioned acceptance of authority.

Conservative intellectual Sir Keith Joseph made explicit reference to the need to reject 'fashionable socialist opinion' and in particular focused attention on a perceived need to amend the Children and Young Persons Act 1969. The outgoing Labour government was depicted as being anti-police, condoning lawbreaking and having ineffective policies for crime control. After the election, the home secretary expanded places in detention centres for young 'thugs' and introduced a regime of 'short, sharp, shocks'. A subsequent White Paper – *Young Offenders* (Home Office 1980) – and the resulting legislation, the Criminal Justice Act 1982, attacked the welfare approach of the Children and Young Persons Act 1969 and there was a significant move away from predestined actor notions of treatment and lack of personal responsibility and a return to rational actor notions of punishment and individual and parental responsibility. In accordance with this rediscovery of the rational actor model, there was also a significant move away from executive decision-making (social workers) and a return to judicial decision-making (courts) and away from the belief in the 'child in need' to what Tutt (1981) has termed 'the rediscovery of the delinquent'. The Criminal Justice Act 1982 was nonetheless 'not an unremittingly punitive statute' (Cavadino and Dignan 1997) for it essentially introduced restrictions on the use of custody for all those under 21 which, in itself, was an indication of the apparent ambiguity of the Conservative government youth justice policy and its outcomes during the following years.

In many ways, juvenile justice policy in the 1980s and 1990s was underpinned by contradictions and inconsistencies. For example, the Criminal Justice Act 1991 espoused an 'anti-custody' ethos, while the government announced the introduction of 'new' secure training units in 1993 and the Criminal Justice and Public Order Act 1994 introduced new tougher sentences for young offenders. Some observed these apparently contradictory measures to be the response of a government that had lost confidence in the ability of the 'experts' to find solutions to the problem of youth offending and it was merely reacting to crises as they arose. However, it is possible to identify an increasing and consistent tendency to deal with young people as adults. Others took a more optimistic view. Gelsthorpe and Morris (1994: 984) observed that:

> The arguments are clearly no longer about 'welfare', 'crime control', or 'justice'. The new philosophies cannot be allied to the political right or left as they once could. Indeed, there is every indication that there is a new political consensus on criminal justice in the 1990s.

Conservative youth justice policy during the 1980s and 1990s clearly provided significant foundations that led to the development of the contemporary youth justice system – regardless of a change in political leadership and the self-proclaimed rupture with the past – and these are considered in this chapter.

The retreat from welfarism

During the 1980s, the 'welfare' approach to youth justice came under increasing attack and not just from the aforementioned right-wing, law-and-order lobby influenced by 'right realist' criminological thinking and the rediscovery of the rational actor model, but also from proponents of a 'progressive' 'back to justice' policy. In particular, there was a fundamental questioning of the ability of social workers to diagnose the causes of delinquency and to treat these with non-punitive methods. Empirical justification for these reservations came with the publication of an influential paper by Robert Martinson (1974) which purported to show that rehabilitation programmes in prison simply 'do not work' and thus the whole rationale for the existence of welfare-oriented intervention strategies was called into question. Moreover, the discretion of social work judgements was criticised as a form of arbitrary power, with many young people, it was argued, the subject of apparently non-accountable state procedures with their liberty often unjustifiably denied (Davies 1982: 33). It was further argued that the investigation of social background is in itself an imposition and social work involvement not only preserves explanations of individual pathology but also undermines the right to natural justice. We are here reminded of that first attempt to introduce legislation into parliament in 1840 that would have enabled magistrates to act as moral guardians of destitute and delinquent juveniles but which was, nevertheless, rejected by the House of Lords because it denied children the right to a jury trial in accordance with the then rational actor model of criminal behaviour and which was discussed in the previous chapter. Such an approach, it was now argued, might place the child or young person in double jeopardy and unintentionally accelerate movement up the tariff.

With the experience of the 1970s, in which the numbers of custodial sentences increased dramatically in the aftermath of the implementation of an at least nominal welfare treatment system, the progressive new justice proponents argued for a return to notions of 'due process' and 'just deserts' along with moves to decriminalise certain (e.g., victimless) offences and a general shift towards using alternatives to custody (Rutherford 1978). As Taylor et al. (1979: 22–3) observe:

> Under English law the child enjoys very few of the rights taken for granted by adults under the principles of natural justice. The law's reference to the child's 'best interests' reflects the benevolent paternalism of its approach. Essentially as far as the courts are concerned, the 'best interests' principle empowers social workers, psychologists, psychiatrists and others to define on the basis of their opinions what is good for the child . . . [The law] does not require that the experts should substantiate their opinions or prove to the court that any course of action they propose will be more effective in promoting the best interests of the child than those taken by the parent or by the child acting on his own behalf . . . A child may find that his/her arguments against being committed to care are perceived as evidence of their need for treatment, as a sign, for example, that they have 'authority problems'.

A classic justice/punishment model solution was thus proposed with a return to the use of determinate sentences based on the seriousness of the offence rather than the profile of individual offenders. In other words; the fundamental rational actor notion of the punishment should fit the crime and not the characteristics and circumstances of the individual offender. This approach, it was argued, would be seen as 'fair 'and 'just' by young people themselves. Moreover, a greater use of cautions by the police for minor offences would help to keep young people out of the courts; but when in court, closer control over social inquiry reports would in turn ensure that intermediate treatment, care orders or other forms of 'community correction' would only be used in the most serious of cases as an alternative to custody, thus helping to avoid the 'net-widening' potential inherent within the system.

While it was recognised that this approach would help overcome some of the ambiguities of a system dogged by the dual concern to both 'care and control' and apprehensions about the 'arbitrary discretion' of social service professionals, the 'back to justice' movement was not without its own critics. Pitts (1996) notes that this renewed faith in legalism was advocated at precisely the same time as 'youth' was yet again the subject of a major moral panic and was thus seen as requiring greater degrees of containment. There is nevertheless little doubt that such debates had considerable influence on, and helped to legitimate, government policy throughout the populist Conservative years between 1979 and 1997.

Populist conservatism and youth justice

The Criminal Justice Act 1982 involved a fundamental attack on the social welfare perspective introduced by the Children and Young Persons Act 1969, with a significant move away from the welfare/treatment model of youth justice towards the justice/punishment model and this was epitomised by new powers of disposal made available to magistrates. Criteria were introduced to restrict the use of care and custodial orders and juveniles were now to be legally represented. Moreover, custodial orders were to be made only in cases where it could be established that the offender had failed to respond to non-custodial measures, where custody was seen as unavoidable for the protection of the public, or where the offence was serious. Offenders had previously been sentenced to an indeterminate period of borstal training with the date of release – which could be up to three years – decided by those running the system. Borstals were now abolished, thus removing any element of indeterminacy from the system, and replaced by a fixed-term youth custody order and the use of imprisonment was abolished for offenders under the age of 21.

There appeared to be little consistency as different sentences were repeatedly introduced and then abolished. Thus, from 1983 a determinate sentence of youth custody was introduced for offenders aged 15 and under 21 with a maximum sentence for those aged under 17 of twelve months. A sentence of custody for life was introduced as the equivalent to life imprisonment when the offender was aged 17 and under 21, while detention sentence orders for males were changed so that the usual sentence ranged from twenty-one days to four months instead of three to six months.

The Criminal Justice Act 1982 appears at first sight to provide clear evidence of the ambiguity and inconsistency of Conservative youth justice policy during the 1980s. It was clearly introduced with the objective of helping to 'restore the rule of law' (Pitts 1996) but at the same time placed significant restrictions on the use of custody for young people. This apparent inconsistency can nevertheless be explained with reference to a legislative strategy which Bottoms (1974) terms 'bifurcation' and which involves separating the treatment of serious offenders from that of minor offenders, with the outcome being that the former are dealt with by overtly punitive means and the latter are dealt with much more leniently.

Pitts (1988) observes that the introduction of shorter detention centre sentences – or 'short, sharp shocks' as they became known – was supplemented by considerable government-instigated publicity, or what is now termed 'spin', which sought to assure the public that while young offenders were being subjected to shorter periods of incarceration, the deterrent effect of these tougher regimes would nevertheless be greater in accordance with the contemporary rational actor model philosophy we will encounter in the following chapter. Many of those designated less serious offenders would now be dealt with by a significant expansion of the Department of Health and Social Security (DHSS) Intermediate Treatment Initiative which was to provide 4,500 'alternatives to custody'. Pitts (1996: 266) observes the somewhat ironic consequences of these policies:

The government was seeking to persuade magistrates to sentence larger numbers of less problematic children and young people, whom they described as 'hooligans', to a brief and relatively inexpensive spell 'inside'. They were also trying to persuade magistrates to divert simultaneously a similar number of more serious young offenders, who attracted much longer and much more expensive custodial sentences (and who, since the mid-1970s, had constituted an important element in the crisis of overcrowding in British prisons) to alternatives to custody, in the community.

The government had nonetheless given magistrates a mixed message. The home secretary, as a politician, had said that we must 'get tough', but the home secretary as a penal administrator had said that we must limit the use of custody. The bench, by and large, had listened to the first and ignored the second. Muncie (1990) observes that the outcome was that the youth custody centre population increased by 65 per cent in the twelve months ending in May 1984, while that of the new-style 'short, sharp shock' detention centres was to actually decline during the same period. Pitts (1996) observes that a policy which had sought to both 'get tough' with a minority of serious and persistent young offenders while, at the same time, actually reducing the incarcerated population had quite simply failed. A successful bifurcation strategy was still sought.

By the mid-1980s the Home Office had enthusiastically discovered and adopted the new public management philosophy, which will be discussed in the following chapter, and had come to pursue a rational cost-effective youth justice process:

> Describing their 'mission' in terms of 'targets', 'minimum standards' and 'performance indicators', they were anti-union, anti-professional and pro-privatization. This was 'full-blown' Thatcherism and it set itself against restrictive practices in the police, the law and the Prison Service.
>
> (Pitts 1996: 267)

The late 1980s nevertheless came to be proclaimed a 'successful revolution' in youth justice policy not least because the number of young people incarcerated was reduced substantially during the period. The numbers aged 17 or under convicted or cautioned decreased from 230,000 in 1981 to 149,000 in 1991 (Hagell and Newburn 1994), while the number of juveniles given custodial sentences was also significantly reduced: 6,700 juveniles were sentenced to custody in 1984, compared with 3,400 in 1988, 2,000 in 1991 and 1,700 in 1992 (Hagell and Newburn 1994). It was the projects developed within the DHSS Intermediate Treatment (IT) Initiative that were seen as a key factor in this reduction, although we should also note that there was a quite substantial 18 per cent drop in the population of 14–16-year-old males during the period 1981–88 (Newburn 2002b).

The DHSS Intermediate Treatment Initiative of 1983 financed the establishment of 110 intensive schemes in sixty-two local authority areas to provide alternatives to custody and practitioners were required to evolve a 'new style of working' with less focus on the emotional and social needs of juveniles and more on the nature of the offence. It was through such means that magistrates were to be persuaded that IT was no longer a 'soft option', but a 'high tariff' disposal and this was achieved, in practice, by the development of inter-agency juvenile panels which by the 1980s existed in most local authorities in England and Wales. The panels, comprising representatives from the welfare agencies, the youth service, the police and education departments, reviewed the cases of apprehended children and young people entering the youth justice system and, where possible, they were diverted away from court.

Perhaps the most significant development throughout the 1980s was the repeatedly affirmed government commitment to the concept of community-based diversionary schemes for young offenders. Diversion had increased in the years following the introduction of the Children and Young Persons Act 1969 with an enormous rise in the numbers cautioned by the Juvenile Liaison Bureau established by the police, but by the 1980s there was a growing recognition of the limitations of custodial or institutional treatment. Custody was extremely expensive – with detention invariably costing considerably more than fee-paying boarding schools – but the vast majority of young offenders coming out of such institutions went on to reoffend (Cavadino and Dignan 1997). Many argued that such institutions acted like schools of crime where offenders perpetuated a delinquent or criminal subculture based on violence and bullying (Hopkins Burke and Hopkins Burke 1995). Treatment in the community was, therefore, considered preferable and no less effective in terms of reconviction rates (Cavadino and Dignan 1997).

Diversionary policies were to continue throughout the 1980s. Consultative documents, circulars to the police, and the Code of Practice for Prosecutors emphasised that prosecution should be used only as a last resort, with a greater use of cautioning encouraged to avoid net-widening (Gelsthorpe and Morris 1994). Moreover, the use of cautions for second and third offences was encouraged, along with the development in some areas of caution-plus schemes, which included some form of supervised activity in the community.

Thus, explanations of decarceration probably lie more in efforts to divert juveniles from court (through increased use of informal cautioning, rather than court appearance) than in diversion from custody once in court (as the intensive IT schemes were designed to do). Home Office Circular 14/1985, for example, encouraged the use of 'no further action' or 'informal warnings' instead of formal action and from then (up to a reversal of the policy in 1994) the number of juveniles brought into the system did decline. Again the practice varied regionally, but in Northampton, in 1985, for example, 86 per cent of juveniles who came to the notice of the police were either prosecuted or formally cautioned; however, by 1989 this figure had been reduced to 30 per cent (McLaughlin and Muncie 1994).

A major theme running through all such developments appears to be a reduction in court processing and custody on the grounds of expense and effectiveness. In 1990–1, it was estimated that keeping an offender in custody for three weeks was more expensive than twelve months of supervision or community service. In addition, 83 per cent of young men leaving youth custody were reconvicted within two years, with the reconviction rate for those participating in community-based schemes substantially lower (McLaughlin and Muncie 1994). A less politically motivated approach to offending therefore appeared to be in prospect when the Criminal Justice Act 1988 introduced further restrictions on immediate custody and finally acknowledged the failure of 'short, sharp shock' regimes by merging detention centre orders and youth custody sentences into a single custodial sentence to be served in a 'young offender institution'.

Pratt (1989) now proposed that the 'welfare' and 'justice' models which had always provided the theoretical foundations and justifications of the youth justice system had been superseded by a depoliticised 'corporatist model' in which a partnership of social workers, youth workers, police and magistrates cooperated to produce a cost-effective mechanism for the effective processing of adjudicated offenders. Youth justice workers were also developing working relationships with local juvenile court magistrates in an attempt to encourage them to divert young offenders away from custody and into 'alternatives to custody' programmes. It was the growing confidence of magistrates in the common-sense 'hard-headedness' of these programmes, and the competence of the workers who staffed them, that were seen as the most important factors in the success of the Intermediate Treatment Initiative.

The process was furthered by the Criminal Justice Act 1991, the provisions of which were enacted in October 1992. This legislation was heralded as a significant policy move away from custody in that it attempted to provide a national consistency to the success of local initiatives and to expand the use of diversionary strategies for juveniles to include young adults (17 to under 21 year olds). The anti-custody ethos of the legislation was justified with the promise of more rigorous community disposals which were not alternatives to custody but disposals in their own right.

'Punishment in the community' was to be the favoured option but at the same time this required a significant change in focus for the juvenile court and the practices of probation and social work agencies. For the latter it meant a shift in emphasis away from the traditional approach of 'advise, assist and befriend' towards tightening up the conditions of community supervision and community service work; for the former it meant the abolition of the juvenile court (which had previously dealt with criminal and care cases) and the creation of youth courts and family courts (created by the Children Act 1989) to deal with such matters separately.

The youth court subsequently became operative in October 1992 and would deal only with criminal cases involving those up to and including those aged 17 years of age. Justice-based principles of proportionality in sentencing or 'just deserts' appeared to provide a more consistent, visible and accountable decision-making process, thus ending a confusion which had haunted the juvenile justice system since the inception of the juvenile justice courts in 1908 (Gibson 1994). Moreover, the rationale for dealing with young offenders was now more in accordance with that for dealing with adults.

The impact of decarcerative measures was, nevertheless, shown to be fragile when, in 1991, the home secretary hastily established a new offence of 'aggravated vehicle taking' carrying a maximum five-year sentence. Two years later, the establishment of 'new' secure training units (akin to the old approved schools) was announced amidst a furore of media and political debate about a small group of supposedly 'persistent young offenders', 'bail bandits', to appease the public outcry following the James Bulger case where two 10-year-old children were found guilty of abducting and killing a 2-year-old child. Prime Minister John Major insisted that 'we should understand a little less and condemn a little more' and comments from police, judges and MPs that official figures showing a decrease in juvenile offending were quite simply 'wrong' also signalled a renewed tough stance on the part of government and a repoliticisation of youth crime. As a result, Home Office Circular 18/1994 advised the police to discourage the use of 'inappropriate' – and in particular, repeat – cautions and to pursue conviction instead. The Criminal Justice and Public Order Act 1994 subsequently introduced new sentences for juveniles aged 10–13 convicted of serious offences, secure training centres and doubling of the maximum sentence of detention in a young offender institution.

Thus, until the late 1980s the Conservative government pursued youth justice policies which sought cost-effective reductions in the incarcerated population in accordance with their reduced state-intervention philosophy. Pitts (1996) observes that this system of justice was to appear totally inadequate for dealing with an unprecedented real increase in the crime rate that was to occur on a significant scale in a socio-economic world devastated by an economic restructuring unprecedented since the great Industrial Revolution of the late eighteenth and early nineteenth centuries and the subsequent mass – invariably youth – unemployment. Pitts (1996: 276) observes support for a draconian intervention from right across the political spectrum:

> The then Home Secretary Kenneth Clarke announced the introduction of the secure training order. Tony Blair, then Labour Party shadow Home Secretary, demanded a regime of 'tough love', a phrase he had borrowed from US President Bill Clinton, in which containment and confrontation in secure units would be tempered by responsiveness to the needs of the offender. The Labour MP Ken Livingstone advocated longer prison sentences, and David Blunkett, then Shadow Health Secretary, called for the return of National Service. It suddenly appeared as if politicians across the entire political spectrum had felt for the last 10 years that things, particularly juvenile things, were 'getting out of hand'. The repoliticisation and remoralisation of youth justice was under way and this time the political Left and Centre were determined to wrest the political issue of 'law and order' from the grasp of the Tories if they possibly could.

Within weeks of becoming home secretary in 1993, Michael Howard, undoubtedly bolstered by apparent cross-party support, commenced a process of revising youth justice policy. Secure training centres were to be rethought along the lines of US-style 'boot camps' to provide tougher and more physically demanding regimes aimed at knocking criminal tendencies out of young offenders. Pitts (1996) observes that the retreat from the highpoint of welfarism exemplified by the Children and Young Persons Act 1969 was apparently now complete. At the same time most observers proposed that a return to the 'short, sharp shock' strategies of the recent past would be no more successful than previously when dealing with a new, potentially dangerous young underclass that had been created as an outcome of economic restructuring and whose formation is discussed later in this book.

For some, populist Conservative youth justice policies had amounted to a 'successful revolution' (Pitts 1996) but it is nonetheless a notion worthy of closer consideration. There was certainly no lack of enthusiasm for the apprehension and incapacitation of offenders with a distinct recognition that the latter need not mean imprisonment. Perhaps the most significant component was the policy and legislative strategy of 'bifurcation' (Bottoms 1977) discussed above. It was in reality a twin-track approach to justice that sought to identify those young people who had briefly stumbled in the pursuit of an 'upward option' of increased commitment to education and training (Cohen 1972) and provide them with the impetus and support to overcome their offending behaviour.

In a social world where the modernist project had been undermined by the emergence of what some social scientists have referred to as the postmodern condition (Lyotard 1984) or at least the fragmentation of modernity and social class (Hopkins Burke 1999a) – which are discussed below – and where the old moral certainties seemed increasingly less appropriate, it is possible to identify discourses emerging from very different locations to justify the implementation of bifurcation strategies. First, from an unequivocal liberal standpoint, there was the enduring influence of labelling theory (see Becker 1963, 1967) and its policy implication of unduly avoiding the criminalisation of young people. Second, the 'punishment in the community' approach was more popular than previously with conservative-minded magistrates because it had been given some 'teeth' by the common-sense 'hard-headedness' of the new 'alternative to custody' programmes. Third, the strategy coincided neatly with the extremely influential anti-state spending discourse within the government that was happy to reduce court processing and custody on the grounds of expense (Pitts 1996). Fourth, there were those – usually probation officers and social workers – who questioned the very effectiveness of custody. During the period 1990–1, 83 per cent of young men leaving youth custody were reconvicted within two years; the reconviction rate for those participating in community-based schemes was, however, substantially lower (McLaughlin and Muncie 1994). In short, there was a considerable range of support for a bifurcation strategy.

The persistent and more serious offenders considered more worthy of a punitive intervention could easily be identified as predominantly belonging to those sections of working-class youth who had failed to take advantage of the economic changes that had transformed Britain during the previous twenty years and had objectively taken a 'downward option', ignoring the need for – or unable to take advantage of – improved education and training (Cohen 1972), and had thus drifted into a non-skilled, unemployable underclass location. At the peak of industrial modernity, there had been informal mechanisms whereby these offenders had been reintegrated back into the fold, as Pitts (1996: 280) pertinently observes:

> In the 1960s it was not uncommon for young people in trouble to avoid a custodial sentence by joining the armed forces. For their part, probation officers would often cite the rehabilitative powers of 'going steady', which usually involved getting a 'steady' job in order to 'save up to get married' and 'put a few things away in the bottom drawer'.

Excluded now from legitimate employment opportunities and presenting themselves as unattractive propositions to young women as partners in long-term relationships, these young men found themselves 'frozen in a state of persistent adolescence' (Pitts 1996: 281). This had important implications for their involvement in crime because the evidence suggests that 'growing up' means growing out of crime (Rutherford 1992) and, stripped of legitimate access to adulthood, these young men now found themselves trapped in a limbo world somewhere between childhood and adulthood long after the 'developmental tasks' of adolescence had been completed (Pitts 1996). Having failed to heed the warnings provided by the welfare and youth justice system, persistent and more serious young offenders were, therefore, to be targeted with a much harsher intervention than those who had been labelled non-problematic.

The new multi-agency forum managerialism was without doubt about recognising the two categories of young miscreants we have identified earlier in this book and setting in motion a twin-track response. On the one hand, there was the great majority who could be diverted from further offending behaviour and reintegrated back into the collective fold; on the other hand, there was the small minority for whom harsher treatment was inevitable. The notion of a new political consensus is nonetheless more suspect. Conservatives and Labour were in agreement over the need for realism but there was a substantial difference in their interpretation of that reality (Hopkins Burke 1999a).

Conservative youth justice policy during the 1980s and 1990s had been for many young people particularly strong on 'the stick' but rather weak on 'the carrot'. There were many complexities and ambiguities to government policy during the period where the closely connected twin concerns of political expediency and pragmatism had led repeatedly to apparent changes in direction but in summary the perceived solution to the problem of offending by children and young people was to catch more of them and send out a clear message that they would get caught and be punished, although this did not have to involve incarceration or, indeed, serious punishment. However, this did not require that all children and young people would be treated the same. Populist Conservative youth justice policy during the period again, and indeed where possible, involved a twin-track approach that differentiated between those who were deemed to have briefly transgressed and could be provided with the support to overcome their offending behaviour (and thus were to receive minor if any punishment) and the persistent and more serious offenders who were deemed to be far more of a problem and considered more worthy of a punitive intervention (and thus were to receive more rigorous punishment). The purpose of 'the stick' was to make young people take responsibility for their actions and become fully aware of the consequences of any illegal transgressions. The latter group of persistent and more serious offenders was nevertheless seriously over-represented among the ranks of those sections of working-class youth who had drifted into a non-skilled, unemployable underclass location. For a fundamental outcome of laissez-faire economic and social policy during that period had been the creation of a socially excluded underclass. Welfare policies, in general, and youth justice policies, in particular, had, at best, done nothing to alleviate that situation, and, at worst, had managed to exacerbate the problem. I have thus elsewhere termed this the 'excluded tutelage' model of youth justice (Hopkins Burke 1999a) and it is summarised in Box 4.1.

Box 4.1 The excluded tutelage model of youth justice

- The solution to the crime problem involves catching more offenders in order to deter others.
- It involves a twin-track approach to justice that differentiates between those who have briefly transgressed and can be provided with the support to overcome their offending behaviour, and the more persistent and serious offenders considered more worthy of a punitive intervention.
- The latter group predominantly consists of members of those sections of working-class youth who have drifted into a non-skilled, unemployable underclass location.
- A failure of government non-interventionist socio-economic policies to significantly address the social exclusion of this group of young people.

Vivian Stern of NACRO, writing in 1996, observes that while other European countries favoured the reintegration of offenders back into the community as being central to social and criminal justice policy, Home Office press releases and Conservative government ministers:

> Use the language of conflict, contempt, and hatred . . . doing good is a term of derision, and seeking to help offenders means that you do not care about the pain and suffering of victims.
>
> (Stern, cited in Brown 1998: 74)

Central to the criminal justice strategy of the New Labour government elected in 1997 was to be significant attempts to reintegrate this socially excluded underclass back into inclusive society. It is this notion of reintegration into the community that enables us to explain the approach to youth justice favoured by

New Labour and which enables us to distinguish its policies from those of its populist Conservative predecessors. It is a distinctive approach that was to be part of a wider set of government strategies that sought to reintegrate those sections of the population that had become increasingly socially and economically excluded during the previous twenty years. I have termed this unwritten and unspoken government strategy 'reintegrative tutelage' and this is summarised in Box 4.2.

Box 4.2 The reintegrative tutelage model of youth justice

- Based on the left-realist notion that crime requires a comprehensive solution and there must be a 'balance of intervention'.
- Young people who commit crime must face up to the consequences of their actions and take responsibility (rational actor model of criminal behaviour).
- An effective intervention needs to address the causes of offending as well as punishing the offender (predestined and rational actor model).
- Part of a wider set of educative and welfare strategies that seek to reintegrate socially and economically sections of society.

The reintegrative tutelage model is discussed further in the following chapter which extensively considers the origins and justifications of the contemporary youth justice system introduced by New Labour via its flagship criminal justice legislation, the Crime and Disorder Act 1998. We will conclude this chapter by returning to the socio-political changes that provide the foundations for our story of the development of the juvenile justice system and indeed its transformation in the following chapter to a youth justice system.

Postscript: young people and the postmodern condition

This first part of the book has – so far – discussed the social construction of children and adolescents, and considered strategies to educate, discipline and control them in the interests of myriad different interest groups, including industrial capitalism, middle-class philanthropists, and the respectable working classes who themselves had a significant self-interest in improved life chances and protection from 'the rabble' or 'rough' working classes in their midst; a story to which we return in Chapter 6. This was followed by a discussion of the official, increasingly legislative and institutional response to the deviance and offending behaviour of children and young people from the beginnings of industrial modernity via the rational actor-inspired justice model and the predestined actor-inspired treatment model to scientific managerialism, corporatism and the election of New Labour in 1997. It is nevertheless a story rooted in notions of modernity and modern society.

We have seen that modern societies at their most confident were fundamentally mass societies with a very high demand for workers and military personnel

(Harvey 1989; Hopkins Burke 1999a, 2001). In such societies people were an important commodity, with children and young people perceived to be economic assets worthy of nurture and protection. There were frequent concerns about the quality of that population with the outcome being increasing state intervention in the socialisation of children and young people and especially their re-socialisation when their behaviour became problematic or indeed criminal. The young nevertheless continued to be at least potential societal assets regardless of the level and extent of their bad behaviour and were always worthy of reintegration into mainstream society. Jock Young (1999) observes this process of societal reintegration to be the overriding welfare and social work strategy of modernity. The situation was to change significantly with the fragmentation of that modernity (Hopkins Burke 1999a) and the arrival of what some social scientists have termed the postmodern condition (Lyotard 1984).

From at least the last three decades of the twentieth century, substantial doubts started to emerge – and again from disparate sources – about the sustainability of the modernist project in an increasingly fragmented social world. The collapse of the post-war socio-political consensus and an intensifying lack of enthusiasm for large-scale state intervention in the socio-economic sphere coincided with a decreasing enthusiasm for grand theoretical explanations in the social sciences. Underlying this disintegration of confidence was the beginning of an economic and political transformation accelerated by the oil crisis of the early 1970s, an abandonment of full employment policies with a decline in economic competitiveness, and a restructuring of the world economy with the rise in the productive capacity of the nations of the Pacific Rim. At the same time, increasingly diverse and fragmented social structures began to emerge in the economic, political and cultural spheres. In the economic sphere, there was a rejection of mass production-line technology in favour of flexible working patterns and a flexible labour force. This involved a weakening of trade unions, a greater reliance on peripheral and secondary labour markets, the development of a low-paid and part-time, often female, labour force, and the shift towards a service, rather than manufacturing, economy. Politically, there was the dismantling of elaborate state planning and provision in the fields of welfare. Meanwhile, most conventional representative democratic systems were proving increasingly inadequate to the task of representing myriad interest groups as diverse as major industrialists and financiers, small business proprietors, the unemployed and dispossessed, wide-ranging gender and sexual preference interests, environmentalists, the homeless and the unemployed (Giddens 1994).

It had been with the emergence of modernity and the needs of a mass industrial economy that children and young people had become an asset rather than a liability to society. The modern epoch was thus epitomised by strategies to control the activities of children and young people via education and discipline with the implicit objective of integration into an inclusive and productive, albeit unequal, society. The period of high modernity – circa 1945–74 – was distinguished by an unwritten social contract secured between government and the people based on full employment and a relatively generous welfare state. The subcultural mechanisms whereby unskilled working-class youth came to accept and reproduce their

role within that economically and socially unequal industrial modernity are discussed at the conclusion of the second part of this book.

It was with the fragmentation of that modernity that whole tracts of the former
industrial working class now appeared superfluous to the requirements of society
and the consequences – either intended or unintended – of subsequent government
policies were to lead to growing social exclusion for this group. The unwritten
social contact of high modernity had collapsed. The total transformation of the
UK economy that occurred during the 1980s brought with it perhaps the last
chance for a now far from confident modern mass society. Mass unemployment
had now arrived:

> On official figures . . . unemployment increased from 4.1 percent of the labour
> force in 1972 to 10.3 percent in 1981. Official figures suggest that the high-
> est level of unemployment in the 1980s in Britain was 12.4 percent in 1983,
> declining to 6.8 in 1990, returning to 11 percent (three million) in 1992, and
> declining again to 8 percent in 1996.
>
> (Taylor 1997: 281)

The end of full employment as a social and political project led to increasing
social exclusion for the residual group of low-skilled workers identified above
and discussed in more detail later in this book. With the arrival of long-term
unemployment many became absorbed into what some cultural and sociological
commentators have referred to as a socially excluded, uneducated and unskilled
'underclass' with little value or use to contemporary society. The second part of
this book will consider the various explanations – or criminological theories – that
have been proposed at various times during the modernist era to explain why it is
that young people offend, and it concludes with a critical discussion of the creation of the socially excluded underclass.

Summary of main points

1 Conservative intellectual Sir Keith Joseph made explicit reference to the need
  to reject 'fashionable socialist opinion' and in particular focused attention on
  a perceived need to amend the Children and Young Persons Act 1969.
2 During the 1980s, the 'welfare' approach to youth justice came under increasing attack and not just from the right-wing, law-and-order lobby but also from
  proponents of a 'progressive' 'back to justice' policy.
3 The progressive new justice proponents argued for a return to notions of 'due
  process' and 'just deserts'.
4 A classic justice/punishment model solution proposed a return to the use of
  determinate sentences based on the seriousness of the offence rather than the
  profile of individual offenders.
5 The late 1980s came to be proclaimed a 'successful revolution' in youth justice policy not least because the numbers of young people incarcerated was
  reduced substantially during the period.

6 A most significant development throughout the 1980s was the repeatedly affirmed government commitment to the concept of community-based diversionary schemes.

7 Pratt (1989) proposed that the 'welfare' and 'justice' models which had always provided the theoretical foundations and justifications of the youth justice system had been superseded by a depoliticised 'corporatist model'.

8 The youth court became operative in October 1992 and would deal only with criminal cases involving those up to and including those aged 17 years of age.

9 The impact of decarcerative measures was shown to be fragile when, in 1991, the home secretary hastily established a new offence of 'aggravated vehicle taking' carrying a maximum five-year sentence.

10 Excluded tutelage refers to a failure of government non-interventionist socio-economic policies to significantly address the social exclusion of groups of young people involved in or at risk of involvement in offending.

Discussion questions

1 Explain the various different critiques of welfarism.
2 Explain the concepts 'just deserts' and 'due process'.
3 What is 'bifurcation' in relation to youth justice?
4 Was there is successful revolution in youth justice during the 1980s?
5 Explain the concept of 'excluded tutelage'.

5 New Labour and the Youth Justice Board

Key issues

1 New Labour, communitarianism and reintegrative shaming
2 The risk society
3 The new public management, quality assurance and the audit society
4 The Audit Commission and the youth justice system
5 Effective and evidence-based practice
6 Reflections on youth justice and the New Labour years

The previous two chapters have told the story of the history of the juvenile justice system from its beginnings to the election of the New Labour government in 1997. This chapter considers the creation of the contemporary youth justice system established in the aftermath of that election and its operation during the 'New Labour' years. The change in terminology is important because the new government sought to signify a clear break with what was perceived as the failings of the previous system and had decided to start again from 'year zero' (Warner 1999). We commence this chapter by considering the origins of the new system via the emergence of New Labour as an electoral force during the mid-1990s and its commitment to the philosophy of communitarianism.

New Labour and communitarianism

The Labour Party has since its formation in the early twentieth century been the principal left-wing political party of the UK.[1] Labour won a landslide 179-seat majority in the 1997 general election under the leadership of Tony Blair but this was its first electoral success for nearly a quarter of century and the first time since 1970 that it had exceeded 40 per cent of the popular vote. Its large majority in the House of Commons was slightly reduced to 167 in the 2001 general election and more substantially to 66 in 2005.

The Labour Party has its origins in the trade union movement and socialist political parties of the late nineteenth century and has continued to call itself a party of democratic socialism. 'New Labour' was an alternative 'brand name' for the party and one which originated in 1994 as part of the ongoing rightwards shift to the centre of the British political spectrum started under the previous leadership of Neil Kinnock (Labour Party 2006). Successive heavy general election defeats had gradually convinced Labour to accept much of the new political settlement brought about by the repeated electoral success of the populist Conservatives. Globalisation had meant there were international pressures for national governments to pursue 'prudent' economic policies and Labour gradually came to accept the need to prioritise economic stability, low inflation and borrowing while encouraging private enterprise. Moreover, de-industrialisation and the decline of the working class and trade union membership meant that Labour's traditional electoral base was being eroded. Gaining the support of an increasingly middle-class electorate was crucial for electoral victory as Britain underwent demographic and economic change.

The term 'Old Labour' nevertheless continued to be used by commentators to describe the older, more left-wing members of the party, or those with strong trade union connections. The name New Labour originates from a conference slogan first used by the party in 1994 and which was later seen in a draft manifesto published by the party two years later called 'New Labour, New Life For Britain' (Labour Party 1996). The term was intended as part of an acknowledged new 'branding' of the party in the eyes of the electorate and coincided with the rewriting of Clause IV of the party constitution and its rejection of its traditional socialist roots epitomised by its commitment to the common ownership of the means of production (Labour Party 2006).

Tony Blair, Gordon Brown, Peter Mandelson and Alastair Campbell are most commonly cited as the creators and architects of New Labour and were among the most prominent advocates of the right-wing shift in European social democracy during the 1990s that came to be known as the Third Way (see Giddens 1998). The use of 'new' echoes slogans widely used in US politics over the years and associated with the Democratic Party, such as New Deal (Roosevelt), New Frontier (Kennedy) and New Covenant (Clinton). What brings together the New Democratic politics introduced by Bill Clinton in the USA and those of New Labour in the UK into a new 'third way' entity is the influential philosophy of communitarianism.

Communitarianism emerged in the USA during the 1980s as a response to what its advocates considered to be the limitations of liberal theory and practice, but significantly diverse strands in social, political and moral thought arising from very different locations on the political spectrum – such as Marxism (Ross 2003) and traditional 'one-nation' conservatism (Scruton 2001) – can be identified within the body of communitarian thought. Its dominant themes are that the individual rights vigorously promoted by traditional liberals need to be balanced with social responsibilities, and moreover, autonomous individual selves do not exist in isolation but are shaped by the values and culture of communities. Communitarians propose that unless we redress the balance towards the pole of community, our society will continue to become normless, self-centred and driven by special interests and power seeking.

The critique of the one-sided emphasis on individual civil or human rights promoted by liberalism is the key defining characteristic of communitarianism. Rights, it was argued, have tended to be asserted without a corresponding sense of how they can be achieved, or for that matter, exactly who will pay for them. 'Rights talk' is thus seen to corrupt political discourse by obstructing genuine discussion and is employed without a corresponding sense of responsibilities (see Emanuel 1991; Glendon 1991; Etzioni 1993, 1995a).[2] Communitarians argue that the one-sided emphasis on rights in liberalism is related to its conception of the individual as a 'disembodied self', uprooted from cultural meanings, community attachments and the life stories that constitute the full identities of real human beings. Dominant liberal theories of justice, as well as much of economic and political theory, presume such a self (see Etzioni 1993). Communitarians shift the balance, arguing that the 'I' is constituted through the 'We' in a dynamic tension. Significantly, this is not an argument for the traditional community with high levels of mechanical solidarity (see Durkheim 1933), repressive dominance of the majority or the patriarchal family, although some on the Conservative fringes do take up that position. Mainstream communitarians are, in fact, critical of community institutions that are authoritarian and restrictive and that cannot bear scrutiny within a larger framework of human rights and equal opportunities. They thus implicitly accept the (post)modern condition that we are located in a complex web of pluralistic communities – or organic solidarity (Durkheim 1933) – with genuine value conflicts within them and within selves.

Etzioni (1993) outlines the basic framework of communitarianism, urging that we start with the family and its central role in socialisation and, moreover, it is argued, employers should provide maximum support for parents through the creation of worktime initiatives such as the provision of crèche facilities and warn us against avoidable parental relationship breakdowns in order to put the interests of children first. Communitarians, consequently, demand a revival of moral education in schools at all levels, including the values of tolerance, peaceful resolution of conflict, the superiority of democratic government, hard work and saving. They also propose that government services should be devolved to an appropriate level, with the pursuit of new kinds of public–private partnerships, and the development of national and local service programmes.

Communitarians in the USA consider themselves to be a major social movement similar to that of the progressive movement in the early twentieth century.[3] Their ideas have been very influential and were to filter into the Clinton administration during the 1990s and beyond. In a pamphlet written shortly after he became prime minister of the UK, Tony Blair (1998: 4) demonstrated his communitarian or 'third way' credentials:

> We all depend on collective goods for our independence; and all our lives are enriched – or impoverished – by the communities to which we belong . . . A key challenge of progressive politics is to use the state as an enabling force, protecting effective communities and voluntary organisations and encouraging their growth to tackle new needs, in partnership as appropriate.

The most familiar and resonant of the 'abstract slogans' used by Blair in the promotion of the importance of community has been the idea that rights entail responsibilities, and this is taken from the work of Etzioni (1993). In contrast to the traditional liberal idea that members of a society may be simply entitled to unconditional benefits or services, it is proposed that the responsibility to care for each individual should be seen as lying, first and foremost, with the individual themselves. For Blair and his sociological guru Anthony Giddens (1998), community is invoked very deliberately as residing in civil society: in lived social relations, and in 'common-sense' notions of our civic obligations. The 'third way' is presented as avoiding what its proponents see as the full-on atomistic egotistical individualism entailed by the Thatcherite maxim that 'there is no such thing as society' and, conversely, the traditional social-democratic recourse to a strong state as the tool by which to realise the aims of social justice, most notably that of economic equality. For Blair, 'the grievous 20th century error of the fundamentalist Left was the belief that the state could replace civil society and thereby advance freedom' (Blair 1998: 4). The state has a role to play, he readily accepts, but as a facilitator, rather than a guarantor, of a flourishing community life.

Dissenters have, however, noted that the implementation of the New Labour agenda seemed to take a rather different course with its character rather more authoritarian – centred more on the usage of the state apparatus to deliver particular outcomes – than is suggested by the rhetorical appeal to the relatively autonomous powers of civil society to deliver progress by itself (see Driver and Martell 1997; Jordan 1998). New Labour neo-communitarian credentials can be clearly identified in the Crime and Disorder Act 1998 and the subsequent establishment of the contemporary youth justice system which was epitomised by the central state control of youth offending teams by a dictatorial Youth Justice Board.

It was argued at the end of the previous chapter that this distinctive New Labour approach to youth justice can be conceptualised as part of a wider government strategic initiative introduced with the intention of seeking to reintegrate those sections of the population that had become increasingly socially and economically excluded during the previous twenty years. We will now consider that neo-communitarian reintegrative tutelage project further.

New Labour and reintegrative tutelage

Two major criminological theoretical influences on New Labour youth justice policy were left realism and reintegrative shaming. Left realism – which will be discussed in more detail in the second part of this book – was a response to the electoral success of the populist Conservatives led by Margaret Thatcher in 1979 by a group of radical criminologists on the political left who were concerned that the debate on crime control had been lost to the political right. These 'new realists' argued for an approach to crime that recognised both the reality and the impact of crime – not least on poor people who were significantly over-represented among the ranks of its victims – but which also addressed the socio-economic context in which it occurred (Lea and Young 1984). Inasmuch as the 'right realists' – who had provided at least a partial intellectual justification for the new Conservative criminal justice perspective – had focused their efforts on targeting the offender in traditional rational actor fashion, 'left realists' with their intellectual foundations in both the predestined and victimised actor traditions emphasised the need for a 'balance of intervention'.

Left realism can be summarised briefly for our purposes here: first, there is recognition of the necessity and desirability of offenders taking responsibility for their actions (rational actor model); and second, it is acknowledged that account must be taken of the circumstances in which the crime took place (predestined actor model). It is an approach that became popularised by the oft-quoted sound-bite of Tony Blair – made when he was shadow home secretary in 1994 – 'tough on crime, tough on the causes of crime'.

The second and less obvious theoretical contribution to New Labour youth justice policy and a significant criminological contribution to the notion of rein-tegrative tutelage is provided by the Australian criminologist John Braithwaite (1989), who has developed a theory of 'predatory' crime – those involving the victimisation of one party by another – where he argues that the key to crime control is a cultural commitment to shaming in ways that he describes as 'reintegrative'. For our purposes here it is sufficient to say that Braithwaite offers a radical reinterpretation and reworking of the labelling theory tradition that we will encounter in the following part of this book. In brief, labelling theories propose that no behaviour is inherently deviant or criminal but only comes to be considered as such when others confer this label upon the act. Central to this perspective is the notion that being found out and stigmatised, as a consequence of rule-breaking conduct, may cause an individual to become committed to further deviance, often as part of a deviant subculture (Lemert 1951; Becker 1963). Braithwaite argues that Western industrial societies have a long established tradition of negative shaming where young offenders become social outcasts and turn to others sharing their plight for succor and support with the inevitable outcome being the creation of a virtual criminal underclass living outside of the respectable society from which they find themselves excluded.

Braithwaite has turned our attention to another tradition among the aboriginal tribes of Australasia and the industrial society of Japan – or at least the low-crime Japan of the 1980s – where shaming is used in a far more positive fashion. Thus, the notion of reintegrative shaming involves a closely linked two-part strategy for intervening in the life of the offender. First, the offending activities of the individual are shamed, with punishment administered where this is felt appropriate, and this will usually involve some form of reparation to the victim. Second, and this is the crucial element, rituals of reintegration are undertaken where the individual is welcomed back into an inclusive society that values their role and person.

The active involvement of victims of crime in the youth justice process was to be a key element of the contemporary youth justice system. Actions to achieve these aims are usually called restorative justice and seek to balance the concerns of the victim and the community with the need to reintegrate the young person into society. They also seek to assist the recovery of the victim and enable all parties with a stake in the justice process to participate in it (Marshall 1998) and these have been shown to be effective in reducing reoffending by young people (Sherman and Strang 1997; Nugent et al. 1999; Street 2000), especially by violent young people (Strang 2000), and provide greater satisfaction for victims (Umbreit and Roberts 1996; Wynne and Brown 1998; Strang 2001). Compliance with reparation has been found to be generally higher in restorative schemes than through the courts (Marshall 1999).

It is the purpose of restorative justice to bring together victims, offenders and communities to decide on a response to a particular crime with the intention of putting the needs of the victim at the centre of the criminal justice system and to find positive solutions to crime by encouraging offenders to take responsibility for their actions. Victims may thus request a restorative justice approach to make an offender realise how the crime has affected their life, to find out information to help put the crime behind them (e.g., why it was the offender targeted them) and to openly forgive the offender.

Whereas 'traditional justice' is about punishing offenders for committing offences against the state, restorative justice is about offenders making amends directly to the people, organisations and the communities they have harmed. The New Labour government was a strong supporter of restorative justice because it gives victims a greater voice in the criminal justice system, allows victims to receive an explanation and more meaningful reparation from offenders, and makes the latter accountable by allowing them to take responsibility for their actions, all with the intention of building community confidence that offenders are making amends for their wrongdoing.

Perpetrators and victims are brought into contact through, first, direct mediation, where victim, offender, facilitator and possibly supporters for each party meet face to face; second, indirect mediation, where victim and offender communicate through letters passed on by a facilitator; or third, conferencing, which involves supporters for both parties and members of the wider community, and is thus similar to direct mediation, except the process focuses on the family as a support structure for the offender. It is this latter approach that is found to be particularly useful when working with young offenders. There were nevertheless prominent concerns about the efficacy of restorative justice in practice and we return to this theme later in this book.

It is nevertheless this notion of reintegration back into the community that enables us to explain the approach to youth justice favoured by the Labour government elected in 1997 and which enables us to distinguish its policies from those of its populist Conservative predecessors. It is a distinctive approach that was part of a wider set of government strategies that sought to reintegrate those sections of the population that had become increasingly socially and economically excluded during the previous twenty years.

New Labour youth justice policies should therefore be understood in the context of a range of other initiatives that were introduced to tackle the causes of crime and criminality among young people – which we will encounter in the following part of the book – and help to reintegrate the economically and socially excluded back into inclusive society.

First, measures were introduced to support families, including assistance for single parents to get off benefits and return to work, to help prevent marriage and family breakdown and to deal with such breakdown, if it was to occur, with the least possible damage to any children.

Second, policies were introduced to help children achieve at school, including: good-quality nursery education for all 4 year olds (and progressively for 3 year olds too); higher school standards, with a particular focus on literacy and numeracy skills in primary schools; steps to tackle truancy and prevent exclusions; the provision of study support out of school hours; and better links between schools and business to help young people make the transition to adult working life.

Third, the provision of opportunities for jobs, training and leisure, through the New Start strategy aimed at re-engaging in education or training youngsters up to 17 who had dropped out of the system; through the welfare-to-work New Deal for unemployed 18 to 24 year olds; and through the creation of positive leisure opportunities, including those which involve young people themselves in preventing crime.

Fourth, action to tackle drug misuse with new initiatives in the criminal justice system, innovative projects showing what schools and the wider community can do and through the work of a new UK Anti-Drugs Coordinator in putting forward a new strategy aimed at young people (Hopkins Burke 1999, 2005).

New Labour neo-communitarianism youth justice nevertheless only makes sense in the context of other socio-political developments that had occurred during the previous two decades. It is to these issues that we now turn our attention and we will start with the concept of the risk society.

The risk society

For most of the twentieth century, crime control was dominated by the 'treatment model' prescribed by the predestined actor model of criminal behaviour, which we encounter in more detail in the next part of this book. This model proposes that criminality is at least partly determined by factors either internal to the individual (physiological or psychological) or by external environmental influences (sociological) and was closely aligned to the powerful and benevolent modernist state which was obliged to intervene in the lives of individual offenders and seek to diagnose and cure their criminal behaviour (Hopkins Burke 2001, 2005). It was the apparent failure of that interventionist modernist project epitomised by chronically high and seemingly ever-increasing crime rates and the corresponding failure of criminal justice intervention which led to new modes of governance.

The outcome has been a new contemporary governmental style organised around economic forms of reasoning which has been reflected criminologically in those contemporary rational actor theories which view crime simply as a matter of opportunity and participation which requires no special predisposition or abnormality. Consequently, there has been a shift in policies from those directed at the individual offender to those directed at 'criminogenic situations' which include – to quote Garland (1996: 19), a major proponent of this viewpoint – 'unsupervised car parks, town squares late at night, deserted neighbourhoods, poorly lit streets, shopping malls, football games, bus stops, subway stations and so on'.

Feeley and Simon (1996) have influentially argued that these changes in styles of governance should be understood as part of a paradigm shift in the criminal process from the 'old penology' – with its central concern of identifying the individual criminal for the purpose of ascribing guilt and blame, and the imposition of punishment and treatment – to the 'new penology' and concerns with developing technique for identifying, classifying and managing groups, who are then catalogued in terms of levels of dangerousness based not on individualised suspicion, but on the probability that an individual may be an offender. Feeley and Simon thus observe that justice is becoming 'actuarial', its interventions increasingly based on risk assessment, rather than on the identification of specific criminal behaviour. We are, it is argued, witnessing an increase in, and the legal sanction of, such actuarial practices as preventive detention, offender profiling and mass surveillance (Norris and Armstrong 1999).

The past thirty years have witnessed an ever-increasing use of surveillance technologies designed to regulate groups as part of a comprehensive strategy of managing danger. This includes the ubiquitous city-centre surveillance systems referred to above, testing employees for the use of drugs (Gilliom 1994) and the introduction of the blanket DNA testing of entire communities (Nelken and Andrews 1999). The introduction of these new technologies often tends to be justified in terms of their ability to monitor 'risk' groups who pose a serious threat to society; however, once introduced, the concept of dangerousness is broadened to include a much wider range of offenders and suspects (see Pratt 1989).

For some – following the influential Ulric Beck (1992) – these trends are indicative of a broader transition in structural formation from an industrial society towards a risk society. Now, this concept is not intended to imply any increase in the levels of risk in society but rather a social formation which is organised in order to respond to risks. As Anthony Giddens (1999: 3) observes, 'it is a society increasingly preoccupied with the future (and also with safety), which generates the notion of risk'. Beck (1992: 21) himself defines risk in such a social formation as 'a systematic way of dealing with hazards and insecurities induced and introduced by modernisation itself'.

Human beings have always been subjected to certain levels of risk but modern societies are exposed to a particular type that is the outcome of the modernisation process and this has led to changes in the nature of social organisation. Thus, there are risks such as natural disasters that have always had negative effects on human populations but these are produced by non-human forces; modern risks, in contrast, are the product of human activity. Giddens (1999) refers to these two different categories as external and manufactured risks. Risk society is predominantly concerned with the latter.

Because manufactured risks are the product of human agents there is the potential to assess the level of risk that is being or about to be produced. The outcome is that risks have transformed the very process of modernisation. Thus, with the introduction of human-caused disasters such as Chernobyl (now in the Ukraine, at that time in the Soviet Union)[4] and the Love Canal crisis (in New York City),[5] public faith in the modernist project declined, leaving only variable trust in industry, government and experts (Giddens 1990). The increased critique of modern industrial practices has resulted in a state of reflexive modernisation with widespread consideration given to issues of sustainability and the precautionary principle that focuses on preventative measures to reduce risk levels. Contemporary debates about climate change and the future of the planet should be seen in the context of debates about the risk society.

Social relations have changed significantly with the introduction of manufactured risks and reflexive modernisation, with risks, much like wealth, distributed unevenly in a population and this, differentially, influences the quality of life. People will nevertheless occupy social risk positions that they achieve through aversion strategies, which differs from wealth positions which are gained through accumulation. Beck (1992) proposes that widespread risks contain a 'boomerang effect' in that individual producers of risk will at the same time be exposed to them, which suggests, for example, that wealthy individuals whose capital is largely responsible for creating pollution will suffer when, for example, contaminants seep into the water supply. This argument might appear to be oversimplified, as wealthy people may have the ability to mitigate risk more easily but the argument is that the distribution of the risk originates from knowledge as opposed to wealth.[6]

Ericson and Haggerty (1997) accordingly argue that in the sphere of criminal justice we are witnessing a transformation of legal forms and policing strategies that reflect the transition to a risk society. Policing has become increasingly proactive rather than reactive and, given that risk assessment is probabilistic rather than determinist, it requires the assignment of individuals and events to classificatory schemes which provide differentiated assessment of risk and calls for management strategies. Offenders are now classified as 'prolific' rather than merely opportunistic and having been designated as such, the individual becomes a candidate for targeting by more intensive forms of surveillance. The emphasis on risk makes everyone a legitimate target for surveillance and – as Norris and Armstrong (1999: 25) pithily observe – 'everyone is assumed guilty until the risk profile assumes otherwise'.

Significantly, many of the programmes of practical action which flow from strategies of 'risk management' are increasingly addressed not by central state agencies such as the police, but to quote Garland (1996: 451), 'beyond the state apparatus, to the organisations, institutions and individuals in civil society' (see also O'Malley 1992; Fyfe 1995). Thus, following the demise of the interventionist welfare state that had been the cornerstone of high modernity (Hopkins Burke 1999a), there was to be an emphasis on individuals managing their own risk and this was to find converts from all parts of the political spectrum (Barry et al. 1996).

Pat O'Malley (1992) observes, therefore, the emergence of a new form of 'prudentialism' where insurance against future risks becomes a private obligation of the active citizen. Responsibilisation strategies are also designed to offload the responsibility for risk management from central government on to the local state and non-state agencies, hence the increasing emphasis on public/private partnerships, inter-agency cooperation, inter-governmental forums and the rapid growth of non-elected government agencies. The composition of such networks allows the state to 'govern at a distance' – to utilise the norms and control strategies of those formerly autonomous institutions identified by Foucault (1971, 1976) – while leaving, to quote Garland (1996: 454), 'the centralised state machine more powerful than before, with an extended capacity for action and influence'.

This author has previously directed our attention not just to the increasing pervasiveness of policing in its various disguises in society but also significantly to our own contribution in the legitimisation of this state of affairs (Hopkins Burke 2004a) and this neo-Foucauldian left-realist variation on the carceral surveillance society – outlined in detail in Chapter 6 – which proposes that in a complex, fragmented, dangerous risk society, it is we the general public, regardless of class location, gender or ethnic origin, that have a material interest in the development of that surveillance matrix (see also Hopkins Burke 2013a 2013b).

Developments that were to occur in the establishment of the contemporary youth justice system reflect these wider societal trends. Social policy, thus, focuses on children 'at risk' and the management of that risk pervades every sphere of activity within the system. The commencement of intervention itself is regulated through a detailed assessment of risk through the Asset profile form, which contains a scoring system that predicts the likelihood of offending and will determine the level of intervention and surveillance the young person will experience (Youth Justice Board 2002). Moreover, the widespread introduction of mechanisms for risk management coupled with the emphasis on interventions to change individual behaviour are a significant contrast to previous approaches such as the emphasis on system management and diversion in the late 1980s and early 1990s, or earlier approaches such as intermediate treatment that characterised the previous orthodoxy of the treatment model.

Most critics of the risk analysis criminal justice model of intervention observe this to be indicative of a contemporary social policy which focuses on the shortcomings of the individual while ignoring significant structural factors such as poverty and unemployment (Goldson and Muncie 2006). It is further argued that this preoccupation with risk has displaced welfare considerations and 'need' and provides an overly confident sense of being able to successfully tackle something as significantly complex as the offending behaviour of young people (Smith 2006).

Three further closely linked influences on the development of the contemporary youth justice system can be identified – the new public management, quality assurance and the audit society – and these all have their origins in the widespread notion that previously the public sector had been poorly managed and was at the time a bottomless conduit of resources while lacking any proper accountability to the public for how this was spent. With the rise of the populist conservatism we encountered in the previous chapter, that state of affairs was to be increasingly challenged in the UK.

The new public management, quality assurance and the audit society

It could be argued that the most important development in the public sector during the past thirty years has been the increasing encroachment of the new public management (NPM), which has involved the transfer of business and market principles as well as management techniques from the private into the public sector. NPM is founded on the neoliberal understanding of the state and economy introduced above and which was epitomised by the regimes of Margaret Thatcher in the UK ('Thatcherism') and Ronald Reagan in the USA ('Reaganomics') where the goal was a slimmed-down, minimal state in which any public activity is significantly reduced and, if undertaken at all, exercised according to business principles of efficiency. NPM is based on the understanding that all human behaviour is motivated by self-interest and, specifically, profit maximisation and is popularly denoted by concepts such as project management, flat hierarchies, customer orientation, abolition of the career civil service, depolitisation, total quality management, and the contracting-out of services, all in the name of market-oriented efficiency (Manning 2005). Cost-effective, efficient private-sector-style management techniques have become increasingly fashionable in the UK and are closely linked to notions of the audit society.

Complex and differentiated contemporary economies require large numbers of managers whose economic function is essentially the coordination of the activities of specialised workers but the nature of managerialism appears to vary between countries according to the dominant disciplinary background of managers. Charlton (1999) observes that in Germany engineers form the most dominant school of managers and, therefore, engineering concepts dominate managerial ideologies. In the UK, the dominant style of managerialism is derived from accountancy because managerial consultancy is dominated by the big accountancy firms and consequently audit-derived concepts and technologies dominate managerialism. The concepts of 'accountability' and 'quality' are, therefore, representative of UK managerial discourse.

The current managerial use of 'quality' was developed and adapted to the needs of managerialism during the last two decades of the twentieth century and what has emerged is a generic, audit-based version of quality control usually termed 'quality assurance' (QA) and this has transformed 'quality' into an abstract requirement for a particular kind of regulatory system. Quality assurance now refers to auditable systems, not guaranteed excellence, while the current era has been described as the audit society because corporate life is increasingly dominated by these accountancy-derived concepts and technologies (Power 1997). Accountability is – as its name implies – one of these concepts and the desirability of 'increased accountability' has become ubiquitous in political, managerial and even journalistic discourse.

Charlton (1999) observes that accountability is assumed in common discourse to be an intrinsically desirable goal. Thus nobody has ever argued that one can have 'too much' accountability and the demand is always for more. Accountability in its technical sense has, nevertheless, almost the opposite meaning to those democratic, egalitarian, radical and 'empowering' values that are associated with the term in general usage. Charlton thus argues that the drive for increased accountability operates as merely an excuse to justify further managerial control with behaviour becoming labelled as unaccountable (hence unacceptable) simply because it is not subject to managerial control, and this is taken (by managers and politicians who wish to control this behaviour) to imply a need to introduce audit systems. The latter can be established to advance the interests of those who have introduced them with autonomy re-packaged as irresponsibility while the subordination of employees and hierarchical control mechanisms is reiterated in terms of 'increased accountability'.

Charlton (2001) observes that QA is a technical managerial term for that type of auditing which is concentrated upon systems and processes rather than outcomes. It is built on the assumption that any properly constituted organisation should be based around a system of auditing systems and processes. In other words, with the introduction of QA only those activities and systems which are transparent to auditing – and thus amenable to comprehensive and self-consistent documentation – are considered appropriate. It is the existence of such documentation that renders all significant organisational activities visible to external gaze.

Since the rise of the 'audit society' and the dominance of managerial discourse over practice, for an organisation to be 'opaque' to auditing, to include significant activities that are not documented is regarded as intrinsically deficient and probably dishonest (Power 1997). Yet, although transparency has become a term of approval among managers and politicians, it is merely a technical term that refers to auditability and, therefore, does not carry any necessary implications of responsibility to the public, or of excellent or desirable practice, especially when auditing is implemented and evaluated by government officials.

The conflation of 'transparency' with probity has arisen because modern managers equate a properly constituted organisation with a fully auditable organisation and this equation is endorsed because, in the accountancy-dominated world of UK managerialism, managers exert control by means of auditing. Transparent organisations are auditable, and auditable organisations are manageable and vice versa. By its concentrations upon systems and procedures, QA provides a mechanism for quantifying almost any aspect of organisational performance that can be given an operational definition – 'quality', 'excellence', 'equity', 'access' or whatever the current terminology happens to be. Any aspects of measured organisational performance may be attached to these terms with no more justification than plausibility, then these can be quantified 'objectively' and judged against pre-established 'performance' criteria. The magic of QA is that what was unmeasurable has been rendered measurable – so long as one does not inquire too carefully into what words such as 'quality' actually mean in operational terms.

Stephenson et al. (2007) observe, in this context, that confidence in the traditional authority of independent professionals wielding invariably unaccountable discretionary power has declined in the public sector and this has been replaced with a dependency on audit and inspection systems. This transformation is nowhere more apparent than in the contemporary youth justice system, where the term 'practitioner' has become the orthodox terminology rather than the previously widely used term 'professional'. The challenge to professionalism by the new public management has, however, not escaped criticism from those who consider these changes in emphasis to reflect a dehumanisation of youth justice with the sole purpose of delivering a cost-effective 'product' (Muncie 2004), the 'zombification of youth justice professionals' (Pitts 2001a) and the replacement of the principled 'systems management of the 1980s with a technocratic management with no principles or independent rationale' (Smith 2003: 3). Stephenson et al. (2007) respond to these criticisms with the observation that unsupervised professional autonomy and discretion may obscure vested interests, problematic perspectives and indeed incompetence. There is, moreover, no necessary conflict between the observation of the rights of children and a managerialist and audit culture. The quality assurance framework for measuring the effectiveness of the contemporary youth justice system, whereby practitioners audit their own performance, which was to become an essential component of the contemporary youth justice system, within a framework of evidence-based practice, is discussed below. We will first consider the impact of the independent public-sector auditing body on the development of that system.

The Audit Commission and the youth justice system

The Audit Commission was an independent body responsible for ensuring that public money is used economically, efficiently and effectively.[7] Its strategic plan published in 2006 presented five objectives which clearly delineate its central role in the public sector audit society:

- to raise standards of financial management and financial reporting in the public sector;
- to challenge public bodies to deliver better value for money;
- to encourage continual improvement in public services so they meet the changing needs of diverse communities and provide fair access for all;
- to promote high standards of governance and accountability;
- to stimulate significant improvement in the quality of data and the use of information by decision-makers.

(Audit Commission 2006)

The Audit Commission (1996) report *Misspent Youth: Young People and Crime* influentially examined – and was highly critical of – what it perceived to be an expensive and inefficient juvenile justice system that was in place at the time.

First, it found that crime committed by young people was a significant problem that had impacted, in particular, on some poor disadvantaged neighbourhoods. Of known offenders, 26 per cent were found to be aged under 18, 40 per cent of offences were concentrated in 10 per cent of geographical areas and the total cost of crime committed by young offenders in terms of public services was £1 billion per annum.

Second, it was proposed that resources could have been better used. The youth court process took four months, on average, from arrest to sentence; the whole process cost around £2,500 for each young person sentenced; half the proceedings commenced were discontinued, dismissed or ended in a discharge; the many different agencies involved did not always agree on the main objectives to be achieved; and the monitoring of reoffending after the imposition of sentences was rare.

Third, proposals were made for improving the youth justice process in the short term. Thus, it was proposed that the court process should be accelerated and the time from arrest to sentence monitored; persistent offenders on community sentences should and could be more intensively supervised; 'caution plus' programmes, compensating victims and addressing offending behaviour were identified as alternatives to the court process; and it was observed that the impact on reoffending of different interventions needed to be monitored regularly.

Fourth, it was recognised that prevention is better than cure and offending by young people at the greatest risk of involvement could be reduced by targeting, piloting and evaluation, with assistance to be given with parenting skills; structured education for children under 5 introduced; support given for teachers dealing with badly behaved pupils; and the provision of positive leisure opportunities.

Fifth, it was proposed that all agencies involved should work together more effectively. All services for children and young people should share information and target areas at the greatest risk, while local residents in those areas should be consulted.

Sixth, it was proposed that central government could provide important assistance. Local authorities should be given a duty to lead in developing multi-agency work, the resources released from court processes could fund local services that reduce offending and all agencies should contribute to monitoring and evaluating preventive programmes.

In summary, the Audit Commission (1996) identified a need for a more effective youth justice system that prevented and reduced youth offending and provided considerably more value for money than the system in place at the time. Central to the new cost-effective, efficient system would be the concept of evidence-based practice.

Effective and evidence-based practice, the human services and youth justice

Stephenson et al. (2007) observe that the general public might reasonably assume that the actions of practitioners in the human services are determined largely by the most up-to-date research findings. Yet they observe that this has often not been the case with studies across most disciplines indicating a variety of reasons why many practitioners only make a relatively limited use of research findings in their day-to-day decision-making. More significant influences on practice were seen to be knowledge gained during primary training, prejudice and opinion, the outcomes of previous cases, fads and fashions and the advice of senior and not-so-senior colleagues who 'have seen it all' (Trinder and Reynolds 2000). Three possible explanations are offered for why this has been the case. First, much of the available research is said to lack methodologies rigorous enough or appropriately consistent to be applied with any degree of confidence. Second, the excessive volume of available research, irrespective of its methodological merits, can often overwhelm practitioners. Third, many simply lack the appraisal skills to assess the methodologies employed and the overall quality of research. Thus, in the arena of social work, the human services and youth justice, interventions were for a long time based upon practice wisdom and intuition rather than proven research.

Evidence-based practice had emerged during the previous decade as a contemporary approach to work in the human services and allows the articulation of a proven basis for interventions and assessments by encouraging practitioners to continuously and consistently challenge their practice and support accountability aspects of such work. This approach enables workers to employ practice interventions that have more informed outcomes, engage clients more effectively in the decision-making process and develop greater professional and personal authority.

The concept of evidence-based practice is therefore a response to concerns that professional practice is not always based on the 'best evidence' or is minimally informed by research knowledge (Carew 1979; Rosen 1994; Darlington and Osmond 2001). As such, it is proposed that it can assist practitioners to identify, call upon and utilise the 'best' research in their daily practice. Moreover, while it discourages guess-work, intuition, unsystematic thinking, uncritical and unreflective practice and heightens the likelihood of critically aware, informed, independent and systematic practitioners who are continually updating and expanding their knowledge bases, it is an approach that seeks to combine the expertise and experience of practitioners with the current 'best' evidence on practice topics and issues. Professional judgement is thus not devalued or substituted but is extended and empowered by external sources of evidence (MacDonald 1998) and this, it is argued, can lead to practices with clients that are helpful, effective and informed (Darlington and Osmond 2001).

Wilcox (2003) nevertheless sounded a note of caution, for an evidence-based approach does not necessarily imply an evidence-led one, as there are other influences and constraints on policy-makers and these include public opinion, the Treasury, European and international law and interest groups. Moreover, some propose that policy should actually be led by values and not research evidence and, indeed, it has been observed that the latter is more likely to influence policy if the findings are relatively uncontroversial, the implied changes fall within the existing capabilities and resources of the programme, or the policy is in crisis and no other options are available (Nutre et al. 2000). In short, evidence-based practice does not mean that all research is taken into account when developing a policy or stratagem, but merely that the evidence which is selected is compatible with the worldview of the government or organisation. Goldson and Muncie (2006) observe that this selective use of evidence by policy-makers has led to a gap between research findings and policy formation and practice development and, moreover, this situation can be compounded by a lack of methodological rigour of some evaluations (Bottoms 2005).

Evidence-based practice in criminal justice was also closely linked with the 'what works' agenda, which had its origins in the title of an influential article written by Robert Martinson (1974) which concluded that, on the basis of then existing research, there was no clear pattern to indicate the effectiveness of any particular method of treatment. The conclusion was contested and Martinson acknowledged that the poor design quality of many research programmes might preclude the detection of any positive outcome but even so, it was only in recent years that a consensus had developed among some academics that some approaches to working with young people who offend appear capable of having an impact on preventing offending.

Stephenson et al. (2007) observe that in order for services to address the question of 'what works?' and reflect this in their day-to-day practice, they require access to sound critical knowledge and information about the impact of current policies and practice, an evidence-led approach to planning provision and an allied training strategy. These issues apply in youth justice services, in particular the need for specialist training for practitioners and managers in identifying 'what works?' The effective practice agenda challenges everyone involved in the contemporary youth justice system to make its provision and outcomes more transparent and to establish the role of knowledge in the application of youth justice policies. There are, however, significant criticisms of the application of the 'what works' approach to the system, with Bateman and Pitts (2005) arguing that – regardless of claims to the value-free, objective application of rigorous research findings to youth justice interventions – the reality is a distortion and selectivity of research findings, the deskilling and wasting of practitioner creativity and justifications that simply fail to reduce offending behaviour.

The increasing emphasis placed on 'value for money', 'effectiveness' and best value by successive governments influenced by the new public management and audit society agenda had nonetheless clearly encouraged youth justice agencies to focus far more clearly on the evidence of effectiveness in these services. Meta-analysis, a statistical tool which facilitates the aggregation of results from different studies, has also been used since the mid-1980s to review a large number of research programmes which, in combination, had confirmed a positive overall effect. Clear trends have been detected concerning the components of programmes with higher or lower levels of effectiveness in reducing offending. The term 'what works?', therefore, refers to that body of research knowledge and the principles deriving from it. Meta-analysis reviews have failed to show that there is any one outstanding approach that is by itself guaranteed to work as a means of reducing reoffending but these studies did, nevertheless, help recover confidence in official circles that there is promising evidence of social interventions which could have a direct and positive effect on people who offend and on their behaviour (see, for example, Lipsey 1992; Lipsey and Wilson 1998; Trotter 1999; McGuire 2000; Andrew et al. 2001). Criticisms of meta-analysis tend to fall into two categories. Thus, some observe that meta-analysis obscures important qualitative information by 'averaging' simple numerical representations across studies, while others argue that research is best reviewed by a reflective expert (Kulik and Kulik 1989).

The Youth Justice Board (YJB), which oversaw the development and introduction of the contemporary youth justice system, identified effective practice as a key element in developing and improving youth justice services and was committed to identifying and promoting such practice throughout the system to ensure that work with young people was as effective as possible and based on best practice and research evidence. It therefore introduced the Key Elements of Effective Practice (KEEPs) documents, which describe the features of effective services and which were to support the identification of staff learning and development needs. The KEEPs also provided the foundations of a simple quality assurance system which was implemented in all youth justice services. These describe effective practice as currently defined and were informed by the latest research, national standards and existing legislation. As new research became available, or as legislation or national standards were to change, the YJB was to revise and reissues the documents to reflect changes in the youth justice system.

The actual work of the contemporary youth justice system and the impact of effective practice is examined in some detail in the third part of this book, which considers the system in the aftermath of the general election in 2010. At that stage a much more detailed critique of that system will be provided. In this final section of the chapter, which completes the story of the development of the juvenile justice system and its transition to a youth justice system, we will make some preliminary reflections on the success and failings of the New Labour project.

Reflections on youth justice and the New Labour years

The contemporary youth justice system established by the New Labour flagship criminal justice legislation the Crime and Disorder Act 1998 introduced a different strategy to that of their populist Conservative predecessors' laissez-faire-driven excluded tutelage approach: a reintegrative tutelage strategy that sought to address both the social contexts in which offending behaviour takes place and the nature of the intervention (Hopkins Burke 1999a). The aim was an inclusive youth justice strategy with significant criminological theoretical influences recognisable in the form of left realism and reintegrative shaming. The former is evidenced in the form of the fundamental communitarian notion that offenders should take responsibility for their actions while, at the same time, the social circumstances in which that behaviour takes place are also addressed; the latter is demonstrated in the form of a restorative justice approach which sought to reintegrate the young offenders back into an inclusive welcoming society.

New Labour produced a plethora of youth justice reforms during the course of their three consecutive terms in office with varying levels of success. Key proposals for reform were initially outlined in the White Paper 'No More Excuses – A New Approach to Tackling Youth Crime in England and Wales', produced shortly after their electoral triumph in 1997. The paper emphasised Blair's 'toughness' agenda and was the precursor of the Crime and Disorder Act 1998 which introduced an entirely restructured apparatus for dealing with offending by children and young people, with the establishment of local inter-agency youth offending teams (YOTs) and local inter-agency partnerships, Youth Offending Boards (YOBs), while introducing an array of new powers and sentencing disposals. The flurry of criminal justice and anti-social behaviour legislation continued and in the ten years between 1997 and 2007, with 3,023 new offences being created (Goldson 2005).

The Crime and Disorder Act 1998 provided the new government with the opportunity to rectify what they considered to be the administrative failings of the system in place at the time. Problematically, a new system introduced with the aim of radically changing youth justice administration and practice would – like all bureaucratic systems – have a logic of its own (Pitts 2003a). The logical inevitability of this new bureaucracy was a significant widening of the net of the criminal justice system. Thus those who might previously have been dealt with informally, by the system or authorities, through practitioner discretion, warnings or cautions, were to now to receive a more formal intervention (Cavadino et al. 2013). This presumably unintended outcome was nonetheless nothing new with a similar situation having arisen in the aftermath of the Children and Young People Act 1969 where – as we saw in Chapter 3 – a newly enlarged system had absorbed a much wider clientele into its interventionist remit. The ultimate outcome on that occasion was that the number of young people receiving custodial sentences rose very significantly. History was now to be repeated with the new youth justice system.

Pitts (2001b) observes that the new youth offending teams were based on the multi-agency youth diversion panels introduced during the 1980s but were devised in such a way that on this occasion far greater numbers were drawn in, compared to those diverted out. He further notes that the new system invariably lacked sufficient resources and infrastructure to deal with the new influx of children and young people and was thus sometimes forced to provide a considerably reduced service, or require a large proportion of additional funding. What is certain is that the new youth justice system – like its predecessor in the 1970s, enabled a new, younger population to come within the formal grasp of the authorities and on this occasion they were well equipped with a whole new range of Child Safety, Child Curfew, Anti-Social Behaviour and Parenting *Orders* which greatly enhanced their interventionist capacity.

The new legislation required that all first-time offenders should be dealt with formally, the caution, previously a decriminalising mainstay of dealing with children and young people, was replaced with the formal Reprimand of which only one was to be issued followed by a Final Warning. The unintended but inevitable outcome was that a very large number of children and young people exhausted these low-level tariff options at a very early stage in their offending career. Consequently, their 'formal' offending career would begin at a far earlier age than had been the case for previous generations, thus making it far more likely that delinquent youths would end up in prison or with a criminal record at an earlier age. This induction into the formal system at such an early stage, through a mixture of stigmatisation, deviancy amplification and administrative drift, seems to have helped accelerate the progress of many young people through it (Pitts 2003a). It is a classic example of net-widening where a large increase in the system leads to more children being absorbed into the system invariably at an earlier age through measures introduced for their own good. Moreover, while the multi-agency youth diversion panels introduced during the 1980s had sought to divert young people from the criminal justice system, the new system was apparently not interested in diversion. Children and young people were now referred to YOTs because the intervention would be beneficial to them and apparently nip their offending career in the bud at an early stage. This clearly did not happen in a lot of cases with unfortunate consequences.

The Youth Justice and Criminal Evidence Act 1999 introduced the Referral Order and effectively removed the Conditional Discharge as a disposal from the system.[8] A young person now found guilty of an offence would be referred to a panel which would decide on the type of programme they should pursue but there would invariably be a restorative justice emphasis on reparation and interventions of that kind (Pitts 2001b). Breach of a Referral Order – and this would only require the young person to miss one session of a programme – will nevertheless lead to reappearance at court. In contrast, breach of a Conditional Discharge required the young person to reoffend, get apprehended and be successfully prosecuted. There are clearly positive aspects of the Referral Order but evidence from Denmark, where a similar intervention was implemented, showed that young people were liable to increased court reappearances with the inevitable likelihood of eventual custody (Cavadino et al. 2013).

The 1999 Act also introduced the Action Plan Order and Reparation Order to strengthen the existing Supervision Order and would be used when an offender failed to complete the requirements of a Referral Order. These community intervention programmes were essentially a 'last chance' for young offenders and were designed to deter those previously not dissuaded. The programmes were touted as 'evidence-based' and there was a presumption that only the most persistent of offenders would continue offending beyond this stage. Pitts (2001b) nevertheless observes the introduction of an overly optimistic new system based on flawed evidence of its likely success. Thus, children and young people who breached any one of these new Orders – or were to reoffend – were very likely to be remanded in custody or 'residence', with the number subsequently sentenced to custody significantly increasing. Thus, only a year after the legislation was enacted in September 2000 there had been an 11.5 per cent increase on the previous year (Prison Reform Trust 2008).

These community punishments were the intended mechanism whereby young offenders would be persuaded to desist from their offending and thus bring about a reduction in the numbers in custody. The outcome was the very opposite. New Labour had such confidence in the 'evidence-based' programmes working to deter children and young people from crime that the Crime and Disorder Act 1998 stated that community penalties could only be imposed on two occasions. Pitts (2003a) noted that 50 per cent of young people sentenced to community penalties subsequently reoffend, and this reality, combined with the custodial punishments handed out for those breaching Orders, combined to hasten the progression of many young people towards imprisonment. Further aspects of the legislation also increased the likelihood of a custodial sentence being received. For example, the 'fast-tracking' of 'persistent' and/or 'serious' young offenders led to the same outcome (Goldson 2008). All this means offenders appearing more frequently in court with each charge dealt with separately, again significantly increasing the possibility of a custodial sentence. Moreover, the definitions of 'serious' and 'persistent' contained within the legislation are ambiguous and controversial. Hagell and Newburn (1994) had found that 'serious' young offenders are generally not persistent and 'persistent' offenders are seldom serious with the outcome that youth jails tend to attract persistent minor offenders who pose minimal risk to the community and who essentially require social help rather than incarceration. A study conducted by S. Jones (2001) of 270 young people involved with a London YOT highlighted that 45 per cent had been placed on the Local Authority Child Protection Register, most had spent time in care and the majority had a parent with recurrent mental health problems.

A further measure which amplified the use of custody was the powers given to youth courts to remand children and young people directly into penal establishments. Jack Straw, the home secretary at the time, sent clear signals to the courts that there would be enough custodial provision available if the court wanted to impose such sentences. Pitts (2001a) notes that this provision, combined with the 'three strikes' sentencing strategy for 'persistent' juvenile offenders, plus the de facto one-strike, 'breach' condition initiated in the Criminal Justice and Court Services Act 2000, demonstrate clearly how penal incapacitation was a central element of New Labour's youth justice policy. It is nevertheless uncertain whether this was intended or simply the unintended consequences of the bureaucratic logic of the system.

In spring 2002 Britain had more youths in custodial settings than at any other time since the establishment of the juvenile justice system in 1908 (Prison Reform Trust 2008) with, at the same time, more children, young people and parents under the supervision of youth justice authorities. Furthermore, between 1995 and 1999 the number of children and young people sentenced to some form of custodial internment in England and Wales (not including persons held under the Mental Health Act) increased by almost 30 per cent (Cavadino et al. 2013). The number of children and young people being placed under lock and key was causing such unease that in October 2002 the United Nations Committee on the Rights of the Child officially reported its 'deep concern' at 'the high increasing numbers of children in custody in England and Wales' (Goldson 2005: 1).

Although these increasing custodial figures were a concern, they were also remarkable as the period witnessed a decline in the crime rate (Solomon and

Garside 2008). While Pitts (2003a) observes that in addition to the increased use of custody, young people were being held for lengthier periods. From 1989 to 1999 the average custodial sentence for boys aged between 15 and 17 increased from 5.6 months to 10.3 months, and for girls it rose from 5.5 months to 7.1 months.

During New Labour's period of governance, young offender institutions (YOIs) were in a state of disarray with most underfunded, over-crowded and mismanaged. In none of the institutions did more than 30 per cent of the inmates receive education, despite the fact that approximately 54 per cent of their number were scoring below GCSE standard in reading ability. Thus, highlighting a paradox in the New Labour youth justice policy, as insufficient education would likely have a negative impact on the reintegration process. Sir David Ramsbothom, chief inspector of prisons, conducted a further investigation into the conditions of YOIs and found that over 50 per cent of young offenders on remand and 30 per cent who were serving a sentence had a diagnosable mental health problem (Forrester-Jones 2006) and these problems were further amplified by rampant drug use, violence and intimidation. Deaths and self-harm incidents were and still are a big problem in YOIs. In 2004, 14-year-old Adam Rickwood became the youngest child to die in penal custody in living memory. Between 1990 and 2005, twenty-nine children died in penal custody; all except two were self-inflicted. In the same time period, sixty-five young people between the ages of 18 and 20 killed themselves while in custody. Furthermore, between 1998 and 2002 there were 1,659 reported self-injury incidents or attempted suicides by child prisoners in England and Wales (Carrabine 2010) demonstrating a stark realisation of the damaging psychological experience prison has on children and young offenders. A report on Feltham YOI in 2001 ended with the damning conclusions that isolation and long periods spent in cells were overwhelming for young prisoners, and the regime there was 'rotten to the core' (BBC 2001). The culmination of these factors resulted in the United Nations Committee further voicing its 'extreme concern' in relation to the experience of children and young people while in detention, including the 'high levels of violence, bullying, self-harm and suicide among child and young prisoners' (Goldson 2005: 1).

As crime and disorder was a focal point of New Labour's youth policies, the dividing lines between education, employment, social welfare services and the criminal justice apparatus became increasingly blurred. The rationale for this integration of services was because 'crime, disorder and social exclusion are intricately linked' (Pitts 2005: 2). Thus by 2002, 52 per cent of street-based youth work projects had entered partnerships with criminal justice and community safety organisations. An example of how services for young people were gradually criminalised under New Labour is that of Connexions (2002). This organisation was established in 2001 as a place for young people to receive education, training and vocational guidance, and it aimed to incorporate street-based youth workers to identify, support and track 'hard to reach young people' not in education. However, the introduction of the Transforming Youth Work Bill 2002 placed the Youth Service at the centre of Connexions, enabling it to contribute to 'cross-cutting preventative strategies, including identification, referral and tracking' (Pitts

2005: 3). Further incorporation was introduced in the Respect and Responsibility White Paper 2003 that identified the Youth Service and Connexions as integral participants of crime reduction partnerships. This affiliation and the contribution to cross-cutting preventative strategies was particularly distressing for youth work professionals, who saw client confidentiality and accountability to the young people they work with to be a necessary ethical principle for their guidance and training to be successful.

A number of independent assessments of New Labour's youth justice policy reform have concluded that YJB claims of success are vastly overstated. The Centre for Crime and Justice Studies conducted a ten-year review of the implementation of these policies and found that their record on reducing youth crime was at best 'mixed' (Solomon and Garside 2008). The report found that the initial targets set for reducing overall youth offending appeared ambitious and promising. In reality the targets were modest and essentially committed the government to sustaining self-reported offending by young people at a similar level to what it had been at the time they were first elected. Yet these targets were not met. Some targets for specific offences such as burglary, vehicle crime and robbery were apparently met but were based on self-report studies and police conviction data, both of which offer an unreliable basis for understanding the extent and trends in youth offending (Cavadino et al. 2013). Solomon and Garside (2008) observe that New Labour's record on youth crime reduction was very limited considering the extent of the reforms introduced and concluded that youth justice agencies do little more than regulate youth crime.

New Labour invested a considerable amount of money and political focus in the contemporary youth justice system, particularly in the establishment of the Youth Justice Board and the YOTs. This was combined with extensive reforms as to the way young people and children are dealt with and convicted by the youth justice system. The sentencing framework and the multi-agency structure of YOTs were innovative at the time and – as we will see in the third part of this book – are still in place today following the change of government in 2010 which demonstrates the appeal and potential of the system that was introduced. Pitts (2005) nevertheless notes that much of the potential of these new policies was undermined by political expediency, and thus important policy initiatives were disrupted because of governmental acquiescence in the face of media criticism. The YOTs have progressed and become 'diverse, locally managed and locally accountable teams that exercise a considerable amount of operational discretion' (Solomon and Garside 2008: 65). They later worked in unison with an array of legal and voluntary agencies, such as Connexions, with the outcome that a more integrated system was developed in order to stop youth offending. Additionally, the Crime and Disorder Act 1998 has pioneered work with parents and victims of crime and initiated the restorative justice approach, and this strategy was an important achievement for all those involved with youth justice.

It is clear that the design of New Labour's youth justice policy had its own bureaucratic logic and this led to far more young people and children being criminalised and subsequently imprisoned than previously, and this was something that the system itself did not have the capacity to deal with. This resulted in YOTs often providing a reduced service with the regimes in many young offender institutions being 'rotten to the core'. The increased incarceration of children and young people still has an impact on the government today as more children receive custodial sentences in England and Wales than most other industrialised democratic countries in the world (Lyon 2014). Moreover, many of the resources that New Labour marshalled to facilitate the increased use of custody came from other areas of social spending, health, education and children's services and was not new money. Peled (2013) notes that, as a result, large sums of money were transferred from policy areas that were critical to challenging the underlying causes of youth offending and which – we might observe – could have made a positive contribution to the New Labour communitarian reintegrative tutelage strategy.

The ambition of New Labour's youth policy reform was certainly commendable and had the YOTs fulfilled their initial aspirations to be teams where a collection of experts from different disciplines came together to 'custom fit' interventions to the assorted needs of young people in trouble, then it would of marked a real breakthrough in the response to youth crime in England and Wales. Goldson (2005: 3) nevertheless observes that YOT '"experts" typically put their subjects through patently ineffective, but politically acceptable, offending programmes'. Thus, in reality, the new youth justice system, although theoretically plausible and could have been successful, 'had a very limited impact on youth crime and victimisation' (Solomon and Garside 2008: 66). It is therefore pertinent to question whether youth justice agencies can actually address the multi-faceted economic and social influences that are the cause of youth offending and we will return to these issues in the last two parts of this book.

Summary of main points

1 This chapter considers the creation of the contemporary youth justice system established after the General Election in 1997 and its operation during the 'New Labour' years.

2 The change in terminology is important because the new government sought to signify a clear break with what was perceived as the failings of the previous system.

3 Communitarianism emerged in the USA during the 1980s as a response to what its advocates considered to be the limitations of liberal theory and practice. Its dominant themes are that individual rights need to be balanced with social responsibilities and were to become very influential with New Labour in the UK.

4 Two major criminological theoretical influences on New Labour youth justice policy were left realism and reintegrative shaming, which is a major influence on the concept of reintegrative tutelage.

5 Whereas 'traditional justice' is about punishing offenders for committing offences against the state, restorative justice is about offenders making amends directly to the people, organisations and the communities they have harmed.

6 New Labour youth justice policies should be understood in the context of a range of other initiatives that were introduced to tackle the causes of crime and criminality among young people and help to reintegrate the economically and socially excluded back into inclusive society.

7 For most of the twentieth century, crime control was dominated by the 'treatment model' prescribed by the predestined actor model of criminal behaviour which proposes that the powerful and benevolent modernist state should intervene in the lives of individual offenders and seek to diagnose and cure their criminal behaviour.

8 It was the apparent failure of that interventionist modernist project epitomised by chronically high and seemingly ever-increasing crime rates and the corresponding failure of criminal justice intervention which led to new modes of governance and in particular the risk society thesis.

9 Three further closely linked influences on the development of the contemporary youth justice system can be identified: the new public management, quality assurance and the audit society, and these all have their origins in the widespread notion that previously the public sector had been poorly managed.

10 The Youth Justice Board (YJB), which oversaw the development and introduction of the contemporary youth justice system, identified effective practice as a key element in developing and improving youth justice services.

Discussion questions

1 Explain the concept of communitariansim and its relationship to liberalism.
2 Explain the concepts of left realism and reintegrative shaming.
3 What is restorative justice and how does it differ from traditional criminal justice?
4 Briefly explain the concepts of the risk society, the new public management, quality assurance and the audit society.
5 What is 'effective practice' in the public services?

Notes

1 Communitarians nevertheless promote the preservation of traditional liberal rights and their extension in non-democratic regimes or those that practise discrimination, but propose that these rights need to be located in a more balanced framework.

2 See Hughes (1998) for an overview of the different variants of communitarianism.

3 Progressivism was the reform movement that ran from the late nineteenth century through the first decades of the twentieth century, during which leading intellectuals and social reformers in the USA sought to address the economic, political and cultural questions that had arisen in the context of the rapid changes brought with the Industrial Revolution and the growth of modern capitalism in America. The progressives believed that these changes marked the end of the old order and required the creation of a new order appropriate for the new industrial age.

4 The Chernobyl disaster was an accident at the Chernobyl Nuclear Power Plant on 26 April 1986, consisting of an explosion at the plant and subsequent radioactive contamination of the surrounding geographic area (see Davidson 2006).

5 Love Canal is a neighbourhood in Niagara Falls, New York, the site of the worst environmental disaster involving chemical wastes in the history of the USA (see Mazur 1998).

6 Certainly the prevalence of cholera which knew no social class boundaries in early Victorian London was a great motivation for the affluent to agree to the provision of public parks and baths. In contrast, reducing the risk of criminal victimisation in contemporary society increasingly means self-imposed self-exclusion for those who can afford it. For centuries the criminal justice system worked in a very simple manner: take away the 'criminals' and put them behind gates and walls segregated from the rest of the population. This method holds true today, except now in risk society people are voluntarily surrounding themselves with concrete and metal fences to escape the so-called 'criminals' of society. Americans, in particular, are scared and residential society is slowly beginning to show it. More and more people are moving into and raising families in 'gated communities'.

7 On 13 August 2010, it was leaked to the media, ahead of an official announcement, that the Commission is to be scrapped, with its functions being transferred to the voluntary, not-for-profit or private sector. In 2009–10 the Commission cost the central government £28m to run, with the remainder of its income coming from audit fees charged to local public bodies. The Commission closed on 31 March 2015.

8 *Absolute Discharge*

A young person is given an absolute discharge when they admit guilt or are found guilty but no further action is taken against them.

Conditional Discharge

A young person receiving a conditional discharge receives no immediate punishment. A period of between six months and three years is set, and as long as a young person does not commit a further offence during this period, no punishment will be imposed. However, if the young person commits another offence during this period, they can be brought back to court and be sentenced for the original offence that they had the conditional discharge for and any new offence.

6   Theorising the development of youth justice

Key issues

1   The orthodox social progress model
2   The radical conflict model
3   The carceral surveillance society model
4   The left realist hybrid model
5   Four models of criminal justice development summarised

This first part of the book commenced by tracing the social construction of young people in the modern era in terms of the concepts of childhood and adolescence and has discussed the tutelage strategies employed to educate, discipline and control this increasingly important section of the population and make them fit for purpose in a modern industrial society. The last three chapters have told the story of a specialist juvenile justice system introduced to deal with those individuals who came to deviate from, and transgress against, the legal and social norms that were a crucial part of that modernist tutelage project.

We have seen that the contemporary youth justice system that was established in England and Wales by New Labour in 1998 was the culmination of often contrasting, conflicting and sometimes ambiguous themes, many of which had been in existence since the beginnings of the tutelage project over 170 years ago. We have thus established that in order to theorise the establishment of the contemporary system – or why it is that it came into existence in the form that it is has – it is essential to locate the discussion in a historical context. It is impossible to make legitimate sense of the present without reflection on the past. As we have seen, fears about rising crime rates among children and young people have been constantly repeated throughout history with the emphasis on 'appropriate parenting' and the 'failing family' being nothing new. This chapter considers this history and the story of the development of a de facto disciplinary tutelage project emerging to remodel young people as fit for purpose in a modern industrial society with a special emphasis on the criminal justice elements developed to deal with miscreants resistant to this project. In this chapter we reconsider that history in the context of four models of criminal justice development devised elsewhere by this author (Hopkins Burke 2013a, 2013b) and which discusses from different theoretical perspectives why it is that the various components of the 'criminal justice system' – or specifically in this case the juvenile or youth justice system – have come to operate in the way that they do and in whose interests they function in modern societies. Four different models of criminal justice development are discussed and these are: (1) the orthodox social progress model; (2) the radical conflict model; (3) the carceral surveillance society model; and (4) the left realist hybrid model.

The orthodox social progress model

The orthodox social progress model is – as its name suggests – the standard non-critical explanation which considers the development of law and the criminal justice system to be predominantly non-contentious. Thus, from this perspective, criminal justice institutions operate neutrally in the interests of all.

The concept of progress in history is the idea of an advance that occurs within the limits of the collective morality and knowledge of humanity and its environment. It is an idea often associated with the Western notion of a straight linear direction as developed by the early Greek philosophers Aristotle and Plato and which was to influence the later Judeo-Christian doctrine. The idea spread during the European Renaissance which occurred between the fourteenth and sixteenth centuries and this marked the end of the static view of history and society which had been characteristic of feudalism. By the eighteenth and nineteenth centuries – and during the great Industrial Revolution that was to transform Western Europe and instigate the rise of modern society – belief in progress was to become the dominant paradigm non-critically accepted by most people.

Social progress is defined as the changing of society towards the ideal and was a concept introduced in early nineteenth-century social theories, especially those of social evolutionists such as Auguste Comte (1798–1857) and Herbert Spencer (1820–1903). The former was a philosopher and social visionary and is perhaps best known for giving a name to the discipline of sociology, which he nevertheless outlined rather than practised. Central to his thought was his search in chaotic times – exemplified by the major transition from predominantly agrarian to urban societies throughout Western Europe – for principles of cultural and political order that were consistent with the apparent forward march of society. Spencer was the major theorist of social evolutionism and held the view that human characteristics are inherited and it was this aspect of his work that was to be a major influence on the development of the predestined actor model of crime and criminal behaviour that we will encounter in the second part of this book. Spencer nevertheless went much further than the natural scientist Darwin and explained evolution as the product of the progressive adaptation of the individual character to the 'social state' or society. His major contribution to the development of sociology is his recognition that human beings develop as part of a process of interaction with the social world they inhabit.

The orthodox social progress model of criminal justice development in the modern era should thus been seen in this evolutionary context. From this perspective, the development of modern societies, their laws and criminal justice systems are the product of enlightenment, benevolence and a consensual society where the whole population shares the same core values and which develops an increasingly progressive humanitarian response to crime and disorder. Cohen (1985) observes that from this liberal perspective the impetus for change is seen to come from developments in ideals, visions, theories, intentions and advances in knowledge. All change is 'reform' and, moreover, this is a term without any negative connotations. All reform is motivated by benevolence, altruism, philanthropy and humanitarianism with the collective outcome of a succession of reforms being progress. Theories of criminal justice – and other associated disciplines such as criminology and psychology – provide the scientific support or knowledge base to inform the particular reform programme, and changes occur when the reform vision becomes more refined and ideas more sophisticated.

Thus, for example, the orthodox social progress perspective on the development of the public police service observes the emergence, expansion and consolidation of a bureaucratic professionalised service to be part of a progressive humanitarian development of institutions considered necessary to respond to crime and disorder in the interests of the whole of society (Reith 1956). The effectiveness of the premodern system of policing had been based on stable, homogeneous and largely rural communities where people knew one another by name, sight and/or reputation. During the eighteenth century, such communities had begun to break down in the face of the rapid transition to an industrial economy, while, at the same time, the unpaid and frequently reluctant incumbents of posts such as the parish constable and the watch failed to carry out their duties with great diligence. Many employed substitutes who were more often than not ill-paid, ignorant and too old to be effective in their duties. The local watch was also often demoralised, drunk on duty and did little to suppress crime.

The fast-expanding towns and cities increasingly became a haven for the poor and those dispossessed of their land as a result of the land enclosures, while the rookeries, slum areas and improvised shelters for the poor grew rapidly as the urban areas expanded to serve the labour needs of the growing industrial machine. These areas were extremely overcrowded, lacked elementary sanitation and were characterised by disease, grinding poverty, excessive drinking, casual violence, prostitution and thieving (Emsley 1996, 2001). From the orthodox social progress perspective, the establishment of the first professional police service in 1829 and its subsequent development occurred in the interest of all groups and classes in a society which needed protection from the criminality and disorder in their midst.

It was thus in this context that contemporary notions of childhood and adolescence were formed or socially constructed at the outset of the modern era. We have seen that children, and increasingly their families, were disciplined, controlled and placed under surveillance and from a social progress perspective this occurred because motivated entrepreneurial philanthropists had genuine humanitarian concerns about poor urban children and young people at risk from the numerous dangers on the streets, which included criminality and a failure to find God. These philanthropists were thus keen to do something about this problem in the interests of the whole of society but not least the children and the parents themselves. It was done for their own good.

Cohen (1985) further observes that, in terms of the orthodox social progress model, criminal justice institutions do not actually 'fail' to achieve their aims and objectives, which might seem to be almost self-evident to the neutral observer. Instead they adapt and modify themselves in the face of changing scientific knowledge, social circumstances and the application of reflective reason. This vision is nevertheless not complacent. The system is recognised to be flawed in practical and even moral terms, bad mistakes are seen to be made and abuses do occur, but from the social progress perspective all these problems can be solved, over time, with the provision of more resources (invariably more money), better trained staff and improved facilities. Thus, all can be humanised and improved with the application of scientific principles and reason.

Cohen (1985) observes that the orthodox social progress model is a contemporary variant of Enlightenment beliefs in progress and its supporters and adherents are the genuine heirs to the nineteenth-century reform tradition. It is in many ways the most important model not least because it represents taken for granted mainstream opinion and is thus the orthodox view held by most people. There is nevertheless a more recent, radical, cynical, ambivalent, critical variant to this liberal reform story which has emerged from the mid-1960s onwards. Yet, while a version critical of the purist version of that history, it can still be conceptualised in the liberal reform tradition not least because of its tendency to propose orthodox solutions to even major significant failure. Cohen (1985: 19), in his discussion of the development of the penal system in modern society, observes the extent of that failure:

> The message was that the reform vision itself is potentially suspect. The record is not just one of good intentions going wrong now and then, but of continual and disastrous failure. The gap between rhetoric and reality is so vast, that either the rhetoric itself is deeply flawed or social reality resists all such reform attempts.

This revisionist variant of the orthodox social progress model thus tells a less idealist account than the purist history. Ideas and intentions are still important and are to be taken seriously, but not as the simple products of humanitarian caprice or even advances in knowledge. They are functional and pragmatic solutions to immediate social changes. Rothman (1971) discusses the establishment and development of the asylum in the USA at the end of the eighteenth century and in doing so provides the original revisionist variant of the social progress model. He observes that in the aftermath of the War of Independence there emerged a new restless, dispossessed, socially mobile potentially dangerous population while there was a simultaneous widespread sense that the old traditional modes of social control based on small self-policing local communities were now seriously outdated. The asylum was hence conceived as a microcosm of the perfect social order, a utopian experiment in which criminals and the insane could be isolated from bad influences and would be changed by subjection to a regime of discipline, order and regulation.

This goal of changing the individual was clearly based on a very optimistic worldview and the parallel notion of the nature of humanity but there was, however, soon to be a widespread proliferation in these institutions. By the late nineteenth century it was clear that they had failed in their honourable rehabilitative intentions and had degenerated into mere custodial institutions. Rothman nevertheless observes that regardless of their failure and widespread derogatory criticisms these institutions were retained and sustained because of their functionality and the enduring power of the rhetoric of benevolence. They simply kept a dangerous population off the streets.

Rothman (1980) develops his argument further by observing degeneration in closed institutions in the early decades of the twentieth century, which occurred regardless of the introduction of a progressive reform package. The outcome of this disappointment was a search for alternatives which was to lead to the ideal of individual treatment, the case-by-case method and the introduction of psychiatric doctrines and attempts to humanise all closed institutions. But yet again none of the programmes turned out the way their designers had intended. Cohen (1985: 20) observes that:

> Closed institutions hardly changed and were certainly not humanized; the new programmes became supplements, not alternatives, thus expanding the scope and reach of the system; discretion actually became more arbitrary; individual treatment was barely attempted, let alone successful. Once again, however, failure and persistence went hand in hand: operational needs ensured survival while benevolent rhetoric buttressed a long discredited system, deflected criticism and justified 'more of the same'.

For Rothman the crucial concept is that of 'convenience' which does not, in reality, undermine the original vision or 'conscience' but actually aids in its acceptance. The managers of the system and their staff come to actively embrace the new programmes and use them to their advantage. A useful political alliance is thus developed between the reformers and the managers and this allows the system to survive even though it appears to be a total failure. Rothman (1980) observes that it is essential that we have a critical understanding of the origins of the original reform vision, the political interests behind them, their internal paradoxes and the nature of their appeal, for this creates a story that is far more complicated than terms such as 'reform', 'progress', 'doing good', 'benevolence' and 'humanitarianism' suggest. This revisionist account provides a significantly more critical account than the simplistic purist version of the orthodox social progress model but it nevertheless remains a liberal model which still believes that things can be improved if we learn the correct lessons from history and research. The radical conflict model to which we now turn our attention goes much further and identifies an inherent problematic contradiction in the very nature of capitalist society.

The radical conflict model

Proponents and supporters of the social progress model – whether in its purist or revisionist form – fundamentally agree that society is characterised by consensus. Proponents of the radical conflict model, in contrast, argue that society is inherently conflict-ridden. Max Weber (1864–1920) influentially argued that conflict is intrinsic in society and arises from the inevitable battle within the economic market place – between different interest groups with different levels of power – over the distribution of scarce material resources. The radical conflict model of criminal justice development is nevertheless heavily influenced by the far more radical account of Karl Marx (1818–83) who – in a simplified account of a complex and highly contested materialist philosophy – goes significantly further than Weber and argues that economic inequality is inherent in society with the outcome being an inevitable conflict between antagonistic irreconcilable social classes. Those who own and control the capitalist mode of production are also in the final analysis in control of the political and civil institutions in society which, in turn, are used to maintain and sustain the capitalist system in the interests of the rich and powerful to the disadvantage of the poor and powerless or, for that matter, anyone not owning capital.

From the radical conflict perspective, it is argued that the story of the development of the criminal justice system during the modern era is neither what it appears to be nor, for that matter, can it be considered to be in any way a 'failure'. For, the new control system served more than adequately the requirements of the emerging capitalist order for the continued repression of recalcitrant members of the working class and, at the same time, continued to persuade everyone (including the reformers themselves) that these changes were fair, humane and progressive.

Thus it is argued from this perspective that the professional police were from their very formation at the beginning of the modern period 'domestic missionaries' with an emphasis on the surveillance, discipline and control of the rough and dangerous working-class elements in society in the interests of the capitalist class (Storch 1975); while recent 'hard' strategies such as zero-tolerance policing, which are ostensibly targeted at socially excluded groups in society, are simply a continuation of that tradition (see Crowther 1998, 2000a, 200b; Hopkins Burke 1998a, 2004a). At the same time, children and their families were disciplined and controlled from the early nineteenth century in the interests of an industrial capitalism which required a fit, healthy, increasingly educated, trained but always obedient workforce. The motor force of history is thus the political economy and the requirements of the dominant mode of production, which in the modern era is capitalism. Ideology is only important in that it succeeds at passing off as fair, natural and just a system which is basically coercive and unfair. It is only the outside observer, uncontaminated by false consciousness,[1] who can really know what is going on.

Rusche and Kirchheimer (1968) provide the earliest version of the radical conflict model in the criminal justice context and they begin from the principle that changes in the mode of production correspond with changing dominant forms of punishment in society. Hence, the origins and development of penal systems were determined by and, thus, must be studied in terms of primarily economic and fiscal forces. Their central argument is that in societies where workers are scarce and work plentiful, punishment is required to make the unwilling work, and when there is a surplus of labour (or a reserve army), harsh punishments are used to keep the workless under control. The status of the labour market thus determines the form and severity of punishment. The reformed prison renders docile the non-compliant members of the working class, it deters others, it teaches habits of discipline and order; it reproduces the lost hierarchy; repairs defective humans to compete in the market place and rehabilitation is used in the interests of capitalism. Increasingly, the state takes on a more and more active role in guiding, coordinating and planning a criminal justice system which can achieve a more thorough, rationalised penetration of the subject population.

Melossi and Pavarini (1981) take this argument further and contend that the functional connection between the prison and society can be found in the concept of discipline. The point is to create a socially safe proletarian who has learned to accept being propertyless without threatening the very institution of property. The capitalist organisation of labour shapes the form of the prison as it does other institutions and nothing can change this. The control system continues to replicate and perpetuate the forms necessary to ensure the survival of the capitalist social order.

Ignatieff (1978) produces a rather different 'softer' version of the radical control model and in doing so rejects the rather simplistic straightforward 'economic determinism' and 'left functionalism'[2] of the purist version and observes the 'complex and autonomous structure and philosophical beliefs' which led reformers to conceive of the penitentiary. It is these beliefs and not the functional necessity of the economic system or the 'fiction of a ruling class with a strategic conception of its functional requirements' which explains why the penitentiary was adopted to solve the 'crisis in punishment' in the last decades of the eighteenth century. Motives were complex. Driven by a perceived disintegration of the society they valued, the reformers sought a return to what they imagined to be a more stable and orderly society. They may well have acted not only out of political self-interest but also out of religious belief and a sense of guilt about the condition of the lower orders.

This revisionist version of the radical conflict model is very similar to that presented by Rothman – and there are clear similarities with the mainstream orthodox social progress model – but there are crucial differences. Ignatieff observes organised philanthropy to be a new strategy of class relations and both the property nature of crime and the role of the prison in containing the labour force are essential to his account. He argues that the new disciplinary ideology of the penitentiary – with its attempt to isolate the criminal class from the rest of the working class – was a response to the crisis years of industrialisation. There was thus a specific class problem to be solved and not a vague sense of unease about 'social change'. Cohen (1985: 24) observes that from this perspective:

> The point of the new control system – reforming the individual through punishment, allocating pain in a just way – was to devise a punishment at once so humane and so just that it would convince the offender and the rest of society of the full moral legitimacy of the law.

In this way the system was far from the failure suggested by the orthodox social progress model; indeed, quite the contrary, it was remarkably successful. The carceral society model to which we now turn our attention takes these arguments further.

The carceral surveillance society model

We have seen that supporters of the orthodox social progress model propose that the development of modern societies, their laws and criminal justice systems are the product of enlightenment, benevolence and a consensual society which develops an increasingly progressive humanitarian response to crime and disorder. Advocates of the radical conflict model essentially reject the consensual view and observe, in contrast, an inherently conflict-ridden society with the development of the criminal justice system as a mode of social control and repression functioning in the interests of the capitalist order. Proponents of the carceral society model do not totally disregard these arguments but consider the situation to be far more complex than that explained by both the social progress and radical conflict models.

It is clear that from the beginning of the modern period many (if not most) philanthropists had genuine humanitarian concerns about those involved (or at risk of involvement) in crime and disorder on the streets. They acted with the best of humanitarian intentions but without completely understanding the full (especially long-term) consequences of their actions. The labelling theorist Howard Becker (1963) helps us to not only understand further the notion of the motivated philanthropist but also the invariably obscure consequences – intentional or unintentional – of their actions. He argues that rules of conduct – including criminal laws – are made by people with power and enforced upon people without power. Thus, rules are made by the old for the young, by men for women, by white people for ethnic minorities, by the middle class for the working class. These rules are invariably imposed upon their recipients against their will and own best interests and are legitimised by an ideology that is transmitted to the less powerful in the course of primary and secondary socialisation. As an outcome of this process, most people internalise and obey the rules without realising – or questioning – the extent to which their behaviour is being decided for them.

Becker observes that some rules may be cynically designed to keep the less powerful in their place but others have simply been introduced as the outcome of a sincere – albeit irrational and mistaken – belief on the part of high-status individuals that the creation of a new rule will be beneficial for its intended subjects. Becker termed the people who create new rules for the 'benefit' of the less fortunate 'moral entrepreneurs'. We should note that this account has resonance with the story of how philanthropic entrepreneurs came to define different categories of children and youth as acceptable and non-acceptable to respectable society while, at the same time, developing strategies to ensure their surveillance, control, discipline and tutelage with the intention of reconstructing the non-acceptable in the form of the acceptable. But, yet again, this account is too simplistic. It is clear that not only did many of these philanthropists have little idea of the actual or potential consequences of their actions but also they might well have become extremely concerned had they recognised that final reality. Indeed, this predominantly liberal labelling perspective fails to take into account the complexities of power and the outcomes of strategies promoted by agencies at the mezzo-level of the institution that often enjoy autonomy from the political centre and implemented by those working at the micro-level of the frontline who often enjoy considerable discretion in the criminal justice field. It is thus the notion of the carceral surveillance society devised by Michel Foucault (1980) and developed by others such as Jacques Donzelot (1980), Stanley Cohen (1985) and David Garland (2001) that helps us to make sense of this situation and provide the fundamental basis of the carceral society model.

From this Foucauldian perspective, power is not simply conceptualised as the privilege of an all-powerful state, although that which it does both possess and wield is clearly *very* significant. Strategies of power are in reality pervasive throughout society with the state only one location of the points of control and resistance. Foucault (1971, 1976) observes that particular areas of the social world – and he uses the examples of law, medicine and sexuality – are colonised and defined by the norms and control strategies a variety of institutions and experts devise and abide by. He argues that these networks of power and control are governed as much by the knowledge and concepts that define them as by the definite intentions of groups.

Power and knowledge are seen to be inseparable. Humanism, good intentions, professional knowledge and the rhetoric of reform are neither in the idealist sense the producers of change nor in the materialist sense the mere product of changes in the political economy. They are inevitably linked in a power/knowledge spiral. Thus forms of knowledge such as criminology, psychiatry and philanthropy are directly related to the exercise of power, while the latter itself creates new objects of knowledge and accumulates new bodies of information.

The State, for its part, is implicated in this matrix of power-knowledge, but it is only part of the story, for in this vein it has been argued that within civil society there are numerous 'semi-autonomous' realms and relations – such as communities, occupations, organisations, families – where surveillance and control are present but where the state administration is technically absent. These semi-autonomous arenas within society are often appropriately negotiated and resisted by their participants in ways that, even now, the state has little jurisdiction.

The carceral society model is thus founded on the work of Michel Foucault, and while complementary to the radical conflict model, it recognises that power is both diffuse and pervasive in society. Agents and experts at all levels of the social world have both access to and control of power and although this is invariably exercised in the overall interests of the capitalist class – or the market economy – in the long run, those involved in its application at the micro-, mezzo- and macro-levels are not always aware of their contribution to the 'grand design'. Cohen (1985) observes that the 'great incarcerations' of the nineteenth century – which put thieves into prison, lunatics into asylums, conscripts into barracks, workers into factories, children into school – are to be seen as part of a grand design. Property had to be protected, production had to be standardised by regulations, the young segregated and inculcated with the ideology of thrift and success, the deviant subjected to discipline and surveillance. The mode of discipline which was represented by the prison belonged to an economy of power quite different from that of the direct, arbitrary and violent rule of the sovereign in the pre-modern era. Power in capitalist society had to be exercised at the lowest possible cost – economically and politically – and its effects had to be intensive and extended throughout the social apparatus in order to gain control of those populations resistant and previously invisible to the disciplinary-control-matrix.

The left realist hybrid model

This author has previously (Hopkins Burke 2004a, 2009) developed a left realist hybrid model which essentially provides a synthesis of the orthodox social progress, radical conflict and carceral surveillance society models but with the additional recognition of our interest and collusion in the creation of the increasingly pervasive socio-control matrix of the carceral society (Hopkins Burke 2004a, 2009, 2013a, 2013b). This model is heavily influenced by left realism – an eclectic and now influential criminological perspective (Hopkins Burke 2014) – which recognises that crime is a real problem for ordinary and invariably poor people who, as we have seen earlier in this book, are often targeted by the criminal element living in their own communities and from whom they require a protection that has not always been recognised or forthcoming (Lea and Young 1984; Matthews and Young 1986, 1992; Young 1994, 1997). We have indeed seen that this criminological perspective was influential with the New Labour youth justice strategy devised at the outset of their three consecutive electoral successes and which was discussed in some detail in the previous chapter.

This author has subsequently employed the left realist perspective in a historical context to demonstrate that the general public has always had an interest in the development of social progress (orthodox social progress model) but this has invariably conveniently coincided with the requirements of capitalism or the market economy (radical conflict model) and which has contributed invariably unwittingly to the construction of the disciplinary-control-matrix that constrains the actions and rights of all. First, in order to explain the development of the public police service from the beginning of the nineteenth century, it is recognised that crime was as a real problem for ordinary people at the time, as it is now, and that the respectable working class has always required protection from the criminal elements in their midst, whether these were termed the 'rough working classes' (nineteenth century) or a socially excluded underclass (twenty-first century) (Hopkins Burke 2004b). Second, this historical variant on the left realist thesis has helped explain the increasing surveillance and control of young people on the streets and elsewhere from the nineteenth century to the present day. Third, it is observed that in the complex fragmented dangerous society that we inhabit, it *us* the general public – regardless of our social class location, gender or ethnic origin – who have a material interest and/or an enthusiasm for the development of the carceral surveillance matrix that restricts the civil liberties or human rights of some individuals or groups (Hopkins Burke 2004c).

The left realist hybrid perspective readily accepts the carceral society thesis that disciplinary strategies are invariably implemented by philanthropists, moral entrepreneurs, professional agents and practitioners who rarely seem to recognise how their often, but sometimes less, humble discourse contributes to the grand overall disciplinary-control-matrix. Thus, the bourgeois child tutelage project with its origins in the nineteenth century, which we have encountered in the previous four chapters of this book, can clearly be viewed in that context.

Proponents of the radical conflict model argue that definitions of crime and criminality are class-based, with the public police service agents of a capitalist society targeting the activities of the socially excluded while at the same time ignoring the far more damaging behaviour of corporate capitalism (see Scraton and Chadwick 1996). Left realists nevertheless consider the situation to be more ambiguous, crucially recognising that crime is a real problem for ordinary people and that it is therefore appropriate that the criminal justice system – of which the police service is a key institution – should seek to defend the weak and oppressed (see Lea and Young 1984; Matthews and Young 1986; Young 1997; Hopkins Burke 1998a; 2004a).

Observed from a left realist perspective, it is apparent that from soon after the introduction of the new police in the mid-nineteenth century there was a widespread – and admittedly at times tacit and fairly grudging – acceptance and support for this body. The police may well have targeted criminal elements within the working class and they might on occasion have taken the side of capital in trade disputes but at the same time their moralising mission on the streets coincided conveniently with the increasing enthusiasm for self-betterment among the great majority that has been described from differing sociological perspectives as 'embourgeoisement' (Goldthorpe 1968–9) and 'the civilising process' (Elias 1978, 1982).

The left realist hybrid perspective thus does not dismiss the orthodox social progress, radical conflict or carceral models of criminal justice development but instead produces a synthesis of the three. For it seems self-evident that the police are an essential necessity in order to deal with conflicts, disorders and problems of coordination necessarily generated by any complex and materially advanced society (Reiner 2000) and hence there is a widespread demand for policing throughout society. Studies have shown that while during the nineteenth century prosecutions for property crime emanated overwhelmingly from the more affluent groups, the poorer sections of society also resorted extensively to the law as victims (see Storch 1989; Emsley 1996; Taylor 1997: Miller 1999; Philips and Storch 1999). Indeed, at crucial times these poorer groups had considerable interest in the maintenance of the status quo and the isolation of a growing criminal class. For example, with the end of the Crimean War came the prospect of a footloose army of unemployed soldiers returning – at the very time that transportation to the colonies had ended – which meant that 'an organised race of criminals' would be roaming the countryside looking for criminal opportunities and from whom all would need protection, affluent or poor (Steedman 1984; Hopkins Burke 1998c, 1999b).

Thus, while working-class antagonism may have been exacerbated by police intervention in recreational activities and labour disputes, a close reading of the issues suggests a more complex situation than previously supposed (Hart 1978). There seems to be little doubt that the police were closely linked with the general increase in orderliness on the streets of Victorian society (Gatrell 1980; Taylor 1997) and this was again widely welcomed. Indeed, it has been argued that the crucial way in which the police affect law enforcement is not by the apprehension of criminals – for that depends on many factors beyond their control – but by symbolising the existence of a functioning legal order, by a having a visible presence on the street and by being seen to be doing something (Gatrell 1980). It is a discourse that coincides neatly with a consistent widespread contemporary public demand for police on the streets frequently expressed in contemporary crime surveys and regardless of the academic policing orthodoxy that has repeatedly stated the service on its own can have little effect on the crime rate (Hopkins Burke 1998a, 1998b, 2004a, 2004b).

The left realist hybrid variation on the carceral society model proposes that there are further interests involved in the creation of the disciplinary-control-matrix and those significantly are ours and those of *our* predecessors. The bourgeois child tutelage project which has its origins in the nineteenth century can clearly be viewed in that context and the accounts of two scholars of young people and criminality – Anthony Platt and Victor Bailey – helps support this thesis.

Platt's (1969) study of the child-saving movement in the USA in the late nineteenth century was concerned with the ways in which certain types of youthful behaviour came to be defined as 'delinquent' and argued that 'the child savers . . . brought attention to . . . and, in doing so, invented – new categories of youthful behaviour which had been hitherto unappreciated' (1969: 3–4). He argues that the movement was related to the changing role of middle-class women who were attempting to rebuild the moral fabric of society. While the changes were of instrumental significance in that they legitimated new career opportunities for these women, they were also symbolic in that they preserved their prestige in a rapidly changing society and institutionalised certain values and ways of life for women, children and the family. Platt characterises the 'child savers' as disinterested reformers because they regarded their cause as a matter of conscience and morality, and not one which would improve their economic or class interests even though their subjective actions contributed to that objective reality.

Bailey (1987) is concerned with developments in juvenile justice during the first half of the twentieth century and reconstructs the social and ideological background of those who promoted reform during that period. He observes how, during the 1920s, a consensus of opinion emerged around the issue of the causes of young offending, which brought together 'social workers, magistrates, penal reform groups, associations of penal practitioners, and the administrators and inspectors of the Children's Branch' who collectively favoured 'the social conception of delinquency' (Bailey 1987: 66). This consensus for reform could nevertheless be located in deeper socio-political conditions, not least the new welfarist brand of liberalism which had flourished at the turn of the twentieth century. Bailey observes that this was a generation of middle-class men and women whose ideas had formed the social policies of the Liberal governments of 1906–14 and they, therefore, inherited not only a social philosophy which recognised social inequalities and their structural roots, but also a political and legal framework in which the scope for state intervention and administrative action was considerably extended and which again we should observe contributed almost subconsciously to the increasing disciplinary-control-matrix.

The left realist hybrid model accepts that all the above accounts – radical conflict, orthodox social progress, carceral surveillance society – are at least partially legitimate for there were, and indeed are, a multitude of motivations for both the implementation and willing acceptance of the increasing surveillance and tutelage of young people. The moralising mission of the entrepreneurial philanthropists and the reforming zeal of the liberal politician and administrator, invariably implemented with the best of humanitarian intentions, were consistently compatible with those of the mill and mine-owners and a government which wanted a fit healthy fighting force but, at the same time, also coincided with the ever increasing enthusiasm for self-betterment among the great majority of the working class as we have seen above. Those who were resistant to that moralising and disciplinary mission – the 'rough working' class of the Victorian era – has subsequently been reinvented in academic and popular discourse as the socially excluded underclass of contemporary society, with the moral panics of today a reflection of those of the past and demands for action remarkably similar.

The radical conflict perspective nevertheless demands some prominence in the left realist hybrid model of criminal justice development because significantly everyone in the nineteenth century – and certainly all of us today – are subject to the requirements and demands of the market economy. Attempts at self-improvement or embourgeoisement were always constrained and restricted by the opportunities provided by the economy – healthy or otherwise – and this will always be the case as recent events following the virtual collapse of the worldwide banking system in 2008 has shown. Children and young people were increasingly disciplined and controlled throughout the nineteenth – and first half of the twentieth – century in a form that was functional and appropriate to the needs of mass modern society and an industrial capitalism which required an abundant, healthy and increasingly skilled workforce. With the fragmentation of that modernity and the subsequent retreat from mass industrialism that was to occur from the last quarter of the twentieth century onwards, the requirements for young people were to change accordingly (Hopkins Burke 1999a, 2008).

In a complex fragmented risk society there is increasing demand for further intrusion and surveillance of lives in the apparent interest of all. There is thus public motivation for the increased policing of the financial services industry, in particular the investment arm of banking, which is entirely understandable in view of the activities of that sector of the economy, in particular, but not exclusively, in the USA and the UK at the end of the first decade of the twenty-first century, which range from gross incompetence at one end of the spectrum to unequivocal criminality at the other. Other policing, surveillance and control intrusions into various parts of the social world are at first sight equally non-problematic and acceptable both to the general public and to informed opinion. Taken individually, these measures may seem both inoffensive and supportable by most law-abiding 'right thinking' people; collectively they are part of an impressive matrix of social control that restricts our freedom as the following examples clearly demonstrate.

The freedom of the authorities to access information on our private lives has grown considerably in the twenty-first century. Data from a wide range of sources – the Office for National Statistics, the National Health Service, the Inland Revenue, the VAT office, the Benefits Agency, Student Finance, our school reports – can now be collated into a file on a citizen, without a court order showing why this should be the case. Legislative proposals in recent years have included phone and email records to be kept for seven years, the extension of child curfews, keeping DNA of those acquitted of crimes and 'ex-suspects', restrictions on travel of those convicted of drug offences, the extension of compulsory finger-printing for those cautioned of a recordable offence and public authorities authorised to carry out speculative searches of the DNA database (Wadham and Modhi 2003). The Social Security Fraud Act 2001 allows for the compilation of a financial inventory from our bank accounts, building societies, insurance companies, telecom companies and the Student Loan Company, while every number on our phone bills may be reverse searched for an address. There may be no evidence that we are involved in fraud for us to be investigated, we may merely belong to a demographic group of people that the authorities feel is 'likely' to be involved in fraud.

The left realist hybrid model of criminal justice development thus proposes that in a complex contemporary society we all have interests in – and indeed a considerable enthusiasm for the introduction of – constraints and restrictions that are placed on particular activities and which restrict the civil liberties or human rights of some individuals or groups in the apparent greater interest. Taken together collectively, these many individual restrictions contribute significantly to the ever-expanding and pervasive disciplinary-control-surveillance-matrix that constrains the lives of all in the carceral society.

Four models of criminal justice development summarised

This chapter has introduced four models for different ways of theorising the development of criminal justice. First, the orthodox social progress model proposes that the development of modern societies, their laws and criminal justice systems is the product of enlightenment, benevolence and a consensual society where the whole population shares the same core values and develops an increasingly progressive humanitarian response to crime and disorder. Theories of criminal justice – and other disciplines such as criminology and psychology – provide the scientific support or knowledge base to inform the particular reform programme and changes occur when the reform vision becomes more refined and ideas more sophisticated. The revisionist variant of the orthodox social progress model tells a less idealist account where the ideas and intentions of the reformers are still seen to be important but where changes occur as functional and pragmatic solutions to immediate social changes. It provides a more critical account than the purist version but nevertheless remains a liberal model which still believes that things can be improved if we learn the correct lessons from history and research and apply them.

Second, the radical conflict model of criminal justice development challenges the notion of a consensual society implicit in the orthodox model and, in contrast, proposes that society is inherently characterised by conflict. From this perspective, the developing criminal justice system has successfully served the requirements of the emerging capitalist order by allowing for the continued repression of non-compliant members of the working class while this oppressive reality is hidden from the general population and the impression given that the changes introduced were fair, humane and progressive. In reality the changes introduced have always been in the interests of the capitalist market economy and its maintenance. A revisionist 'soft' variant of the radical conflict model proposes that changes in the development of criminal justice did not simply occur because of the functional requirements of capitalism for the motives of those involved were many and complex. Thus, reformers may well have ultimately acted out of political self-interest but benevolent motives and genuine concerns about the welfare of the target pollution were also involved.

Third, proponents of the carceral society model of criminal justice development consider both the social progress and the radical conflict models to be too simplistic and – while recognising the strengths of each and in particular the complementary nature of the latter – recognise that power is both diffuse and pervasive in society with agents and experts at all levels of the social world having both access to and control of power. This diffuse power is nevertheless invariably and ultimately exercised in the overall interests of the capitalist class or market economy, although those involved in its application at the micro- and mezzo-levels are not always aware of their contribution to the 'grand design'.

Fourth, the left realist hybrid model of criminal justice development does not completely dismiss the social progress, radical conflict or carceral surveillance models but recognises the least partial strengths of each. It thus produces a synthesis of the three while, going a step further, recognising the interest and collusion of the general public – and that means *us* – in the creation of the increasingly pervasive socio-control matrix of the carceral society. It is a model moreover influenced by left realist criminology which recognises that crime and disorder is a real problem for poor people who are targeted by – and are the principal victims of – a criminal element living in their own communities and from whom they require a protection that has not always been recognised or forthcoming. This model proposes that the general public has since the beginnings of the modern era always had an interest in the development of social progress that has conveniently coincided with the requirements of capitalism – or the market economy – and have contributed invariably unwittingly to the construction of the disciplinary-control-matrix. It is accepted that each of the other perspectives are to some extent legitimate for there were and are a multitude of motivations for both implementing and accepting the increasing surveillance and control of a potentially dangerous population on the streets and elsewhere.

Conclusions

The development of a juvenile/youth justice system to specifically target the apparently perpetual social problem of criminal behaviour by children and young people can be at least partially explained by the orthodox social progress model of criminal justice development, because it is obvious that many – if not virtually all – of those involved in this element of the much wider and ever increasing surveillance and disciplinary project targeted at children and young people throughout the modern era have done so with the best of benevolent and invariably humanitarian intentions, even though there is some dispute over definitions of these terms which seem to change over time. It is nevertheless clear that the increasing development of an intrusive and pervasive child surveillance system has occurred in the final instance in the interests of a capitalist market economy (radical conflict model) which has come under increasingly competitive economic pressures in contemporary neoliberal Western societies. There is a pressing cost-effective demand to both discipline and control a fast expanding, increasingly superfluous sub-population of society, while the role of the expert, frontline professional and practitioner in the construction of that all-seeing, all-encompassing disciplinary-surveillance-matrix is also very apparent, regardless of any humanitarian intention. It is nevertheless the left realist hybrid model which demonstrates how we, the general public, have a socially constructed interest in the control of out-groups of young people – and indeed their elders – who are the contemporary 'folk devils' who apparently threaten our well-being. It is this concern about these groups of young people that has helped to bring about an enforced mechanical social solidarity and a not always unknowing commitment to the carceral surveillance society and its containment project.

The commitment of the great majority in society to the mainstream social project and their willing support of the surveillance of supposedly high-risk, high-threat groups such as disaffected, dispossessed and disillusioned young people will be further considered later in this book.

Summary of main points

1　The contemporary youth justice system which was established in England and Wales by New Labour in 1998 was the culmination of often contrasting, conflicting and sometimes ambiguous themes, many of which had been in existence since the beginnings of the tutelage project over 170 years ago.
2　This chapter reconsiders the history of that tutelage project in the context of four models of criminal justice development.
3　The orthodox social progress model is the standard non-critical explanation which considers the development of law and the criminal justice system to be predominantly non-contentious. Thus, criminal justice institutions operate neutrally in the interests of all.
4　From this perspective, children and increasingly their families were disciplined, controlled and placed under surveillance because motivated entrepreneurial philanthropists had genuine humanitarian concerns about poor urban children and young people at risk.
5　The revisionist variant of the orthodox social progress model tells a less idealist account which argues that changes and developments are functional and pragmatic solutions to immediate social changes.
6　From, the radical conflict perspective, the tutelage project served more than adequately the requirements of the emerging capitalist order for the continued repression of recalcitrant members of the working class and in this case young people.
7　The carceral surveillance society model has its foundations in the work of Michel Foucault and recognises that power is both diffuse and pervasive in society. Agents and experts at all levels of the social world have both access to and control of power, although this is invariably exercised in the overall interests of the market economy.
8　Those agents, experts and professional involved in the application of power at the micro-, mezzo- and macro-levels are not always aware of their contribution to the 'grand design'.
9　The left realist hybrid model provides a synthesis of the orthodox social progress, radical conflict and carceral surveillance society models but with the additional recognition of our interest and collusion in the creation of the increasingly pervasive surveillance matrix.
10　The left realist hybrid model accepts that all accounts – radical conflict, orthodox social progress, carceral surveillance society – are at least partially legitimate for there were, and are, a multitude of motivations for both the implementation and the willing acceptance of the increasing surveillance and tutelage of young people.

Discussion questions

1   What was the youth justice disciplinary/tutelage project with its origins in the nineteenth century?
2   Explain the social progress model of criminal justice development.
3   Explain the radical conflict model of criminal justice development.
4   Explain the carceral surveillance society model of criminal justice development.
5   Explain the left realist hybrid model of criminal justice development.

Notes

1   False consciousness is a term used by some Marxists for the way in which material, ideological and institutional processes in capitalist society mislead members of the proletariat.
2   Left functionalism – Jock Young argues that most 'Marxism' is little more than a form of functionalism that replaces the interests of 'society' with those of the 'ruling class'. Especially 'Instrumental Marxism' (e.g., Ralph Milliband).

Part II

Explaining offending behaviour by children and young people

7 Youth offending as rational behaviour

Key issues

1 Pre-modern explanations of criminal behaviour
2 The rational actor model of criminal behaviour
3 The Classical School and its aftermath
4 Populist conservative criminology
5 Contemporary rational actor theories
6 The rational actor model and the youth offender reconsidered

---

The first part of this book discussed the social construction of childhood and adolescence as particular categories of human development and the various methods utilised and developed over time for the socialisation and disciplining of young people as a group functional to the requirements of industrial modernity. Chapters 3 to 5 discussed the development of increasingly sophisticated attempts to respond and intervene in the lives of children and young people who had deviated from defined acceptable norms of behaviour.

Throughout the first part of the book, reference was made to explanations of why young people deviate from the norms of society and become involved in offending behaviour. This second part of the book discusses the different explanations – or criminological theories – that have been proposed at different times during the era of industrial modernity to explain offending behaviour by children and young people. It provides a discussion which is complementary to the author's *Introduction to Criminological Theory* (Hopkins Burke 2001, 2005, 2009, 2014) and thus uses the same explanatory models of crime and criminal behaviour introduced and developed in those texts. Thus, this chapter discusses youth offending in terms of the rational actor model, which proposes that involvement in criminal behaviour is very much a matter of choice. The explanations discussed in the following three chapters are, however, fundamentally underpinned by both the predestined actor model, which proposes that criminality can be explained in terms of factors, either internal or external to the human being that cause or determine them to act in ways over which they have little or no control, and the victimised actor model, which proposes offenders to be themselves the victims of an unjust and unequal society which targets and criminalises the behaviour and activities of disadvantaged sections of society. It will nevertheless become increasingly obvious to the reader that these three models are not mutually exclusive. Young people do make choices but those available to them are significantly constrained by the life circumstances in which they find themselves. They may appear poor choices to make from our point of view but could well make considerable sense from the perspective of the young person. We shall commence our discussion of the rational actor by locating it in the pre-modern context from which it originally emerged.

Pre-modern explanations of criminal behaviour

All human societies throughout history have sought to explain why it is that some of their number break the rules of the group. The purpose is to identify the basis of social solidarity, reasons for disorder, and subsequently the implementation of sanctions against those who contravene the established norms of behaviour (Durkheim 1933; Hopkins Burke 2001, 2005, 2009, 2014). Many pre-modern explanations of criminal behaviour were grounded in spiritualism and naturalism; that is, involvement in criminality could be explained by an inappropriate relationship with supernatural powers. Offences were, therefore, spiritual 'sins' or crimes against the natural order and punishments were said to be carried out in accordance with nature or to be divinely sanctioned. This presumption of a linkage between order, disorder and non-human influences became part of the body of laws and traditions in many pre-modern societies, albeit with a number of cultural adaptations. Thus, two early theories of delinquency that were extremely influential in premodern medieval Western Europe were those of naturalism[1] and demonology.[2]

It was observed in the first part of this book that concepts of childhood, adolescence and juvenile delinquency are relatively recent social constructions, as is the notion of a separate juvenile or youth justice system. Pre-modern societies certainly considered young offenders to be nothing more than little versions of adult criminals and, very often, this approach was rooted in the presumption – offered by both naturalism and demonology – that explanations of criminal behaviour are indistinguishable from criminal causation, and therefore all such behaviour should be similarly punished. From a perspective where criminal behaviour was the outcome of an inappropriate relationship with natural or supernatural phenomena, it made perfect sense to respond to contaminated individuals in the same way, which invariably meant the termination of their ungodly lives. Differential responses to different categories of people in such circumstances would simply have been irrational.

With the rise of modernity in Western Europe, explanations of offending behaviour came to focus on the personal responsibility of individuals. These new theories simply rejected naturalism and demonology as explanations of delinquency and criminality and were heavily influenced by the rationality and humanitarianism which was the basis of European Enlightenment philosophy (Hopkins Burke 2001, 2005, 2009, 2014).

The rational actor model of criminal behaviour

Hopkins Burke (2001, 2005, 2009, 2014) identifies three models – or traditions – of explaining criminal behaviour: the rational actor, the predestined actor and the victimised actor models. Variants of the latter two models are discussed in the following three chapters while the former is the focus of this one. The rational actor model has its origins in the Classical School of the late eighteenth century and proposes that criminal behavior is the outcome of individual rational choice and has its theoretical foundations in the human desire for the pursuit of pleasure and aversion to pain. Because of this emphasis on human rationality, it is argued that offenders should be held personally accountable for criminal and delinquent acts and be punished accordingly. Since the calculus for making this choice is the acquisition of a benefit from criminal behaviour (pleasure), it is argued that society must develop policies to increase the costs for this benefit (pain). Thus, punishment should become increasingly harsher as the extent of criminal behaviour becomes greater and more serious, and the costs of crime must, therefore, always outweigh the possible benefits that might be obtained from the criminal act. Box 7.1 summarises the main points of the rational actor model of criminal behaviour.

Box 7.1   The rational actor model of criminal behaviour

- Crime is an outcome of rationality and free will.
- People choose to engage in criminal rather than conformist behaviour.
- Criminality is morally wrong and an affront against social order and the collective good of society.
- Civil society must necessarily punish criminals to deter individual wrongdoers and other would-be criminals.
- Punishment should be proportional to the nature of the criminal offence and never excessive.
- Punishment must also be a guaranteed response to criminal behaviour and delivered quickly.

The Classical School and its aftermath

It was the two key Classical School theorists – Cesare Beccaria in Italy and Jeremy Bentham in Britain – writing in the late eighteenth century who established the essential components of the rational actor model. Beccaria considered that criminals owe a 'debt' to society, and he advocated the then radical proposition that punishment should be swift, certain and proportional to the seriousness of the crime. In short, the punishment should fit the crime.

Beccaria provides the essential foundations of the rational actor model which is based on the concepts of free will and hedonism. He proposes that human behaviour is essentially purposive and based on the pleasure–pain principle and that punishment inflicted should reflect that principle: thus, fixed punishments for all offences must be written into the law and not be open to the interpretation, or the discretion, of judges; the law must be applied equally to all citizens regardless of social status, the sole function of the court is to determine guilt, there should be no mitigation and all that are guilty of a particular offence should suffer the same prescribed penalty.

The philosopher Jeremy Bentham promoted the ideas of Beccaria in England during the late eighteenth and early nineteenth centuries and argued that human beings rationally seek pleasure and avoid pain. Rational people can thus be easily deterred from criminal deviance by the threat of punishment, but the criminally minded will conclude that the pleasure derived from crime outweighs the pain of punishment and are not easily dissuaded. Bentham nevertheless went further and argued that deterrence was far more likely to be achieved by the certainty of punishment and by making the severity of each punishment surpass any benefit derived from the crime.

This argument appears at first sight both plausible and even attractive but significantly these early rational actor theorists had deliberately and completely ignored differences between individuals. First offenders and recidivists were treated exactly the same, solely on the basis of the particular act that had been committed; children, the 'feeble-minded' and the insane were all treated as if they were fully rational and competent. Thus, the appearance in court of people who were unable to comprehend the proceedings against them did little to legitimise the new judicial orthodoxy and it became increasingly recognised that people were not equally responsible for their actions. The outcome was that a whole range of experts gradually came to be invited into the courts to pass opinion on the degree of reason that could be expected of the accused and judges were now able to vary sentences in accordance with the degree of individual culpability argued by these expert witnesses.

It was this theoretical compromise that led to the emergence of a modified criminological perspective that came to be termed the neo-Classical School and which informs the justice/punishment model of youth justice outlined in Chapter 3. In this modified variant of the rational actor model, ordinary sane adults were still to be considered fully responsible for their actions, and all equally capable of either criminal or non-criminal behaviour, but it was now recognised that children – and in some circumstances, the elderly – were less capable of exercising free choice and were, therefore, less responsible for their actions. We have here an early recognition that various innate predisposing factors may actually cause or determine human behaviour: a perception that was to provide the foundation of the predestined actor model that we will encounter in the following three chapters and which was to increasingly provide the basis of the welfare/treatment model of youth justice that was again outlined in Chapter 3.

It was significantly these revisions to the penal code that admitted into the courts for the first time non-legal 'experts' including doctors, psychiatrists and, later, social workers. These professionals were gradually introduced into the criminal justice system in order to identify the impact of individual biological, psychological and social differences and the purpose of this intervention was to determine the extent to which offenders were responsible for their actions. The outcome was that sentences became more individualised and dependent on the perceived degree of culpability of the offender and on mitigating circumstances. Moreover, it was now recognised that a particular punishment would have a differential effect on different people and, consequently, punishment came increasingly to be expressed in terms of punishment appropriate to the rehabilitation of the individual. From this time onwards, punishment came to fit not the crime but the perpetrator.

Populist conservative criminology

The rational actor model was to go into increasing decline as an explanation of the offending behaviour of children and young people but was to return to favour with the rise of the 'new' political right – or populist conservatism – that came to political power in 1979 and which we encountered in Chapter 4. At that time conservative writers were mounting a vigorous moral campaign against various forms of 'deviance' and during the general election held during that year, the Conservative leader, Margaret Thatcher, made crime a major election issue for the first time in post-war Britain. Her general concern was to re-establish 'Victorian values' and to this end targeted the supposedly permissive society of the 1960s and its perceived legitimisation in 'soft' social science. In criminology, this perceived liberal indulgence was epitomised, first, by the predestined actor model of criminal behaviour – which had been the enduring dominant orthodoxy of criminological explanation in the twentieth century – with its focus on discovering the causes of crime and, having first located them, offering treatment and rehabilitation rather than punishment, but, second, even more so with the more radical variants of the 'victimised actor' model and their critique of an unfair and unequal society and their policy assumptions of understanding, forgiveness and non-intervention that were gaining increasing popularity with the idealistic but at that time still electorally viable political left.

Right-wing intellectuals observed that it was not merely that left-wing and liberal thought had simply failed to see the problems inherent in 'soft' approaches to crime, discipline and education but this so-called progressive theorising had itself provided a basis for the acceleration of the permissive syndromes in question. High levels of criminality and disorder were blamed not only on the weakening sources of social authority, the family, schools, religion and other key institutions, but even more so on the corrosive influence of the surrounding culture with its emphasis on rights rather than obligations and the celebration of self-expression to the point of self-indulgence, instead of promoting self-control and self-constraint (Tzannetakis 2001). The populist conservatives thus argued that in such a de-moralising culture, it was clear that crime and violence would inevitably flourish. Real problems and sociological apologies alike had to be confronted, and an attempt made to reassert the virtue and necessity of authority, order and discipline (Scruton 1980, 1985).

In social policy in general (Morgan 1978) and in the area of crime and deviance in particular (Dale 1984), an assault was mounted on liberal and radical left trends. Empirical justification for this attack on the self-styled forces of socially progressive intervention came from the publication of an influential paper by Robert Martinson (1974) – discussed elsewhere in this book – which purported to show that rehabilitation programmes in prison simply 'do not work' and thus the whole rationale for the existence of a welfare-oriented probation service, in particular, was called into question. Consequently, we were to see the enthusiastic reintroduction of the idea of retributive punishment and arguments for the protection of society from danger. From this populist conservative perspective, punishment is essentially about devising penalties to fit the crime and ensuring that they are carried out, thus reinforcing social values. In short, this concern to treat the miscreant as an offender against social morality, and not as a candidate for reform, can be seen as a contemporary form of the rational actor model, but one with a distinctly retributive edge (Hopkins Burke 2014).

Contemporary rational actor theories

Three groups of contemporary rational actor model theories have come very much to prominence with the revival of the tradition: (i) contemporary deterrence theories, (ii) rational choice theories and (iii) routine activities theory.

Contemporary deterrence theories

Contemporary deterrence theories are founded on the twin principles that punishment must occur quickly after the offence has occurred and be certain to happen. Thus, if the punishment is sufficiently severe, certain and swift, it is argued that the rationally calculating individual will decide that there is more to be lost than there is to be gained from offending and not become involved (Zimring and Hawkins 1973; Gibbs 1975; Wright 1993). It is moreover proposed that the certainty of being caught and being processed by the criminal justice system is a significantly more effective deterrent than the severity of punishment imposed (Akers 1997).

There are two variations of the deterrence doctrine and it is proposed that these operate in different ways. In the case of 'general deterrence', the apprehension and punishment of offenders in society demonstrates clearly to the population as a whole what will happen to them if they break the law (Zimring and Hawkins 1973); while, in the case of 'specific deterrence', it is the apprehended and punished individual offender who learns from their specific experience of the futility of involvement in criminality. The high rate of recidivism (or repeat offending) nevertheless challenges the effectiveness of deterrence as a crime control strategy. Reoffending rates for young people leaving custody remain high, although there has been a small reduction in the past few years. Thus, the proven re-offending rate for juvenile offenders released from custody between April 2011 and March 2012 was 69.3 per cent. This represents a fall of 3.3 percentage points compared to the previous twelve months and a fall of 7.5 percentage points since 2000 (Ministry of Justice 2014).

Moreover, there are clearly problems with the notion that even fully rational adults – if there are such people – accurately calculate the rewards and risks associated with crime but this is clearly more problematic in the case of immature children and young people who may have a limited sense of rationality and, therefore, cannot legitimately be held fully responsible for their actions. Contemporary rational choice theories help us explore this notion further.

Contemporary rational choice theories

The earlier and less sophisticated variants of rational choice theory tended to compare the decision-making process adopted by offenders with straightforward economic choice where the person chooses the activity – legal or illegal – that offers the best return (Becker 1968), very much in accordance with the pleasure/pain dichotomy of Bentham's hedonistic calculus. Thus, it was argued that offending could be prevented by reforming the law with the introduction of more rigorous and punitive punishment and the introduction of more effective criminal justice administration in order to alter the equation and make crime appear appreciably less attractive. Perhaps not surprising, this early variant was accused of implying too high a degree of rationality by comparing criminal choices too closely with marketplace decisions, and, at the same time, failing to explain expressive non-economically motivated criminal activity such as vandalism (Trasler 1986; Long and Hopkins Burke 2015). Certainly, it would appear an inappropriate theory for explaining the behaviour of children or adolescents who have long been recognised as possessing a less developed sense of rationality.

A more sophisticated, highly influential variant of rational choice theory has, however, been developed by Clarke and Cornish, who define crime as 'the outcome of the offender's choices or decisions, however hasty or ill-considered these might be' (Clarke 1987: 118). Thus, from this perspective, offenders invariably act in terms of limited or bounded forms of rationality. They will not always obtain all the facts needed to make a wise decision and the information available will not necessarily be weighed carefully or appropriately, but they will make a decision that is perfectly rational in the context of their lives, experiences, cultural background and knowledge base. Moreover, Clarke (1987) is not entirely dismissive of the predestined actor model tradition that we will encounter in the following three chapters, and suggests that most of the factors seen as predisposing an individual to commit crime can be interpreted in terms of their influence on offender cognitive decision-making. It is thus proposed that individuals respond to situations in different ways because they bring with them a different history of psychological conditioning. Hence, children and young people brought up in different social environments with different socialisation experiences are likely to make very different decisions when confronted with similar circumstances and criminal opportunities, which is a key concept for rational choice theorists. Significantly, a child brought up in a geographical location where criminality is common, their family and friends are actively involved in illicit activities that appear to bring them easily obtained material rewards, while access to legitimate opportunities appear both limited and implausible, could well consider criminal involvement to be a very rational choice for them. Thus, growing up in an area where the schools are poor, good jobs non-existent and university well off the radar for the average young person, literally getting on your usually too small bicycle and delivering that package for the man, or more accurately an elder boy, makes perfect sense, while helping to set up a future criminal career.

Routine activities theory

Routine activities theory is, to some extent, a development of the rational choice theory key concept of criminal opportunity which proposes that for a personal or property crime to occur there must be at the same time and place a perpetrator, a victim, and/or an object of property (Felson 1998). The criminal act can take place if there are persons or circumstances in the locality that encourage it to happen but, however, it can be prevented if the potential victim or another person is present who can take action to deter it from happening.

Cohen and Felson (1979) have taken the elements of time, place, objects and persons to develop a 'routine activities' view of crime events and these have been placed into three categories of variables that increase or decrease the likelihood that persons will be victims of 'direct contact' predatory – personal or property – crime. The first variable is the presence in the locality of motivated offenders, those looking to commit offences or those who will do so if a reasonable criminal opportunity presents itself. Cohen and Felson observe – albeit in a US context but one which is easily transferable to the UK – that the great majority of motivated offenders walking the streets looking for criminal opportunities are young males. Second, it is necessary to have available suitable targets, either in the form of a person to rob or property to enter (burglary) or steal. The third identified variable was the absence of 'capable guardians' against crime. Therefore, the probability that a crime will take place is enhanced when there are one or more persons in the locality who are motivated to commit a crime, a suitable available target or potential victim, and the absence of formal or informal guardians who could deter the potential offender.[3]

Cohen and Felson argue that it is the fundamental changes in daily activities related to work, school and leisure that have occurred during the past seventy years that have placed more people in particular localities at particular times. This has both increased their accessibility as targets – or victims – of crime while at the same time they are away from home and unable to guard their own property and possessions.

Moreover, Felson (1998) places less emphasis on the significance of formal guardians – such as the police – because he has concluded that crime is a private phenomenon which is largely unaffected by state intervention. Natural crime prevention and deterrence are now emphasised and Felson argues that it is ordinary people, oneself, friends, family or even strangers that are the most likely capable guardians. In this later work he has also applied routine activities theory to four crime categories other than property variants:

- Exploitative (robbery, rape)
- Mutualistic (gambling, prostitution, selling and buying drugs)
- Competitive (fighting)
- Individualistic (individual drug use, suicide).

Felson has thus identified a fourth variable that enables a criminal event to take place – the absence of an 'intimate handler', a significant other; for example, a parent or girlfriend – who can impose informal social control on the offender. A potential offender must escape the 'intimate handler' then find a crime target without being under the surveillance of this 'capable guardian'. There is clearly a social class differential factor in existence here. Middle-class children are far more likely to spend their leisure time in the family home or taking part in super-vised organised activities such as music or sport, while working-class children are more likely to be unsupervised, out on the almost mythical 'street', at risk of becoming involved in offending opportunities.

Much routine activity theory research and discussion concentrates on the interlinked areas of crime targets and the lack of appropriate guardians. Thus, Cohen and Felson (1979) developed their concept of the 'household activ-ity ratio', that is, the percentage of all households that are not husband–wife families, or where the wife is employed outside the home, and argue that such households are more vulnerable because their members are away from home more and are thus less able to function as guardians of their property. Cohen et al. (1981) subsequently developed a more formalised version of routine activi-ties theory, which they named 'opportunity' theory and which considers the elements of exposure, proximity, guardianship and target attractiveness as vari-ables that increase the risk of criminal victimisation. Others propose that routine activities theory is merely a way of explaining why people become victims of crime and that it fails to explain why it is that some people engage in criminal behaviour and others do not (Akers 1997). Thus, there is a taken-for-granted assumption with this perspective that such people exist and that they commit crimes in certain places, at times when the opportunities and potential victims are available, but it tells us absolutely nothing about these people and their motivations, why it is that *they* commit crime.

The predestined actor model discussed in the following three chapters provides us with numerous suggestions for the identity of many motivated offenders. For as the evidence shows, it is often children and young people who are to be found wandering the streets during those times when adults are at work and who are motivated to offend, or at least are prepared to take advantage of crime oppor-tunities when they arise, not least when they are in the company of likeminded others, in particular when they are truanting or excluded from school, or even when on their way home from school when, for example, they descend in groups on shopping malls. Or in the following years, having left school with inadequate educational qualifications, they often find themselves excluded from access to legitimate economic opportunities.

The rational actor model and the youth offender reconsidered

The original rational actor model theorists had emphasised the rationally calculating, reasoning, human being who could be deterred from choosing to commit criminal behaviour by the threat of a fair and proportionate punishment. Moreover, they had proposed that all citizens should be treated equally in terms of a codified and rationalised legal system. The purist version of that explanatory system nevertheless fell into decline because it became clear that not all people – and children and young people in particular – are capable of making purely rational decisions for which they can be held legitimately responsible. Thus, the revised version of the rational actor model, which came to the fore with the rise of the political 'new right' in the last quarter of the twentieth century, came to implicitly accept the predestined actor notion that there are different categories of human beings with different levels of reasoning. From this perspective, it is accepted that young people do make decisions which are rational for them in the circumstances in which they find themselves and in terms of their life experience and knowledge. In some of these circumstances crime and criminality can be a very rational choice.

The rational actor model proposes that children and young people *choose* to offend because it makes rational sense to them in the context of their lives. Offending choices are more attractive than legitimate activities, which are usually unavailable to them or of limited value. Deterrence theory suggests that children and young people can be deterred from criminality by the threat or imposition of rigorous penalties but recidivism rates suggest that this strategy has not been very successful. The other strategy implication is to improve the life chances of the juvenile so they have access to good quality, legitimate opportunities that make offending a less rational choice. Offenders will desist from criminal behaviour when they are provided with such rational alternatives.

Summary of main points

1   The rational actor model has its origins in the Classical School of the late eighteenth century and proposes that criminal behaviour is the outcome of individual rational choice and has its theoretical foundations in the human desire for the pursuit of pleasure and aversion to pain.
2   Because of this emphasis on human rationality, it is argued that offenders should be held personally accountable for criminal and delinquent acts and punished accordingly.
3   Since the calculus for making this choice is the acquisition of a benefit from criminal behaviour (pleasure), it is argued that society must develop policies to increase the costs for this benefit (pain).

4 Significantly these early rational actor theorists deliberately ignored differences between individuals and it became increasingly recognised that people were not equally responsible for their actions.

5 The outcome was that a whole range of experts gradually came to be invited into the courts to pass opinion on the degree of reason that could be expected of the accused and judges were now able to vary sentences in accordance with the degree of individual culpability argued by these expert witnesses.

6 It was this theoretical compromise that led to the emergence of a modified criminological perspective that came to be termed the neo-Classical School and which informs the justice/punishment model of youth justice.

7 The rational actor model was to go into increasing decline as an explanation of offending behaviour but was to return to favour with the rise of the 'new' political right and three groups of contemporary rational actor model theories have come very much to prominence with the revival of the tradition: (i) contemporary deterrence theories, (ii) rational choice theories and (iii) routine activities theory.

8 Contemporary deterrence theories are founded on the twin principles that punishment must occur quickly after the offence has occurred and be certain to happen.

9 Contemporary rational choice theories propose that offenders invariably act in terms of limited or bounded forms of rationality.

10 Routine activities theory proposes that for a personal or property crime to occur there must be at the same time and place a perpetrator, a victim, and/or an object of property.

Discussion questions

1 What are the basic fundamentals of the rational actor model of criminal behaviour?

2 What was the 'neo-Classical' compromise?

3 Explain contemporary deterrence theories.

4 Explain contemporary rational choice theories.

5 Explain routine activities theory.

Notes

1 Naturalism refers to the ancient practice of linking human affairs to the natural world and inferring that human behaviour is thus derived from the forces of nature. Just as the tides are affected by the sun and the moon, so too are human passions and fortunes. All that is necessary is for humans to become adept at understanding how the forces of nature work, and develop the ability to interpret these forces. Naturalism is therefore a deterministic theory of criminal causation, because it eliminates notions of individual responsibility and the ability to choose courses of action (Vold et al. 1998).

2 For many centuries, humans believed that evil creatures – demons or devils – wielded great influence over humans, sometimes possessing them and making them commit

offences against the greater good. Criminal behaviour and delinquency were manifestations of conflict between creatures of evil and chaos against deities of goodness and order. Demonology is thus – like naturalism above – a deterministic theory of criminal causation where the individual has no choice in their behaviour (Hopkins Burke 2005).

3 The term 'target' has been used in preference to that of 'victim' because the acquisition of property or money was seen to be focus of the great majority of criminal behaviour.

8 Biological explanations of youth crime

Key issues

1 Physiological constituents and youth criminality
2 Biochemical explanations
3 Altered biological state theories
4 Socio-biological theories
5 Conclusions

We saw in the previous chapter that the rational actor model of criminal behaviour proposes that human beings possess free will and are, therefore, free to choose the behaviour of their own choice. The predestined actor model, in contrast, rejects this emphasis on free will and replaces it with the doctrine of determinism which claims to account for criminality in terms of factors – either internal or external to the individual – which cause them to act in ways over which they have little or no control. From this perspective, the individual is both predestined to be a criminal while being a different category of humanity from non-criminals. Box 8.1 summarises the main points of the predestined actor model of criminal behaviour.

Box 8.1 The predestined actor model of criminal behaviour

- The rational actor emphasis on free will is rejected and replaced with the doctrine of determinism.
- From this positivist standpoint, criminal behaviour is explained in terms of factors, either internal or external to the person that cause – or determine – them to act in ways over which they have little or no control.
- The individual is thus in some way predestined to be a criminal.
- Criminals are in some way different from non-criminals.
- There are three basic formulations of the predestined actor model: biological, psychological and sociological.
- All three variants incorporate the same fundamental determinist assumptions.
- Treatment of the offender is proposed, rather than punishment.

There are three basic formulations of the predestined actor model: biological, psychological and sociological. All three variants, nevertheless, incorporate the same fundamental assumptions, and although each is discussed separately, they become increasingly non-exclusive; for example, biologists came to embrace sociological factors, while at times it is often difficult to differentiate between biological and psychological explanations. This chapter considers the biological variant of the predestined actor model and is divided into three sections. First, there is a consideration of those theories which propose that the young person has been born with a physiological predisposition to commit crime. Second, there is a discussion of altered biological states where criminal behaviour is at least influenced by the consumption of alcohol, drugs or poor diet. Third, there is an examination of socio-biological theories which propose that biological predispositions are activated in different ways in diverse environmental conditions, often dependent on the socialised upbringing of the young person.

Physiological constituents and youth criminality

Early biological explanations of criminal behaviour have their origins in the work of the Italian school at the end of the nineteenth and the beginning of the twentieth centuries and although these theories were primitive by the standards of today, they significantly established an enduring research tradition that has persisted to this day. Cesare Lombroso (1876) argued that criminals are a physical type distinct from non-criminals with physical characteristics suggestive of earlier forms of evolution. It is an approach considered simplistic and naïve today, yet Lombroso had made an important contribution to the development of criminological explanations by recognising in his later work the need for multifactor accounts that include not only hereditary, but also social, cultural and economic factors. These latter important factors were emphasised by his successors Enrico Ferri and Raffaele Garofalo.

Ferri (1895) argued that criminal behaviour can be explained by studying the interaction between physical, individual and social factors, influentially proposing that crime could be controlled by improving the social conditions of the poor, thus advocating the provision of subsidised housing, birth control and public recreation facilities. Garofalo (1914) returned to evolutionary arguments and proposed that some members of society have a higher than average sense of morality because they are superior, further evolved, members of the group, while conversely, true criminals lack properly developed altruistic sentiments and, moreover, have psychic or moral anomalies that they have inherited. From this perspective, criminals are a different category of humanity from non-criminals and this remains a key tenet of purist predestined actor model philosophy. Later biological explanations of criminal behaviour were to become increasingly more sophisticated but the notion of inherited criminal characteristics continues to be central with evidence to support this supposition obtained from three sources: criminal family studies; twin studies; and adopted children studies.

Criminal family studies

Criminal family studies have their origins in the work of Dugdale (1877), who traced 709 members of the Juke family and discovered that the great majority had been either criminals or paupers; Goddard (1914), who traced 480 members of the Kallikak family and found that a large number of them had been criminals; and Goring (1913), who conducted a study of 3,000 prisoners and found strong associations between the criminality of children, their parents and siblings, even if they had been separated from each other at an early age. Problematically, none of these studies was able to distinguish between biological and environmental factors in establishing criminal causality, a weakness that later twin and adoption studies sought to overcome but ultimately with limited success.

Lange (1930) examined a group of men with a prison record and found that in 77 per cent of cases involving identical twins, both brothers had such a record; however, in the case of non-identical twins, only 12 per cent of brothers both had a prison record; while only 8 per cent of ordinary brothers, near to each other in age, were both found to have records. Christiansen (1968) examined official registers over an extended time period and found that in the case of identical male twins where at least one brother had a criminal record, the same applied to 36 per cent of the other twins. This was only the case with 12 per cent of the non-identical twins.

A problem with twin studies is the lack of clarity about the sort of characteristics that are supposedly inherited as variations might reveal themselves in quite different forms of behaviour (Trasler 1967). For example, some pairs of twins in Lange's study had committed very different types of offences from each other and it could well be the case that a predisposition to offend is inherited but the actual form of offending is determined by other factors. Christiansen interestingly did not actually claim that inherited characteristics were the only or even the dominant factor and proposed that twin studies could increase our understanding of the interaction between the environment and biological traits. It is nevertheless a significant criticism of twin studies that they cannot accurately assess the balance between the effects of inherited characteristics and those of the environment. Twins are more likely than ordinary siblings to share similar experiences in relation to family and peers and it is indeed possible that such similarities will be greater in the cases of identical twins.

More recent research conducted by Rowe and Rogers (1989) has supported both inherited characteristics and environmental explanations of criminality. Collecting data from self-report questionnaires involving 308 sets of twins in the Ohio State school system in the USA, they concluded that environment partly determines the similarity of behaviour of same-sex and identical twins and could lead them to develop similar offending behaviour. Moreover, as twins are usually brought up together, it becomes virtually impossible to reach any firm conclusion as to the role of inherited characteristics alone (Rowe 1990). It is adopted children studies that have sought to overcome this methodological predicament.

It would seem that in the case of adopted children – where contact with a criminal parent has obviously been limited – any association between criminal behaviour can be attributed to inherited characteristics with a greater degree of certainty. Thus, Hutchings and Mednick (1977) found that 48 per cent of young males with a criminal record and 37.7 per cent with a record of minor offences had a birth father with a criminal record. However, among young males without a criminal record, only 31.1 per cent had a birth father with a record. Interestingly, an adoptee was even more likely to have a record where both the birth and adoptive father had previous convictions.

A later wide-ranging study found a similar though slightly less strong correlation between birth parents and their adoptee children (Mednick et al. 1984). Again the most significant results were when both birth and adoptive parents were criminal and the researchers concluded that there was an inherited characteristic element that was transmitted from the criminal parents to their children that increased the likelihood of their offspring becoming involved in criminal behaviour. It should be noted, however, that adoption agencies try to place children in homes situated in similar environments to those from which they came and there remains a possibility that it is upbringing, not inherited characteristics, that 'causes' criminal behaviour. It might well be the case that some people are genetically endowed with characteristics that render them more likely to 'succumb to crime' (Hutchings and Mednick 1977: 140).

There have been attempts in more recent years to identify a link between the level of intelligence and criminal behaviour. Hirschi and Hindelang (1977) found that IQ, as a predictor of offending behaviour, is at least as good as any other major social variables and is also strongly related to social class and ethnic group. Thus, because offending behaviour is viewed as being the province of lower-class young people from ethnic minorities, this relationship implies that such people have lower IQs. It is an argument that has received a great deal of understandable criticism. For example, Menard and Morse (1984) argued that IQ is merely one of the ways in which young offenders are disadvantaged in society, citing societal and institutional response to these disadvantages as the real explanation for offending behaviour. In general, critics note that the way in which IQ tests are constructed provides advantages to those who are middle class and white and in reality do not measure innate intelligence, but rather some other ability, such as a facility in language or cultural concepts.

Genetic structure explanations

Genetic structure explanations of criminal behaviour consider abnormalities in the genetic structure of the offender with crucial identified defects being related to the sex chromosomes. People usually have twenty-three pairs of chromosomes, forty-six in all, with the sex of a person determined by one of these pairs. The normal complement in a female is XX and in a male XY but in some men an extra chromosome has been found. Klinefelter et al. (1942) discovered that sterile males often display a marked degree of feminisation together, sometimes, with low intelligence and increased physical stature and it was later found that these men had an extra X chromosome. A later study conducted among Klinefelter males in psychiatric institutions discovered an abnormally high incidence of criminal behaviour among the research subjects, which suggested they are over-represented among homosexuals, transvestites and transsexuals.

Later studies examined incarcerated criminals and focused on men with an extra Y chromosome, in order to test the hypothesis that they might be characterised by extra maleness, and thus more aggressive. Casey in 1965 and Neilson in 1968 conducted the first major studies at the Rampton and Moss Side secure hospitals, respectively, and discovered that such men tended to be very tall, generally of low intelligence, often with EEG abnormalities and histories of criminal and aggressive behaviour, with theft and violent assault their characteristic offences.

Price and Whatmore (1967) noted that men with an extra Y chromosome tend to be convicted at an earlier age than other offenders, come from families with no history of criminality, have a tendency to be unstable and immature without displaying remorse, and have a marked tendency to commit a succession of apparently motiveless property crimes. Witkin et al. (1977) explained the over-representation of such men in institutions to be the result of their slight mental retardation.

A range of criticisms has been made of genetic structure theories. First, almost all the research has been concentrated on inmates in special hospitals and has revealed more evidence of psychiatric disorder than criminality. Second, there does not appear to be any fixed and identifiable XYY syndrome, which means the concept is not useful in predicting criminal behaviour. Third, the offending behaviour of some young males with an extra X chromosome may actually be due to anxiety in adolescence about an apparent lack of masculinity. Fourth, all the young male offenders with an identified extra Y chromosome have come from working-class backgrounds. It is possible that because they are tall and well built, they may be defined as 'dangerous' by judges and psychiatrists, and, therefore, more likely to be incarcerated than fined. Finally, and perhaps crucially, there are thousands of apparently perfectly normal and harmless people in the general population who have either an extra X or Y chromosome.

Advances in genetic science in recent years have nevertheless led to a revival of claims that aspects of criminality can be explained by genetic factors. Significantly, the discovery that some traits of personality can be explained by a genetic component (Jones 1993) does greatly strengthen the possibility that some criminal behaviour can be explained by a genetic susceptibility triggered by environmental factors. This is an observation to which we return later in this chapter.

Criminal body types

A further category of biological positivism has its foundations directly in the Italian school tradition of emphasising body type. Hooton (1939) thus controversially concluded that criminals are organically inferior to other people and that low foreheads, in particular, were an indication of physiological inferiority, but his work was not surprisingly widely condemned for its racist overtones and failure to recognise that the prisoners studied represented only those who had been caught, convicted or imprisoned. Sheldon (1949) shifted attention to offending male youths, seeking to link different types of physique to temperament, intelligence and offending behaviour. He therefore categorised the physiques of the boys by measuring the degree to which they possessed a combination of three different body components: first, *endomorphs* tended to be soft, fat people; second, *mesomorphs,* muscular and athletic; *third*, ectomorphs had a skinny, flat and fragile physique. Sheldon concluded that most offenders were mesomorphs and moreover because the youths came from parents who were offenders, the factors that produce criminal behaviour are inherited. Glueck and Glueck (1950) found offenders to have narrower faces, wider chests, larger and broader waists, bigger forearms and upper arms than non-offenders, with approximately 60 per cent mesomorphic. The researchers, like their predecessors in this tradition, nevertheless failed to establish whether the mesomorphs were offenders because of their build and disposition, because their physique and dispositions are socially conceived as being associated with offenders, or whether poverty and deprivation affected both their body build and offending behaviour.

Body type theories can be legitimately criticised for ignoring different aspects of the interaction between the physical characteristics of the person and their social circumstances. Thus, poor people tend to have an inferior diet and be small in stature; while young people in manual occupations – and this was a time when such employment was widely available and undertaken from those in the poorer sections of society – are likely to acquire an athletic build. The over-representation of such people among convicted criminals may simply be explained by a variety of socio-cultural, rather than biological, factors. Gibbons (1970) thus argued that the high proportion of mesomorphs among offenders is due to a process of social selection and that the nature of their activities is such that deviants will be drawn from the more athletic members of that age group. Cortes and Gatti (1972) nevertheless observe that such arguments falsely accuse biological explanations of being more determinist than they actually are. They propose that as physical factors are essential to the social selection process, human behaviour has both biological and social causes. This point is revisited later in this chapter.

Biochemical explanations

Biochemical explanations of offending behaviour are similar to the altered biological state theories we will encounter below but differ in that the relevant substances are either already present in the body of the individual or are created by some internal physiological process.

It has long been recognised that male animals – of most species – are more aggressive than females and this has been linked to the male sex hormone, testosterone (Rose et al. 1974; Keverne et al. 1982). The relationship between sex hormones and human behaviour appears to be nonetheless more complex, although testosterone has been linked with aggressive crime such as murder and rape. In most men testosterone levels probably do not significantly affect levels of aggression (Persky et al. 1971; Scarmella and Brown 1978) but studies of violent male prisoners do suggest that testosterone levels have an effect on aggressive behaviour (Kreuz and Rose 1972; Ehrenkranz et al. 1974).

Problematically, these studies have not differentiated between different forms of aggression but others have sought to address these problems. Olwens (1987) thus conducted a study of young men with no marked criminal record and found a clear link between testosterone and both verbal and physical aggression, with a further distinction identified between provoked and unprovoked aggressive behaviour. Provoked aggression tended to be more verbal than physical in response to unfair or threatening behaviour by another person; unprovoked aggression was violent, destructive and involved activities such as starting fights and making provocative comments. The relationship between testosterone and unprovoked violence was, nevertheless, found to be indirect and would depend on other factors such as how irritable the particular individual was. Schalling (1987) discovered that high testosterone levels in young males were associated with verbal aggression but not with actual physical aggression, which suggests a concern to protect their status by threats. Low-testosterone-level boys would tend not to protect their position, preferring to remain silent. Neither study suggests a direct link between testosterone and aggression but in a provocative situation it is those with the highest levels of testosterone who are more likely to resort to violence.

Ellis and Coontz (1990) observe that testosterone levels peak during puberty and the early twenties and that this correlates with the highest crime rates. They claim that this finding provides persuasive evidence for a biological explanation of criminal behaviour and that it explains both aggressive and property crime, arguing that sociological researchers have failed to explain why it is that this distribution exists across all societies and cultures. There is, nevertheless, no evidence of a direct causal relationship between criminal behaviour and the level of testosterone. The link may be more tenuous, with testosterone merely providing the environment necessary for aggressive behaviour to take place.

Hypoglycaemia or low blood sugar levels – sometimes related to diabetes mellitus – may result in irritable, aggressive reactions, and may culminate in sexual offences, assaults and motiveless murder (see Shah and Roth 1974). Shoenthaler (1982) discovered that by lowering the daily sucrose intake of incarcerated young offenders it was possible to reduce the level of their anti-social behaviour. Virkkunen (1987) has, moreover, linked hypoglycaemia with other activities often defined as anti-social such as truancy, low verbal IQ, tattooing and stealing from home during childhood. Hypoglycaemia has also been linked with alcohol abuse; if consumed regularly and in large quantities, the ethanol produced can induce hypoglycaemia and increase aggression (Clapham 1989).

The relationship between adrenaline and aggressive behaviour is a similar area of study to that involving testosterone with both involving a relationship between a hormonal level and aggressive anti-social behaviour. Schachter (cited in Shah and Roth 1974) had found that injections of adrenaline made no difference to the behaviour of normal prisoners but a great difference to psychopaths but Hare (1982) found that when threatened with pain, criminals exhibit fewer signs of stress than other people. Mednick et al. (1982) discovered that not only do certain, particularly violent, criminals need stronger stimuli to arouse them, but also once they are in a stressed state they recover more slowly to their normal levels than do noncriminals. Eysenck (1959) had offered a logical explanation for this relationship some years previously, proposing that individuals with low stress levels are easily bored, become quickly disinterested in things around them, and crave exciting experiences. Thus, for such individuals normal stressful situations are not disturbing but they are exciting and enjoyable, something to be savoured and sought after. Rather like skydiving or extreme sports, which are a legal way of meeting these needs if the person has the resources to get involved in these activities.

Baldwin (1990) suggests that the link between age and crime rates can be partially explained by considering arousal rates, observing that children quickly become used to stimuli that had previously excited them and hence seek ever more thrilling inputs. The stimulus received from criminal type activities also declines with age, as does the level of physical fitness, strength and agility required to perform many such activities. Baldwin interestingly explains both the learning of criminal behaviour and its subsequent decline in terms of stimuli in the environment. The question is then posed as to whether the production of adrenaline is biologically or socially dictated.

Altered biological state theories

Altered biological state theories are those which link behavioural changes in the individual with the introduction of an external chemical agent, and these can be divided into the following categories: allergies, diet, alcohol and other drugs.

Allergies and diet

There have been suggested links between irritability and aggression that may lead individuals in some circumstances to commit criminal assault, and allergic reactions to such things as pollen, inhalants, drugs and food. Research on the criminological implications of allergies is ongoing but studies indicate two main reactions in these patients: first, emotional immaturity characterised by temper tantrums, screaming episodes, whining and impatience; second, anti-social behaviour characterised by sulkiness and cruelty.

More recent research has sought to bring together earlier work on blood sugar levels, allergies and other biochemical imbalances and the basic premise of the resulting 'biochemical individuality' theory is that each person has an absolutely unique internal biochemistry. We all vary in our daily need for each of the forty-odd nutrients – minerals, vitamins, carbohydrates, etc. – required to stay alive and healthy. From this idea flows the concept of 'orthomolecular medicine', which proposes that many diseases are preventable and treatable by proper diagnosis, vitamin supplementation and avoidance of substances that would bring on an illness or preclude a cure. Prinz et al. (1980) propose that some foods, and in particular certain additives, have effects that may lead to hyperactivity and even criminality. A low level of cholesterol has often been linked with hypoglycaemia, particularly when alcohol use has been involved (see Virkkunen 1987).

At first sight, it might appear strange to link criminal behaviour with vitamin deficiency but there is nevertheless evidence for an active role for biochemical disturbance in some offences of violence and some quite impressive results have been obtained in the orthomolecular treatment of some mental disorders. For example, Vitamin B3 (niacin) has been used successfully to treat some forms of schizophrenia (see Lesser 1980; Pihl 1982; Raloff 1983); while there is evidence that addiction to both drugs and alcohol may be related to unmet individual biochemical needs.

Substance abuse is usually brought about by the intake of drugs in the widest generic sense. Some of these drugs are legal and freely available, such as alcohol, which is drunk, and glues and lighter fluids, which are inhaled. The medical profession prescribes some, such as barbiturates, while others – such as cannabis, amphetamines, LSD, MDA or 'ecstasy', opiates (usually cocaine or heroin) – are only available illegally.

Alcohol, young people and criminality

Alcohol is more significant for criminality than any other drug, not least because it is legal and its extremely common usage makes it readily available. It has moreover long been associated with anti-social activity, crimes and criminality. Saunders (1984) calculated that alcohol was a significant factor in about 1,000 arrests per day or over 350,000 a year in the USA at that time. Flanzer (1981) had estimated that 80 per cent of all cases of family violence in the USA involved the consumption of alcohol, while De Luca (1981) estimated that almost a third of the cases of violence against children in the home were alcohol related. More general studies have discovered a strong link between alcohol and general levels of violence (Collins 1988; Fagan 1990).

Alcohol and young people are closely linked in the public mind in the contemporary UK, although this has not always been the case. In the inter-war period, young people aged 18–24 were the lightest drinkers in the adult population and the group most likely to abstain. Nor did alcohol play a significant part in the youth culture that came into existence in the 1950s, this being more likely to involve the coffee bar than the pub. It was not until the 1960s that pubs and drinking became an integral part of the youth scene. By the 1980s, those aged 18–24 years had become the heaviest drinkers in the population and the group least likely to abstain (Institute of Alcohol Studies 2005a).

By the year 2002, hazardous drinking, that is, drinking bringing the risk of physical or psychological harm now or in the future, was most prevalent in teenagers and young adults. Among females, hazardous drinking reached its peak in the age group 16–19, with just under one-third (32 per cent) having a hazardous drinking pattern. Among males, the peak was found in the 20–24 age group, with just under two-thirds (62 per cent) having a hazardous drinking pattern (Office for National Statistics 2001). These changes were moreover accompanied by a decline in the age of regular drinking. Thus nowadays most young people are drinking regularly – though not necessarily frequently – by the age of 14 or 15. One survey found that more than a quarter of boys aged 9–10 and a third a year older reported drinking alcohol at least once in the previous week, normally at home (Balding and Shelley 1993).

Most surveys suggest that there is a growing trend of drinking for effect and to intoxication. A related aspect is the partial merging of the alcohol and drug scenes in the context of youth culture, with alcohol being one of a range of psychoactive products now available on the recreational drug market. A large survey of teenagers in England, Wales and Scotland found that by the age 15–16 'binge drinking' is common, as is being 'seriously drunk' (Beinart et al. 2002). In this study, binge drinking was defined as consuming five or more alcoholic drinks in a single session. The growth in binge drinking may be regarded as particularly significant as there is evidence that drinking – and especially heavier drinking – in adolescence increases the likelihood of binge drinking continuing through adult life (Jefferis et al. 2005).

Alcohol is associated with a wide range of criminal offences – in addition to drink-driving and drunkenness – in which drinking or excessive consumption defines the offence. Alcohol-related crime has thus become a matter of great public concern. In England and Wales, approximately 70 per cent of crime audits published in 1998 and 1999 identified alcohol as an issue, particularly in relation to public disorder (Home Office 2000).

The term 'alcohol-related crime' normally refers to offences involving a combination of criminal damage offences, drunk and disorderly and other public disorder offences involving young males, typically 18–30 and occurring in the entertainment areas of town and city centres. However, a whole range of offences are linked to alcohol and these do not necessarily occur in the context of the night-time economy, and in 1997, Jack Straw, the then shadow home secretary, pledged a New Labour government to 'call time' on drunken thugs:

> Every year, there are almost 1.5 million victims of violent attacks committed by people under the influence of drink (excluding domestic violence). Every weekend, people avoid their town and city centres for fear they will be attacked or intimidated by drunken youth.
>
> (Jack Straw, cited in Institute of Alcohol Studies 2005b: 1)

A study conducted for the Home Office in 1990 found that growth in beer consumption was the single most important factor in explaining crimes of violence against the person (Home Office 1980) while research also shows that a high proportion of victims of violent crime are drinking or under the influence of alcohol at the time of their assault, and a minimum of one in five people arrested by police test positive for alcohol (Bennett 2000). An all-party group of MPs investigating alcohol and crime was advised by the British Medical Association that alcohol is a factor in 60–70 per cent of homicides, 75 per cent of stabbings, 70 per cent of beatings and 50 per cent of fights and domestic assaults; the Police Superintendents' Association reported that alcohol is a factor in 50 per cent of all crimes committed; and the National Association of Probation Officers advised that 30 per cent of offenders on probation and 58 per cent of prisoners have severe alcohol problems which is a significant factor in their offence or pattern of offending (All-Party Group on Alcohol Misuse 1995).

Illegal drug use

Drug taking does not have as long an association with criminal behaviour as alcohol consumption. It was only at the beginning of the twentieth century that drugs were labelled as a major social problem and came to be regulated. Drugs are chemicals and once taken alter the chemical balance of the body and brain. This can affect behaviour but the way that it is altered varies according to the type and quantity of the drug taken (see Fishbein and Pease 1990; Pihl and Peterson 1993). The biological effects of cannabis and opiates such as heroin tend to reduce aggressive hostile tendencies, while cocaine and its derivative crack are more closely associated with violence. Interestingly, some see both alcohol and drug misuse as intrinsically wrong and thus in need of punishment; others see them as social and personal problems requiring understanding and treatment. The first solution has generally been applied in the case of (illegal) drugs, while the second has tended to be more acceptable in the case of (legal) alcohol.

In 2001/2, 15 per cent of men and 9 per cent of women aged 16 to 59 in England and Wales said that they had taken an illicit drug in the previous year. Among those aged 16 to 24, 35 per cent of males and 24 per cent of females said they had done so in the previous year. The most commonly used drug by young people was cannabis, which had been used by 33 per cent of young men and 22 per cent of young women during that time period. Ecstasy was the most commonly used Class A drug, with higher use among those aged 16 to 24 than those aged 25 to 59. In 2001/2, 9 per cent of males and 4 per cent of females aged 16 to 24 had used ecstasy in the previous year. Since 1996 there has been an increase in the use of cocaine among young people, especially among males; in contrast, the use of amphetamines and LSD has declined (Institute of Alcohol Studies 2005a). Drug use has been found to be widespread among school pupils, although there has been a decrease in prevalence since 2003. In that year 21 per cent of pupils admitted having taken a drug during the previous year; this figure had decreased to 18 per cent by 2004 (Department of Health 2005).

Breaking the link between drugs and other criminal behaviour has been a key feature of government anti-drug strategies since the mid-1990s (CDCU 1995; UKADCU 1998). Recent studies estimate the cost of drug offences to the criminal justice system as £1.2 billion (Brand and Price 2000) and the social costs of class A drugs have been estimated to be nearly £12 billion (Godfrey et al. 2002). Research on offender populations in the UK reveal that acquisitive crime (particularly shoplifting, burglary and fraud) are the primary means of funding drug consumption

(Edmunds et al. 1999; Bennett 2000; Coid et al. 2000). The evidence points to users of heroin and cocaine (particularly crack) as the most likely to be prolific offenders (Bennett 2000; Stewart et al. 2000).

The NEW-ADAM research programme has found that those who report using heroin, crack or cocaine commit between five and ten times as many offences as offenders who do not report using drugs. Although users of heroin and cocaine/ crack represent only a quarter of offenders, they are responsible for more than half (by value) of acquisitive crime (Bennett et al. 2001). Links between problematic drug use and crime are nevertheless complex. Edmunds et al. (1999) suggest that experimental drug use can pre-date contact with the criminal justice system and become problematic after extensive criminal activity. For those engaged in crime prior to drug use, their offending behaviour can increase sharply.

Socio-biological theories

Some of the studies reviewed above which propose that certain individuals have been born with a physiological condition which predisposes them to commit crime really do point to biological explanations of criminality, but this appears to be the case with only a tiny minority of offenders. Closer investigation of individual cases suggests that social and environmental background is at least equally as important. Evidence nevertheless suggests that in cases where the biology of the individual has been altered through the introduction of a foreign chemical agent – such as diet, alcohol and/or illegal drugs – behaviour can be substantially changed and involvement in criminal activity may well follow. In recent years, moreover, there has been a concerted attempt to rehabilitate biological explanations by incorporating social and environmental factors into a 'multifactor' integrated theory approach which explains criminal behaviour (Vold et al. 1998). It is thus argued that the presence of certain biological predispositions – and the introduction of foreign chemical agents – may increase the likelihood, but not determine absolutely, that an individual will engage in criminal behaviour. These factors generate criminal behaviours when they interact with psychological and social factors.

Mednick and his colleagues (1977, 1987) propose that all individuals must learn to control natural urges that drive us towards anti-social and criminal behaviour. This bio-social theory acknowledges that the learning process takes place in the context of the family and during the course of interaction with peer groups, but proposes that punishment responses are mediated by the autonomic nervous system. If the reaction is short-lived, the individual is said to have rewarded him or herself, and criminal behaviour is inhibited. A slow physiological recovery from punishment nevertheless does little to teach the individual to refrain from undesirable behaviour and it is proposed that offenders are those who experience slow autonomic nervous system responses to stimuli.

Jeffery (1979) argues that individuals are born with particular biological and psychological characteristics that may not only predispose them to, but also actually *cause* certain forms of behaviour. This 'nature' is independent of the socialisation process that occurs within the social environment but it is recognised that there is a good deal of interaction between the physical environment and the feedback mechanisms that exist in human biochemical systems. Jeffery observes that it is poor people who are more likely to experience a poor quality diet and be exposed to pollutants with the resulting nutrients and chemicals transformed by the biochemical system into neurochemical compounds within the brain. Poverty thus leads to behavioural differences which occur through the interaction of individual and environment. This argument has been taken up and developed by key 'right realist' criminological theorists.

James Q. Wilson was a major influence on the development of the 'right realist' explanation of criminal behaviour that was so influential in the rehabilitation of the rational actor model of criminal behaviour we encountered in the previous chapter. It is in his work with Richard Herrnstein where he offers a more definitive account of the underlying causes of crime, synthesising both biological and environmental factors in an integrated criminological theory (Wilson and Herrnstein 1985): an amalgam of gender, age, intelligence, body type and personality factors which constitute the individual human being who is projected into a social world where they learn what kind of behaviour is rewarded in what circumstances.

Wilson and Herrnstein (1985) are heavily influenced by the psychological behaviourism of B.F. Skinner – which we will encounter in the next chapter – and propose that individuals learn to respond to situations in accordance with how their behaviour has been rewarded and punished on previous occasions. From this 'operant conditioning' perspective it was now proposed that the environment can be changed to produce the kind of behavioural response most wanted from an individual. Thus, in order to understand the propensity to commit crime, it is important to understand the ways in which the environment might operate on individuals, whose constitutional make-up might be different, to produce this response. Within this general learning framework the influence of the family, the school and the wider community is located.

Central to this explanation of offending behaviour is the notion of conscience. Wilson and Herrnstein (1985: 125) support the conjecture made by Eysenck – again to be encountered in the next chapter – that 'conscience is a conditioned reflex' and propose that some people during childhood have so effectively internalised law-abiding behaviour that they could never be tempted to behave otherwise. For others, breaking the law might be dependent upon the particular circumstances of a specific situation, which suggests a less effective internalisation of such rules. For yet others, the failure to appreciate the likely consequences of their actions might lead them into criminal behaviour under any circumstances. In other words, the effectiveness of something termed 'the conscience' may vary in terms of the particular physiological constitution of the individual and the learning environment in which they find themselves.

These three different elements – constitutional factors, the presence and/or absence of positive and negative behavioural reinforcement, alongside the strength of the conscience – provide the framework in which Wilson and Herrnstein seek to explain crime, proposing that long-term trends in the crime statistics can be explained primarily by these factors. First, shifts in the age structure of the population will increase or decrease the proportion of young males in the population who are likely to be temperamentally aggressive and to have short-term horizons. Second, changes in the benefits and cost of crime will change the rate at which crimes occur. Third, broad social and cultural changes in the level and intensity of the investment made by society in terms of families, schools, churches and the mass media will affect the extent to which individuals at risk of becoming involved in offending behaviour are willing to postpone gratification and conform to rules.

Conclusions

This chapter has considered three general categories of biological explanations of youth offending. The first proposes that the young person is born with a physiological component of some kind that in some way predisposes them towards criminal behaviour. The second proposes that behaviour is heavily influenced by the introduction of external agents to the human body such as pollutants, poor diet, alcohol and drugs. The particular combination of individual biological predisposition and external agent is likely to lead to differential outcomes; thus while for some alcohol might fuel aggressive tendencies, others might become more passive than usual. A third category of socio-biological theories takes that argument a stage further and proposes that biological predispositions are activated in very different ways in different environmental conditions, often dependent on the socialised upbringing of the young person. From this latter perspective the solution to the problem of young offending is to change the environment of the young person in some way, which is similar to the propositions of the cognitive behaviourist and sociological theories that we will encounter in the next two chapters.

Summary of main points

1 The predestined actor model rejects the rational actor model emphasis on free will and replaces it with the doctrine of determinism which claims to account for criminality in terms of factors – either internal or external to the individual – which cause them to act in ways over which they have little or no control.
2 The individual is both predestined to be a criminal while being a different category of humanity from non-criminals.
3 Early biological explanations of criminal behaviour have their origins in the work of the Italian school at the end of the nineteenth and the beginning of the twentieth centuries.
4 Later biological explanations of criminal behaviour were to become increasingly more sophisticated but the notion of inherited criminal characteristics continues to be central with evidence to support this supposition obtained from three sources: criminal family studies; twin studies; and adopted children studies.

5 Genetic structure explanations of criminal behaviour consider abnormalities in the genetic structure of the offender with crucial identified defects being related to the sex chromosomes.

6 Biochemical explanations of offending behaviour are similar to the altered biological state theories but differ in that the relevant substances are either already present in the body of the individual or are created by some internal physiological process.

7 Altered biological state theories are those which link behavioural changes in the individual with the introduction of an external chemical agent, and these can be divided into the following categories: allergies, diet, alcohol and other (invariably) illegal drugs.

8 In recent years there has been a concerted attempt to rehabilitate biological explanations by incorporating social and environmental factors into a 'multi-factor' integrated theory approach which explains criminal behaviour.

9 It is argued that the presence of certain biological predispositions – and the introduction of foreign chemical agents – may increase the likelihood, but not determine absolutely, that an individual will engage in criminal behaviour.

10 From this socio-biological perspective, the solution to the problem of young offending is to change the environment of the young person in some way, which is similar to the propositions of the cognitive behaviourist and socio-logical theories that we will encounter in the next two chapters.

Discussion questions

1 What are the basic fundamentals of the predestined actor model and what are the three categories?

2 How do genetic theories explain offending behaviour by children and young people?

3 How do biochemical explanations explain offending behaviour?

4 How do altered biological states theories explain offending behaviour?

5 In what ways do socio-biological theories enhance the earlier biological positivist perspective?

9   Psychological explanations of youth crime

Psychological explanations of offending behaviour direct our attention to the mind of the individual and it is here that we encounter notions of the 'criminal mind' or 'personality'. For purist advocates of the psychological variant of the predestined actor model – or psychological positivists – there are patterns of reasoning and behaviour that are specific to offenders and these remain constant regardless of their different social experiences. There are three broad categories of psychological theories of crimes and while the first two groupings, psychodynamic and behavioural learning theories, have firm roots in the predestined actor tradition, the third group, cognitive learning theories, reject much of the positivist tradition and, in their incorporation of notions of creative thinking and, thus, choice are, in many ways, more akin to the rational actor model of criminal behaviour. Each tradition, nevertheless, proposes that the personality is developed during the early formative childhood years of the individual through a process of learning, much of which is subconscious.

Psychodynamic theories

Psychodynamic explanations of criminal behaviour have their origins in the extremely influential work of Sigmund Freud (1856–1939) and his theories about how our personalities develop as an outcome of our intimate relationships – or lack of these – with our parents and, in particular, our mother. His assertion that sexuality is present from birth and has a subsequent course of development is the fundamental basis of psychoanalysis and it is one that has aroused a great deal of controversy. Freud had originally proposed that it was the experience of sexual abuse in childhood that is the basis of all neurosis, but he subsequently changed his mind: the abuse had not actually taken place but was merely fantasy. It is this notion of the repressed fantasy that is the core tenet of the psychoanalytic tradition.

Within the psychoanalytical model, the human personality has three sets of interacting forces. First, there is the id or primitive biological drives. Second, there is the superego – or conscience – that operates in the unconsciousness but which comprises values internalised through the early interactions of the child, in particular those with their parents. Third, there is the ego or the conscious personality, which has the important task of balancing the demands of the id against the inhibitions imposed by the superego, as the child responds to external influences (Freud 1927).

Freud himself proposed two different explanations of offending behaviour, with the first viewing certain forms of criminal activity – for example, arson, shoplifting and some sexual offences – as essentially reflecting a state of mental disturbance or illness. His theory of psychosexual development proposes a number of complex stages of psychic development that may easily be disrupted, leading to neuroses or severe difficulties in adults. Crucially, a disturbance at one or more of these stages in childhood can lead to criminal behaviour in later life. Of central importance to the psychosexual development of the child is the influence of the parents and the nature of the relationship the child has with them. Significantly, many of these influences are unconscious, with neither the child nor its parents aware of the impact they are having on each other. This is an important recognition, for, in a sense, it reduces the responsibility of the parents for producing children that become offenders.

Freud's second explanation of criminality proposes that offenders possess a 'weak conscience', the development of which is of fundamental importance in the upbringing of the child. A sense of morality is closely linked to guilt, and those possessing the greatest degree of unconscious 'guilt' are likely to be those with the strictest consciences and the most unlikely to engage in criminal behaviour. Guilt is something that results not from committing crimes, but rather from a deeply embedded feeling that develops in childhood, the outcome of the way in which the parents respond to the transgressions of the child. It is an explanation of criminal behaviour that has led to a proliferation of tests attempting to measure conscience or levels of guilt, with the belief that this would allow a prediction of whether the child would later become an offender.

The Freudian approach is firmly embedded in the predestined actor model of criminal behaviour: unconscious conflicts or tensions determine all actions; the purpose of the conscious (ego) is to resolve these tensions by finding ways of satisfying the basic inner urges by engaging in activities sanctioned by society, such as playing organised sport or involvement in drama or artistic activities. The subsequent Freudian tradition was concerned with elaborating the development of the ego more specifically.

Aichhorn (1925) thus argued that at birth a child is unaware of – and obviously unaffected by – the norms of society around it but has certain instinctive drives that demand satisfaction. The child is, at that time, in an 'asocial state' and the task is to bring it into a social state, but when the development process is ineffective he or she remains asocial. Thus, if the instinctive drives are not acted out, they become suppressed and the child is in a state of 'latent delinquency'. Given outside provocative stimuli, this latent delinquency can be translated into actual offending behaviour.

Aichhorn concluded that many of the offenders with whom he had worked had underdeveloped consciences and proposed that this was the outcome of the absence of an intimate attachment with their parents while children. The proposed solution was to rescue such children and place them in a happy environment where they could identify with adults in a way they had previously not experienced and develop their superegos. Two further categories of offender were identified: first, there were those with fully developed consciences but who had clearly identified with parents who were themselves criminals; and second, there were those who had been allowed to do whatever they liked by overindulgent parents.

Healy and Bronner (1936) conducted a study of 105 pairs of brothers where one was a persistent offender and the other a non-offender and found that only nineteen of the former and thirty of the latter had experienced good-quality family conditions, therefore suggesting that circumstances within a household may be favourable for one child but not the sibling. It was proposed that the latter had not made an emotional attachment to a 'good parent', hence impeding the development of a superego. The researchers also found that siblings exposed to similar unfavourable circumstances might react differently, with one becoming an offender while others do not. From this perspective, offenders were considered to be more emotionally disturbed and needed to express their frustrated needs through deviant activities; non-offenders, however, channelled their frustrated needs into socially accepted activities.

Kate Friedlander (1947, 1949) argued that some children simply develop an anti-social behaviour or a faulty character that leave them prone to deviant behaviour; while Redl and Wineman (1951) similarly argued that some children develop a delinquent ego and a subsequent hostile attitude towards authority because they have not developed a good ego and superego.

John Bowlby (1952) influentially argued, in a study published by the United Nations, that offending behaviour takes place when a child has not enjoyed a close and continuous relationship with its mother during its formative years. He studied forty-four juveniles convicted of stealing and referred to the child guidance clinic where he worked and compared them with a control group of children – matched for age and intelligence – which had been referred but not in connection with offending behaviour. Problematically, no attempt was made to check for the presence of criminal elements in the control group, thus exposing the study to methodological criticism (Morgan 1975). Bowlby nevertheless found that seventeen of those with convictions for stealing had been separated from their mothers for extended periods before the age of 5, in contrast to only two of the control group. Fourteen of the convicted group were found to be 'affectionless characters', persons deemed to have difficulty in forming close personal relationships, but none of the controls was thus labelled.

Maternal deprivation theory was to have a major and lasting influence on the training of social workers (Morgan 1975) while other researchers have sought to test it empirically. Their findings have tended to suggest that the separation of a child from its mother is not, in itself, significant in predicting criminal behaviour. Andry (1957) and Grygier (1969) thus both indicated a need to take account of the roles of both parents. Naess (1959, 1962) found offenders were no more likely to have been separated from their mothers than were non-offenders. Little (1963) found that 80 per cent of a sample of boys who had received custodial sentences had been separated from at least one parent for varying periods but found separations from the father more common. Wootton (1959, 1962) found no evidence that any effects of separation of the child from its mother will be irreversible. She accepts that a small proportion of offenders may be affected in this way but observes a lack of information about the extent of maternal deprivation among the non-offending population. Rutter (1981), in one of the most comprehensive examinations of the maternal deprivation thesis, concludes that the stability of the child/mother relationship is more important than the absence of breaks and proposes that a small number of substitutes can carry out mothering functions, without adverse effect, provided that such care is of good quality. The crucial issue is thus considered to be the quality of child-rearing practices and this aspect is considered in the following studies.

Glueck and Glueck (1950) found that the fathers of offenders generally provided lax and inconsistent discipline; the use of physical punishment by both parents was common and the giving of praise rare. Parents of non-offenders used physical punishment more sparingly and were more consistent in their use of discipline. McCord et al. (1959) later agreed that the consistency of discipline is more important than the degree of strictness; while Bandura and Walters (1959) found that the fathers of aggressive boys are more likely to punish such behaviour in the home while approving of, and even encouraging, it outside.

Hoffman and Saltzstein (1967) identified and categorised three types of childrearing techniques: first, power assertion involves the parental use of – or threats to use – physical punishment and/or the withdrawal of material privileges; second, love withdrawal is where the parent withdraws – or threatens to withdraw – affection from the child, for example, by paying no attention to it; third, induction entails letting the child know how its actions have affected the parent, thus encouraging a sympathetic or empathetic response. The first technique primarily relies on the instillation of fear, while the other two depend on the fostering of guilt feelings in the child.

Hoffman and Saltzstein offer five explanations for the association to be found between moral development and the use of childrearing techniques. First, an open display of anger and aggression by a parent when disciplining a child increases the dependence of the latter on external control, while dissolving both the anger of the former and the guilt of the latter more rapidly. Second, love withdrawal and induction, and the anxiety associated with them, have a longer-lasting effect so that the development of internal controls are more likely. Third, where love withdrawal is used, the punishment ends when the child confesses or makes reparation, and this is referred to as engaging in a corrective act; while, in the case of physical punishment, there is likely to be a lapse of time between it being carried out and the child performing a corrective act. Fourth, withholding love intensifies the resolve of the child to behave in an approved manner in order to retain love. Fifth, the use of induction is particularly effective in enabling the child to examine and correct the behaviour that has been disapproved of.

Hoffman and Saltzstein conclude that young people who have been raised through the use of love withdrawal or induction techniques develop greater internalised controls and are less likely to engage in offending behaviour. However, young people raised on the power assertion method depend on the threat of external punishment to control their behaviour and, therefore, will only remain controlled as long as that risk is present, certain and sufficiently intense. It is of course only internal controls that are likely to be ever-present.

A number of studies have gone beyond childrearing practices to assess the relevance of more general features of the family unit in the causation of criminal behaviour. Some of these have suggested that a 'broken home' – where one of the birth parents is not present – may be a factor in the development of offending behaviour and note that most of these early studies pre-1970s took place when the two-parent nuclear family was very much the norm and the term 'single-parent family' unknown.[1] Glueck and Glueck (1950) found that 60 per cent of the offenders came from a broken home, compared with only 34 per cent of their control group and in Britain, Burt (1945) and Mannheim (1948) previously found that a high proportion of offenders came from such homes.

Others perceptively note that the 'broken home' is not a homogenous category and that a range of different factors need to be considered (Mannheim 1948; Bowlby 1952; Tappan 1960). Nye (1958) and Gibbens (1963) thus observed that offending behaviour is more likely to occur among children from intact but unhappy homes. West (1969) echoed the observations of Wootton (1959) about the difficulties of defining a broken home: his study with Farrington (1973) found that about twice as many offenders, compared with controls, came from homes broken by parental separation before the child was ten years old. Comparing children from a home broken by separation with those homes broken by the death of a parent, more children from the former were found to be offenders. Moreover, 20 per cent of the former group became recidivists, whereas none of those from the second group did.

Monahan (1957) suggested that broken homes were far more common among black than white offenders; while Chilton and Markle (1972) later found that the rate of family breakdown is in general much higher in the case of black than white families and suggested that this may explain why it is that more black young offenders come from broken homes. Pitts (1986) claimed a link between criminality and homelessness and found that African-Caribbean youths tend to become homeless more than their white counterparts.

Two more recent studies conducted in the UK have reported that broken homes and early separation predicted convictions up to age 33 where the separation occurred before age 5 (Kolvin et al. 1990) and predicted convictions and self-reported offending behaviour (Farrington 1996). Morash and Rucker (1989), nevertheless, found that although it was single-parent families who had children with the highest rates of deviancy, these were also the lowest-income families. Thus, the nature of the problem – broken home, parental supervision, low income – is unclear but by this time the notion of single parents as a lifestyle choice was much more common.

Behavioural learning theories

Behavioural learning theories assume at their most basic level that the behaviours we learn in our childhood formative years are caused, strengthened or weakened by external stimuli in our environment and are thus acquired as an automatic invariably subconscious response to an environmental stimulus without thought or reflection. They have their origins in the work of Ivan Petrovich Pavlov and B.F. Skinner. Pavlov famously studied the processes involved in very simple, automatic animal behaviours (e.g., salivation of his dog in the presence of food), finding that responses that occur spontaneously in response to a natural (unconditioned) stimulus could be made to happen (conditioned) to a stimulus that was previously neutral (e.g., a light). If you consistently turn the light on just before feeding the animal, then eventually the animal will salivate when the light comes on, even though no food is present. This conditioning can be undone and if you continue to present the light without the food, eventually the animal will stop salivating. To some extent the conditioning process is specific to the exact stimulus presented but it can also be generalised to other similar stimuli and, for behaviourists, the notion of differential conditioning is the key to understanding how learning works.

B.F. Skinner extended the behaviourist conditioning principle to active learning, where the animal has to do something in order to obtain a reward or avoid punishment. The same principle nevertheless applies: the occurrence of the desired behaviour is increased by positive reinforcement and eventually extinguished by non-reinforcement. Learned behaviours are much more resistant to extinction if the reinforcement has only occasionally been used during learning and the behaviour can be differentially conditioned so that it occurs in response to one stimulus and not another. In a sense all operant conditioning – as this is what this type of learning is called – is differential conditioning, where the animal learns to produce certain behaviours and not others, because only these receive reinforcement.

Operant conditioning – sometimes referred to as instrumental conditioning – is thus a method of learning that occurs through rewards and punishments that become associated with that behaviour. Through operant conditioning, an association is made by the individual child or young person between a particular behaviour and the consequences that arise from their involvement and there are many examples to be observed throughout the social world. Thus, children complete homework to earn a reward from a parent or teacher, or employees finish projects so as to receive praise or promotions. In these examples, the promise or possibility of rewards causes a qualitative increase in behaviour, but operant conditioning can also be used to reduce less desirable activities. For example, a child may be told that they will have privileges withdrawn if they misbehave or talk in class and this it is this potential for punishment that may lead to a decrease in disruptive behaviour.

Hans Eysenck sought to build a general theory of criminal behaviour based on the psychological concept of conditioning, although it is not easy to categorise. Eysenck was a behaviourist who considered learned behaviours to be of great significance but primarily considered personality differences to be a product of our individual genetic constitution, and he is predominantly interested in temperament. He thus argues from the biological predestined actor perspective that individuals are genetically endowed with certain learning abilities but these are conditioned by stimuli in the environment. At the same time, he accepts the rational actor model premise that crime can be a natural and rational choice activity where individuals maximise pleasure and minimise pain. Eysenck essentially proposes that people learn the rules and norms of society through the development of a conscience which they acquire through learning the outcomes of what happens when you take part in certain activities; in other words, good behaviour is rewarded and bad behaviour is punished.

Eysenck describes three dimensions of personality – extroversion (E), neuroticism (N) and psychoticism (P) – and each takes the form of a continuum that runs from high to low, with scores obtained by the administration of a personality questionnaire. Each of these personality dimensions has distinct characteristics, thus someone with a high E score is outgoing and sociable, optimistic and impulsive; a high N person is anxious, moody and highly sensitive; those with low scores on these continuums present the very opposite of these traits.

Eysenck (1977) argues that various combinations of different personality dimensions within an individual affects their ability to learn not to offend, and consequently the level of offending in which they engage. Thus, someone with a high E and a high N score, a neurotic extrovert, will not condition well; a low E and N score, a stable introvert, is, however, the most effectively conditioned. Stable extroverts and neurotic introverts come somewhere between the two extremes.

Various researchers subsequently sought to empirically test Eysenck's theory. Little (1963) thus compared the scores for convicted young offenders on the extroversion and neuroticism dimensions and found that neither appeared to be related to repeat offending. Hoghughi and Forrest (1970) compared scores for neuroticism and extroversion between a sample of convicted youths and a control group with no convictions and found that while the former rated higher on the neuroticism scale they were actually less extroverted than their controls. This is a finding that could be explained by the possibility that it is the actual experience of incarceration itself that could make a young person neurotic. Hans and Sybil Eysenck (1970) tested incarcerated young offenders on all three personality dimensions and followed up this research on their release, finding that two-thirds had been reconvicted and all these scored significantly higher in relation to extroversion than the others. Allsopp and Feldman (1975) conducted a self-report study and found a significant and positive association between scores for E, N and P levels of anti-social behaviour among girls between 11 and 15 years of age, with the strongest association found in relation to psychoticism. A study of schoolboys conducted the following year reached similar conclusions (Allsopp and Feldman 1976). The association between psychoticism and criminal behaviour has nevertheless been the subject of very little research, although Smith and Smith (1977) and McEwan (1983) found a positive relationship between psychoticism and repeat offending. The work of Allsopp and Feldman (1975, 1976) and McGurk and McDougall (1981) does, however, suggest that combinations or clusters of scores for the three dimensions are more important than scores for individual dimensions.

There seems to be considerable uncertainty and ambiguity about the validity and veracity of Eysenck's theory. In a major review of his work, David Farrington (1994a) does suggest that there is a link between offending and impulsiveness but could find no significant links with personality and hence no evidence of the existence of a 'criminal personality'.

Cognitive learning theories

We have seen that both psychodynamic and behavioural learning theories have clear foundations in the predestined actor model of criminal behaviour but later more sophisticated variants of those traditions became more readily accepting of rational actor model notions of, albeit limited, choice. They nevertheless both remained committed to the central notion of psychological positivism, which proposes that there are patterns of reasoning and behaviour specific to offenders that remain constant regardless of their different social experiences. The third psychological tradition – cognitive or social learning theories – have their foundations in a fundamental critique of the predestined actor model and explain human behaviour in terms of a three-way, dynamic reciprocity in which personal factors, environmental influences and behaviour continually interact.

The behavioural learning theorists emphasised the role of environmental stimuli and overt behavioural response, but significantly failed to explain why it is that people attempt to organise, make sense of and often alter the information they learn. Thus, there emerged a growing recognition that mental events – or cognition – could no longer be ignored (Kendler 1985). Cognitive psychologists controversially proposed that by observing the responses made by individuals to different stimuli it is possible to draw inferences about the nature of the internal cognitive processes that produce those responses.

Many of the ideas and assumptions of cognitivism have their origins in the work of the Gestalt psychologists of Germany, Edward Tolman of the USA and Jean Piaget of Switzerland. Gestalt psychologists had emphasised the importance of organisational processes in perception, learning and problem-solving and proposed that individuals were predisposed to organise information in particular ways (Henle 1985). Tolman (1959) had been a prominent learning theorist, at the time of the behavioural movement, but subsequently developed a distinctively cognitive perspective including internal mental phenomena in his perspective of how learning occurs. Piaget (1977) constructed a highly influential model of learning founded on the idea that the developing child builds cognitive structures – mental 'maps', schema or networked concepts – for understanding and responding to physical experiences in their environment. Piaget further asserted that the cognitive structure of a child increases in sophistication with development, moving from a few innate reflexes such as crying and sucking to highly complex mental activities.

B.F. Skinner (1984) had argued, from an operant conditioning perspective, that the person must actively respond if they are to learn, and cognitive behaviourists share that view but, at the same time, emphasise mental rather than physical activity. This social learning theory proposes that behaviour may be reinforced not only through actual rewards and punishments, but also through expectations that are learned by watching what happens to other people. Thus, ultimately, the person will make a choice as to what they will learn and how.

An early proponent of the notion that crime is simply a normal learned behaviour was Gabriel Tarde (1843–1904), who argued that criminals are primarily normal people who by accident of birth are brought up in an atmosphere in which they learn crime as a way of life. His 'laws of imitation' were essentially a cognitive theory in which the individual was said to learn ideas through the association with other ideas with behaviour said to follow. People simply imitate and copy one another in proportion to how much contact they have with each another. These three 'laws of imitation' – (i) the law of close contact, (ii) the law of imitation of superiors by inferiors, and (iii) the law of insertion – all sought to describe and explain why people become involved in criminal behaviour (Tarde 1969).

First, the law of close contact proposes that individuals in close intimate contact with one another imitate the behaviour of each other. Thus, if a child or young person is regularly in the company of people involved in deviant or criminal behaviour, they are more likely to imitate the behaviour of these individuals than they would others with whom they had little association. In this way direct contact with criminal behaviour is said to produce more criminality. Second, the law of imitation of superiors by inferiors proposes that youngsters imitate older individuals and that crime among young, poor or lower-class people is really their attempt to imitate wealthy, older, high-status people. Certainly, young people, 'hanging out' on the street tend to take their cues and be heavily influenced by older children as we shall see later in this book. Third, the law of insertion proposes that new activities and behaviours are superimposed on old ones and subsequently either reinforce or discourage previous customs. This law refers to the power said to be inherent in newness or novelty where new fashions are said to replace old 'customs'. Thus, for example, illicit drug taking may become popular among a group of young people who had previously favoured alcohol. This group may nevertheless find a combination of both substances to be even more pleasurable than when used on their own and this could lead to an increase in both drug and alcohol use. The replacement of the knife by the gun as a weapon of choice among young people has also been cited as an example of where a new criminal custom replaces an older one.

The work of Gabriel Tarde has had a considerable impact on the study of deviance and social control. Social psychologists have proposed that patterns of illicit drug use can have their origins in the observation of parental drug use, which begins to have a damaging effect on children as young as two years old. This has been found to be particularly problematic when children imitate the behaviour of parents with drug-related personality problems. Wills et al. (1996) found that children whose parents use illicit drugs are more likely to have persistent drug-use problems than the children of non-users, because one is more exposed intimately to the activity than the other. Children and young people nevertheless respond to peer group influences more readily than adults because of the crucial role these relationships play in identity formation. Their greater desire for acceptance and approval from their peers makes them more susceptible to peer influences as they adjust their behaviour and attitudes to conform to those of their contemporaries. Significantly, young people 'commit crimes, as they live their lives, in groups' (Morse 1997a: 108) and this important concept of deviant subcultural groups is discussed in more detail in the following chapter. More indirectly, the desire of children and young people for peer approval could affect the choices that they make, without any direct coercion. Morse (1997b) observes that peers may provide models for behaviour that adolescents believe will assist them in accomplishing their own ends.

Gabriel Tarde was a major influence on Edwin H. Sutherland, whose later differential association theory has had an understandably significant impact on criminological explanation. Sutherland first used the term 'differential association' to explain interaction patterns, by which offenders were restricted in their physical and social contacts to association with like-minded others, and later proposed that crime is a learned activity much like any other. He argued that it is the frequency and consistency of contacts with patterns of criminality that determine the chance that a person will participate in systematic criminal behaviour (Sutherland 1939). The basic cause of such behaviour is the existence of different cultural groups, with different normative structures, within the same society that have produced a situation of differential social organisation.

Sutherland later revised his theory to argue that criminal behaviour occurs when individuals acquire sufficient sentiments in favour of criminality to outweigh their association with non-criminal tendencies. Those associations or contacts that have the greatest impact are those that are frequent, early in point of origin or the most intense. It was not necessary to explain why a person has particular associations because this involved a complex of social interactions and relationships, but he maintained that it was the existence of differential social organisation that exposed people to varied associational ties. Differential association thus remains in contrast to other psychological explanations, in that it retains a dominant sociological argument that the primary groups to which people belong exert the strongest influence on them.

Burgess and Akers (1968) later revised the principles of differential association in the language of operant conditioning and proposed that criminal behaviour can be learned both in non-social situations that are reinforcing and through social interaction in which the behaviour of other persons helps to reinforce that behaviour. Akers (1985) later revised the theory further and focused on four central concepts. First, differential association is considered the most important and refers to the patterns of interactions with others that are the source of social learning and which can be either favourable or unfavourable to offending behaviour. Moreover, the indirect influence of more distant reference groups such as the media is now also recognised and we might want to consider here the contemporary issue of Internet access which can bring like-minded people together from all around the world (Hopkins Burke and Pollock 2004) and, of course, social media. Second, definitions reflect the meanings that a person applies to their own behaviour; for example, the wider peer group might not define recreational drug use as deviant. Third, differential reinforcement refers to the actual or anticipated consequences of a particular behaviour. Thus, it is proposed that children and young people will do things that they think will result in rewards and avoid activities that they think will result in punishment. Fourth, imitation involves observing what others do but whether a decision is made to imitate that behaviour will be dependent on the characteristics of the person being observed, the actual behaviour the person engages in and the observed consequences of that behaviour for others. If the observed young person – or persons – appears to be 'cool' and is engaged in deviant or criminal activities that likewise appear to be 'cool', rewarding and/or pleasurable, it is likely that the behaviour will be imitated. Conversely, if neither the person or persons involved in the behaviour nor the activity in which they are involved is 'cool', imitation is unlikely to occur.

Akers et al. (1979) propose that the learning of criminal behaviour takes place through a specific sequence of events. It starts with the differential association of the individual with others who have favourable definitions of criminal behaviour and they provide a model to be imitated and which is socially reinforced. Thus, primarily differential association, definitions, imitation and social reinforcements explain the initial participation of the individual child or young person in criminal behaviour. After the individual has commenced offending behaviour, differential reinforcements determine whether the person will continue with that behaviour. Akers (1992) argues that the social learning process explains the link between the social structural conditions we will encounter in the following chapter and the behaviour of individuals.

The emergence of learning theories has led to the development of a range of behaviour modification treatment strategies introduced with the intention of changing behaviour. As the above theorists had proposed that behaviour is related to both the setting in which the offence takes place and the consequences of involvement in such activities, strategies were developed to modify both the environment in which the offence took place and the outcomes of the behaviour. Bringing about change through modification of the environment is called stimulus control and is a standard technique in behaviour modification (Martin and Pear 1992). It is most apparent in situational crime prevention where the intention is to reduce offending by either reducing the opportunity to commit an offence or increasing the chances of detection (Hopkins Burke 2014).

Similarly, there is a range of established methods that seek to modify the consequences that follow a given behaviour and such techniques are widely used not just with convicted offenders, but also in most mainstream schools as a means of controlling children. This approach has encouraged books on positive parenting, where 'praise is much more potent than criticism or punishment'. Strategies that focus explicitly on overt behaviour are often termed behaviour therapy, although the basic underpinning theory is the same as that which informs behaviour modification. By the 1970s the notion of skills training in the health services was developed and quickly became widespread in the form of assertion, life and social skills training, the latter becoming widely used with a range of offenders (Hollin 1990a).

A number of particular techniques have become associated with more recent cognitive-behavioural practice, including self-instructional training, 'thought stopping', emotional control training and problem-solving training (Sheldon 1995). The rationale under-pinning this approach is that by bringing about change of internal – psychological and/or physiological – states and processes, this covert change will, in turn, mediate change at an overt behavioural level. Changes in overt behaviour will then elicit new patterns of reinforcement from the environment and so maintain behaviour change. These cognitive-behavioural methods have been widely used with young offenders (Hollin 1990b) where social skills training, training in problem-solving and moral reasoning techniques have been popular and have been shown to have some success in reducing offending (McGuire 2000) and provide the rationale for many contemporary youth justice interventions with young offenders and which we will encounter in the third part of this book.

Conclusions

Psychological explanations of crime and criminal behaviour have firm foundations in the predestined actor model of criminal behaviour and it is the implication of both psychodynamic and behaviourist learning traditions that there is such a thing as the criminal mind or personality and that this in some way determines the actions of the individual. The causes are dysfunctional, abnormal emotional adjustment or deviant personality traits formed in early socialisation and childhood development, and as a result of these factors, the individual is destined to become a criminal. The only way to avoid that destiny is to identify the predisposing condition and provide some form of psychiatric intervention that will in some way ameliorate or preferably remove those factors and enable the individual to become a normal law-abiding citizen.

The more recent cognitive learning approach involves a retreat from the purist predestined actor model approach. First, there is recognition of the links between the psychology of the individual and important predisposing influences or stimuli available in the social environment, but the behavioural learning theorists accept that point. It is the second recognition that is the important one. Offenders now have some degree of choice and they can, therefore, choose whether or not to imitate the behaviours of others. There may be a substantial range of factors influencing their decision and these may suggest to the individual that in particular circumstances – when the opportunity arises – criminal behaviour is a rational choice to make. Thus, we can see here the links between recent cognitive learning theories and contemporary variants of the rational actor model. In short, the active criminal can in favourable circumstances choose to cease offending or alternatively an individual living in circumstances where criminal behaviour is the norm can choose not to take that course of action in the first place. From this perspective, crime is not an inevitable destiny.

Summary of main points

1   Psychological explanations of offending behaviour direct our attention to the mind of the individual and it is here that we encounter notions of the 'criminal mind' or 'personality'.

2   For purist advocates of the psychological variant of the predestined actor model – or psychological positivists – there are patterns of reasoning and behaviour that are specific to offenders and these remain constant regardless of their different social experiences.

3   There are three broad categories of psychological theories of crime: the first two groupings, psychodynamic and behavioural learning theories, have firm roots in the predestined actor tradition; the third group, cognitive learning theories, reject much of the positivist tradition and in many ways are more akin to the rational actor model of criminal behaviour.

4   Each tradition proposes that the personality is developed during the early formative childhood years of the individual through a process of learning, much of which is subconscious.

5   Psychodynamic explanations of criminal behaviour have their origins in the extremely influential work of Sigmund Freud and his theories about how our personalities develop as an outcome of our intimate relationships – or lack of these – with our parents and, in particular, our mother.

6   The Freudian approach is firmly embedded in the predestined actor model of criminal behaviour: unconscious conflicts or tensions determine all actions; the purpose of the conscious (ego) is to resolve these tensions by finding ways of satisfying the basic inner urges by engaging in activities sanctioned by society, such as playing organised sport or involvement in drama or artistic activities.

7   Behavioural learning theories assume at their most basic level that the behaviours we learn in our childhood formative years are caused, strengthened or weakened by external stimuli in our environment and are thus acquired as an automatic invariably subconscious response to an environmental stimulus without thought or reflection.

8   Operant conditioning is a method of learning that occurs through rewards and punishments that become associated with that behaviour. Through operant conditioning, an association is made by the individual child or young

person between a particular behaviour and the consequences that arise from their involvement and there are many examples to be observed throughout the social world.

9　Cognitive or social learning theories have their foundations in a fundamental critique of the predestined actor model and explain human behaviour in terms of a three-way, dynamic reciprocity in which personal factors, environmental influences and behaviour continually interact.

10　Cognitive psychologists controversially proposed that by observing the responses made by individuals to different stimuli it is possible to draw inferences about the nature of the internal cognitive processes that produce those responses.

Discussion questions

1　Explain the concept of the criminal mind.
2　Explain the origins of psychodynamic theories.
3　What are behaviourist theories?
4　In what way does cognitive or social learning theories differ from their psychodynamic and behaviourist predecessors?
5　What are the treatment implications of cognitive theories?

Note

1　A nuclear family or elementary family is a family group consisting of a pair of adults and their children. This is in contrast to a single-parent family, to the larger extended family and to a family with more than two parents.

10 Sociological explanations of youth crime

Key issues

1 The social disorganisation thesis
2 Robert Merton and anomie theory
3 Deviant subculture theories
4 Social control theories
5 Victimised actor model theories
6 Critical criminology revisited

We saw in the previous two chapters that both the biological and psychological variants of the predestined actor model of criminal behaviour locate the primary impulse for offending in the individual, whether it is a biological predisposition or criminal personality. We nevertheless found that in both cases the influence of environmental factors is highly significant. Thus, an individual may well have certain physiological tendencies but these are only likely to be activated in a deviant or criminal fashion when particular environmental conditions are present; moreover, altered biological states, whether these are the product of poor diet, alcohol or drug use, are very likely to be the outcome of social influence. Personalities – whether they be 'criminal' or otherwise – are clearly the creation of social or environmental circumstances and are highly dependent on the nature of the socialisation experiences of the young person, the quantity and quality of parenting and the peer groups encountered in the geographical location in which the young person lives. The sociological variant of the predestined actor model which is considered in this chapter rejects individualist explanations of criminality and examines the environmental factors that are seen as significant in the creation of crime and criminal behaviour. It is a tradition which is very much informed by the increasingly influential social theory of Emile Durkheim and his concerns with the social problems created by rapid social change (see Hopkins Burke 2014).

The social disorganisation thesis

Emile Durkheim and the division of labour in society

Durkheim (1933) argued that earlier forms of pre-modern society were characterised by high levels of mechanical solidarity while, in contrast, more developed
industrial modern societies could be differentiated by an advanced stage of
'organic' solidarity. The former were epitomised by the conformity of the group
where there is a likeness and a similarity between individuals who have very
much the same experiences of life, attitudes and beliefs which bind them together
as close-knit, like-minded communities with shared values but where, conversely,
the ability of an individual to develop a sense of personal identity or uniqueness is
severely restricted. Thus, such pre-industrial societies had very intense and rigid
collective consciences where members held very precise shared ideas of what is
right and wrong. There were, nevertheless, individuals who transgressed against
the norms of the group and in these cases the law was used as a means to maintain that uniformity. Moreover, repressive and summary punishments were used
against individuals and minority groups that transgressed against the collective
conscience of the majority.

This punishment of dissenters served a useful functional purpose by emphasising their inferiority while at the same time encouraging commitment to the
majority viewpoint. Thus, in this sense crime is a normal feature of societies with
high levels of mechanical solidarity. Punishment performs a necessary function
by reinforcing the moral consensus – or worldview – of the group and any reduction in behaviour defined as criminal would as a necessity lead to other previously
non-criminal activities becoming criminalised. Durkheim takes this argument
further and claims that a society with no crime would be abnormal. The imposition of rigorous controls that make crime impossible would seriously restrict
the potential for social progress. Individuals who challenge the boundaries of the
social consensus are in reality functional rebels who are necessary for the healthy
development of society (Taylor et al. 1973).

Durkheim argues that with greater industrialisation societies develop
greater levels of organic solidarity with a more developed division of labour
and (sometimes very) different groups that are nonetheless dependent on each
other. Social solidarity is now less dependent on the maintenance of uniformity
between individuals and more on the management of the diverse functions of
different groups. A certain degree of uniformity, nevertheless, remains essential
or else social cohesion would be impossible. Significantly, for Durkheim, the
division of labour is a progressive phenomenon; its emergence does not mean
the inevitable collapse of morality, but the manifestation of a new content for
the collective conscience.

In pre-modern societies dominated by mechanical solidarity the emphasis is on
the obligation of the individual to society, but with modern organic formations,
the focus is increasingly on the obligation of society to the individual. Now to

give the maximum possible encouragement to individual rights does not mean that altruism – that is, self-sacrifice for others – will disappear; on the contrary, moral individualism is not unregulated self-interest but the imposition of a set of reciprocal obligations that bring individuals together into social solidarity (Durkheim 1933). Here lies the essential originality of Durkheim's interpretation of the division of labour and which provides the intellectual underpinnings of the radical moral communitarianism we will encounter in the concluding chapter of this book.

Adam Smith, the founder of free-market economics, had argued that the specialisation of economic exchange is simply an effect of the growth of wealth and the free play of economic self-interest, but, for Durkheim, the real significance of the division of labour lies in its moral role, for it is a source of restraint which is placed upon otherwise unbridled self-interest and as a result provides the basis of a cohesive society. Durkheim had considered the cohesion of nineteenth-century laissez-faire society, with its wholly unregulated markets, its arbitrary inequalities, its restrictions on social mobility and its 'class' wars, to be a dangerous condition. Such imperfect social regulation leads to a variety of different social problems, he argued, including crime.

Durkheim provides a three-fold typology of deviants. The first typology is the biological deviant who is explained by the genetic or psychological malfunctioning we encountered in the previous two chapters, and these can be present in a normal division of labour. The other two typologies are linked to the nature and condition of the social system and are present in an abnormal or forced division of labour. The second typology, the functional rebel, is therefore a 'normal' person who is simply reacting to a pathological society, rebelling against the existing, inappropriate and unfair division of labour and indicating the existence of strains in the social system. For Durkheim, such a person expresses the true 'spontaneous' or 'normal' division of labour as opposed to the artificial 'forced' or 'pathological' one currently in operation (Taylor et al. 1973). The third typology, skewed deviants, is those who have been improperly socialised into a disorganised pathological society and are the usual focus of the student of deviance and criminal behaviour.

Durkheim presented two central arguments to explain the growth of crime and criminal behaviour in modern industrial societies with a pathological division of labour. First, such societies encourage a state of unbridled 'egoism' – the notion that individuals should pursue their own rational self-interest without reference to the collective interest of society – and that this is contrary to the maintenance of social solidarity and conformity to the law. Second, the likelihood of inefficient regulation is greater at a time of rapid modernisation, because new forms of control have not evolved sufficiently to replace the older and now less appropriate means of maintaining solidarity. In such a period, society is in a state of normlessness or 'anomie'; a condition characterised by a breakdown in norms and common understandings.

Durkheim notably claimed that without external controls human beings have unlimited needs and it is thus appropriate for society to indicate the extent of acceptable rewards for their endeavours. This all works reasonably well in times of social stability, he argues, but at times of economic upheaval, society is unable to control the aspirations of individuals. Thus, during an economic depression, people are forced to lower their sights, a situation which some will find intolerable and yet when there is an improvement in economic conditions social equilibrium will break down, with uncontrollable aspirations released. Both situations can lead to increased criminality – the first through need, the second through greed. This social disorganisation thesis was later developed by the American structuralist sociologists based at the University of Chicago.

American structuralism

The Chicago School sociologist Ernest Burgess (1928) produced an influential model for understanding the social foundations of crime in complex industrial societies, arguing that as modern cities expand in size, their development is patterned socially and they grow radially in a series of concentric zones or rings. Burgess observed that commercial enterprises were located in the central business district and the most expensive residential areas were in the outer suburbs, away from the bustle of the city centre and the homes of the poor but it was the 'zone in transition' – containing rows of deteriorating tenements and often built in the shadow of ageing factories – that was the centre of academic attention. The outward expansion of the business district led to the constant displacement of residents, and as the least desirable living area, the zone was the focus for the influx of waves of immigrants who were too poor to reside elsewhere. Burgess observed that these social patterns weakened family and communal ties and resulted in 'social disorganisation' and criminal behaviour.

Clifford Shaw and Henry McKay (1972) found that crime levels were highest in the slum neighbourhoods of the zone of transition regardless of which racial or ethnic group resided there and, significantly, as these groups moved to other zones, their offending rates correspondingly decreased. It was this observation that led the researchers to conclude that it was the nature of the neighbourhoods – not the nature of the individuals who lived within them – that regulated involvement in crime.

Shaw and McKay emphasised the importance of neighbourhood organisation in allowing or preventing offending behaviour by children and young people. They noted that in more affluent communities, parents fulfilled the needs of their offspring and carefully supervised their activities. In the zone of transition, families and other conventional institutions were strained, if not destroyed, by rapid urban growth, migration and poverty. Left to their own devices, young people in this zone were not subject to the social constraints placed on their contemporaries in the more affluent areas, and were more likely to seek excitement and friends in the streets of the city.

Shaw and McKay concluded that disorganised neighbourhoods help produce and sustain 'criminal traditions' that compete with conventional values and can be 'transmitted down through successive generations of boys, much the same way that language and other social forms are transmitted' (Shaw and McKay 1972: 174). Thus, young people growing up in socially disorganised inner-city slum areas characterised by the existence of a value system that condones criminal behaviour could readily learn these values in their daily interactions with older adolescents.

Shaw and McKay fundamentally argued that offending by children and young people can only be understood by reference to the social context in which young people live. In turn, this context itself is a product of major societal transformations brought about by rapid urbanisation and massive population shifts. Young people born and brought up in the socially disorganised zone of transition are particularly vulnerable to the temptations of crime, as conventional institutions disintegrate around them; they are given little supervision and are free to roam the streets where they are likely to become the next generation of carriers of the criminal tradition in the area.

In short, the US variant of social disorganisation theory called for efforts to reorganise communities with treatment programmes that attempt to reverse the criminal learning of offenders. From this perspective, it is argued that young offenders should be placed in settings where they will receive pro-social reinforcement; for example, through the use of positive peer counselling.

Robert Merton and anomie theory

Durkheim had proposed that human needs or aspirations are 'natural' in an organic society, that is, in the sense that they are socially constructed by reference to other individuals and groups and then a ceiling is placed upon material aspirations by a benign and neutral state. His US successor, Robert Merton, in contrast, argued that needs are usually socially learned, while – and this is the central component of his argument – there are social structural limitations imposed on access to the means to achieve these goals. Merton (1938) distinguished between cultural goals, that is, those material possessions, symbols of status, accomplishment and esteem that established norms and values encourage us to aspire to, and are, therefore, socially learned; and institutionalised means, which is the distribution of opportunities to achieve these goals in socially acceptable ways. He observes that it is possible to overemphasise either the goals or the means and the outcome of this situation is social strains, or 'anomie'.

Deviant, especially criminal, behaviour results when cultural goals are accepted, for example, and people would generally like to be materially successful, but where access to the means to achieve that goal is limited by the position of individuals in the social structure. Merton outlined five possible reactions – or adaptations – that can occur when people are not in a position to legitimately attain internalised social goals. First, conformity is a largely self-explanatory adaptation whereby people tend to accept both the cultural goals of society and the means of achieving them, even if they find their social ascent to be limited, they still tend not to 'deviate'. Second, retreatism is the least common adaptation, being those who reject both the dominant social goals and the means of obtaining them and are, therefore, a category of social 'drop-outs'. Third, ritualism is where a person adheres to rules for their own sake and takes pleasure and pride in ultra-conformity. Fourth, rebellious people are those who not merely reject the dominant norms but also wish to change the existing social system and its goals. Finally, the innovator – the usual focus for the student of criminal behaviour – is keen to achieve the standard goals of society, wealth, fame or admiration, but, probably due to blocked opportunities to obtain these by socially approved means, embarks on novel, or innovative, routes.

Many 'innovative' routes exist in complex organic societies, so much so that some innovators may be seen to overlap with 'conformists'; for example, the sports, arts and entertainment industries frequently attract, develop and absorb 'innovators', celebrating their novelty in contrast to the conformist or ritualist, and thus providing opportunities for those whose circumstances may frustrate their social ascent through conventionally prescribed and approved routes. In short, the innovator may be seen to overemphasise the goals of achievement over the means. Thus, conventionally regarded success may be achieved by any means that seem appropriate to the innovator, who strives to overcome barriers by adopting any available strategies for attaining their objective and this includes, appreciably, involvement in criminal behaviour. Merton's thesis has attracted criticisms (see Hopkins Burke 2014 for a full discussion) but has remained extremely influential and this is readily apparent in the discussion of deviant subcultures to which we now turn.

Deviant subculture theories

Deviant subcultural criminological explanations emerged in the USA during the 1940s and 1950s, and although there are different variations, all share a common perception that certain social groups have values and attitudes that enable or encourage them to become involved in offending behaviour. Young people come together and engage in activities, which may or may not be deviant or criminal, because these appear to be 'cool' and the individual can gain 'respect' from their peers by becoming involved.

Albert Cohen (1955) influentially argued that youth offending was prevalent among lower-class males and that the most common variant was the juvenile gang and, moreover, these delinquent subcultures were said to have values that were in opposition to those of the dominant culture. Emerging in the slums of some of the largest cities in the USA, subcultures were said to have their foundations in class differentials, parental aspirations and school standards. Cohen observes that the family position in the social structure determines the nature of the problems the child will encounter later in life. They will experience status frustration and strain and adapt into a 'corner boy', 'college boy' or 'delinquent boy'. Corner boys were observed to lead conventional lifestyles and make the most of the situation in which they found themselves, spending most of their time with peers from whom they could receive status and support in group activities. There were few of these boys, nevertheless, and their chances of obtaining material success were limited because their academic and social limitations prevented them from achieving middle-class standards. Delinquent boys, however, come together to define status with their offending behaviour serving no real purpose, often discarding or destroying what they have stolen, they are a simply a short-term hedonistic subculture. Cohen observes that offending tends to be random and directed at people and property; they often act on impulse, often without any consideration or thought for the future but nevertheless remain loyal to each another and allow no one to control their behaviour. Stealing, in the gang context, serves as a form of achieving peer status within the group, there is no other motive. It is simply 'cool'.

Cohen's work has received both praise and criticism and it certainly provides some answers to questions that had remained unresolved by the earlier anomie theories, and his notion of status deprivation has been usefully adopted and adapted by subsequent researchers. Significantly, he fails to explain why it is that some members of delinquent subcultures eventually become law-abiding even when their social class position is fixed and their access to good legitimate opportunities limited.

Miller (1958) rejected the notion that youth offending has its foundations in working-class opposition to middle-class values, emerging as a response to living in the brutalised conditions of the slums and it was environmental experience which generates offending behaviour. Miller uses the concept of focal concerns – and not values – to describe important aspects of being involved in this working-class subculture. First, there is an ever-present concern with *trouble*: both getting into trouble and staying out of it are very important daily preoccupations which can mean obtaining respect from one's peers or ending up in prison. Second, *toughness* represents a further commitment to breaking the law and being a problem to others, with machismo and daring emphasised as a means of gaining and maintaining respect. Third, *smartness* is the ability to gain some advantage by outsmarting or conning others, with prestige and respect often the reward for those demonstrating such skills. Fourth, *excitement* is living on the edge and doing dangerous things for 'the buzz' and again which are 'cool'. Fifth, *fate* is seen as being of crucial concern to the lower class, with many believing their lives are subject to forces outside their control. Sixth, *autonomy* signifies being independent, not relying on others and a rejection of authority. You are out on that street doing what you want with your friends and you are not being told 'what to do' by 'them' until you are caught of course. Miller's theory has attracted considerable support but others have noted that he fails to explain why it is that many – if not most – lower-class people actually conform to societal norms.

Cloward and Ohlin (1960) combine strain, differential association and social disorganisation perspectives in their differential opportunity theory and propose that delinquent subcultures flourish among the lower classes, but take different forms, with the means to achieve illegitimate success no more equally distributed than those for legitimate success. They propose the existence of three different types of deviant subculture and argue that the capacity for each to flourish is dependent on the locality in which they develop and the availability of deviant opportunities. First, criminal gangs emerge in those areas where conventional – as well as non-conventional – values of behaviour are integrated by a close connection of illegitimate and legitimate businesses. It is a type of gang substantially more stable than the following two where older criminals serve as role models, teach the necessary criminal skills and provide available opportunities and a career structure for the younger generation. Second, the conflict or violent gang is a non-stable and non-integrated grouping which exists where there is an absence of a stable criminal organisation and the members of which seek a reputation and respect for toughness and destructive violence. Third, the retreatist gang is equally unsuccessful in the pursuit of illegitimate as well as legitimate opportunities and is seen to be a double failure, retreating into a world of sex, drugs and alcohol.

Spergel (1964) identified an 'anomie gap' between aspirations, expected occupations and income; finding that the extent of this differed significantly between offenders, non-offenders and different subcultures. He thus rejected Cloward and Ohlin's subculture categories and replaced them with his own three-part typology: first, a racket subculture which is said to develop in areas where organised adult criminality is already in existence and highly visible; second, a theft subculture, involving offences such as burglary, shoplifting, taking and driving away cars, would develop where a criminal subculture was already in existence but not very well established; and third, conflict subcultures, involving gang fighting and the pursuit of 'reputation' where there is limited or no access to either criminal or conventional activities. Drug misuse was found to be common to all subcultures as part of the transition from adolescent delinquent activity to either conventional or fully developed criminal activity among older adolescents and young adults.

These early US deviant subcultural theories while telling a plausible tale which makes intuitive sense to the observer have nevertheless been widely criticised for being overly determinist, with offenders seen to be not only different from non-offenders but also in some way committed to an alternative 'ethical' code making involvement compulsory. While it is extremely likely that some young people are so strongly socialised into the mores of a particular worldview – or mechanical solidarity – through membership of a particular ethnic group, the upbringing of their parents and the reinforcing influences of neighbourhood groups or gangs, that they do not challenge this heritage in any way, it also likely that many others have less consistent socialisation experiences and have a far more tangential relationship to such deviant behaviour, although they may be at considerable risk of being drawn into a far deeper involvement.

The most comprehensive critique of the highly determinist early deviant subculture tradition is provided by Sykes and Matza (1957), who observe that their criminological predecessors simply failed to explain why it is that most young offenders 'grow out' of their criminality. Their drift theory proposes that juveniles sense a moral obligation to be bound by the law, and if that bond remains in place, they will remain law-abiding most of the time. It is when that bond is not in place that the young person will drift between involvement in legitimate and illegitimate activities. Most young offenders actually hold values, beliefs and attitudes very similar to those of law-abiding citizens and, indeed, they actually recognise an obligation to be bound by the law, and this being the case, the issue remains as to how it is that these young males can justify their involvement in criminality. The answer proposed is that they learn 'techniques' which enable them to 'neutralise' their law-abiding values and attitudes temporarily and thus drift back and forth between legitimate and illegitimate behaviours. Sykes and Matza observe that at times – and this might well be most of the time – such young people participate in conventional activities but nevertheless shun such involvements while engaging in offending behaviour. In such situations the young offender disregards the controlling influences of rules and values and utilises techniques of neutralisation to 'weaken' the hold society has over them. In other words, these techniques act as defence mechanisms that release the young person from the constraints associated with the moral order.

Matza (1964) simply rejects the notion that young offenders maintain a set of values independent from the dominant culture; they actually do appreciate the culturally held goals and expectations of the middle-class but feel that the pursuit of such behaviour would be frowned upon by their peers and not considered to be 'cool'. Moreover, such beliefs remain almost unconscious – or 'subterranean' – because delinquents fear expressing these to their peers. It is when the young person reaches a situation where they can admit this appreciation to a close friend that both will simply grow out of offending. Of course some never do this and it is these young people who invariably develop adult criminal careers.

Early British deviant subcultural studies tended to follow the lead of the US theories discussed above and seek to operationalise these in a local context. John Mays (1954) thus argued that in some areas, the residents share a number of attitudes and ways of behaving that predispose them to criminality and these attitudes have existed for years and are passed on to newcomers. He found working-class culture to be intentionally criminal; it is just a different socialisation, which, at times, happens to be contrary to the legal rules. Criminal behaviour, in particular adolescent criminal behaviour, is not therefore, a conscious rebellion against middle-class values but arises from an alternative subculture that has been adopted over the years in a random sort of way.

Terence Morris (1957) similarly argued that social deviancy is common among the working classes and that it is the actual characteristics of that class that create the criminality. Forms of anti-social behaviour exist throughout society but the way in which it is expressed differs. Criminal behaviour is largely a working-class expression. The family controls middle-class socialisation, it is very ordered and almost all activities are centred on the home and the family; in contrast, the socialisation of the working-class child tends to be divided between family, peer group and street acquaintances, with the latter likely to have a less ordered and regulated upbringing. The peer group is a much stronger influence from a much earlier age among the working classes and they encounter controls only after they commit a crime and when they are processed by the criminal justice system. The whole ethos of the working class, according to Morris, is oriented towards anti-social and criminal, rather than 'conventional', behaviour.

David Downes (1966) conducted a study among young offenders in the East End of London and found that a considerable amount of offending took place but this mostly happened in street-corner groups, rather than organised gangs. Status frustration did not occur to a significant degree among these young males; instead, their typical response to lack of success at school or work was one of 'dissociation', a process of opting out rather than reaction formation. There was an emphasis on leisure activities, not on school or work, with a dominant interest in commercial forms of entertainment rather than youth clubs with their middle-class orientation. Access to leisure pursuits was significantly restricted by a lack of money and youngsters would take part in offending to find excitement and a 'buzz'. Peter Wilmott (1966) also conducted a study of teenagers in the East End of London and reached much the same conclusions as Miller in the USA, finding that adolescent offending behaviour was simply part of a general lower working-class subculture. Teenagers became involved in petty crime simply for the fun and 'togetherness' of the shared activity experience which again is simply 'cool'.

Howard Parker (1974) conducted a survey of unskilled adolescents in an area of Liverpool with a high rate of youth offending and found a pattern of loosely knit peer groups with criminality a central activity. Young males shared common problems such as unemployment, while leisure opportunities were limited and, consequently, some of their number had developed a temporary solution in the form of stealing car radios. The community in which they lived largely condoned this behaviour as long as the victims were from outside the area.

Pryce (1979) studied African-Caribbean youngsters in the St Paul's area of Bristol and found that their parents had arrived in the UK during the 1950s with high aspirations but had been relegated to a cheap labour force and both genera-tions were subject to racism and discrimination which contributed to a pattern of 'endless pressure'. There appeared two types of anomic adaptation to this pressure: one was to be stable, conformist and law-abiding, the other was to adopt an expres-sive, disreputable rebellious 'rude-boy' attitude. Younger African-Caribbeans, by now encountering widespread unemployment among their number, were significantly more likely to reject conformity and adopt the second response.

These earlier British deviant subculture studies are extremely important because they draw our attention to specific historical factors, in particular the level of economic activity, and to the importance of a structural class analysis in helping to explain subcultural youth offending (Hopkins Burke and Sunley 1996, 1998). They also demonstrate that different groups within the working class had identified distinct problems in terms of negative status and had developed their own solutions to their perceived problems.

Studies of deviant youth subcultures conducted in the USA since the late 1960s have predominantly focused on issues of violence, ethnicity and poverty. Wolfgang and Ferracuti (1967) identified a 'subculture of violence' where there was an expectation that the receipt of a trivial insult should be met with vio-lence and the failure to respond in this way was greeted with social censure from the peer group. Curtis (1975) adapted this theory to explain violence among US blacks, arguing that the maintenance of a manly image was essential and individuals who were unable to resolve conflicts verbally were more likely to resort to violence in order to assert their masculinity. Behaviour was seen to be partly a response to social conditions and partly the outcome of the ideas and values absorbed from the subculture of violence.

More recent US research has proposed that poverty is unequivocally the root cause of gangs and the violence they produce. Miller (1958) had argued that lower-class delinquency was a normal response to socio-cultural demands but in his later writings he essentially adopts a 'culture of poverty' view to explain the self-perpetuation of gang life, a view that emphasises the adaptational aspects of the gang to changing socio-economic circumstances (Miller 1990). The most popular recent theory to explain criminal behaviour among poor young invariably black people in inner-city USA is, nevertheless, William Julius Wilson's (1987) 'underclass theory' where he argues that groups in socially isolated neighbourhoods have 'few legitimate employment opportunities; while inadequate job information networks and poor schools not only give rise to weak labour force attachment but also raise the likelihood that people will turn to illegal or deviant activities for income' (Wilson 1991: 462).

Wilson has been accused of failing to address the issues of gang formation and explain the development of specific types of gang problems (Hagedorn 1992) but, nevertheless, a number of observers assume a close correlation between gangs, gang violence and the development of a socially excluded underclass (Krisberg 1974; Anderson 1990; Taylor 1990). Poverty is central to the underclass thesis and various writers recognise that the absence of economic resources leads to compensatory efforts to achieve some form of economic and successful social adjustment (Williams 1989; Moore 1991; Hopkins Burke 1999a). It is in this context that Spergel (1995: 149) argues that 'a sub-culture arises out of efforts of people to solve social, economic, psychological, developmental, and even political problems', an argument to which we will return later in this chapter.

The concept of deviant subculture was subsequently revised and revitalised by radical neo-Marxist sociologists and criminologists based at the Birmingham Centre for Contemporary Cultural Studies in the UK during the 1970s (see Brake 1985; P. Cohen 1972; S. Cohen 1973; Hebdige 1976, 1979). These researchers observed that youth subcultures arise at particular historical 'moments' as cultural solutions to the same structural economic problems created by rapid social change identified earlier by Durkheim – and Merton in a rather different way – as an anomic condition. The central concern of these studies was to locate the historical and environmental context in which particular youth subcultures arose and the details of 'style' adopted. The focus was on two broad areas: mainstream youth and delinquency and expressive or spectacular youth subcultures.

The two major studies of mainstream youth subcultures are those of Willis (1977) and Corrigan (1979), both being concerned with the transition from school to work among urban lower working-class adolescent boys. The 'problem' of these boys was found to be an alien or irrelevant education system followed by the prospect of a boring and dead-end job (or, nowadays, training and the benefits queue, see Hopkins Burke 1999a) and the 'solution' was a 'culture of resistance' manifested in truancy and petty offending. Spectacular youth subcultures – such as Teddy Boys, Mods, Skinheads and Punks – involve the adoption, by young people of both sexes, of a distinctive style of dress and way of using material artefacts combined, usually, with distinctive lifestyles, behaviour patterns and musical preferences. Both variants of subculture invariably involve a contemporary manifestation of parent culture values that have been adapted to the changed socio-economic circumstances in which the group finds itself.

The Birmingham studies represented an important development of the earlier deviant subcultural tradition – which had recognised that deviance often occurs in response to economic or status deprivation – and identified that particular subcultures – or status groups – have arisen as a response to the economic problems encountered by particular groups. Hopkins Burke and Sunley (1996, 1998) note that these studies presume a linear development of history where different subcultures arise, coalesce, fade and are replaced as economic circumstances change; for example, the Mods were a product of the upwardly mobile working-classes during the optimistic 1960s (Hebdige 1976, 1979; Brake 1980), whereas the Punks were a product of the 'dole-queue' despondency of the late 1970s (Hebdige 1979; Brake 1980, 1985).

Hopkins Burke and Sunley (1996, 1998) subsequently observed the coexistence of a number of different subcultures and propose these to be an outcome of a fragmented society where different groups of young people have coalesced to create solutions to their specific socio-economic problems. Central to this account is the possibility of choice. The simultaneous existence of different subcultures enables some young people to choose the solution to their problem from the various subcultures available, although that choice will be crucially and significantly constrained by structural factors.

The early deviant subcultural studies – and indeed the work of the Birmingham School – tended to suggest that young people had limited choices, if any, between the subculture available, at a particular time and in their geographical location, and a life of conventionality. This more contemporary – or postmodernist – interpretation of youth subcultures enables us to recognise that individuals, and different groups of young people, not all members of the traditional working class, but in existence concurrently at the same historical moment, have had very different experiences of the radical economic change that has engulfed British society since the late 1970s and which has accelerated significantly during the first decades of the twenty-first century with disastrous consequences for many young people. This is a story to which we will return later in this book.

Social control theories

Social control theories are part of a long established tradition, with strong foundations in both the rational actor and the predestined actor models of criminal behaviour, and they are fundamentally founded in a conception of human nature which proposes that there are no natural limits on elementary human needs and desires. People will always want and seek further economic reward and it is not therefore necessary to seek motives for engaging in criminal activity. Human beings are born free to break the law and will only refrain from doing so under particular circumstances, and it is these fundamental rational actor model assumptions that provide the foundations of the later influential social control theories.

Criminological theories, under whatever guise, usually view conformity to be the natural state of humanity; in other words, criminal behaviour is simply abnormal and it is this orthodox way of thinking about crime that social control theory seeks to challenge. Thus, the central question asked from this perspective is not the usual, 'why do some people commit crimes?' but rather, 'why do most of us conform?' The unifying factor in the different versions of control theory is the assumption that crime and deviance are only to be expected when social and personal controls are in some way inadequate and fail to restrain the individual from criminal involvement.

Early control theories attached much importance to psychological factors. Reiss (1951) distinguished between the effects of 'personal' and 'social' controls, proposing that the former arise when individuals internalise the norms and rules of non-deviant primary groups to such an extent that they become their own; the latter are founded in the ability of external social groups or institutions to make rules or norms effective. Conformity involves simple acquiescence and does not require the internalisation of rules and norms within the value system of the individual. Reiss proposed that personal controls are far more important in preventing deviance than external social controls.

Nye (1958) sought to locate and identify the factors that encourage conformity in adolescents and focused his attention on the family, which because of the affectional bonds established between members were considered to be the most important mechanism of social control. Nye identified four modes of social control generated by the family. First, direct control is imposed through external forces such as parents, teachers and the police using direct restraint and punishment. Second, individuals themselves in the absence of external regulation exercise internalised control. Third, indirect control is dependent upon the degree of affection that an individual has for conventional significant others. Fourth, control through alternative means of needs satisfaction works by reducing the temptation for individuals to resort to illegitimate means of needs satisfaction. Though independent of each other, these four modes of control were considered mutually reinforcing and to work more effectively together.

Reckless (1967) later sought to explain why it is that despite the various 'push' and 'pull' factors that may tempt individuals into criminal behaviour, most people resist these pressures and remain law-abiding citizens. He argued that a combination of control factors, both internal and external to the individual, serve as insulators or 'containments' but he, nevertheless, attached much more importance to internal factors, arguing that these tend to control the individual irrespective of the extent of external environment change and he identified four key components. First, individuals with a strong and favourable self-concept are better insulated against those 'push' and 'pull' factors which encourage involvement in criminal activity. Second, goal orientation is the extent to which the individual has a clear direction in life oriented towards the achievement of legitimate goals such as educational and occupational success. Third, frustration tolerance is where contemporary society – with its emphasis on individualism and immediate gratification – might generate considerable frustration. Fourth, norm retention is the extent to which individuals accept, internalise and are committed to conventional laws, norms, values and rules and the institutions that represent and uphold these.

Reckless (1967: 476) described the process by which norm retention is undermined, thus making deviance more possible, as one of norm erosion and involves 'alienation from, emancipation from, withdrawal of legitimacy from and neutralisation of formerly internalised ethics, morals, laws and values'. This idea of individuals being able to neutralise formerly internalised norms and values to facilitate deviant or offending behaviour were, of course, a prominent element in the drift theory of David Matza we encountered above.

Travis Hirschi (1969) made the most influential contribution to later social control theory and observed that at their simplest level all such theories share the basic assumption that offending behaviour occurs when the bond of an individual to legitimate society is weak or broken. Four elements of this social bond were identified. First, attachment refers to the capacity of individuals to form effective relationships with other people and institutions; in the case of children and young people, with their parents, peers and school. Second, commitment refers to the social investments made by the individual to conventional activities that could be put at risk by engaging in deviant behaviour. Third, involvement refers to the simple reality that a person may be too busy doing conventional things to find time to engage in deviant activities. Fourth, beliefs are a set of impressions and convictions that are in need of constant reinforcement and which are closely connected to the pattern and strength of attachments an individual has with other people and institutions. These four variables, though independent, are also highly interrelated and, it is argued, help to prevent law-breaking activities in most people. It is this theory that has been so influential within the contemporary youth justice system and provides the theoretical foundations on which the work of youth offending teams is based, although this is rarely acknowledged.

Subsequent research has tended to find that the aspects of the social bond most consistently related to offending behaviour are those of the family and the school (Thomas and Hyman 1978; Thompson et al. 1984) and there is substantial evidence that juveniles with strong attachments to their family are less likely to engage in offending behaviour unless of course the family is involved in criminality, whereupon family attachment can be a negative factor. The evidence on the association between attachment and commitment to school (particularly poor school performance, not liking school, low educational and occupational aspirations) and delinquency is even stronger.

Hirschi's original formulation of control theory did not escape criticism and he himself acknowledged that it overestimated the significance of involvement in conventional activities and under-estimated the importance of offending friends and these problems appear to have emanated from the assumption of a natural motivation towards offending behaviour (Box 1981; Downes and Rock 1998). Other critics noted that the theory cannot account for the specific form or content of deviant behaviour; there is thus a failure to consider the underlying structural and historical context in which criminal behaviour takes place and while it clearly considers primary deviance among adolescents, habitual 'secondary deviance' appears to be outside its conceptual remit. Other researchers subsequently sought a solution to these identified defects by integrating control theory with other theoretical perspectives.

Elliot et al. (1979) developed a model that sought to expand and synthesise anomie theories, social learning and social control perspectives, and their starting point is the assumption that individuals have different early socialisation experiences which lead to variable degrees of commitment to the conventional social order and these initial social bonds can then be reinforced by positive experiences at school and in the wider community. The structural dimension is most explicit with their analysis of the factors that serve to loosen social bonds such as limited or blocked opportunities, which include economic recession and unemployment.

Stephen Box (1981, 1987) was to integrate control theory with a labelling/ conflict perspective we will encounter below and argue that differential policing practices, and institutional biases at different stages of the criminal justice system, all operate in favour of the most advantaged sections of society and very much to the detriment of its less favoured citizens. This is not simply a product of discriminatory decision-making criteria made on the basis of the individual characteristics of the suspect, nevertheless, for such outcomes can be a response to structural social problems of which the individual is merely a symbol. Stigma, disadvantage and a sense of injustice engendered by the consequential criminalisation process, particularly when it is perceived as discriminatory, provide further impetus towards criminal behaviour (Box 1981).

Box (1987) later uses his version of social control theory to help us understand how the impact of economic recession – such as that experienced in Britain during the 1980s – could lead to an increase in criminal activity. First, by further reducing legitimate opportunities and increasing relative deprivation, recession produces more 'strain' and, therefore, more individuals with a motive to deviate, particularly among the economically disadvantaged. In such cases, the commitment of the individual to society is undermined because their access to conventional modes of activity has been seriously reduced. Second, by undermining the family and conventional employment prospects, the ability and motivation of an individual to develop an attachment to other human beings, who might introduce a controlling influence in his or her life, is substantially reduced.

John Braithwaite's (1989) theory of 'predatory' crime – that is, crimes involving the victimisation of one party by another – builds upon and integrates elements of control, labelling, strain and subcultural theory and proposes that the way to reduce crime is to have a commitment to 'reintegrative' forms of shaming. Braithwaite makes a crucial distinction between the negative shaming identified by the labelling theorists that we shall encounter below, and which leads to stigmatising and the outcasting of the individual, and that which is reintegrative and ends disapproval with rituals of forgiveness. The latter approach is seen to control crime while the former merely pushes offenders towards criminal subcultures which become increasingly attractive to the stigmatised because they can provide emotional and social support.

Braithwaite observes that participation in these groups can also supply criminal role models, knowledge on how to offend and techniques of 'neutralisation' that taken together can make the choice to engage in crime more attractive, likely and, indeed, rational. Therefore, a high level of stigmatisation in a society is a key factor in stimulating the formation of criminal subcultures in particular among children and young people. Braithwaite claims that individuals are more susceptible to positive reintegrative shaming when they are enmeshed in multiple relationships of interdependency and it is thus communitarian societies that shame the most effectively. It is such societies or cultures – constituted of dense networks of individual interdependencies characterised by mutual help and trust – rather than individualistic societies that are more capable of delivering the required more potent shaming that is reintegrative. This is a crucial observation and the contemporary philosophy of communitarianism was, as we have seen, very influential with New Labour in the UK and the development of the contemporary youth justice system.

Both Box and Braithwaite sought to rescue the social control theory perspective from its emphasis on the individual, or more accurately family culpability, that had made it so popular with Conservative governments in both the UK and the USA since the 1980s. Box has clearly located his radical reformulation of social control theory within the victimised actor model we will encounter below (Box 1981, 1987) but it is the notion of 'reintegrative shaming' developed by Braithwaite that was so influential with New Labour.

Gottfredson and Hirschi (1990) combined rational actor model notions of crime with a predestined actor model theory of criminality in order to produce an inevitably flawed 'general theory of crime' which ambitiously sought to explain all criminality. Crime is defined as acts of force or fraud undertaken in the pursuit of self-interest, and the authors propose that the vast bulk of criminal acts are trivial and mundane affairs that result in little gain and require little in the way of effort, planning, preparation or skill, and their 'versatility construct' considers crime to be essentially interchangeable, that is, low-level criminals turning their hand to any crime opportunities that arise. Thus, the characteristics of ordinary criminal events are simply inconsistent with notions of specialisation or the 'criminal career'. Since the likelihood of criminal behaviour is also closely linked to the availability of opportunity, the characteristics of situations and the personal properties of individuals will jointly affect the use of force or fraud in the pursuit of self-interest. This central concept of their explanation of criminality – low self-control – is not confined to criminal acts, it is also implicated in many 'analogous' acts, such as promiscuity, alcohol use and smoking, where such behaviour is portrayed as the impulsive actions of disorganised individuals seeking quick gratification.

Gottfredson and Hirschi turn to the predestined actor model in order to account for variations in self-control among individuals and they argue that the main cause is 'ineffective parenting'. They propose from a behaviourist perspective that failure to instil self-control early in life cannot easily be remedied later, any more than effective control, once established, can be later undone. According to this 'stability postulate', levels of self-control will remain stable throughout the life course and thus by asserting that crime is essentially interchangeable while the propensity to become involved in criminality remains stable throughout the life course, the theory has no need to provide separate explanations for different types of crime, nor for primary or persistent secondary deviation.

Problematically though, even if the proposition that low self-control is a causal factor in some or even most types of crime is accepted, it is questionable whether we can accept a straightforward association between low self-control and ineffective parenting. Although the literature discussed elsewhere in this book does suggest a relationship between parenting and offending behaviour, this is compromised and complicated when structural factors are considered. For example, while her study of socially deprived families in Birmingham did find that parental supervision was an important factor in determining adolescent offending behaviour, Harriet Wilson (1980: 322–3) warned against the misinterpretation of her findings, arguing that it is the position of the most disadvantaged groups in society, and not the individual, which is in need of significant improvement.

Hirschi (1995) more recently and influentially argued that policies designed to deter (the rational actor model) or rehabilitate (the predestined actor model) will continue to have little success in reducing criminal behaviour, proposing that effective state policies are those that support and enhance socialisation within the family by improving the quality of childrearing practices with the focus on the form, size and stability of the family unit. Thus, there should always be two parents for every child, no more than three children in a family and the relationships between parents and children strong and durable. Moreover, it is not young teenage mothers who are a problem that causes offending behaviour in children; it is having a mother without a father. Effective policies are thus those that focus not on preventing teenage pregnancies, but on maintaining the involvement of the father in the life of the child. Hirschi argued most successfully that these policy reforms will strengthen family bonds, increase socialisation and create greater self-control in the child that will make it unlikely that they will become involved in criminality.

Victimised actor model theories

The victimised actor model of criminal behaviour is a more recent criminological tradition that proposes – with increasingly radical variants – that the criminal is in some way the victim of an unjust and unequal society; thus, it is the behaviour and activities of the poor and powerless in society that are targeted and criminalised, while the sometimes dubious activities of the rich and powerful are simply ignored, or not even defined as criminal. Box 10.1 summarises the main points of the victimised actor model of criminal behaviour.

Box 10.1   The victimised actor model of criminal behaviour

- The criminal is in some way the victim of an unjust and unequal society.
- The behaviour and activities of the poor and powerless sections of society are targeted and criminalised.
- The dubious activities of the rich and powerful are ignored or not even defined as criminal.
- Neither punishment nor treatment of offenders is proposed but a radical restructuring of society to eradicate or least significantly reduce unequal power relations.

Labelling theories

Labelling – or social reaction – theories are the first to be considered and these have unequivocal foundations in the victimised actor model. They were considered a radical new form of criminological explanation during the late 1960s and early 1970s, focusing on social processes, including reactions and counteractions, and came to consider how 'labels' are developed, negotiated, exchanged and applied to people (see Wilkins 1964; Cohen 1972). It is the central proposition of labelling theories that in the case of all social behaviours it is the reactions of other people, or an audience, that is the important variable in the ongoing process of action. For example, crashes on the stock exchange produce panic as a reaction, and this panic leads to more selling, which amplifies the original panic. Social reaction theorists propose that the same occurs in the case of youth offending. Thus, for example, the influential deviant subculture theorist Albert Cohen (1955), who we encountered above, had emphasised the negative and malicious characteristics of young offender activities and how these engender a strong societal reaction which can lead to young offenders being categorised as abnormal and thus helps the authorities denounce them as unacceptable. The outcome of this reaction formation is the denial of legitimate opportunities for young people labelled as deviant and this in itself encourages them to revert to illegitimate opportunities and thus the cycle is perpetrated.

Societal reaction is thus a significant component in explaining youth offending. Stan Cohen (1972) instigated an interest in the activities of prominent agents of social reaction – especially those in the media – and devised the now almost household term 'moral panic'. His account of how the media amplified the initially rather innocuous mod and rocker 'riots' that occurred at Clacton at Easter 1964 are now well known to students of deviancy and the main points of his account are clear: the media stereotyped and polarised the contending groups (not only mods and rockers, but young people in general and the police) and increased the sensitivity of the participants thus encouraging further delinquent behaviour. This is a famous analysis, but still rather a speculative one which ends with an important note of caution: that we still do not know very much about the effects of labels on individuals, although there are reasons to believe that these are complex.

Social reactions have been studied at the micro-level and this brings us to the classic work of Howard Becker (1963), who argues that since social groups create rules, they also create deviants or outsiders; in other words, if you have no rules, you have no deviancy. Deviancy is consequently not about the quality of the act itself, but of the social process of recognition and rule enforcement and our attention is hence directed to the rule-makers and enforcers – the 'moral entrepreneurs' – as much as to deviants. Morality is therefore an enterprise, not just a simple natural social process and our attention is directed to the values of those who have the power to label. This involves a critique of those values because these can no longer be seen as natural or neutral, and in this sense, the approach takes the side of the disadvantaged (Becker 1967). The work of Becker is the usual source of radical variants of labelling theory and this work implies there is no need to explain deviance in the first place, that it is simply a very common social activity, a normal one, which only becomes abnormal when it too is so labelled by an outside audience. The application of the label thus confirms the initial diagnosis and becomes a self-fulfilling prophecy, launching young people on a deviant career from which they will have increasing difficulty leaving. In this way the legitimate choices available to the young person are now significantly reduced.

Conflict and radical theories

Conflict and radical theories have developed the labelling and social reaction thesis further and sought to explain crime and criminal behaviour in terms of the unequal nature of the socio-political structure of society. Conflict theorists take a pluralist stance and propose that society consists of numerous groups all involved in struggle to promote their interests in the economic marketplace, while the radical versions are invariably informed by different interpretations of Marxist social and economic theory. Despite these differences in emphasis, both groups have a common concern with the social struggle for power and authority. There subsequently developed among young radicals in the UK during the early 1970s a concern to restore some dignity to the deviant person and restore meaning to their deviant actions, to regard them as knowing people responding rationally, albeit sometimes rebelliously, to their circumstances which invariably means crucially reduced legitimate opportunities for legitimate success. The classic text in this tradition is Taylor et al. *The New Criminology* (1973) which, while drawing heavily on labelling theory, argued that the power to criminalise, make laws and prosecute offenders, or particular groups that are perceived to be offenders, is a function of the state.

There are at the current time two variants of the radical criminological tradition: one version, 'left realism', is considered below; the other, critical criminology, is the only version with unequivocal foundations in the victimised actor model. Critical criminologists have defined criminality in terms of the concept of oppression and observe that some groups in society – the working class, women and ethnic minority groups – are the most likely to suffer oppressive social relations based upon class division, sexism and racism. Criminal behaviour among such groups is seen to be the rational outcome of the interaction between the marginalisation, or exclusion, from access to mainstream institutions and that of criminalisation by the state authorities. The latter involves a process in which the law, agencies of social control and the media associate crime with particular groups who are subsequently identified and targeted as a threat. Scraton and Chadwick (1996) argue that this process is used to divert attention from economic and social conditions, particularly at times of acute economic change that could provide the impetus for serious political unrest. Criminalisation can thus be used to justify harsher social control measures that are often taken against economically and politically marginalised groups who have few means of resisting these initiatives.

This author has previously used the term 'the schizophrenia of crime' to refer to the apparently contradictory duality of attitude to criminal behaviour that is a significant characteristic of contemporary post-industrial society (Hopkins Burke 2005, 2007, 2014). Thus, on the one hand, there is a widespread populist public demand for a rigorous intervention against criminality that has made the 'war against crime' a major political issue and has seen the main political parties seeking to outbid each other for electoral gain with a consequential major expansion in situational crime-prevention strategies epitomised by the ubiquitous existence of closed-circuit television cameras (Hopkins Burke 2004b), a whole raft of crime control legislation that has placed increasing restrictions on our civil liberties and human rights (Hopkins Burke 2004c), and the introduction of rigorous 'zero-tolerance-style' policing interventions (see Hopkins Burke 1998a, 2002, 2004a). On the other hand, criminality is observed to be widespread to the virtual point of universality, with many people having committed criminal offences at some stage in their life – not least when they were children and young people – with a great many continuing to do so. There is therefore a considerable moral ambiguity about crime and criminal behaviour in contemporary society which sends out confused measures to many young people, not least because of the widely advertised pleasure of criminality and doing crime which clearly conveys a widely received message that doing crime is 'cool' (Hopkins Burke 2007).

Cultural criminologists have examined the pleasures to be enjoyed from engaging in deviant and criminal activities (Katz 1988; Presdee 2000) and identified the long-established tradition of 'carnival' functions as a playful and pleasurable resistance to authority where those normally excluded from the exercise of power celebrate their anger at this exclusion. Presdee (2000) argues that the outcome of living in a world dominated by scientific rationality and social control has been the fragmentation of organised carnival with its fragments distributed far and wide in acts of transgression and crime and thus, from this perspective, many pleasurable activities such as rave culture, drug taking, body modification, binge-drinking, Internet use, joy riding and sado-masochist activities contain many elements of the carnivalesque and crime; while the much reported and discussed deviant activity of the past thirty years, football hooliganism, can be conceptualised in this context (Hopkins Burke 2005). From this perspective, crime is simply normal, non-pathological, enjoyable and understandable in the context of the nature of the neoliberal society in which we live and is a highly significant point to which we return at the end of this chapter

Left realism

Left realism as a criminological perspective recognises the almost universal pleasures and attractions of involvement in criminality but at the same time accepts that these activities have victims which include – particularly in the case of young offenders – many of the perpetrators themselves, for whom a life of criminality and involvement with the criminal justice system is not going to be a happy one.

Left realism has its origins in the writings of a group of British criminologists, some of whom had been in the forefront of the radical criminology of the 1970s, which emerged in response to four closely interconnected factors. First, there was a reaction to what they perceived to be 'left idealism' (see Young 1994): the extreme positions that their previous associates in the radical/critical criminological tradition had now developed into the critical criminology above. Second, there was a response to the ever-increasing criminal victimisation that was so readily apparent and where poor people were overwhelmingly the victims. Yet, it seems extremely unlikely, that these writers and researchers would have so readily discovered this new reality – or have been motivated to do so – but for the important impetus provided by the other two factors (Hopkins Burke 2001, 2005). Thus, third, there was the crucial rise to prominence and power of the populist conservatives or the 'new right' and, fourth, the rediscovery by right realist criminologists of the rational actor model of crime and criminal behaviour that was discussed in Chapter 5.

This group of criminologists on the left of the political spectrum – such as Jock Young, John Lea and Roger Matthews – became increasingly worried during the 1980s that the debate on crime control had been successfully appropriated by the political right. The critical criminologists, by denying that working-class crime was a real problem and concentrating instead on 'crimes of the powerful' and the politics of oppression, were ignoring the plight of working-class victims of predatory crime. Moreover, successive electoral defeats of the British Labour Party convinced them that they had allowed the political high ground to be captured by the new populist Conservatives with the rediscovered rational actor model gaining increasing favour with the Home Office. Lea and Young (1984) thus observed the need for a 'radical realist' response to the populist Conservatives: one which recognised the impact of crime but which at the same time addressed the context in which it occurred.

For left realists, crime, then, is a real problem that must be addressed. Lea and Young deal with the argument that corporate crime is more important: yes, 'crimes of the powerful' do exist and are to be condemned, but the effects of corporate crime are generally widespread, while those of direct-contact crime are concentrated. Corporate crime may indeed cause financial loss and even death and danger, but the real problem for those living in high-crime areas is posed by predatory offenders in their midst. Left realism thus takes into account the immediate fears that people have and seeks to deal with them.

From a left realist perspective, crime is a real problem for ordinary people that must be taken seriously, and central to their crime control strategy is the proposition that crime requires a comprehensive solution: there must be a 'balance of intervention' against both crime and the causes of crime. For the British New Labour government, unquestionably influenced by this criminological discourse, it was to be an approach to crime and criminal behaviour summarised and popularised by the oft-quoted sound bite of Prime Minister Tony Blair when previously shadow home secretary, 'tough on crime, tough on the causes of crime'. The first part of that equation proposes that offenders should accept and take responsibility for their actions and is in theoretical accordance with the prescriptions of the rational actor model; the second part proposes a tough stance on the causes of crime by targeting both those individual and structural factors which, in some way, encourage criminality and is thus in accordance with not only the predestined actor model but also – and most appropriately for a socialist political party, however much they sought to disguise that fact – rooted most firmly in the victimised actor model. The theoretical justification for that governmental approach – and it is one that sets it apart from its political opponents and predecessors in government – is offered by the following realist examination of the creation of an apparently criminal 'underclass'.

An analysis of a socially excluded underclass – whose members are over-represented among the ranks of convicted offenders – when conducted from a left realist perspective requires that we consider theoretical inputs from each of the three models of criminal behaviour. First, the structural model of the underclass – incorporating accounts by Dahrendorf (1985), Field (1989), Jordan (1998) and from the USA, William Julius Wilson (1987, 1991) discussed above – is usually associated with the political 'left' and has its theoretical foundations firmly located in both the conflict, radical and critical variants of the victimised actor tradition and the sociological predestined actor model tradition. Primarily various forms of social exclusion, poverty, material deprivation and patterns of inequality are emphasised and it is recognised that entry into and membership of this class are explained by the inadequacy of state-provided welfare services, changes in the labour market and exclusion from full citizenship. Second, the behaviourist or culturalist model, however – incorporating accounts from James Q. Wilson and Herrnstein (1985) Murray (1990, 1994) and Herrnstein and Murray (1994) – is usually associated with the new political 'right' or populist Conservatives and has its theoretical foundations in the rational actor model and the biological variant of the predestined actor model. This model of the underclass came to prominence during the 1980s following the rise in the number of long-term unemployed, the fast-expanding lone parent population, increased welfare dependency and rising crime and disorder and it is argued, from this perspective, that the provision of state welfare erodes individual responsibility by giving people incentives not to work and provide for themselves and their family. Moreover, it is argued that the 'controls' and social bonds that stop individuals and communities from behaving badly, such as stable family backgrounds and in particular positive male role models, do not exist for many members of this underclass. Left to their own devices without the controls and rewards of the labour market but provided with basic support by the welfare system, young people are free to develop with other like-minded others a deviant invariably criminal subcultural solution to their socially excluded existence.

Research evidence has shown that non-participation in the labour market fails to contribute, in any simple way, to the creation of a distinctive subculture (Westergaard 1995; Levitas 1996; Marshall et al. 1996; Crowther 1998) and people can – or at least could – remain unemployed for many years, surviving on a very limited income while remaining law-abiding citizens. However, it is important to recognise that there has been a real problem of crime and anti-social behaviour inflicted on some invariably poor working-class communities by gangs of socially excluded, usually young males living in their midst (Campbell 1993; Jordan 1998).

This author has proposed elsewhere that a left realist analysis requires the development of a process model of the underclass that both locates the structural preconditions for the emergence of this social grouping while at the same time examining the nature of their behavioural response to the predicament in which they find themselves (Hopkins Burke 1999, 2005) and it is an analysis which provides a theoretical justification for a balanced intervention in their lives. The structural preconditions for the emergence of an underclass were undoubtedly the collapse of the unwritten post-war social contract between governments and the unskilled working class in advanced industrial societies which had been fundamentally founded on the provision of full employment and the safety net of a relatively generous welfare state. With the major economic restructuring that occurred during the late 1970s and throughout the 1980s, non-skilled young people, in particular young males, entering into the labour market became increasingly over-represented among the ranks of the unemployed, and at the same time, changes to social security entitlement in 1988 – instigated by the populist Conservatives with the conscious intention of eradicating welfare dependency – had meant that 16 and 17 year olds lost their automatic right to benefits while 18 to 24 year olds saw a dramatic reduction in the amount of money they could claim. Caroline Adams, from the charity Action for Children, estimated at the time that this was a contributory reason why 75,000 16 and 17 year olds had no source of income whatsoever (Hopkins Burke 1998c). In short, the collapse of the economic basis of their existence provides the structural element of a process model of the creation of an underclass (Hopkins Burke 2000).

The behavioural response of this group has its origins in changes to familial living arrangements encouraged by the aforementioned economic upheaval. The ideal type of nuclear family of industrial modernity (Parsons 1951) had been based on a division of labour and interdependency between men and women that had made considerable sense with the former invariably the main breadwinner and the latter the provider of home conditions to support the man and nurture and socialise the next generation. It was a rational arrangement because there were very few – if any – realistic alternatives available to either man or woman but in changed socio-economic circumstances it was a form of social arrangement that was to become less of a rational choice for potential participants. Feminists have observed that, stripped of their role as the breadwinner, 'workless' men now had little to offer women and their children other than the erratic affection, violence and child abuse that had often been present in working-class families (Campbell 1993). Moreover, in a situation where the modernist state was quite understandably prepared to place women and children at the head of the queue for welfare benefits and 'social' housing provision, the former had relinquished their economic dependency on men to become dependent upon an increasingly inadequate welfare state (Field 1989).

Many young men were now stripped of the informal controls of waged employment and family responsibilities that had previously restrained their wilder excesses and which had brought them back into the fold of conforming non-offending by their early twenties. Unskilled and poorly educated, they were now completely superfluous to the long-term requirements of post-industrial society. Unable to obtain legitimate employment opportunities and appearing as unattractive propositions to young women as partners and fathers for their children, many of these young men found themselves 'frozen in a state of persistent adolescence' (Pitts 1996: 260). Moreover, these restricted life chances had significant implications for their involvement in criminal behaviour because the evidence suggests that growing out of crime is simply part of growing up (Rutherford 1992). Pitts (1996: 262) observes that 'stripped of legitimate access to adulthood these young men were trapped in a limbo world somewhere between childhood and adulthood long after the developmental tasks' of adolescence had been completed. Now into their second – or even third – generation of what is a workless underclass in some geographical localities, this widely ostracised grouping had become stereotyped as inherently criminogenic and drug-ridden, with images that are frequently racialised (see Rose 1999; Parenti 2000; Bauman 1998a, 2000).

In conclusion, it is important to reiterate our previous recognition that the left realist perspective has been extremely influential with the New Labour government elected in 1997. There was a readily identified need for a balanced intervention that tackles both offending behaviour and the social and environmental conditions that support and encourage that behaviour with the intention of seeking to reintegrate back into included society the socially excluded 'underclass' identified above, as part of a major government project – or 'big idea' – that this author has previously termed 'reintegrative tutelage' and which was introduced in the third of this book. Pitts (2001a), nevertheless, observes in this context that while New Labour accounts of the origins of the socially excluded underclass have tended towards the structural with the logical outcome being a challenge to social inequalities and the provision of legitimate life chances for young people, their actual proposed solutions tended to tackle the behavioural/culturalist facets of teenage pregnancy, bad behaviour and welfare dependency with no impact whatsoever on the major structural issues with which they were faced. Recent critical criminological discourses explain how the reintegrative tutelage project was doomed to failure.

Postscript: critical criminology revisited

Simon Winlow and Steve Hall (2013) continue their ongoing critique of neoliberal society to which we have referred elsewhere in this book and have questioned what the term 'social exclusion' actually means and explore the manner in which it is represented in contemporary society. Their analysis focuses on the central issue of what actually happens to 'the social' when increasing numbers of people – and the number increases significantly during every economic downturn – are cut adrift from its organising logic, its economic transactions, relations, customs, codes, cultural norms and meaningful political representation.

Winlow and Hall seek to establish a framework for understanding how it might be possible to transcend the dominance of the current neoliberal hegemony at a time when so much of the current critique has lost its critical edge. They argue that because of the ever-increasing atomisation of society – where we all are little more than a collection of free-floating individuals – we are all being excluded in crucial ways from 'the social'. This has become the case because the social itself no longer really exists in neoliberal society where everybody is a man, or woman, from nowhere. They argue that in a world where Britain and the rest of the developed industrial world is experiencing a fast acceleration of social atomisation there is a need to ask exactly who is being excluded and from what and why and they propose that the answer is essentially everybody and nobody because there is little to be excluded from in contemporary neoliberal society.

Winlow and Hall observe that the problem for the political left is, of course, that if society itself no longer really exists, and everybody buys into the neoliberal individualist model, there is no collective ground or public space from which to elaborate or construct effective opposition. They are in particular critical of the shortcomings of the liberal-left in confronting the ahistorical, post-political, neoliberal, capitalist landscape and its failure to provide any real scrutiny or opposition, focusing on their abandonment of their socialist principles and the decline in progressive and oppositional politics. It is abandonment, they argue, in the failure of the left to fully comprehend the seductive appeal of the neoliberal politico-economic system that wipes out social responsibility and appeals to individual desire and drive. In other words, since neoliberalism is already anti-social and against any idea of community, the left absolutely cannot afford to let its socialist principles slide out of sight, moving away from oppositional politics and towards arguing for incremental change to mitigate for the worst excesses of capitalism. In this way the liberal left becomes complicit in the reproduction of neoliberal society.

Winlow and Hall (2013) seek to change society through critical thinking aimed at inspiring a return to the oppositional and progressive politics currently so sorely missing in the post-political neoliberal (a)society; although like many of their predecessors in this pro-revolutionary endeavour, they wish to radically change society without really outlining the nature of that world post-revolution. They are thus followers of Slavoj Zizek who seeks revolutionary change without really outlining what that world will look like after the event with the assumption that things cannot be worse than they now are. We will return to these themes in the concluding chapter of this book.

Summary of main points

1   The sociological variant of the predestined actor model rejects individualist explanations of criminality and examines the environmental factors that are seen as significant in the creation of crime and criminal behaviour.

2   It is a tradition very much informed by the increasingly influential social theory of Emile Durkheim and his concerns with the social problems created by rapid social change.

3   The Chicago School produced an influential model for understanding the social foundations of crime in complex industrial societies, arguing that as modern cities expand in size, their development is patterned socially and they grow radially in a series of concentric zones or rings.

4   Robert Merton distinguished between cultural goals, that is, those material possessions, symbols of status, accomplishment and esteem that established norms and values encourage us to aspire to, and are, therefore, socially learned; and institutionalised means, which is, the distribution of opportunities to achieve these goals in socially acceptable ways.

5   Deviant subcultural criminological explanations emerged in the USA during the 1940s and 1950s and although there are different variations, all share a common perception that certain social groups have values and attitudes that enable or encourage them to become involved in offending behaviour.

6   Young people come together and engage in activities, which may or may not be deviant or criminal, because these appear to be 'cool' and the individual can gain 'respect' from their peers by becoming involved.

7   Earlier British deviant subculture studies are important because they draw our attention to specific historical factors, in particular the level of economic activity, and to the importance of a structural class analysis in helping to explain subcultural youth offending.

8   Social control theories are part of a long-established tradition which propose that people will always want and seek further economic reward and it is not therefore necessary to seek motives for engaging in criminal activity. Human beings are born free to break the law and will only refrain from doing so under particular circumstances.

9   Travis Hirschi (1969) made the most influential contribution to later social control theory and observed that at their simplest level all such theories share the basic assumption that offending behaviour occurs when the bond of an individual to legitimate society is weak or broken.

10 The victimised actor model of criminal behaviour proposes – with increasingly radical variants – that the criminal is in some way the victim of an unjust and unequal society. It is the behaviour and activities of the poor and powerless in society that are targeted and criminalised, while the sometimes dubious activities of the rich and powerful are simply ignored, or not even defined as criminal.

Discussion questions

1   How does Emile Durkheim explain motivations for criminal behaviour in industrial societies?
2   How does Robert Merton explain criminality?
3   Explain the fundamental components of subcultural theories.
4   How do contemporary social control theorists explain offending behaviour by young offenders?
5   How do labelling theories explain criminal behaviour by children and young people?

Part III

The contemporary youth justice system and its critics

11 The Coalition, the Big Society and youth justice policy

Key issues

1 The demise of New Labour and the arrival of the Coalition
2 The Big Society
3 Coalition youth justice policy
4 General election 2015 – the Conservatives prevail

The first part of this book concluded by exploring the origins and foundations of the contemporary youth justice system with the emergence of New Labour as an electoral force and its commitment to the philosophy of communitarianism, the notion of reintegrative tutelage (and its constituent criminological perspectives of left realism, reintegrative shaming and restorative justice), the risk society, the new public management, quality assurance and the audit society, the Audit Commission and its influential critique of the then juvenile justice system, and effective and evidence-based practice. This third part of the book considers the operation of the contemporary youth justice from its outset, the changes that were subsequently made, not least following the electoral demise of New Labour and the aftermath.

The demise of New Labour and the arrival of the Coalition

The New Labour Government had been elected in May 1997 with a huge majority and appeared committed to pursuing progressive social policies backed up by the empirical research evidence that had been gathering dust during the long years of the previous Conservative regime. Where research findings did not exist, then resources would be made available so that the appropriate studies could be conducted. These were good times to be a researcher in the areas of criminology and criminal justice. The Crime and Disorder Act 1998 was the new government's major flagship criminal justice legislation which was intended to transform criminal justice in the UK.

In the area of young people and crime, the long-established juvenile justice system was to be replaced with a new youth justice system via the auspices of the newly created Youth Justice Board for England and Wales with a significantly large budget which epitomised the self-confident optimistic times. There was of course academic and some professional resistance to these developments. Some observed a new punitive turn in youth justice policies while others (such as this author) recognised a positive potential with the proposed left realist-inspired 'balanced intervention', where young offenders would be required to take responsibility for their actions but, at the same time, a great emphasis would be placed on addressing the personal and social conditions that had impacted on their lives and which could encourage them to make the 'wrong' decisions in life.

All this would be located in the context of a government programme of 'reintegrative tutelage' (Hopkins Burke 1999a), which would seek to reintegrate into mainstream society those large sections of the population who had become economically excluded from the good life as an outcome of the laissez-faire free-market economic policies implemented by the previous Conservative administrations. These governments had presided over a major restructuring of the UK economy with a major transition away from manufacturing to the service industries (such as financial services including the ubiquitous investment banking), leaving many in the traditional working-class communities high and dry on the economic scrapheap. Never mind. New Labour socio-economic policy would sort it all out. From the vantage point of today (August 2015 and two lost general elections later), all that optimism seems absurdly naïve and embarrassing.

New Labour proceed to win an unprecedented further two general elections, but while considerable resources were spent on further reintegrative social policies, amid a continuing feeling of 'never had it so good' (to use Prime Minister Harold Macmillan's famous phrase from the 1959 general election) which continued to be enjoyed by large sections of the middle classes (in particular, those in the burgeoning public sector with their regular annual increment-enhanced pay increases), some nonetheless were becoming aware that this extended (worldwide) economic boom was being unnaturally sustained through a mountain of credit. Cutbacks in government spending were occurring long before the final worldwide economic collapse in 2008 and New Labour was losing much of its natural support (to the Liberal Democrats), not least because of its involvement in an extremely unpopular (many said illegal) war in Iraq. The prison population was forever expanding, even though we were advised by official statistics and criminologists working in these areas that we were in the middle of a significant worldwide 'crime drop'. Not that anyone outside this relatively small quantitatively driven group believed this to be the case, perhaps because the crime which was taking place seemed nastier and more violent than ever. Certainly, the self-confidence and optimism of post-1997 UK criminology seemed to be in decline. Then came the economic collapse of 2008 and from then onwards the world was going to be a very different place.

Virtually no one had heard the term 'credit crunch' before 2008 but from that date it was to enter into extremely widespread usage with most people coming to know that it has something to do with banks being far less inclined to lend money than they had previously. Many would-be first-time house buyers were to find it extremely difficult to get mortgages as lenders demanded large deposits and suddenly became very selective to whom they were willing to lend money. Similarly, those looking for a personal loan to buy a car or home extension or go on a foreign holiday were to discover that the easy credit, which had enabled them to live a high consumption lifestyle in the past, was no longer as easy to obtain.

The 2008 credit crunch was one element of a global financial crisis that was to lead to a major (indeed, unprecedented in recent times) economic recession, with many business collapses, rising unemployment and, in many countries (such as the UK), a new austerity politics aimed at reducing high and unsustainable levels of national debt. For the majority of ordinary working people, the consequences were to be felt directly in pay freezes, reduced hours, redundancies and an uncertain (but far from optimistic) future. This was all dramatically symbolised on 15 September 2008 when the US investment bank Lehman Brothers effectively collapsed after 158 years in business, threatening all of its 26,000 workers around the world with the loss of their jobs. But the collapse of Lehman Brothers was a far from unique event.

The fifth largest US bank, Bear Sterns, valued at $18 billion in 2007, was bought by JPMorgan Chase for just $240 million in March 2008, and another household name, Merrill Lynch, agreed to be taken over by the Bank of America. The two largest US mortgage lenders, Fannie Mae and Freddie Mac, which together accounted for $5.3 trillion worth of mortgages (half of all US home loans), had to be bailed out by the US government, as their possible collapse was considered a threat to global financial stability. Another huge mortgage lender, Washington Mutual, also failed and was closed down by the US regulatory authorities and sold to JPMorgan Chase.

Financial analysts traced the origins of the US banking crisis to risky lending practices, especially on home loans. As part of their growth strategy, many US banks had provided a large number of loans to home buyers with poor credit-histories – a practice known as 'sub-prime lending'. These loans were then rolled into portfolios including other assets and bonds and sold to investors around the world. However, between 2004 and 2006, US interest rates rose from 1 per cent to over 5 per cent, and default rates on sub-prime mortgages rose to record levels as people could not afford their rising monthly repayments. Global investors suffered huge losses as a result and the US housing market slumped as banks became very wary of lending to each other and ready credit availability ceased.

Because the financial system is now global, the US crisis began to spread round the world. Investment banks in Europe, China, Australia and elsewhere all suffered losses and the credit crunch (a severe shortage of credit or money) pushed the global economy into recession. In the UK, Ireland and France, major banks were effectively taken into government ownership (nationalised) to prevent them from collapse. National governments across Europe and the European Central Bank intervened, making more money available to banks, hoping that this would encourage them to start lending again. But this strategy did not work, with the outcome being a major global economic recession, bringing business failures, rising unemployment, higher living costs and with the middle-classes (in particular, those public sector employees who had done so well during the previous artificially extended economic boom) being increasingly absorbed into the ranks of socio-economic exclusion, previously the preserve of those involved in manual occupations.[1]

The 2010 British general election produced an inconclusive result with no single party able to form a government, with the eventual outcome being that the first coalition government since the Second World War was formed between the Conservatives and the Liberal Democrats. The centrepiece of the subsequent coalition agreement was the Conservative Party's economic policy of eliminating the UK's structural deficit by 2015, based primarily on public spending cuts rather than on tax rises (a policy which subsequently appeared to have been remarkably unsuccessful, although, at the time of writing, there appears to be no realistic alternative). The 2010 spending review announced a series of measures aimed at achieving this goal, including an average 19 per cent cut across departmental budgets, an extra £7 billion in cuts to the welfare budget on top of £11 billion already announced, and a major reform of public-sector pensions (HM Treasury 2010).

There was an identified synergy between the Liberal Democrat's long-standing focus on localism and the decentralisation of power and Prime Minister David Cameron's pre-election idea of the 'Big Society'. The Coalition announced a vision of Britain as a bottom-up 'Big Society' in which the state withdraws from many of its current (expensive) obligations, to be replaced by strong citizens' groups (cheap) and reinvigorated communities. In a sense, this is an extension of the idea (evident in both 1980s 'Thatcherism' and under New Labour's version of communitarianism) that the state should promote an 'age of responsibility' which focuses on individual behaviour (Lister 2011). Critics nevertheless suggested that the concept of the Big Society provides little more than an ideological smokescreen, covering the increasing pace of privatisation and enormous spending cuts. Critics also note that without the legal right to welfare (or an obligation of the state to provide it), voluntary efforts are unlikely to be sufficient to replace reliable state provision (Charlesworth 2010). This is a remarkably different socio-economic context to social and criminal justice policy from that offered during those heady overly optimistic days when the contemporary youth justice system was first created by New Labour in 1998.

Austerity measures remain very much in place following the 2015 general election and influential voices have foreseen their long-term continuation. Two influential think tanks have warned that austerity measures in the UK could still be in place when the 2020 election takes place. The Institute for Fiscal Studies and the Institute for Government (both of them far from radical left-wing outfits) have said, 'we are still as far away from the (budget deficit) target as we were in 2010 . . . Indeed, it would not be surprising if not just 2015 but also 2020 was an "austerity" election' (BBC 2013). These warnings came in a briefing ahead of the Spending Review on 26 June. Chancellor George Osborne had predicted in 2010 that he could balance the budget within four years, but that is now not expected to happen until 2018–19. While the government remained committed to most of its plans made in 2010, there was to be less growth than expected, which subsequently reduced the amount of money the government collected in taxes. The warning of extended austerity was based on the experience in Canada in the 1980s and 1990s, when the government needed to bring the budget deficit under control: 'If the UK experience proves to be as drawn out as the Canadian one, we should expect not just 2015 but also 2020 to be an austerity election', the briefing said (BBC 2013). Some of us actually think that it will take longer than that and austerity will be the economic orthodoxy in Europe for the foreseeable future. This certainly was the context in which the youth justice system would operate under the Coalition and which it is likely to do for sometime at least.

The Big Society

The Big Society is a political ideology that was developed during the early twenty-first century and which proposes 'integrating the free market with a theory of social solidarity based on hierarchy and voluntarism'. It is conceptually founded on a mix of a Conservative variant of communitarianism and libertarian paternalism. Its origins can be traced back to the 1990s, and to early attempts to develop a non-Thatcherite or post-Thatcherite brand of UK conservatism such as that proposed by David Willets and his Civic Conservatism[2] and the revival of Red Toryism[3] (Blond 2010). Some commentators propose that the 'Big Society' evokes Edmund Burke's idea of civil society and thus the concept can be clearly located in the context of one-nation conservatism[4] (Norman 2010).

The term 'Big Society' was devised by Steve Hilton as director of strategy for the Conservative Party, and the idea is particularly associated with party leader David Cameron, who was a strong supporter. The idea became the flagship policy of the 2010 UK Conservative Party general election manifesto and formed part of the subsequent legislative programme of the Conservative–Liberal Democrat Coalition Agreement. The intention was to create a climate that empowered local people and communities, building a 'big society' that would take power away from politicians and give it to people.

Cameron, now prime minister, launched the initiative in July 2010 with a speech at Liverpool Hope University, where he was accompanied by screenwriter and television producer Phil Redmond.[5] Five main priorities were outlined: first, more powers were to be given to local communities through a process of localism and devolution; second, people were to be encouraged to take an active role in their communities through volunteerism; third, power was to be transferred from central to local government; fourth, support was to be given to co-ops, mutual societies, charities and social enterprises; and fifth, there was a promise of open/ transparent government, not least through the publication of government data (Norman 2010).

The proposed plans included setting up a Big Society Bank and a Big Society Network to fund projects, and introducing a National Citizen Service. Lord Wei, one of the founders of the Teach First charity, was appointed by David Cameron to advise the government on the Big Society programme and carried out the role until May 2011, when Shaun Bailey and Charlotte Leslie were moved into the Cabinet Office to work on the project (Szreter and Ishkanian 2012).

The Big Society Network was established in 2010 in order to generate, develop and showcase new ideas to help people to come together in their neighbourhoods to do good things and was owned by a charity called the Society Network Foundation. During its first four years of existence, the organisation was funded with approximately £2 million of National Lottery money and public-sector grants. However, in July 2014, a National Audit Office report criticised the way that money was allocated to and used by the network and *The Independent* newspaper claimed that the Charity Commission had begun an investigation into alleged misuse of funds by the network. Later that year, the Big Society Network was put into administration, owing money to the government and an application was made to the Charity Commission to have the organisation wound up.

Big Society Capital, the Big Society Bank, was launched in 2011. Major UK banks agreed to provide £200 million in funding for the organisation in addition to money made available from dormant bank accounts under the Dormant Bank and Building Society Accounts Act 2008. The UK government's intention was to unlock £78bn in charitable assets for the 'Big Society' and in order to create a demand for the funds, it was announced that up to 25 per cent of public service contracts were to be transferred to the private and voluntary sector. The Big Society Awards were established in November 2010 in order to recognise community work done in the UK that demonstrates the 'Big Society'. Over fifty awards had been presented by the start of 2015. The National Citizen Service is a voluntary personal and social development programme for 16- and 17-year-olds in England. It was piloted in 2011 and two years later there were 30,000 young people taking part. The Localism Act 2011 contained a section on community empowerment with new rights created for charitable trusts, voluntary bodies and others to apply to local authorities to carry out services provided by the authority. In addition, lists of *Assets of Community Value* were compiled which included shops, pubs and playing fields, which were privately owned, but which were of value to the community. If such an asset was later sold, the Act made it easier for the community to bid for and take over the asset. Free schools (otherwise known as charter schools) were introduced by the Academies Act 2010, making it possible for parents, teachers, charities and businesses to set up and run their own schools. Between 2010 and 2015 more than 400 free schools were approved for opening in England, representing more than 230,000 school places across the country (Gregory and Joseph 2015).

While some responded to the policy favourably and David Cameron continued to defend it, its aims were questioned by other commentators from all sides of the political spectrum. In March 2010, the *Daily Telegraph* wrote: 'we demand vision from our would-be leaders, and here is one who offers a big one, of a society rebuilt from the ground up'. In April 2010, *The Times* described the 'Big Society' as 'an impressive attempt to reframe the role of government and unleash entrepreneurial spirit'. Later in the same year (and now post-election), *The Spectator* said that 'Cameron hoped to lessen financial shortfalls by raiding dormant bank accounts. It's a brilliant idea in theory' (Szreter and Ishkanian 2012).

Questions were now asked concerning originality. Two days after the launch of the initiative in Liverpool, an article in the *Liverpool Daily Post* argued that community organisations in the city such as Bradbury Fields show that Cameron's ideas are already in action and are nothing new, and that groups of community-based volunteers have for many years provided 'a better service than would be achieved through the public sector'. Simon Parker, director of the New Local Government Network, nevertheless responded that although 'there is little in the coalition government's agenda that is entirely novel, what is new is the scale of change required'. While Ben Rogers, in an opinion piece published in the *Financial Times*, suggested that 'the most interesting thing about [Cameron's] speech [to the Conservative Party Conference] were its sections on the "Big Society"', and that 'most of the political problems Mr Cameron faces, from cutting crime to reducing obesity, can only be met if residents and citizens play their part'. However, Rogers went on to say that 'the state has so far invested very little in teaching the skills that could help people make a contribution', thus highlighting what he perceived to be a fundamental flaw in the programme. David Cameron responded that the policy's lack of novelty did not detract from its usefulness and that it should be judged on its results (Szreter and Ishkanian 2012).

The implementation of the Big Society policies nevertheless coincided with large-scale cuts in public expenditure programmes, which were implemented to address the aforementioned macro-economic concerns. In 2010 David Cameron indicated that such cuts were temporary and to be enacted purely from economic necessity. However, in 2013 he said he had no intention of resuming spending once the structural deficit had been eliminated, since his aim was to create a 'leaner, more efficient state'. This led critics to conclude that the Big Society is merely a mechanism for reducing the size of the state. Labour leader Ed Miliband said that the Conservatives were 'cynically attempting to dignify its cuts agenda, by dressing up the withdrawal of support with the language of reinvigorating civic society and suggested that the Big Society is a "cloak for the small state"' (Gregory and Joseph 2015).

Of the political weeklies, the *New Statesman* said 'Cameron's hope that the Big Society will replace Big Government is reminiscent of the old Marxist belief that the state will "wither away" as a result of victorious socialism. We all know how that turned out. Cameron has a long way to go to convince us that his vision is any less utopian.' Also referring to Marx, the award-winning political cartoonist Steve Bell in *The Guardian* on 21 January 2011 and the *Guardian Weekly* newspaper a week later adapted Marx's slogan 'From each according to his ability, to each according to his need' for the Big Society: '*from each according to their vulnerability, to each according to their greed*' (Gregory and Joseph 2015).

Loira Charlesworth (2010) compared the system to the Old Poor Law, and suggested that 'any voluntary system for the relief of poverty is purely mythical'; while Anna Coote, head of Social Policy at the independent think tank New Economic Forum, wrote that 'if the state is pruned so drastically . . . the effect will be a more troubled and diminished society, not a bigger one'. In November 2010 a report by NEF suggested that 'there are strong, sensible ideas at the heart of the "Big Society" vision . . . [but] for all its potential [it] raises a lot of questions, which become more urgent and worrying in the light of public spending cuts'. TUC general secretary Brendan Barber concluded that 'the logic of this is that [Cameron's] ideal society is Somalia where the state barely exists'. Cameron responded by observing that the Big Society ideology pre-dated the implementation of cuts to public services, that the reduction in the size of the state had become inevitable, and that Big Society projects are worthwhile whatever the state of the economy (Gregory and Joseph 2015).

Ed West in the *Daily Telegraph* predicted in 2010 that 'The Big Society can never take off', placing the blame on the socialist ideology held by some of the British public. Mary Riddell, also writing in the *Daily Telegraph*, said 'the sink or swim society is upon us, and woe betide the poor, the frail, the old, the sick and the dependent', whilst Gerald Warner felt that 'of all the Blairesque chimeras pursued by David Cameron, none has more the resonance of a political epitaph than "Big Society"'. Sir Stephen Bubb, chief executive of ACEVO, welcomed the idea of the Big Society but claimed that David Cameron was 'undermining' it. His concerns were about cuts in government money going to charities coming 'too far and too fast'. He later said the project had become a 'wreck'. Steven Kettell of the University of Warwick wrote of the intrinsic 'problems surrounding the government's call to put religious groups at the centre of the Big Society agenda' (Gregory and Joseph 2015).

In April 2012 criticisms were raised concerning the shortage of Big Society policies across government, such as the lack of employee-owned mutuals and social enterprises, in public sector reforms, as well as the introduction of a cap on tax relief for charitable giving in the 2012 Budget. A report published in May 2012 suggested that the £3.3 billion cuts in government funding to the voluntary sector between 2012 and 2015 had greatly reduced the capacity of voluntary groups to implement Big Society projects. Bernard Collier expressed concern that the policy's lack of localism was 'favouring big charities' and ignoring the 'potential contribution of local voluntary and community organisations' (Gregory and Joseph 2015).

In 2014, former Cameron aide Danny Kruger claimed that although the relevant legislation had been put in place, the policy had been downgraded from its original role due to a lack of leadership. At the same time, a Centre for Social Justice report suggested that the policy was having least effect in the poorest areas in the country where it would be most useful. Cameron responded that the public sector had already failed to prevent the poorest parts of the country becoming so, and that there were examples of the Big Society having been effective in poor areas (Gregory and Joseph 2015).

During the course of the 2010–15 government, the Big Society declined as an instrument of government policy. Cameron did not use the term in public after 2013 and the phrase ceased to be used in government statements. The collapse of the Big Society Network in 2014 and criticism of the prime minister's relationship with it were followed by a critical final Big Society Audit published by *Civil Exchange* in January 2015 which highlighted cuts in charity grants and restrictions on the right to challenge government policy through the courts as undermining Big Society ideals. It was noted that charities have had a decreasing role as government contractors due to policies which favoured the private sector and pointed out that the centralisation of the British political system has not significantly decreased, with no noticeable upsurge in volunteering and social action concentrated in the wealthiest places. The Cabinet Office responded that the *Civil Exchange* report did not fairly reflect 'the significant progress made'. In response to a parliamentary question claiming that the Big Society had failed, the government said that 'cynics' were 'entirely wrong' and that 'some of the changes we have introduced are irreversible'. Shortly before the 2015 election, David Cameron proposed a law that would give some employees the right to three days of paid annual leave to do voluntary work. The proposal appeared in the Party's manifesto, along with a guarantee of a place on the National Citizen Service for all children and an increase in the use of social impact bonds. However, the Big Society did not form a significant part of the Conservative Party's election strategy, being replaced instead by an emphasis on economic stability and border controls (Gregory and Joseph 2015).

Coalition youth justice policy

Following the 2010 general election and the creation of the Coalition, the government announced plans to abolish the Youth Justice Board and locate the role of dealing with youth offending within the Ministry of Justice as part of its cost-cutting axing of over 150 government quangos.[6] In November 2011 the government – on the verge of being defeated in the House of Lords on the issue – relented and announced that the YJB would not be abolished. The Ministry of Justice said the youth justice system still needed reform, but 'following careful consideration', the board would be saved. For Labour, Shadow Justice Secretary Sadiq Khan welcomed the government change of mind and observed that the YJB has a proven track record in reducing crime and that is why so many groups campaigned for its survival with such enthusiasm, although he added that the work of the board was 'still being undermined by severe cuts to youth offending teams, which work within communities to cut crime and anti-social behaviour'. Juliet Lyon, director of the Prison Reform Trust, said the government had 'shown that it is prepared to listen to reason . . . [and that] by holding on to the Youth Justice Board it can build on an impressive drop in youth crime and continue to reduce the numbers of children and young people getting into trouble' (Grimwood and Strickland 2013).

The reprieve for the YJB was widely popular among penal pressure groups and, indeed, among critical criminologists who had never previously favoured the board. Opposition to abolition was now focused on concerns that its replacement by a unit within the Ministry of Justice would mean the gradual erosion of an independent focus on youth justice issues within Whitehall. Losing the joint sponsorship of the YJB by the Department for Education was bad enough, but incorporation by a prison service-dominated national offender management service would have been catastrophic for youth justice (Grimwood and Strickland 2013).

The YJB had never been allowed to express much of an independent voice and the current board found favour with penal pressure groups and among liberal opinion in the House of Lords because there were, in Kenneth Clarke and Crispin Blunt, government ministers who were trying to reduce the number of young people entering the justice system. The YJB shared that ambition.

This had not been the case under New Labour, who had closed what it called the 'justice gap' by setting targets for offences brought to justice. Publicly questioning the wisdom of those policies was regarded by Labour home secretaries as treachery, as a previous chief executive Rod Morgan had discovered. The latter observed that it was easy to mock the idea of the 'Big Society', particularly during a period of stringent public expenditure cuts, but observed, as we saw above, that it was intended as more than volunteering. The intention was to devolve responsibility for budgets and priority setting, and restoring to professional decision-makers the exercise of discretion and the relief of frontline staff from excessive bureaucracy. The YJB had not previously been a progressive guide in this regard and the existence of a central policy quango would be positioned uncomfortably with a policy of localisation (Morgan 2010).

The support for the survival of the Youth Justice Board which now arose from youth offending team managers requires some cautious reflection. Their status within local authority structures had been strengthened by their proclaimed accountability to the YJB, yet rather than becoming the multidisciplinary teams working in close partnership with children's services that was originally envisaged, YOTs may have actually become criminal justice silos with the arguments for and against abolition of the YJB finely balanced (Morgan 2010).

An evaluation of New Labour's youth justice reforms by the National Audit Office in 2004 noted improvements brought about by the Youth Justice Board but pointed to weaknesses in the management of sentence delivery and the development of the custodial estate (National Audit Office 2004). In the same year, the Audit Commission found that the new system was a considerable improvement on the old one, with young offenders being dealt with more quickly and being more likely to receive an intervention, although it also made some criticisms (Audit Commission 2004). In 2006 the Centre for Crime and Justice Studies (CCJS) based at King's College London had called for a 'fundamental shift' in approach which should consist of: (1) greater prevention, with an emphasis on addressing the educational and mental health difficulties underlying much offending behaviour; (2) limits placed on the way we criminalise young people with a more appropriate system of prosecution and courts; (3) a wider range of community-based and residential provision for the most challenging young people and a phasing out of prison custody; and (4) new organisational arrangements, with the Children's Department in the Department for Education and Skills taking the lead (Garside and McMahon 2006).

In May 2008, the CCJS published a further audit of Labour's youth justice reforms, which suggested that problems still remained: despite the huge investment, self-reported youth offending had not declined and the principal aim of the youth justice system set out in the Crime and Disorder Act 1998, 'to prevent offending by children and young persons', had not been achieved in any significant sense. Fundamental questions needed to be asked about whether the youth justice agencies could really address the complex economic and social factors which it was recognised are the cause of so much youth offending. Thus, more effective solutions need to be found outside the youth justice system in the delivery of coordinated services through mainstream local authority children's and young people's provision and more effective children's services (Solomon and Garside 2008).

A major review of the governance and operating arrangements of the Youth Justice Board, by Dame Sue Street, was published in March 2010 and argued that much had changed, much had been achieved, but the YJB should be strengthened. It was observed that in order to make future progress, build on its success and adapt to the changing world in which it operated, the YJB needed to take a firm grip of its responsibilities, provide clearer leadership and direction on the delivery of youth justice and prioritise public protection alongside the welfare of young people. This would mean having a strong YJB with clarity of role and relationships, delivering better outcomes for young people and their communities, and using its unique position between central and local government to provide trusted and expert advice to ministers (Street 2010).

There are a number of policy papers and speeches which show the development and themes of Conservative Party criminal and youth justice policy. In a Green Paper 'Prisons with a Purpose' published in March 2008, the Conservatives described the need for reform to the prison system which should, they said, be in the spirit of Jeremy Bentham and Elizabeth Fry. Youth crime and the needs of young offenders would nevertheless be considered separately with the party publishing its contract for young people in May 2010. In the section on crime, the contract promised to focus support on prevention and intervention to tackle youth crime in the most deprived communities. In its manifesto, the party again referred to the importance of rehabilitation as a means of reducing reoffending and suggested that young offenders would receive specialist support in education, mentoring and drug rehabilitation. In order to reform the system of rehabilitation further, it was proposed to: (1) apply the party's flagship criminal justice policy 'payment by results' reforms[7] to the youth justice system; (2) engage with specialist organisations to provide education, mentoring and drug rehabilitation programmes to help young offenders go straight; and (3) pilot a scheme to create Prison and Rehabilitation Trusts so that just one organisation is responsible for helping to stop a criminal reoffending. The Liberal Democrats, in their 2010 general election manifesto, set out proposals which would '[make] the justice system work to rehabilitate criminals and reduce crime' and did not distinguish between adult and young offenders (Grimwood and Strickland 2013).

The Coalition document published on 20 May 2010 mentioned the government's aims for the justice system but made no explicit mention of young offenders, although it did announce a review of sentencing. One change that was made quickly after the government took office was the assumption by the Ministry of Justice of all responsibility for youth justice – a responsibility which had been previously shared between the Ministry of Justice and the Department for Education. In announcing the change, the Ministry of Justice suggested it would increase clarity and accountability and there was speculation that the Youth Justice Board might be abolished as part of moves to save money but, as we have seen above, these changes did not take place (Grimwood and Strickland 2013).

Changes to out of court disposals for young people were made by the Legal Aid, Sentencing and Punishment of Offenders Act 2012, which abolished reprimands and warnings and introduced youth cautions. The intention of the new disposal is to provide a proportionate and effective response to offending behaviour which could be used for any offence provided that the statutory criteria are satisfied: first, the police are satisfied that there is sufficient evidence to charge the youth with an offence; second, the youth admits the offence to the police; and third, the police do not consider that the youth should be prosecuted or given a youth conditional caution for the offence. The police nevertheless cannot issue a youth caution for an offence that is indictable only in the case of an adult without the authority of the CPS. Significantly, there was now no statutory restriction on the number of youth cautions that a youth can receive and, moreover, the person may receive a youth caution even if he or she has previous convictions, reprimands, warnings, youth cautions and youth conditional cautions. These were to be significant changes which reversed the orthodoxy introduced at the outset of the contemporary youth justice system and we will revisit this point when we examine the workings of the system in detail in the following two chapters.

A further proposed change was to be a substantially increased use of restorative justice strategies building on the role being performed by volunteer youth offender panel members and by ensuring that referral orders would have a strengthened restorative approach. The intention was to support panel members to increase their skills and confidence in using restorative justice in referral orders where the victim was prepared to participate. It was recognised that restorative justice was already a key part of the youth justice system but the Coalition wanted to encourage a much wider implementation, drawing on the experience of successful youth conferencing in Northern Ireland. The intention was to ensure the effective use of sentencing for young offenders and simplify out of court disposals while, at the same time, proposing greater use of discretion by the police and prosecutors (Grimwood and Strickland 2013).

A further Green Paper, 'Transforming Youth Custody – Putting Education at the Heart of Detention', was published in February 2013. Again, the government set out the case for change and argued that while the principal aim of the youth justice system is to prevent offending by children and young people, it should achieve this through a combination of preventative early intervention, punishment for those who break the law and rehabilitation to get young offenders back on the right track.

The paper argued that the system was failing, particularly in the context of youth offending and reoffending. Thus, as we have seen earlier in this book, 73 per cent of young offenders who are released from custody reoffend within twelve months, which suggests that the vast majority of those in youth custody were already set upon a life of crime, while a period in detention was having little or no impact on the likelihood that they would break the law again and continue on a career trajectory that will inevitably lead to adult prison. The paper recognised that the boys and girls in youth custody are some of the most complex and disengaged in society, and their behaviours have often become entrenched despite the hard work of some dedicated practitioners. It was nevertheless argued that this is not an excuse, either for them or for the youth justice system, not to do better (Grimwood and Strickland 2013).

Custody, it was proposed, may actually represent a rare period of stability in otherwise chaotic lives, and as such presents a key opportunity to set these young people on the path to a better life, combining the education and wider support that motivates, challenges and achieves results with young people, and which can be continued and built upon after release. This, the paper said, called for a significant programme of cross-government reform with the emphasis on improving education. The vast majority of young people in custody had at some point been excluded from school and about half of those entering Young Offender Institutions (YOIs) had literacy or numeracy levels well below those expected at their age. The quality of education in the youth secure estate was observed to be patchy and young offenders often missed out on the required hours of education. Poor educational achievement and engagement were linked to an increased risk of offending and so education was central to the response to this problem. The Children and Families Bill would introduce Education, Health and Care Plans for young people with the most complex needs and would place duties on local authorities and YOTs to work together when assessing the needs of young offenders with special educational needs. YOTs would thus be involved when local authorities drew up Education, Health and Care Plans for young people who had been in custody (Grimwood and Strickland 2013).

The Green Paper argued that with such disappointing results, the costs of youth custody – at an average cost of £100,000 per annum per place – were far too high. Efficiencies were expected to yield savings across the youth secure estate by 2014/15, but a new approach could drive down costs still further and the case for change was (it was argued) compelling. Contracts for many secure training centres and secure children's homes, as well as for education provision in public sector YOIs, were due to expire in 2013 and 2014. The Ministry of Justice was continuing to adjust the capacity of the youth secure estate, to match demand. These factors meant that now was a good time, it was argued, to take a fresh look and to consider a 'truly transformative' new approach. The paper's 'vision for reform' produced four significant proposals. First, education would be at the heart of the proposed radical reforms to youth custody. Second, building on the reforms brought about by the Free Schools and Alternative Provision and Special Free Schools programmes and the government's curriculum reforms, Secure Colleges – to be provided by a diverse range of providers, drawing in both education expertise and security experience (perhaps in strategic partnerships) – would have education at their heart. Third, education would be tailored to young people in custody. Depending on the background and prior experience of the young offender, this might encompass basic educational skills such as literacy and numeracy, higher-level qualifications or vocational skills. Moreover, with the raising of the school participation age to 17 from 2013 and 18 from 2015, post-16 provision should reflect mainstream provision. Fourth, there should be structure and rigour in the education provided, which might be delivered in classrooms, vocational workshops or through music, sport or catering at mealtimes (Grimwood and Strickland 2013).

The consultation paper also observed that young people in custody (some of whom would be looked-after children or care leavers) often had social, emotional and health needs which needed to be taken into consideration because without that, they might not make educational progress. It was observed that health providers and those who could help offenders develop thinking skills and improved emotional well-being could play a part here in helping young offenders to turn their lives around. The paper observed that the comparatively small number of girls in the custodial population had many complex needs and some aspects of custody impacted differently on them. It was thus crucial that custody met their needs. Specialist provision should continue to be available for those children in custody who were especially damaged and in need of support services (Grimwood and Strickland 2013).

Box 11.1 outlines the prevailing cost-effective model of youth justice during the years of the Coalition government. At a time of major economic recession and a perceived need for austerity socio-economic policies, this is an approach to youth justice based on the need to obtain value for money and thus reducing the expense of intervention very much in contrast to the high-cost approach of its New Labour predecessor.

Box 11.1 The cost-effective model of youth justice

- Based on the notion that there should be proportionate and effective response to offending.
- Custodial sentences should only be used as a last resort with a greater use of cautioning and restorative justice interventions.
- Emphasis on prevention, early intervention and keeping young people out of the youth justice system.
- Emphasis on professional discretion, localism and less central government control.
- A cost-effective approach to youth offending located in the context of austerity socio-economic policies.

Postscript: general election 2015 – the Conservatives prevail

The general election held on 7 May 2015 provided the Conservative Party with an overall majority and the ability to govern without the need for a Coalition partner. It is clearly early days at the time of writing (August 2015) and there are so far no clear suggestions as to the future of government youth justice policy agenda and whether or not they will continue to pursue the cost-effective approach of their coalition predecessors. We will return to possible futures for the youth justice system in the final part of this book. In the following chapter we will consider the parameters of the contemporary youth justice system established by New Labour and the Crime and Disorder Act 1998 and reflect on this in the context of the changes brought about by the Coalition Government 2010–15.

Summary of main points

1 The New Labour government was elected in May 1997 and announced that the long-established juvenile justice system was to be replaced with a new youth justice system via the auspices of the newly created Youth Justice Board for England and Wales with a significantly large budget which epitomised the self-confident optimistic times.

2 The 2008 credit crunch was one element of a global financial crisis that was to lead to a major (indeed, unprecedented in recent times) economic recession, with many business collapses, rising unemployment and, in many countries (such as the UK), a new austerity politics aimed at reducing high and unsustainable levels of national debt.

3 The 2010 British general election produced an inconclusive result with no single party able to form a government, with the eventual outcome being that the first coalition government since the Second World War was formed between the Conservatives and the Liberal Democrats.

4 Austerity measures remain very much in place following the 2015 general election and influential voices have foreseen their long-term continuation.

5 The Big Society is a political ideology that was developed during the early twenty-first century and which proposes 'integrating the free market with a theory of social solidarity based on hierarchy and voluntarism'. It is conceptually founded on a mix of a Conservative variant of communitarianism and libertarian paternalism.

6 The implementation of the Big Society policies coincided with large-scale cuts in public expenditure programmes which were implemented to address the aforementioned macro-economic concerns. During the course of the 2010–15 government, the Big Society declined as an instrument of government policy.

7 Following the 2010 general election and the creation of the Coalition, the government announced plans to abolish the Youth Justice Board and locate the role of dealing with youth offending within the Ministry of Justice as part of its cost-cutting axing of over 150 government quangos.

8   In November 2011, the government relented and announced that the YJB would not be abolished. The reprieve for the YJB was widely popular among penal pressure groups and, indeed, among critical criminologists who had never previously favoured the board.

9   An evaluation of New Labour's youth justice reforms by the National Audit Office in 2004 noted improvements brought about by the Youth Justice Board but pointed to weaknesses in the management of sentence delivery and the development of the custodial estate.

10   The Coalition document published on 20 May 2010 mentioned the government's aims for the justice system but made no explicit mention of young offenders, although it did announce a review of sentencing.

Discussion questions

1   What brought about the Conservative and Liberal Democrat Coalition?
2   What is the Big Society and how successful has it been?
3   Why was the Youth justice Board not abolished as originally planned?
4   What youth justice policy initiatives were introduced by the Coalition government?
5   What do you consider will guide Conservative youth justice policies in the following years?

Notes

1   It is worth elaborating on these events in some detail because a) they have provided the socio-economic conditions in which youth justice and, indeed, the wider public sector will have to operate for the foreseeable future and b) very many people in the UK believe the subsequent Conservative Party propaganda that the Labour Party itself was fully responsible for the global economic collapse. Not only is that argument clearly untrue but also, at the time, the Conservative Party in opposition fully supported the economic measures taken by the government to avert economic disaster and were prepared to match their spending plans at the time of the 2005 general election.

2   'Civic conservatism' is a form of modern conservatism developed by the Conservative intellectual David Willetts, which was introduced in his 1995 pamphlet 'Civic Conservatism'. The idea focuses on the institutions between the state and individuals as a policy concern rather than merely thinking of individuals and the state as the only agencies. The pamphlet wished to 'place the free market in the context of institutions and values which make up civil society'. The examples of these institutions were the 'network of voluntary organisations', from hospitals to guilds, which had been 'weakened if not destroyed by the advance of the State' (Willetts 1995: 15–18).

3   A Red Tory is an adherent of a progressive Conservative political philosophy, tradition and disposition in Canada similar to the High Tory tradition in the UK and is contrasted with 'Blue Tory' or 'Small-c'.

4   One-nation conservatism is a form of British political conservatism that views society as organic and values paternalism and pragmatism. The phrase 'One-nation Tory' originated with Benjamin Disraeli (1804–81) who became Conservative prime minister in February 1868. He devised it to appeal to working-class men as a solution to worsening divisions in society. As a political philosophy, one-nation conservatism reflects the belief that societies exist and develop organically, and that members within them

have obligations towards each other. There is particular emphasis on the paternalistic obligation of the upper classes to those classes below them.

5 Phil Redmond CBE (born 10 June 1949) is an English television producer and screen-writer from Huyton, Lancashire, who is well known for creating several popular television series such as *Grange Hill* (BBC One, 1978–2008), *Brookside* (Channel 4, 1982–2003) and *Hollyoaks* (Channel 4, 1995–). For over twenty years he also ran his own independent production company, Mersey Television, before selling the company in 2005. Redmond also created the daytime legal drama, *The Courtroom*, which was cancelled after thirty-eight episodes.

6 A quango is a semi-public administrative body outside the civil service but receiving financial support from the government, which makes senior appointments to it.

7 Payment by results (PBR) is a new form of financing that makes payments contingent on the independent verification of results. PBR is a cross-government reform priority.

12 The contemporary youth justice system

Key issues

1   The Youth Justice Board and youth offending teams
2   Radical new measures
3   The youth Court and its disposals
4   The Coalition and a decline in entry to the youth justice system

In this chapter we consider the parameters of the contemporary youth justice system established by the Crime and Disorder Act 1998, subsequent changes that were made and developments that occurred during the period of the New Labour governments between 1997 and 2010, and subsequent changes that were made and occurred following the general election in 2010 and the Coalition agreement between the Conservatives and the Liberal Democrats.

The Youth Justice Board and youth offending teams

The Youth Justice Board (YJB) for England and Wales was established by the Crime and Disorder Act 1998 (CDA 1998) and is a non-departmental public body, sponsored by the Home Office, which supervises the operation of youth offending teams (YOTs) and all those working in the contemporary youth justice system as a whole.[1] The CDA 1998 placed a statutory duty on the YJB and all those working in the contemporary youth justice system to give primary consideration to the principal aim of preventing offending by children and young people and this was to be achieved through six key objectives: first, the swift administration of justice; second, ensuring that young people face up to the consequences of their offending; third, ensuring that the risk factors associated with offending are addressed in any intervention; fourth, ensuring that punishment is proportionate to the seriousness and frequency of offending; fifth, encouraging reparation by young offenders to their victims; and sixth, reinforcing parental responsibility.

The CDA 1998 significantly introduced new structures at local and national level in order to provide the framework of an institutional youth offending response. Youth offending teams brought together staff and wider resources from the police, social services, the Probation Service, and education and health in the delivery of youth justice services, with the scope to involve others, including the voluntary sector, in a multi-agency response.[2]

D.W. Jones (2001) observed an openly acknowledged New Labour YJB policy of suppressing all youth justice knowledge and practice prior to the introduction of the new system but, at the same time, noted a widespread challenge to this 'year zero' thesis from academics and practitioners. Thus, Goldson (1999) had been concerned from the outset that youth justice practitioners with extensive prior experience and expertise in working with offending children and young people had been disillusioned and alienated by the speed of change and called for a return to first principles, citing the substitution of 'offending' for 'justice' in the title of the new practitioner teams which, he argued, symbolised a move whereupon those in trouble were to be considered primarily 'offenders' rather than 'children' as under the previous juvenile justice regime (Goldson 2000a). Walsh (1999) similarly noted in this context that the new contemporary youth justice system appeared to be more concerned with the maintenance of social order than with the welfare of the child; Goldson (2000b) perceived 'crude' policy formulations invariably 'underpinned by condemnatory rhetoric'; and Campbell (1999) accused the government of considering children to be 'an unruly constituency' to be patrolled, policed and trained, which – as the evidence presented in this book shows – is absolutely nothing new and has been the case since the beginnings of industrial modernity and the social construction of notions of childhood, adolescence and delinquency. Hogg (1999) observed the CDA 1998 to be simply 'the latest step to enforce social cohesion by coercion' and a major challenge to the principles of the Children Act 1989 which had prioritised the welfare of the child.[3] Muncie (1999b: 59) noted that under the new regime misbehaviour and crime were now synonymous and that 'a logic of prevention' and 'risk management' was being used to justify any number of repressive and retrograde strategies for intervening in the lives of young people in trouble. He considered this to be part of 'the dehumanisation of the youth crime issue' at the expense of cost-effective management performance indicators and observed a contemporary 'institutionalised intolerance' (Muncie 1999c). Diduck (1999) noted that 'the rhetoric of morality trips off the tongues of both the New Right and the New Labour communitarianism'.

Concerns about the limited resources estimated by the government to implement the new system were expressed by various commentators, who, at the same time, acknowledged that these were rather optimistically dependent on savings to be made elsewhere in the system (Cavadino 1997a; Padfield 1998). Newburn (1998) raised similar concerns about the need for appropriate levels of funding for YOTs.

Others observed significant potential problems with the whole notion of multi-agency working in the context of the new youth justice system. Goldson (2000a) thus proposed that the distancing of the management and accountability of YOTs from social services children and family teams would lead to the welfare needs of children being undermined and replaced by a focus on their offending. Muncie (1999b) expressed disquiet about the likelihood of maintaining equity of power and influence between the different agencies; Jackson (1999: 142) identified 'little acknowledgement of differing agency policies, practices, philosophies and priorities'; while Harvey (2000: 141) added that 'different social agencies have different histories, agendas and responsibilities – reflected in very different cultures and discourses'. Progressive developments in the contemporary youth justice system were nevertheless subsequently identified, which can be attributed to close and committed inter-agency working (Smith 2007).

Pickford (2000: 10–11) nevertheless noted that the new system brought with it the inevitability of net-widening and, therefore, 'even greater State intervention in, and control of, the lives of marginalised communities lacking social or economic power', arguing that YOT practitioners 'represent occupations which have a tendency to categorise any anti-social behaviour as troublesome and as requiring a more punitive approach'. Smith (2007: 208) subsequently observed the accuracy of the net-widening prediction noting pertinently that:

> As they move into the criminal sphere, more young people are being formally processed (rather than receiving informal sanction); they are being drawn into the justice system younger, for more relatively minor offences; and they are experiencing formal and recordable disposals earlier in their offending careers. The loss of the option to administer second and subsequent cautions following the 1998 legislation almost certainly ensures quicker progression to court, where the option of a Conditional Discharge is effectively removed, and more demanding and intrusive programmes are imposed at an earlier stage, effectively compressing the sentence tariff. At the same time, the opportunities for non-compliance, failure and breach action are inevitably increased.

Radical new measures

The Crime and Disorder Act 1998 introduced radical new measures with the intention of transforming the youth justice system. Thus, crucial to this new system was the replacement of police cautioning with reprimands and final warnings. Reprimands were now given to first-time offenders for minor offences but *any* subsequent offending – and these included minor offences – would result in either a final warning or a charge. For some the net-widening inevitability of these provisions was apparent from the beginning. Muncie (1999b) expressed concern that young people were being consistently set up to fail; while Justice (2000) observed the lack of explicit legal assistance that was to be made available to children who could acquire a criminal record at an early stage of their lives. Bell (1999: 202) noted that as 'the police are particularly poor judges of the quality of their own evidence' many young people were 'likely to accept a Final Warning (and the consequent criminal record) in cases where the evidence did not merit it' while the police would assume 'the role of investigator, prosecutor, judge and jury'. Butler and Drakeford (1997: 218) found incomprehensible the replacement of a cautioning system which they – and many practitioners – considered to have been 'the one demonstrable success of youth justice in the United Kingdom since the war'.[4] The Youth Justice Board (2002) subsequently acknowledged an increase from 52 per cent to 70 per cent in the use of final warning programmes during the period 2000 to 2001/2, despite significant evidence that questioned their value (Hine and Celnick 2001).

The final warning inevitably initiated an immediate referral – via a referral order – to a local YOT, which would then assess the young person and – unless considered inappropriate – prepare a rehabilitation, or 'change', programme designed to tackle the reasons for the offending behaviour in order to prevent any repeat episodes. This process of risk assessment was also to involve contacting the victim to assess whether victim/offender mediation (restorative justice) or some form of reparation to the victim or community would be appropriate. Wonnacott (1999: 287) nevertheless argued that the idea of the 'contract' – between the young person and the YOT – which underpins the notion of the referral order is a deception, because it is based on a fundamental imbalance of power and concludes that 'a contract agreed under compulsion is not a contract at all'. Ball (2000) argued that these orders would fail to achieve the desired twin objectives of restorative justice and reduction of youth offending and, moreover, could well result in disproportionate sentencing for minor, first offenders, and more severe punishment of those who are unable to keep to their 'contract'.

Wedd (2000) argued that the referral order placed the reflexive practitioner into potential conflict with their client and that the likely outcome would be an institutionalised bullying and unfairness, arguing that 'being invited to agree to a contract in a room full of adults may make the youngster feel under unfair pressure', and urged solicitors to arrange to be outside the panel hearing and for the young offender to seek legal advice if in doubt about the proceedings (see also Ashford and Chard 2000). Goldson (2000b) suggested that the referral order could well be incompatible with international treaties, standards and rules for youth justice; while Crawford and Newburn (2003) later observed that the principle of 'voluntarism' had now been eradicated from all stages of the youth justice process and that the failure to comply – or the commission of further offences – would put young people on the fast track to a 'persistent young offender' designation, therefore qualifying them for even more intrusive forms of constraint and surveillance, regardless of the gravity of their actions. These orders and processes undoubtedly provided significant foundations for the net-widening propensities of the new youth justice system and were – as we saw in the previous chapter – to be replaced by a Coalition government highly concerned at the cost of administration.

The CDA 1998 introduced reparation orders, which require offenders to make specified reparation to their victim, if he or she consents, or to the community at large. Reparation might involve writing a letter of apology, apologising to the victim in person, cleaning graffiti or repairing criminal damage for which the offender has been responsible. The purpose of the order is to help young offenders understand and face up to the consequences of their actions, and offer some practical recompense to victims. The reparation must, however, be commensurate with the seriousness of the offence for which the order is being given, but may not exceed a total of twenty-four hours in aggregate. The YOT, meanwhile, is responsible for coordinating arrangements for the provision of reports to the courts and communicating with the victim to ascertain whether reparation is appropriate.[5]

There were, again, significant concerns about the implementation of reparation orders in practice. Dignan (2000), reporting on the evaluation of pilot projects, raised concerns about the inconsistency between the time necessary to engage sensitively with victims and the pressure to accelerate young offenders through the youth justice process. The same author – although a keen advocate of reparation and generally favourable to the orders – was concerned that they would become 'simply another way of punishing offenders', within the broader context of New Labour 'toughness' rhetoric, arguing that this would undermine their potential, as would the failure to seek consent of the offender, the absence of standards and safeguards for the restorative justice processes, and the 'hidden agenda' of punitiveness lying behind police support for the Orders (Dignan 1999). Akester (2000) argued that referral orders were likely to be undermined by the way that they are conceived in the CDA 1998, which was totally contradictory to the informality and flexibility that had been shown to work elsewhere; while Justice (2000) raised concerns that the procedures indicate the letter, but not the spirit, of cooperation. Bell (1999: 209) noted that Reparation Orders might well comprise a form of 'junior community service' which is contrary to child employment and health and safety laws, while Haines (2000) observed that the emphasis on the restorative principle removes the focus from the best interest of the child and transfers it to the victims. Walklate (1998: 220), meanwhile, argued that in reality very few orders had been applied for or granted but are there if the need should arise.

The long-established rule of *doli incapax*, which had presumed that a child under 14 does not know the difference between right and wrong, was to be 'modernised' by the CDA 1998.7 Cavadino was a major critic of the significant abolition of the rebuttable presumption that a child is *doli incapax* and is, therefore, incapable of understanding that certain behaviour is seriously wrong and the implications for them of becoming involved in such criminality. He observes that the existence of the presumption had previously made 'lawyers, magistrates and judges stop and think about the degree of responsibility of each individual child' aged 10–13 years (Cavadino 1997a: 4; Cavadino 1997b: 164). Ashford (1998) proposed that abolition would have 'dire consequences' for children, giving them criminal records from the age of 10; Fionda (1999) accused the government of 'a dangerous blindness to the incapacities of childhood'; while Haydon and Scraton (2000: 429) argued that the government had simply polarised 'serious wrong and simple naughtiness, without acknowledging the terrain that lies between'.

Morris and Gelsthorpe (2000), drawing on their significant experience in researching and monitoring the application of restorative justice in the Antipodes, also viewed the reparation order as being 'at odds with restorative values', observing that the family group conferences in the southern hemisphere were used for medium to serious offences or with persistent offenders. They observed that the British examples typically cited to support the reparation order – such as the Thames Valley Police project (Young and Goold 1999) – are located merely on the margins of the criminal justice system, deal with low-level incidents of criminality, and are often an alternative to 'no further action' or 'warnings'. Wasik (1999) argued that the orders fail to adequately address the complex issue of who really is the victim. Thus, if the parents of the offender are distressed by the offence, then they could be entitled to reparation. The legislation could clearly be interpreted in this way but, on the other hand, these very same parents can also be punished by a parenting order (see below).

The CDA 1998 introduced child safety orders, whereby a Family Proceedings Court can subject a child under the age of 10 to an order if they commit an act which might have been conceived as an offence if they were over 10 (the age of criminal responsibility), and child curfew schemes, to keep children in this age group off the streets. Both Fionda (1999: 45) and NAPO (1998) observed at the outset that these orders and schemes abandoned the minimum age of criminal responsibility via 'the back door' and effectively 'reduced the age of criminal responsibility to zero'.[6] Idriss (2001) proposed that curfew schemes are generally unworkable and in some cases members of the public have been put at risk. Piper (1999: 406) observed that the child safety order is essentially a supervision order (with requirements) but notes that it has none of the safeguards built into its use which govern other supervision orders, whether through welfare or criminal routes (see also Hayes and Williams 1999). The child supervision order was nevertheless never intended as a punishment. It was designed to help the child improve their behaviour and is likely to be used alongside work with the family and others to address any underlying problems.

The rule of *doli incapax*, which had presumed that a child under 14 does not know the difference between right and wrong, was to be 'modernised' by the CDA 1998. Paul Cavadino was one of the major critics of the significant abolition of the rebuttable presumption that a child is *doli incapax* and is, therefore, incapable of understanding that certain behaviour is seriously wrong and the implications for them of becoming involved in such criminality. He observed that the existence of the presumption had previously made 'lawyers, magistrates and judges stop and think about the degree of responsibility of each individual child' aged 10–13 years (Cavadino 1997a: 4; Cavadino 1997b: 166). Ashford (1998) proposed that abolition would have 'dire consequences' for children, giving them criminal records from the age of 10; Fionda (1999) accused the government of 'a dangerous blindness to the incapacities of childhood'; while Haydon and Scraton (2000: 429) argued that the government had simply polarised 'serious wrong and simple naughtiness, without acknowledging the terrain that lies between'.[7]

Some of the most concerted criticisms of any part of the CDA 1998 were in relation to the Anti-Social Behaviour Order (ASBO), which was a civil order designed to respond to alleged anti-social behaviour but with the power of imprisonment on breach (Ashworth et al. 1998). The minimum length of an ASBO was for two years and anyone from the age of 10 could become subject of an order if their behaviour is deemed to be anti-social. The actual content 'consist[ed] of prohibitions . . . [these] can range from prohibiting an individual from entering a specified area to a more general statement prohibiting them from acting in an anti-social manner in the local authority area' (Campbell 2002: 3).

Critics argued that the ASBO gave power to local officials to criminalise conduct in a way which was in total contradiction to other strategies to reduce social exclusion and that it had 'inappropriately low' standards of proof, could be made without the defendant being heard, and could prohibit conduct which was wholly legal. The ASBO was, moreover, originally introduced with the main aim of placing restrictions on the anti-social behaviour of adults, but that situation was to change and children seemingly became the main focus of concern (Howard League for Penal Reform 2005). Squires and Stephens (2005: 25) observed that 'much of the government's actions on anti-social behaviour have been driven precisely by a concern to address such perceptions about young people slipping "out of control"'.

Hopkins Burke and Morrill (2002, 2004) observed that the ASBO was a significant communitarian initiative introduced with the intention of protecting the rights of citizens whose lives have been blighted by others who behaved in anti-social ways in their communities, but concluded at that time that the balance may well have shifted too much in favour of communities at the expense of individual liberties and human rights. Due-process values had been sacrificed in the increased pursuit of crime control outcomes with, in particular, a worrying potential to absorb further – in a widening net – a whole group of relatively non-problematic young people who, left pretty much to themselves, it is argued, could probably grow out of their anti-social activities and become respectable members of society. The situation did not improve, with the excessive length and blanket coverage of some orders rendering them both extremely difficult to enforce and liable to the claim that they were simply irrational reactive responses to problems which could have been dealt with in another way (Smith 2007). Fletcher (2005), for example, alerts us to the case of a 15-year-old boy with Aspergers syndrome[8] who was made the subject of an ASBO with the condition that he did not stare over the neighbour's fence, which was a feature of his behaviour.

Many criticisms of the ASBO have their origins in the complexities found in defining the term 'anti-social behaviour' itself, with Burney (2005: 2) stating that the term 'has no clear identity'. The Home Office (2004) nevertheless defined anti-social behaviour as 'acting in a manner that caused or was likely to cause harassment, alarm or distress to one or more persons not of the same household (as the defendant)' and the following examples are cited: nuisance neighbours, rowdy and nuisance behaviour, yobbish behaviour and intimidating groups taking over public spaces and vandalism, graffiti and fly-posting. However, these are only a small selection of the behaviours and acts that were covered within the parameters of the guidance, although it is clear from just this small selection that the scope of this term is far reaching.

Even the legislation addressing anti-social behaviour failed to provide further clarity, which created inevitable difficulties in deciding what behaviours should be targeted as unacceptable and where usually acceptable behaviour becomes classified as anti-social. Squires (2006: 226) observed that 'there are potentially no limits to which can be construed as "antisocial behaviour"'. However, the Home Affairs Committee sees the openness of the phrase positively, concluding 'that this "flexibility" was more a positive feature than a negative one' (Thomas 2005: 6). This interpretation, it is argued, allows the community itself to decide what forms of unacceptable behaviour are having a negative impact upon them rather than having to abide by government guidelines prescribing what acts are to be considered within the parameters of anti-social behaviour.

In May 2012, the Coalition government announced plans to replace the ASBO (BBC 2012) and the Anti Social Behaviour Act 2014 subsequently replaced the now discredited order with the Criminal Behaviour Order (CBO). The government proposed that the new order would give agencies and communities what they needed to deal with the hard-core of persistently anti-social individuals who it was observed were also engaged in criminal activity. The court could thus make a criminal behaviour order against the offender if two conditions are met: first, the person has engaged in behaviour that caused or was likely to cause harassment, alarm or distress to one or more persons not of the same household as the offender; and second, the court considers that making the order will help in preventing the offender from engaging in such behaviour.

There were nevertheless significant differences with the ASBO. Thus, the court may make a criminal behaviour order against the offender only if it is made in addition to a) a sentence imposed in respect of the offence, or b) an order discharging the offender conditionally. Moreover, if the offender is under 18, the prosecution must find out the views of the local youth offending team before applying for a criminal behaviour order.

A criminal behaviour order is granted for a specific period of time and if it includes a requirement, it must specify the person who is to be responsible for supervising compliance. It may include provision for the order (or a prohibition or requirement included in the order) to cease to have effect if the offender satisfactorily completes an approved course specified in the order. Breaching the order would nevertheless have tough criminal sanctions with a maximum sentence of five years in prison.

An example given by the Home Office (2012) seeks to illustrate how the Criminal Behaviour Order will enable agencies to deal more effectively with anti-social behaviour: thus, a young person convicted of criminal damage after having broken the window of an elderly person's house following an ongoing campaign of harassment. Under the previous system, they could be prevented from going near their victim's house, but under the new system, the same order could also require them to make good the damage to the victim's window and engage with a mentoring programme to address the reasons why they were harassing the victim.

The criminal behaviour order is essentially replacing the infamous ASBO (Anti-Social Behaviour Order) and one of the reasons that the latter was notorious was because so many were breached, and also because it gave a lot of the holders of such orders 'street credibility' amongst their peers. It was thus cool to have one in some neighbourhoods.

The new Criminal Behaviour Order is targeted at people who have both committed a crime and are engaging in anti-social behaviour. The government itself refers to hard-core offenders and it does thus seem improbable that attendance on a course will make a serious impact with what Hopkins Burke and Hodgson (2015) refer to 'anti-social families'. Moreover, in the example cited above, there does seem to be a contradiction between keeping away from the victim but, at the same time, 'making good the damage' to the window. Clearly the outcomes of the new order will need to be closely monitored and it does seem that ant-social behaviour of this magnitude tends to be committed by adults and far less by children (Hopkins Burke and Hodgson 2015).

The youth court and its disposals

The youth court was given new sentencing and remand powers by the CDA 1998 and the Youth Justice and Criminal Evidence Act 1999. Young people aged between 10 and 17 inclusive are now mainly dealt with in the youth courts by specially trained magistrates and no person is allowed to be present unless authorised by the court.[9]

Exceptions to this regulation are members and officers of the court, parties to the case (normally including parents/guardians), their legal representatives, witnesses and bona fide representatives of the media. Proceedings can be reported in the press but the young person may not generally be identified. A child or young person will, in general, be tried in the youth court unless any of the following apply: he or she is charged with homicide (e.g., murder or manslaughter), when they are sent to the Crown Court for trial; he or she is aged 14 or over and is charged with a 'grave crime' (an offence for which an adult could be imprisoned for at least fourteen years), indecent assault or dangerous driving. These cases are sent to the Crown Court if the magistrates conclude that if convicted, the appropriate sentence would be more than they have the power to give; or he or she is charged jointly with another person aged 18 or more, when both should be dealt with in the Crown Court. Young people aged under 17 who are charged and not released on bail will usually be remanded to local authority accommodation. Conditions such as a curfew can be imposed on the child and the authority. With effect from 3 December 2012, whenever a court refuses bail to a child or young person (aged 10–17), the court is required to remand the child to local authority accommodation unless certain conditions are met, in which case the court may instead remand the child to Youth Detention Accommodation. Every such child (whether remanded to Youth Detention Accommodation or to local authority accommodation) will now be treated as 'Looked After' (formerly known as being in care) by their designated local authority.

Courts have the power to order a secure remand direct to local authority accommodation. This provision is available for females aged 12 to 16 and males aged 12 to 14 where the child is charged with or convicted of a violent or sexual offence, or one where an adult could be sentenced to 14 years or more imprisonment. This provision is also available for the same age groups if there is a recent history of absconding while remanded to local authority accommodation and if the young person is charged or convicted of an imprisonable offence committed while remanded. Additionally, the court must be of the opinion that only a remand to secure accommodation would be adequate to protect the public. In the case of boys aged 15 and 16, secure remands will generally be to prison service accommodation. In exceptional cases where the boy is deemed vulnerable, the remand may be made to secure local authority accommodation.

Detention and training orders (DTOs) were introduced and came into effect on 1 April 2000 and are the new main custodial sentence for juveniles; they replaced the secure training order for 12- to 14-year-olds and detention in a young offender institution for 15- to 17-year-olds. A DTO is a two-part sentence which combines a period in custody with a period spent under supervision in the community. Subject to provisions for early or late release, half the term of the order is spent in custody and half under supervision in the community. The emphasis is on clear sentence planning to ensure that time in custody is spent constructively and this is followed by effective supervision, support on release and, significantly, positive reintroduction to the community. This disposal is available for 12- to 17-year-olds for any imprisonable offence sufficiently serious to justify custody under section 1 of the Criminal Justice Act 1991. Moreover, if the child or young person is aged 12 to 14, the court must be of the opinion that he or she is a persistent offender. The DTO is available to the youth court and the Crown Court. The court can impose an order of between four and twenty-four months provided it does not exceed the maximum term that could be imposed on an adult offender by the Crown Court. Anyone found guilty of murder committed when under the age of 18 must be sentenced to 'detention during Her Majesty's pleasure'. A person aged under 18 convicted of an offence other than murder for which a life sentence may be passed on an adult may be sentenced to 'detention for life'.[10]

A range of non-custodial sentences were introduced and consolidated. Where the youth court considered it to be appropriate, young offenders may be given absolute and conditional discharges as is the case for adults. Young offenders aged 16 can receive a probation order, a community service order, or a combination order in the same way as adults. Young offenders aged 10 to 17 may also be fined and in certain cases their parent or guardian can be ordered to pay.

Supervision orders can be given to any young offender and can last between three months and three years. These require that the young person is supervised by a probation officer, the local authority or a member of the YOT. They are required to meet with their supervisor at regular intervals and can be required to undertake what are known as 'specified activities' to help them address their offending behaviour. The CDA 1998 allowed an element of reparation to be attached to the order and this works in the same way as the reparation order discussed above.

The aim of the attendance centre order was that the offender should be 'given, under supervision, appropriate occupation and instruction' and it could be given to any offender aged between 10 and 20. For those 18 or over, the maximum period of the order was thirty-six hours, but in the case of those aged under 18 the order would be for twelve hours unless there are exceptional circumstances, when it might be reduced or increased. The order required the young person to attend a local centre for a maximum of three hours per day where they usually received instruction on social skills and physical training. This order was abolished under the Criminal Justice and Immigration Act 2009.

Action plan orders (APOs) were designed to provide a short but intensive and individually tailored response to offending behaviour, so that the causes of that offending as well as the offending itself could be addressed. This might include making reparation to the victim if this is considered appropriate and the latter consents. Certain requirements are placed on the young offender, who is supervised by a caseworker, and the orders must last for three months in total. Holdaway et al. (2001) were nevertheless critical of the approach they observed in some areas which they attributed to staff with prior youth offending experience under the previous juvenile justice regime bringing 'old ways of working' with them and turning APOs into 'mini-supervision orders'. The models of intervention observed could, therefore, be characterised as essentially 'correctional' although others have observed a strong welfare element including family support, assistance with accommodation or addressing issues arising from school exclusion (Smith 2007).

Parental bind-overs were introduced for where it is judged that parents or guardians have not exercised proper care and control over the child or young person. These require the former to exercise proper care and control or be liable for the sum specified which may not exceed £1,000. In the case of young persons under 16, courts must give reasons for not binding over parents or guardians. Parental bind-overs are discretionary for courts in the case of 16- and 17-year-olds and the period of the bind-over may not exceed three years or until the young person reaches the age of 18.

Parenting orders can be given to the parents/carers of young people who offend, play truant from school, or who have received a Child Safety Order, Anti-Social Behaviour Order (subsequently replaced by the Criminal Behaviour Order), or Sexual Offences Prevention Order. These do not result in the parent/carer getting a criminal record and the recipient will normally be required to attend counselling or guidance sessions for a period of up to three months. They may also have conditions imposed on them such as attending meetings with teachers at their child's school, ensuring their child does not visit a particular place unsupervised or is at home at particular times. These conditions can last for a period up to twelve months and a parent/carer can be prosecuted for failing to keep the requirements of the order.

Several commentators argued at the outset that the imposition of parenting orders would inevitably increase tension between parents and children and could lead to more parents requesting the local authority to accommodate their children (Cavadino 1997a; Childright 1998; Hogg 1999; Drakeford and McCarthy 2000). Moreover, Hogg (1999) observed that the imposition of financial penalties on families that are dependent on state support would render them less functional. Padfield (1998) claimed there was no evidence that parenting orders would work; while Hogg (2000) expressed surprise at the lack of research into the nine years' experience of parental bind-overs introduced in 1988. Gelsthorpe and Morris (1999) were particularly concerned about an inherent assumption of 'wilful neglect' on the part of parents and the apparent belief that the latter would respond to coercion rather than advice and assistance; Goldson (1999b) observed the orders to be 'fundamentally at odds' with all other child welfare principles,[11] while Bell (1999: 199) remarked that for parents, read 'women', as the imposition of such orders would almost certainly be gendered. Gelsthorpe (1999) thus noted that the 'war on crime' had simply become a 'war on parents' and believed that 'the stigmatisation and potential resentment' felt by parents could exacerbate rather than alleviate difficulties. Smith (2007) subsequently observed that parents were to be persuaded – or when that fails coerced – into ensuring conformity among their children. Pitts (2000: 10) had previously suggested that the contemporary youth justice system reflects this kind of agenda and targets both young people and their parents:

> The new professional practices in the form of cognitive-behavioural treatment, reparation and mediation and mentoring all strive to make good these defects in their behaviour, beliefs and attitudes of young offenders and their parents, and to instill in them a new, disciplined, capacity for self-regulation.

Monaghan (2000: 154) predicted a significant increase in remands to care and custody with the introduction of the contemporary youth justice system and was concerned that a failure to develop confidence in the Young Offender Panel would lead to more punitive disposals, in 'a sentencing arena with more snakes and fewer ladders' (see also Ball 1998: 423). The subsequent conviction statistics are, nevertheless, ambiguous. Thus, while overall crime levels appear to have fallen, those proceeded against and found guilty were steadily increasing in number by 2004 (Home Office 2005a). Conversely, the number of young people – aged 10 to 17 – being proceeded against for more serious (indictable) offences was declining sharply from their peak in 2001. The proportion of young people being processed – cautioned or found guilty – was also falling (1,671 per 100,000 population compared with 1,962 per thousand in 1998). This suggests a decline in the rate at which young people were being processed and subsequently sentenced for more serious offences (Smith 2007). Bateman (2006), nevertheless, observes a significant readiness to instigate formal interventions at the lower end of the scale, which was reflected in a persistently high use of custody, identifying a 55 per cent increase in custodial disposals during the period 1992 to 2003, which is far higher than anywhere else in Europe. Smith (2007) observed that the evidence suggests that reforms progressively implemented from 2000 onwards had little effect on the use of custody: in March 2000, there were 2,650 young people in secure facilities, and by March 2006, this figure was 2,785, although there was some fluctuation in the intervening years.

Both Bateman (2005) and Goldson (2006) observed a political need for senior government figures to 'appear' tough on crime and, therefore, the persistent reliance on a comparatively high use of custody. This, nevertheless, appears to be contrary to the principal objective of the contemporary youth justice system which is to prevent offending by young people. In the following chapter we will examine evidence-based effective practice in that system and consider how it does seek to achieve the principal aim of significantly reducing criminality by children and young people.

Postscript: the Coalition and a decline in entry to the youth justice system

In Chapter 1 of this book we discovered that one of the most significant findings from our brief review of the statistics of young people in the youth justice system was the recognition that there has been a major decline in recent years in the number of young people entering the system. There was a reduction of 50 per cent during the five years of the Coalition government alone. At first sight, this statistic suggests a remarkable success story for the contemporary youth justice system but this is nevertheless a questionable supposition. The evidence contained in our subsequent discussion in this book suggests that the net-widening propensities of the newly introduced youth justice system led to the significant increase in numbers initially absorbed. Reductions in those numbers occurred with measures introduced to address the issue of net-widening, not least the abolition of the 'final warning' in the Coalition years and the return to a much more liberal use of police cautions.

Summary of main points

1 The Youth Justice Board (YJB) for England and Wales was established by the Crime and Disorder Act 1998 (CDA 1998) and is a non-departmental public body, sponsored by the Home Office, which supervises the operation of youth offending teams (YOTs) and all those working in the contemporary youth justice system as a whole.

2 Critics noted from the outset the inevitable net-widening propensities of the new system.

3 The CDA 1998 introduced radical new measures with the intention of transforming the youth justice system. Crucial to this new system was the replacement of police cautioning with reprimands and final warnings. There has since been a return to a police cautioning system.

4 The CDA 1998 introduced reparation orders, which require offenders to make specified reparation to their victim, if he or she consents, or to the community at large as part of a restorative justice strategy.

5 The long-established rule of *doli incapax*, which had presumed that a child under 14 does not know the difference between right and wrong, was to be 'modernised' by the CDA 1998 and was widely criticised.

6 Child safety orders were introduced whereby a Family Proceedings Court can subject a child under the age of 10 to an order if they commit an act which

might have been conceived as an offence if they were over 10 (the age of criminal responsibility), and child curfew schemes, to keep children in this age group off the streets.

7   Some of the most concerted criticisms of any part of the CDA 1998 were in relation to the Anti-Social Behaviour Order (ASBO), which was a civil order designed to respond to alleged anti-social behaviour but with the power of imprisonment on breach.

8   The Coalition government announced plans to replace the ASBO (BBC 2012) and the Anti-Social Behaviour Act 2014 subsequently replaced the now discredited order with the Criminal Behaviour Order (CBO).

9   The youth court was given new sentencing and remand powers by the CDA 1998 and the Youth Justice and Criminal Evidence Act 1999. Young people aged between 10 and 17 inclusive are now mainly dealt with in the youth courts by specially trained magistrates and no person is allowed to be present unless authorised by the court.

10   There has been a major decline in recent years in the number of young people entering the youth justice system – a reduction of 50 per cent during the five years of the Coalition government alone.

Discussion questions

1   Explain the concept of net-widening and why this would be an inevitable feature of the new system.
2   Why were reprimands and final warnings replaced by a system of police cautions?
3   What does the 'modernisation' of *doli incapax* mean?
4   What were the criticisms of the ASBO and why was this eventually replaced?
5   Why do you think that there has been a large reduction in the number of young people entering the youth justice system in the past few years?

Notes

1   The Youth Justice Board consists of between ten and twelve members appointed by the secretary of state, including people who have extensive recent experience of the youth justice system.
2   Youth offending teams were established and came into being from 1 April 2000.
3   See also Gelsthorpe and Morris (1999), Stern (1998) and Sclater and Piper (2000).
4   See also Reid (1997).
5   A reparation order cannot be combined with a custodial sentence, or with a community service order, a combination order, a supervision order or an action plan order.
6   See also the Family Policy Studies Centre (1998), Walsh (1999), Hayes and Williams (1999).
7   I have found that the rebuttal of the presumption of *doli incapax* to be one of the most misunderstood changes introduced by the CDA 1998. I will offer a brief explanation. The presumption of *doli incapax* had simply meant that courts would presume that the child did not know the difference between right and serious wrong. This meant that

the prosecution would need to prove that the child did understand that what they were doing was seriously wrong. The rebuttal of the presumption now meant that the onus was on the defence to prove that their client did not understand. There is thus, a complete reversal of emphasis.

8 Asperger's disorder is a milder variant of autistic disorder. Both Asperger's disorder and autistic disorder are in fact subgroups of a larger diagnostic category termed either autistic spectrum disorders (mostly in European countries) or pervasive developmental disorders (PDD) in the USA. Affected individuals are characterised by social isolation and eccentric behaviour in childhood. There are impairments in two-sided social interaction and non-verbal communication.

9 The Criminal Justice Act 1991 s.70 had previously established the youth court as a successor to the juvenile court and this had dealt with offenders up to and including those aged 16.

10 Since the Criminal Justice and Court Services Act 2000 became law, all convicted defendants aged 18 or over at the time of conviction are sentenced as adults.

11 See also Newburn (1998).

13 Effective youth justice in practice

Key issues

1　Risk and effective practice in the youth justice system
2　Youth justice effective practice
3　Assessment of risk and intervention planning
4　Risk and protective factors
5　Implementing intervention

We have seen how the contemporary youth justice system was designed and implemented via the Crime and Disorder Act 1998 by a New Labour government with a commitment to communitarianism. Moreover, we saw how this system could be located in the context of other significant socio-political developments of the past three decades. First, there is the notion of the risk society and the recognition of a need to identify, eradicate but essentially manage criminological risks. Thus, the contemporary youth justice system was very much founded on the assessment and management of individuals and their risk of offending. Second, there was the influence of the new public-sector management, quality assurance and the audit society, which are all part of an agenda to promote management competence, quality of service delivery and value for money in the public services. Thus, the Audit Commission report *Misspent Youth* (1996) was influentially critical of a youth justice system it judged expensive, inefficient and failing to reduce youth offending, recommending in its place a more rigorously managed and evaluated multidisciplinary youth justice system using the latest research to inform a practice effective in challenging and reducing youth offending. Since the demise of New Labour and its replacement by the Conservative/Lib Dem Coalition following the general election in 2010, we have also seen the introduction of two further closely linked contextual factors which were to have a significant impact on the administration of the contemporary youth justice system. First, the 'Big Society' – which was the Conservative Party variant of communitarianism – places a greater emphasis on self-help and charitable intervention where possible rather than expensive state employment. Second, in an era of austerity and a perceived need to pay back the huge national economic deficit as quickly as possible – thus, instigating major public cutbacks – a practical pragmatic response to youth justice, which encouraged the informal disposal of young offenders with custodial options being very much a last resort, gained favour. This approach was termed the 'cost-effective model of youth justice' in Chapter 11 of this book.

This chapter considers the work of the contemporary youth justice system in practice. We have seen that the system implemented and overseen by the Youth Justice Board through the medium of local youth offending teams (YOTs) was very much founded on the notion of effective evidence-based practice. We have nevertheless seen that notions of evidence-based policy and practice and their application to youth justice were to receive fairly extensive criticism while, at the same time, it was observed that a wide range of policy initiatives appeared to either ignore some of the research and evaluation evidence, while those strategies that were introduced seem to have been based on carefully selected findings that were complementary to the dominant government worldview. Stephenson et al. (2007: xvi) nevertheless both acknowledge and challenge these criticisms, observing that the YJB was to take a far less dogmatic perspective than other areas in the criminal justice system, with far more opportunity given for the development of a workforce that reflected critically on the research evidence and used it 'creatively to come up with solutions to demanding policy initiatives within the constantly challenging, uncertain, and often frustrating world of youth justice'. In this chapter we examine the role and significance of the identified key areas of effective practice – and the evidence on which they are based – in a multi-agency youth justice system with the central aim of reducing youth offending, while incorporating the changes that have occurred since the system was first introduced.

Risk and effective practice in the youth justice system

The identification and management of risk was, as we have seen, to become central to the contemporary youth justice system and the research which was considered in the opening chapter of this book supports the notion that young people who have one or more risk factors present in their lives are far more likely to be involved in criminal behaviour. The contemporary youth justice system was very much influenced from the outset by the work of Utting and Vennard (2000), who identified four categories of risk factors in the research literature. First, they identified family factors which involve low income, poor parental supervision, harsh or erratic discipline, physical abuse, parental conflict, having a parent with a criminal record, and having parents or carers whose attitudes condone or even support anti-social or criminal behaviour. Second, there are educational factors which entail low educational achievement, aggressive and disruptive behaviour (including bullying), lack of commitment to school (including truancy), and attending a disorganised school with poor academic standards and a lack of classroom discipline. Third, there are community factors which involve the ready availability and acceptability of illegal drugs, growing up in a disadvantaged area with a high population turnover, community disorganisation and neglect, and a lack of attachment and commitment to the neighbourhood among residents. Fourth, there are individual/peer factors which are hyperactivity and impulsivity, rebelliousness, alienation and a lack of social commitment to law-abiding society, attitude which condones law-breaking, early involvement in offending behaviour and having friends involved in crime and/or whose attitudes condone law-breaking. Critics noted the absence of important structural factors such as unemployment and poverty which, although included in the research literature, are not cited (see Pitts 2003b) but it is also reasonable to contend that each of the apparently individualised risk factors is in some way linked to social class location and the absence of legitimate access to the appropriate life chances.

Utting and Vennard (2000) also identify three categories of protective factors which the research literature suggests help defend a young person against the pressure to become involved in criminal behaviour and these are very much based on the relatively recent variants of social control theories established by Travis Hirschi (1969) and which we encountered in the second part of this book. First, there are social bonding factors where children enjoy strong bonds of affection with law-abiding parents, family members and other significant people in their lives. Second, there are healthy beliefs and clear standards where families, schools and behavioural norms in the wider community guide children away from crime, drugs and other anti-social behaviour. Third, there are opportunities, skills and recognition where children have available legitimate and satisfying opportunities within their families, schools, peer groups and communities to make a positive contribution; moreover, when they have the cognitive and social skills to take advantage of those opportunities, and when their contribution receives praise and encouragement.

The contemporary youth justice system thus sought from the outset to eradicate – or often more realistically reduce – those significant risk factors identified by research, which were found to exist in the life of the young person, while, at the same time, encouraging and strengthening those factors considered to offer protection against involvement in criminal behaviour.

Youth justice effective practice

In the rest of this chapter we shall consider how different key elements of the Youth Justice Board effective practice agenda contribute to the implementation of the contemporary youth justice system. These key areas of effective practice that are considered here are not mutually exclusive but are closely interconnected and form part of a system for identifying and responding to youth offending. We shall look at these areas of intervention in the following categories: (i) assessment of risk and intervention planning; (ii) risk and protective factors; and (iii) implementing intervention. It should be noted that the subdivision of these areas of intervention into these categories is simply a matter of social scientific convenience which helps us to understand the contribution of each to the contemporary youth justice system. These areas could be legitimately categorised in other ways – and perhaps in a different chronological order – and Stephenson et al. (2011) do this in their far more detailed discussion of effective practice in the contemporary youth justice system, to which the reader is referred.

Assessment of risk and intervention planning

Assessment, planning and supervision

Assessment, planning and supervision were considered to be essential elements of practice with young people at all stages of the contemporary youth justice system because they guide and shape all subsequent work which is conducted. Good practice in these areas was identified as being essential for ensuring that: first, all work conducted in YOTs and the secure estate contributes to the aim of reducing offending; second, young people receive a good-quality service that is relevant to their needs; and, third, there is available evidence to show the effectiveness of work that has been conducted. These three core tasks were considered to be closely linked activities that inform planning and which need to be periodically revised. There is recognition that young people present a complex and constantly changing mix of attitudes, circumstances, problems and positive factors and it is thus considered essential to regularly review progress and revise planned interventions. The increasing range of the latter offered by a variety of service providers is seen to present both an opportunity and a challenge and differences in the intensity, length, structure and aims of each one means that careful decisions need to be made about the allocation of young people to interventions which are appropriate for them. Effective assessment, planning and supervision are, therefore, considered essential to an effective youth justice intervention.

Fundamental to the ability of young people to effectively participate in the process of assessment, planning and supervision and other aspects of the contemporary youth justice system is recognised to be the nature of their individual learning style and this is likely to be influenced by factors such as age, maturity, levels of literacy or educational achievement. It is, therefore, essential that the methods and materials used in all interventions are appropriate to the stage of development of the young person.

Building self-esteem has been identified as an important part of the learning process (Andrews 1995; Strachan and Tallant 1997), while Gardner (1993) refers to 'multiple intelligences' to describe the different ways in which people think and solve problems. These include, for example, 'verbal and linguistic' abilities (understanding and expressing ideas through language), 'bodily-kinaesthetic' skills (gaining knowledge through feedback from physical activity) and 'visual-spatial' intelligence (learning directly through images and thinking intuitively without the use of language). It is, therefore, proposed that learning experiences should be designed with these differences in mind, while assessment should also take into account the diverse family, ethnic and cultural backgrounds of young people.

The assessment of risk and need then provides the foundations of planning and supervising interventions (Chapman and Hough 1998; Coulshed and Orme

1998) and the Youth Justice Board itself (2001b) identified three reasons why good-quality assessment in youth justice is essential. First, it provides a key contribution to effective practice and helping to prevent offending by young people. Second, it is crucial in helping to meet the needs of young people who offend and ensuring that interventions are appropriate to the particular circumstances of each young person. Third, it is in the interests of public protection and the wider community by identifying young people likely to reoffend or cause serious harm to others.

However, there have been significant criticisms of the assessment of risk and planning in the contemporary youth justice system. Two evaluations of the Asset risk assessment tool used in YOTs discovered that it had a predictive accuracy of 67 per cent (Baker et al. 2002, 2005) and various other critics were concerned at its low predictive value (Smith 2006). Others questioned the fundamental validity of the actuarial approach to assessment. First, it has been argued that risks associated with the young person are identified without necessarily addressing their needs. Second, young people have been said to be stereotyped and demonised, which consequently facilitates a culture of control. Third, it avoids traditional criminal justice concerns for justice, fairness and due process in the interests of removing potential risks. Fourth, it simply promotes an over-simplified technical fix to the complex and ambiguous reality that is offending behaviour by young people (Pitts 2001a; Smith 2006).

It was in the context of these criticisms that a new enhanced assessment tool has been introduced in July/August 2015. AssetPlus is a new assessment and planning interventions framework developed by the YJB to replace Asset and its associated tools. The stated intention has been to design and provide a holistic end-to-end assessment and intervention plan, allowing one record to follow a child or young person throughout their time in the youth justice system. AssetPlus importantly focuses on the professional judgement of practitioners and the intention is that better-focused intervention plans will improve outcomes for children and young people.

The rationale for the introduction of AssetPlus acknowledges that assessment and intervention planning are demanding professional tasks requiring high levels of knowledge and skill. Thus, while structured assessment tools or frameworks can assist with these tasks, it is recognised that they will be of most use if individual practitioners and organisations see them as supporting professional practice, rather than replacing it (Baker et al. 2011). Thus, the new framework builds on previous assessment tools used in the youth justice setting, incorporating both the lessons learned from their use since 2000 and new insights from research and the academic literature. It is also designed to reflect the changing context for practice in which greater emphasis is now being placed on flexibility and the importance of professional discretion (Munro 2011).

Assessment will now involve identifying risk and protective factors in the life of a young person, but it is recognised that it is insufficient to just to note their occurrence (YJB 2008; Case 2007; Baker et al. 2011). Thus, different factors will interact with each other in different ways at different points in time; for example, there will be interactions between a young person's personal situation, their attitudes and their social setting. There are a number of theories exploring these connections and mechanisms (e.g., Sampson and Laub 1993; Thornberry 2005; Wikström and Sampson 2009) and the relevance for the assessment practice centres on the importance of explaining the significance of factors in the life of a young person at particular points in time and/or in relation to particular behaviours. Second, it is important to understand the perceptions young people have of the choices they face and their views of the costs/benefits associated with offending or anti-social behaviour (Kemshall et al. 2006; Sharland 2006; Ward and Bayley 2007; Boeck and Fleming 2011). Third, there may be similarities with other behaviours. Thus, the 'Good Lives Model' (GLM) suggests that people who offend are – like everyone else – trying to obtain primary human goods such as a sense of belonging or knowledge and skills (Ward and Maruna 2007). The GLM also suggests that people pursue secondary goals – such as friendships or work, for example – as means to achieve these primary goods. If young people find it difficult to achieve these goods through pro-social means, they may try to obtain them through offending or anti-social behaviour (McNeill 2009). It is recognised that as the GLM is a relatively new model there is a need for more empirical research regarding its validity and there may be some cases where it is less appropriate (Andrews et al. 2011) but it is proposed that it can provide a useful perspective when working with young people and will be relevant for intervention planning.

The new assessment and planning framework is also founded on a more sophisticated understanding of the relationship between the much-used concept of 'risk' and the behaviour of children and young people. Indeed, some have questioned whether 'risk' is an appropriate concept to use when working with young people (e.g., Gray 2005; Muncie 2006; Kemshall 2008; O'Malley 2008). Several key points nevertheless emerge from the literature that have particular relevance to the new framework. First, it is important to have a clear concept of 'risk' and it is argued that the framework reflects the description given by Carson and Bain (2008: 39) as:

> An occasion when one or more consequences (events, outcomes and so on) could occur. Critically (a) those consequences may be harmful and/or beneficial and (b) either the number and/or the extent of those consequences, and/or their likelihood, are uncertain and/or unknown.

There are, moreover, two key elements of 'risk' – impact and likelihood (Kemshall et al. 2006; Carson and Bain 2008). Risk is not an inherent characteristic of a young person but rather depends on particular situations and circumstances. Thus, assessments of impact and likelihood can vary frequently and/or rapidly as the circumstances and opportunities facing a young person change. Risk should not be the only focus of work with young people but neither can it be completely ignored (McNeill 2009; Whyte 2009) as practitioners have a responsibility to work towards preventing adverse outcomes. 'Risk' and the Risk Need Responsivity model continue to be useful, for example, in highlighting cases requiring intensive resources and/or immediate action (Andrews and Bonta 2010).

Final warnings

Final warnings were – as we have seen elsewhere in this book – introduced at the outset of the contemporary youth justice system in order to replace the use of police cautions for young people with the intention of tackling offending behaviour at the earliest stage, while endeavouring to divert young people away from further criminality. Research had suggested the benefits of efficient and appropriate risk and needs assessment at the intake point in the youth justice process (Mears and Kelly 1998) but it was observed that there should be a regular review of intervention content against original intent to make sure that it remained true to its original aim.

Research indicated that – as we have seen in this book – it is not unusual for young people to commit minor offences. Moreover, while the majority of young people who are apprehended by the agents of the contemporary youth justice system will commit one offence and no more, a minority will go on to engage in more serious anti-social behaviour (Farrington 1995, 1996; Jessor and Jessor 1997). For the majority of first-time offenders, the impact of being apprehended will be enough, it was argued, to prevent further offending and, therefore, no further input would be required from the youth justice system. If they were to reoffend, however, then they could be assessed to see whether they were likely to commit further offences while, at the same time, being given help and support to try to stop them reoffending, in the form of structured interventions.

The CDA 1998 thus states that a reprimand should be given for a first offence, with a final warning given for the second offence; the latter should normally be accompanied by some form of intervention. Research nevertheless indicated that – and our knowledge of the labelling theory tradition supports this supposition – early entry into the youth justice system can lead to increased offending. It was therefore considered essential that the degree of the final warning intervention was commensurate with the degree of risk presented by the young person and practitioners were required to ensure strategies were in place to graduate interventions incrementally to make sure they were appropriate in each instance (Dunkel 1996; Hallet and Hazel 1998).

Strategies of gradual intervention can be observed throughout the criminal justice process (Feest 1990) and can include: first, at entry stage, reprimand and/or mediation; second, at processing stage, final warning, unconditional and conditional discharges; third, at the remand stage, bail supervision; fourth, at the conviction stage, reparation, restorative interventions, referral order/young offender panels, sentence deferment; fifth, at the threshold of custody, Intensive Supervision and Surveillance Programme (ISSP) or other intensive interventions.

It was therefore argued that graduated interventions should be seen as filters: where at each stage of the criminal justice process, different groups may be filtered from an initial cohort of alleged offenders; the precise nature of these filtering systems and their eligibility criteria, however, would differ between youth justice systems (Dunkel 1996; Hallet and Hazel 1998; Neubacher et al. 1999). Thus, in this context, the European Commission had urged member states to develop graduated interventions for young people, with the emphasis on education and social reintegration (Dunkel 1996) and the case for these with first- and second-time less serious offenders was undoubtedly strong. In England and Wales, 80 per cent of those cautioned for a first-time offence did not return to the notice of the police within two years; however, the rate of reoffending increased significantly as subsequent cautions were given (Rutter et al. 1998). Effective intervention at this early stage was considered vital. Moreover, it was argued that successful early intervention did not merely have benefits for the individual young person, the cost saving to society – in terms of public perception of crime and the financial gain – would be considerable (Cohen 1998).

The Legal Aid, Sentencing and Punishment of Offenders Act 2012 thus abolished reprimands and final warnings and replaced them with a new system of youth cautions and youth conditional cautions which came into force on 8 April 2013. The Coalition government and the YJB had come to accept the growing evidence that the final warning schema was accelerating the progress of more children and young people into the more punitive aspects of the youth justice system. In its place, the new formal youth out-of-court disposal framework, it is argued, provides a proportionate and effective resolution to offending and supports the principal statutory aim of the youth justice system of preventing offending by children and young people. The new provision stipulates that in dealing with any offence committed by a child or young person aged 10 to 17 years of age the police may: 1) take no further action; 2) use a community resolution, for example, an instant apology and reparation for a minor first-time offence; 3) a youth caution; 4) a youth conditional caution; or 5) charge the child or young person with the offence.

A youth caution can be used as an alternative to prosecution in certain circumstances for any offence where the child admits the offence, there is sufficient evidence for a realistic prospect of conviction but it is not in the public interest to prosecute. A youth conditional caution is a youth caution with conditions attached to it which may, for example, include a requirement to pay a financial penalty or a requirement to attend at a specific place for a specified number of hours. Where there is no reasonable excuse for non-compliance with those conditions, criminal proceedings may be brought. Clearly the public interest is a very flexible and negotiable concept which can change according to political priorities.

Risk and protective factors

We have identified throughout this book risk factors linked to offending by young people and these were summarised above by Utting and Vennard (2000), albeit without the explicit inclusion of significant structural factors such as poverty and unemployment previously identified in the research literature. It is, nevertheless, proposed here that these apparently invisible factors are implicitly taken into account as the following discussion clearly shows. The key areas of effective practice for identifying and responding to these risk and protective factors in the contemporary youth justice system are parenting; education, training and employment; substance misuse; and mental health.

Parenting

The research evidence shows that children who are subject to harsh, neglectful or inconsistent parenting are at a significantly increased risk of involvement in offending when they reach the age of adolescence. Furthermore, adverse family factors have a marked effect on the development of children and potential future problems include prenatal and perinatal factors, poor supervision and discipline, and family conflict (see Hopkins Burke 2014). McCord (1982) had found offending to be common in men raised in broken homes without affectionate mothers and also in families experiencing conflict where parents stayed together. Studies conducted in both the UK and North America show that children are more likely to become offenders if a parent or older sibling has been involved in crime (Farrington 1995).

Living in impoverished family circumstances is also a recognised predictor of criminogenic tendencies. The Cambridge Longitudinal Study identified an increased risk of self-reported offending (Farrington 1992a, 1992b) and found that boys who came from low-income families were twice as likely to have a criminal record at age 18 than those whose families were adequate or comfortable. It was also found that around 55 per cent of boys observed to be poorly supervised at 8 years of age had been convicted of offences by the age of 32, compared with a third of the overall sample, while conflict between two parents was also shown to carry an increased risk of later delinquency for boys. Loeber and Stouthamer-Loeber (1986) found four interrelated parenting factors – neglect, family conflict, deviant behaviour and attitudes on the part of parents, and disrupted family life – to be linked to behavioural problems and delinquency. However, it has been shown that parental involvement in the form of 'at-home good parenting' has a significant positive effect on the achievement and adjustment of children even after all other factors influencing attainment – such as the quality of schools and even poverty – has been taken into consideration, and this is to be found across class and ethnic boundaries (Desforges and Abouchaar 2003).

Reinforcing the responsibilities of parents in addressing the offending and antisocial behaviour of their children has therefore been a key objective of the youth justice system from the outset and was the basis for the introduction of the parenting order. Notably, family-focused work has been found to be more effective than interventions that focuses solely upon parents or on young people (Kumpfer and Alvarado 1998) and family learning has also been shown to be effective in helping young people to move forward towards training and employment or reintegration into mainstream provision.

It is when their children become teenagers that parents experience demands that they often feel ill-equipped to deal with; while teenagers themselves are responding to physical, emotional and lifestyle changes that have a profound impact on them. Moreover, these challenges, for both parents and teenagers, can be located in the context of major shifts in recent years in the social structure as well as in political responses to parenting, teenagers and the family (Coleman and Roker 2001). The changes external to families such as actual or relative poverty can, therefore, intensify the changes within.[1]

Parenting is thus one of the key risk and protective factors identified in relation to the offending or anti-social behaviour of young people (Farrington 1996; Rutter et al. 1998) and it is proposed that the provision of support to parents can contribute to the reduction of offending and anti-social behaviour by young people (Alexander et al. 1976; Borduin et al. 1995; Wasserman et al. 1996; Henggeler et al. 1997; Gordon and Kacir 1998). Parents referred to parenting interventions in the contemporary youth justice system have been found to present substantially higher levels of need; in particular, managing the difficult behaviour of the child, setting boundaries, disciplining the child and improving school attendance, among others.[2]

While section 8 of the Crime and Disorder Act 1998 provides courts with powers to impose parenting orders, parenting programmes can be offered on a voluntary basis. Such programmes do nevertheless carry the risk that parents feel stigmatised – negatively labelled or blamed – and it has been found that this is more likely to be the case for those referred via compulsory routes. It is therefore recognised that services working with parents on compulsory orders can expect to meet considerable hostility and scepticism from the outset and it is has been found to be especially helpful when programmes focus on parenting strengths, rather than weaknesses. Parenting interventions within the youth justice system should thus have clear aims and objectives related to identified need and to reducing parenting risk factors and strengthening protective factors (Kumpfer et al. 1996). Interestingly, psychodynamic interventions that focus on the child and its individual development, rather than structural family interventions, have been found to actually result in a deterioration of family functioning (Szapocznik et al. 1989).

Ghate and Ramella (2002) noted that the parenting risk and protective factors identified above need to be seen in the context of other invariably significant structural factors, such as impoverished neighbourhood, family poverty and poor housing, which may also impact considerably on parenting and family functioning. Thus, the available research shows that there is simply no one 'correct' model of parenting that will address the diverse needs of all parents and their children. It is, therefore, considered appropriate to choose from a menu of optional interventions following a full assessment of need (Stephenson et al. 2011).

The Anti-Social Behaviour Act 2003 gave YOTs a statutory power to make a parenting contract and in return to help parents deliver their part of the contract. These contracts can provide a formal structure for work with parents on a *voluntary* basis, encouraging an effective partnership between the YOT and the parents. The parent cannot be compelled to enter into a parenting contract; there is no obligation on the YOT to offer one; while, moreover, there is no penalty for refusing to enter into or failing to comply with one. However, previous failure to cooperate with support offered through a contract is a relevant consideration for a court when deciding whether to make a parenting order. A contract thus provides more formality when a YOT is attempting to secure voluntary cooperation from parents.

When parents are unwilling to engage with parenting support on a voluntary basis and a YOT assesses that a parent could be supported to improve the behaviour of the child, YOTs can apply for a free-standing parenting order or recommend a parenting order linked to a child's conviction or another order. However, before applying for an order, YOTs should normally have made every effort to engage with parents on a voluntary basis whether or not through a contract. Any parent or guardian of a child or young person including birth and step-parents and carers may enter into a parenting contract or can be made subject to a parenting order if the relevant conditions apply.

The evaluation of the YJB's parenting programmes has shown that few fathers have been involved in parenting programmes. However, when both parents are participating in the upbringing of a child, even when they live separately, a parenting intervention has been found likely to be more effective if both the mother and father are involved, unless there are reasons why this would be unsuitable, for instance, a parent is estranged because of domestic violence or abuse (Ghate and Ramella 2002).

Education, training and employment

Parsons and Howlett (2002) significantly identified educational failure, permanent exclusion or non-attendance at school as the risk factors with the highest correlation to youth offending. In fact, longitudinal research has long established that children who are performing poorly from late junior school are more likely to become involved in offending than those performing adequately or well (see Wolfgang et al. 1972). Official statistics reviewed earlier in this book suggest that young people excluded from school commit 30 per cent of domestic burglaries and 40 per cent of street robberies.

Hodgson and Webb (2005) nevertheless alert us to oversimplified deterministic interpretations of the link between school exclusions and offending by children and young people. Thus, in their sample, 82 per cent of the young people interviewed stated they were no more likely to offend subsequent to being excluded, while 55 per cent stated they were less likely to offend during their exclusion period. Often, this was because on being excluded, they were 'grounded' by their parents, thus alerting us to the importance of multiple risk factors and the inevitable interconnection between them. It is nevertheless the 45 per cent who are criminologically interesting.

Thus, the Cambridge longitudinal study showed that between 44 per cent and 48 per cent of secondary school truants were offenders, compared with 14 to 16 per cent of non-truants (Robins and Hills 1966), while research among offenders in custody aged 17 to 20 has shown that almost one in four could not write their name and address correctly, more than two out of three could not fill in a job application form and a half had difficulty telling the time (Elliot and Voss 1974).

This is bad news for most young people released from custody, for around half of all jobs require some basic maths and more than 90 per cent require communication skills (Literacy Working Group 1999). On release from prison, around 66 per cent of offenders have such poor literacy and numeracy skills that they are excluded from 96 per cent of jobs (Prison Service 1989). Moreover, adults with poor basic skills are more likely to end up in unskilled or semi-skilled, low-grade work; be unemployed more often and for longer periods; have children with poor basic skills; live in overcrowded conditions or be homeless; and have a criminal record. They are also less likely to receive even basic, on-the-job training; vote; or participate in their local communities (Basic Skills Agency 2002). The Youth Justice Board has consequently placed a high priority on the education and training of young people at risk of reoffending and this concern has remained consistent with the change of government as we have seen previously in this book.

Stephenson et al. (2011) observed that only 35 per cent of young people in the contemporary youth justice system, at any one time, may actually be in full-time education, training or employment, and noted the existence of cases where young people had received no education for several years (see also Youth Justice Board 2002; Baker et al. 2002). Academic failure at school is widely recognised as being endemic among young offenders and thus raising educational attainment is identified as one of the most effective means of reducing the risk factors associated with criminal behaviour. Ayers (1999) had proposed that the route to rehabilitation for the vast majority of young people is through the attainment of very normal milestones – such as learning to read and write, gaining qualifications, getting a job, entering further education and training – which are often denied to them due to their marginalised status. Stephenson et al. (2011) observes that there is a whole multitude of schemes and strategies that have been introduced in recent years with the intention of getting excluded and offending young people back into education, and subsequently, training and employment but there are nevertheless very limited research and evaluation findings to demonstrate their success.

There are nevertheless some very notable exceptions. Summer Arts Colleges (SACs) are intensive educational projects designed for young people on Detention and Training Orders (DTOs) and subject to Intensive Supervision and Surveillance (ISS). They re-engage these young people in education, training and employment through the provision of vibrant arts experiences. Summer Arts Colleges were originally launched as part of the Youth Justice Board and Arts Council England's strategic partnership, and at the time of writing, over 165 have been run by Unitas on their behalf, reaching more than 2,000 young people in England and Wales. Young people on Summer Arts Colleges work with a unique combination of artists, literacy and numeracy practitioners, and youth justice practitioners. The aim is to: first, increase educational engagement and facilitate transition into mainstream education, training and employment after the programme; second, provide a structured, full-time, arts-based project, combining arts enrichment and arts appreciation activities, and explore possible routes into employment and careers within the arts; third, reduce levels of (re)offending among participants during the project and in the following months; and fourth, work with the arts to improve literacy and numeracy skills and to achieve an accreditation through the Arts Award.

Tarling and Adams (2013) carried out an evaluation of the colleges for the five years 2007 to 2011 and reached very positive conclusions. Over 1,800 young people from 76 YOTs in England and Wales participated in Summer Arts Colleges between 2007 and 2012 and their characteristics were: (1) typically, male (83 per cent) and white (70 per cent) with an average age of 16.4 years; (2) almost one in three had been in the care system (31 per cent); (3) nearly one-fifth (18 per cent) had statements of special educational need; (iv) over two-thirds were either on a Supervision Order, a Youth Rehabilitation Order (YRO) or the community phase of the Detention and Training Order, with almost three out of five of the young people having Asset scores in the medium–high or high-risk bandings; (6) almost half (41 per cent) were not in education, employment or training (NEET); (7) fewer than one in five of the young people had educational qualifications, despite the majority being above school-leaving age; (8) around four out of five young people had literacy (79 per cent) and numeracy skills (83 per cent) below that expected of a typical 11-year-old (Level 1). At first sight, this might appear to be a rather unpromising cohort of very active young offenders.

The outcomes were nevertheless remarkably successful. The proportion of young people achieving Level 1 for literacy and numeracy skills almost doubled between starting and completing the programme (literacy 21 per cent pre and 39 per cent post; numeracy 17 per cent pre and 31 per cent post): (1) over two-thirds of young people increased their literacy and numeracy scores (70 per cent and 69 per cent respectively); (2) among those young people who completed the Summer Arts College, 87 per cent achieved the Bronze Arts Award and 7 per cent achieved the higher Silver Arts Award (at the same time, the average rate of offending almost halved between the thirteen weeks before the Summer Arts College [8.6] and the period in which the young people were participating in the programme [4.5]); (3) the average rate of offending nevertheless increased slightly during the thirteen-week period immediately following the Summer Arts College [to 5.8].

The evaluation nevertheless found strong evidence for the success of the programme in achieving its intended aims and objectives. The initiative successfully engaged young people at considerable risk of (re)offending. Completion rates and attendance levels were high, as was the proportion achieving a national qualification, the Arts Award. There were significant improvements in basic skills. Progression to further education, training and employment following the programme was achieved by the great majority of young people who completed. Importantly, the positive education, training and employment outcomes were also achieved by those young people most at risk – those who were previously NEET. The remarkable educational outcomes of this programme were accompanied by significant reductions in offending, particularly during the programme, and to a lesser extent in the subsequent months. Unusually, the outcomes of this national programme have improved as it has increased substantially in size and been replicated in a wide range of environments. The continuing refinement of the project model has resulted in significant productivity gains and substantial cost benefits.

While the number of young people in custody has been reduced significantly during the last ten years, those incarcerated continue to have very high rates of academic underachievement. Thus, 17 per cent of sentenced young people in custody have a statement of special educational needs, compared to 3 per cent of the general population; 88 per cent of young men and 74 per cent of young women in custody had been excluded from school at some point; 36 per cent of young men and 41 per cent of young women in custody were under 14 when they last attended school; 65 per cent of young people in young offender institutions have had a period of non-attendance at school on their record; 36 per cent of young people in young offender institutions have a negative attitude towards education, training and employment (Ministry of Justice 2015).

Substance misuse

The relationship between substance misuse and offending by young people has been long established and was discussed in the second part of this book. The British Crime Survey 1998 had found that 50 per cent of all young people under the age of 20 had used some kind of illegal drug but 70 per cent of those who were the subject of supervision orders reported substance misuse. The Audit Commission (1996) found that almost two-thirds of young male prisoners admitted to using drugs at some time, cannabis being the drug most often mentioned; moreover, 15 per cent of young offenders had been found to have a problem with either alcohol or illegal drugs with the figure rising to 37 per cent among those classed as persistent or serious offenders (DPAS and SCODA 2000; NACRO 2000).

A later Home Office study involving nearly 300 young people from YOTs across England and Wales found that almost all had used alcohol (91 per cent) and tobacco (85 per cent), with cannabis (86 per cent) and ecstasy (44 per cent) being the most commonly tried illegal drugs. There were nevertheless relatively few heroin or crack cocaine users, and use of these significantly more serious drugs was not generally that frequent (Hammersley et al. 2003). A total of 40 per cent or more of the sample felt that there was some relationship between their substance use and their offending, and while this does not suggest a simple causal relationship between drug use and offending behaviour, the authors found a strong correlation between the two. First, the factors relevant to the early onset and development of drug taking and involvement in juvenile crime were found to overlap significantly. Second, a strong association between the early onset of drug taking and the likelihood of a subsequent escalation into more problematic drug use was found. Third, it was proposed that drugs and crime experiences of young people may be mutually reinforcing.

These findings clearly have implications for the planning of youth justice interventions. First, it would appear that early intervention initiatives to address common risk factors will be of benefit to both drug prevention and crime reduction initiatives. Second, responses to known drug taking by young people who offend should thus address in parallel those factors relevant to both drug taking and offending behaviour. Third, responses to all young people who offend should also be sensitive to their possible involvement with drugs and include the provision of appropriate services where needed (DPAS and SCODA 2000).

We should nevertheless note that levels of drug and alcohol use among young people have fallen by around a third since 2001. At the same time, the number of proven offences by young people, the number entering the youth justice system, the numbers in custody and the reoffending rates for those under 18 has also fallen significantly as we saw in Chapter 1. Nevertheless, the UK still has some of the highest levels of cannabis use and binge drinking among young people in Europe. There are around 13,000 hospital admissions linked to young people's drinking each year and a marked increase in deaths due to cirrhosis or liver disease in younger adults. Early substance misuse has a significant impact on education. Regular drinking before age 14 equates to a penalty of three GCSE grades at age 16. There were almost 9,000 school exclusions because of drugs or alcohol in 2008/09 (Ministry of Justice 2013).

Mental health

Adolescence is a key developmental stage and it has long been recognised as a time of major growth and change. The concept is – as we have seen in this book – culturally determined and adolescent disturbance must thus be seen within the context of normal development within a particular culture during a certain time period. It is as a developmental stage fundamentally concerned with the negotiation of two specific and interrelated tasks. First, adjusting to the impact of puberty, which involves the adolescent in concerns about questions of sexual orientation and negotiating intimate relationships, separation from parents and the establishment of an individual identity. Second, during this period, there is a shift from accepting rules and boundaries imposed by others to setting them for oneself. Adolescents thus begin to challenge the rules which adults have established.

Definitions in 'mental health' can cause confusion about what is being described and communicated and here the term is used in a broad sense, as described by Hagell (2002), indicating 'a level of symptoms of mental ill health that have led to impairment in day-to-day life'. This term does not necessarily mean that young people are clearly diagnosable as having a major mental illness, but it does assume that they are affected enough by the poor status of their health to cause them problems.[3]

Several studies have conclusively shown that adolescents in prison and other secure establishments show very high rates of psychiatric disorder. Many young offenders have more than one psychiatric disorder and – especially those in secure conditions – often have a range of complex needs, while there is a consensus that this high prevalence rate of disorders can be explained by a range of factors (Rutter et al. 1998; Hagell 2002; Communities that Care 2001). First, risk factors in young people known to be associated with offending have also been shown to be strongly associated with mental health problems and these include family dysfunction/discord and exposure to poor parenting practices, such as a lack of supervision, and harsh and erratic discipline. Over a third of young people in prison have been looked after by the local authority, and as a group, young offenders report high levels of previous physical, sexual and emotional abuse (Boswell 1995). Schooling and employment factors include high rates of school exclusion and poor academic attainments and high levels of unemployment; individual child characteristics include learning difficulties and hyperactivity; with other factors including neighbourhood and community issues. Second, the reality of interactions with the criminal justice system may very well lead to anxiety and/or depression, particularly in children, who may be relatively unsupported by families and have few coping resources. Within prison, young people may experience further stress, being separated from families and being exposed to further psychological and physical intimidation.

Dyer and Gregory (2014) observe that the health, psychological, social and financial burdens of crime – and violence in particular – are well established, with youth crime being a significant public health problem. It is young people who are the most likely to be the victim of youth crime, however, victims can include peers, parents, siblings, strangers, professionals, intimate partners and vulnerable others. Youth homicides account for 41 per cent of the formal figures and homicide is a leading cause of death among adolescents (World Health Organisation 2011). Youth violence is not just limited to interpersonal aggression. The nature of the crime can be as diverse as the range of victims and can include serious and life threatening interpersonal violence, fire-setting/arson, theft, vandalism and various behaviours considered anti-social. Indeed, adolescents account for a disproportionate amount of perpetrated rapes and child abuse (Radford et al. 2011; Vizard et al. 2011). In order to intervene with this population, it is essential to assess and understand the nature of the risk posed and the factors that contributed to the onset, development and maintenance of the problems. Thus, the importance of contemporary practice guidelines which, as we have seen, advocate the use of formalised risk assessment approaches. Providing timely interventions to high-risk young people is essential. For some, it will need to reflect proactive early intervention; for others, it will need to be reactive or crises led. Whilst high rates of mental health problems have been identified in offending populations, a clear causal link between mental disorder and offending has not been established (Johnstone 2013).

The relationship between mental health and offending behaviour is complex and idiosyncratic, and often the diagnostic label (e.g., conduct disorder) merely describes the offending behaviour rather than facilitating understanding of the mechanism of risk. Given the inability of the empirical evidence to inform our understanding in this regard, it is suggested that the relationship between psychological and mental health presentation and risk be understood via individualised formulations, generated on a case-by-case basis. This method is arguably the most appropriate, given what we know about the complexity and co-morbidity of mental health concerns in this population. Only the structured professional judgement (SPJ) paradigm provides an appropriate methodology for reaching such conclusions.

Implementing intervention

The previous group of key areas of effective practice focus on the issue of risk and protective factors in the lives of young people but the following category more specifically addresses the lives of apprehended young offenders and the role of contemporary youth justice interventions in their lives. These are: (1) offending behaviour programmes; (2) neighbourhood prevention; (3) mentoring; (4) restorative justice; (5) intensive supervision and surveillance programmes; (6) remand management; and (7) resettlement.

Offending behaviour programmes

Offending behaviour can be prevented at one of three levels: (i) *primary prevention* includes long-term developmental projects to improve the overall life opportunities of disadvantaged families and children; (ii) *secondary prevention* includes work with children or young people at risk of involvement in delinquency; (iii) tertiary prevention entails work with adjudicated young people, that is, those who have already appeared before the courts and been convicted of offences (Guerra et al. 1994).

Offending behaviour programmes are designed to prevent – or at least reduce – offending by children and young people and research evidence shows that they can make a significant contribution to the reduction of criminality. While such work is likely to be focused primarily on the tertiary level in most services, it may also be undertaken at the secondary level in some instances (Buckland and Stevens 2001; NACRO 2001a) and can be undertaken in secure establishments for young offenders, in YOTs or within voluntary-sector agencies.

The impact of offending behaviour programmes has been found, on the whole, to be positive (Lipsey 1995; Dowden and Andrews 1999), and when interventions have been studied in controlled experimental trials, they have resulted in a reduction in recidivism compared with control samples and therefore have been perceived as worthwhile in public policy terms (Lipsey 1999). Studies have nevertheless found substantial variability in outcomes depending on a range of other factors (Lipsey 1995; Lipsey and Wilson 1998) and it has been clearly established that there is no single solution to the problem of offending behaviour or in helping to reduce its frequency or severity. Thus, methods that might well work in one context, with one selected sample, may work less well in others. Decisions regarding the approach best adopted in a given setting for a particular group, therefore, need to consider a number of variables.

Effective interventions have been found to be those which focus on identified risk factors and utilise methods that actively engage young people in learning new skills or changing thought patterns or attitudes associated with offending (Andrews 1995). These factors are sometimes called 'criminogenic needs' or 'dynamic' risks because they may change over time, and the most effective programmes of intervention have been found to be those which employ interpersonal skills training, behavioural interventions such as modelling, graduated practice and role-playing, cognitive skills training, mentoring linked to individual counselling with the close matching of young people and mentors on key background variables, structured individual counselling within a reality therapy or problem-solving framework, and teaching family homes which involve specially trained staff acting in a parental role (Andrews et al. 1990; Hollin 1995; Lipsey and Wilson 1998; Redondo et al. 1999).

Significantly, punitive sanctions or other elements of a deterrence-based approach to the prevention of reoffending – including incarceration, boot camps, 'scared straight' and home confinement – have all been found to be ineffective. There is simply no evidence that they are a reliable means of achieving this end and their net effect has been sometimes to increase it (Gendreau et al. 1993; Baron and Kennedy 1998). Other programmes shown to be ineffective include those vocational training activities which have no associated links to real prospects of employment (and these are, in fact, associated with increased recidivism), wilderness or 'outdoor challenge' programmes (unless they include high-quality training or therapeutic aspects), open-ended individual counselling which is diffusely focused, or unstructured group programmes using experiential therapies or activities focused solely on personal development (Lipsey 1995; Lipsey and Wilson 1998; Petrosino et al. 2000; Wilson and Lipsey 2000). Effective offending behaviour programmes are, therefore, those that focus on the provision of long-term material benefits to young people such as proper employment opportunities and, thus, address significant structural issues in their lives.

Targeted neighbourhood prevention programmes

Stephenson et al. (2011) pertinently observe that crime does not affect everyone equally with perhaps 40 per cent of youth crime taking place in 10 per cent of neighbourhoods. These criminogenic localities are those which are characterised by major structural issues such as high unemployment, lack of investment in physical and social capital, and numerous risk factors, which impact on the lives of young people and the communities in which they live (Hope 2001). New Labour government policy thus focused much attention on these geographical locations as part of its reintegrative tutelage strategy. Stephenson et al. (2011) nevertheless observe that this plethora of government initiatives was not always seen as benign, with critics observing increased surveillance and social control over certain areas and, at the same time, the net-widening potential of some of these measures to draw increasing numbers of young people into the contemporary youth justice system (Smith 2003; Goldson and Muncie 2006). Social crime-reduction methods are thus those that seek to change these underlying social conditions that permit – or even encourage – involvement in criminal behaviour through diversion from crime.

The Youth Inclusion Programme (YIP) and Splash projects were the flagship neighbourhood prevention programmes introduced by the YJB and both were established in response to the Audit Commission (1996) report which had argued for preventative activity to be targeted at those young people most at risk and in areas of high deprivation and criminal activity by young people.

The YIP was established in 2000 by the YJB in seventy of the most deprived neighbourhoods, and despite the voluntary nature of the project design, aimed to focus on the fifty most at-risk 13- to 16-year-olds and engage them in a wide range of constructive activities. The membership of the core fifty changed and regular reviews ensured that young people moved in or out of this category as appropriate. In order to discourage stigmatisation and labelling, many activities were open to other young people who lived in the neighbourhood and, indeed, many young people in the core fifty were unaware of their status (Hopkins Burke and Orrock 2003).

In June 2003, the objectives of the YIP were revised with the overall aim to reduce youth crime in the local neighbourhood and there were three supporting targets. First, to ensure that at least 75 per cent of the identified target group (the core fifty) were engaged with and that these received at least five hours of appropriate interventions per week. Second, the reduction of arrest rates among the engaged target group by 70 per cent compared with the figure for the previous twelve months. Third, to ensure 90 per cent of those in the engaged group were in suitable full-time education, training or employment. Like many youth work projects, the YIP provided a wide range of activities, but it broke with the idea of generic youth work provision and placed its emphasis on evidence-led practice and focused project management (Stephenson et al. 2011).

Splash schemes targeted young people in the school holidays in order to deter them from crime and anti-social behaviour. They were largely led by local police forces in partnership with agencies involved in youth provision. Splash Extra was launched in response to the Street Crime Initiative launched by the government in March 2002 and focused on ten police force areas. Within this initiative, the YJB were asked to set up schemes in high-crime neighbourhoods adopting the original Splash model of delivery and extending the target age group to 9- to 17-year-olds (Hopkins Burke and Orrock 2003).

Peer influence on anti-social behaviour appears to be at its strongest during adolescence and in the factor most associated with an increased risk of convictions as a young adult, after controlling for other factors (Patterson and Yoerger 1997). Studies suggest that negative peer pressure occurs because anti-social young people tend to gravitate towards each other rather than additional peer pressure per se being a risk factor. Furthermore, young repeat offenders who desist from crime by the age of 19 were found less likely to associate with delinquent friends. One of the robust strategies of the aforementioned neighbourhood programmes was thus to include offenders in activities with more law-abiding and compliant young people and in many cases – and in order to avoid labelling and stigmatisation – the most at-risk young people were again unaware of their status.

Work done with the families and community involvement also enhanced the protective factors that combat negative peer pressure. Hawkins and Catalano (1992) had found that when young people have a genuine stake in their families, schools and communities, they are less likely to get involved in anti-social acts that place their relationships in jeopardy. Honey and Mumford (1986) have suggested that peer-led approaches to changing behaviour are more credible to young people and have the added benefit of affecting the peer educators themselves, who may gain in self-esteem, self-confidence and social skills.

There are currently various prevention programmes that work to keep young people away from crime that are run within local communities and which can involve parents and families. Young people are placed on these programmes if they have been in trouble with the police, they are 'at risk' of committing a crime or are involved in anti-social behaviour. Attending one of these programmes is voluntary. The young person and their parents or carers have to be happy with everything before it starts.

Mentoring

Stephenson et al. (2011) observe that mentoring in the contemporary youth justice system is a voluntary one-to-one relationship between a young person and a supportive adult. It is nevertheless more than simple befriending and the aim is to help bring about constructive changes in the life and behaviour of the young person. Shea (1992) proposed that a mentor can be defined 'as someone who helps others to achieve their potential'. Mentoring is nevertheless a natural part of child development and most young people will identify with one or more adults that provide them with support and guidance outside the family context. Young women have been found more likely to identify mentoring to be significant in their lives than young men (Blyth et al. 1982).

The revised disposal and sentencing options that were introduced by the Crime and Disorder Act 1998 incorporated a number in which mentoring may play a part. Participation on a mentoring scheme is nevertheless voluntary and not part of an order to which a young person might be subject.[4] The main purpose of mentoring is to benefit the young person and this can only happen if their agenda is at the heart of the relationship. Successful mentoring relationships are thus associated with active listening, ongoing training for mentors, the establishment and maintenance of a 'youth driven' agenda, time to develop trusting relationships and reciprocity, and constructive attempts by the mentor to affect the behaviour of the young person (Brewer et al. 1995; Scales and Gibbons 1996; Philip 1997; St James Roberts and Samlal Singh 2001; Clayden and Stein 2002).

The role of the mentor is, as we have seen, to provide support, guidance and coaching to a young person (Brewer et al. 1995), and where interaction is 'youth driven', it is more likely to be successful (Styles and Morrow 1992). There is nevertheless some evidence that mentoring may be at its most effective where there is some attempt not simply to establish a positive relationship between the mentor and the young person, but where the former seeks to reinforce positive patterns of behaviour by the latter through praise and/or reward (Fo and O'Donnell 1974; Tierney and Grossman, with Resch 1995).

Retention of young people in mentoring programmes has been found to be maximised where there is a goal-focused relationship (Brewer et al. 1995) and the framework and structure of this will depend on the age of the young person, level of maturity, risk or level of offending behaviour, developmental and cultural needs and issues particular to the locality. The learning needs of young people can be addressed in both group and one-to-one settings and in matching mentors and young people; while procedures should be developed that take into account the preferences of young people and that of their families and the volunteers (Clayden and Stein 2002). Matching along cultural or gender lines is sometimes not possible, nor in every case is it necessarily desirable. It is essential nevertheless that the cultural and other needs of the young person are recognised and respected and that an attempt should be made to meet them. The mentor must understand the cultural and community background of the young person (Rhodes et al. 1992, 1995).

Between 2001 and 2004, the YJB supported eighty community mentoring projects in England and Wales with the intention of providing mentoring for young people who had offended or were at risk of doing so. The National Evaluation Programme (St James Roberts et al. 2004) found that the mentoring projects succeeded in some respects, in particular, in the reintegration of the targeted young people into education, training and the community. The critical question nevertheless concerned their relative effectiveness and cost. Because mentors are unsalaried community volunteers, one possible benefit of mentoring lies in its value for money. Considered in this context, the findings were found to be less positive. The mentoring programmes were discovered to be substantially more expensive than alternatives that could produce similar benefits, such as the YJB education training and employment (ETE) schemes. Compared to the average cost per ETE programme for a young person of £2,300, the mentoring programmes examined cost several times as much. Furthermore, many young people referred to the projects refused to take part or did not engage with their mentors, while many volunteers failed to become mentors. As a result, only 2,045 of 4,828 young people referred to the projects received mentoring, raising additional concerns about the cost-effectiveness of the project.

The reluctance of young offenders to take part in mentoring or other community intervention programmes was found to be thoroughly documented, which raised crucial questions about their appropriateness as a stand-alone intervention, and highlighted significant issues about service value and cost. The failure to find evidence of improvements in behaviour, literacy and numeracy using formal assessments raised doubts as to whether the project-identified improvements were substantial enough to make a significant, lasting difference to the mentored young people. The evaluation team observed that, considering that an average mentoring programme contained eight meetings – perhaps twenty contact hours overall – it would be surprising if the result did 'immunise' these young people permanently against the many difficulties they faced.

Restorative justice

The active involvement of victims of crime in the youth justice process is a key element of the contemporary youth justice system. Strategies to achieve these aims are usually called restorative justice and seek to balance the concerns of the victim and the community with the need to reintegrate the young person into society. It was thus a central component of the New Labour reintegrative tutelage project and has since been even more strongly promoted by the Coalition and subsequent solo Conservative governments, not least because of its cost-effective potential. Such strategies seek to assist the recovery of the victim and enable all parties with a stake in the justice process to participate in it (Marshall 1998) and also they have been shown to be effective in reducing reoffending by young people (Sherman and Strang 1997; Nugent et al. 1999; Street 2000), especially by violent young people (Strang 2000), and provide greater satisfaction for victims (Umbreit and Roberts 1996; Wynne and Brown 1998; Strang 2001). Compliance with reparation has been found to be generally higher in restorative schemes than through the courts (Marshall 1999).

The Crime and Disorder Act 1998 had incorporated the use of reparation to victims in final warnings (now replaced by youth cautions), action plan orders and reparation orders (Home Office 1998a). Restorative approaches to arranging reparation can also be used in the context of pre-court work, including final warnings and bail support. The New Zealand conferencing system for young offenders enables restorative work to be undertaken as an alternative to the formal criminal justice system at any stage of the process, so serious and/or persistent offenders can be included where this is appropriate (Justice 2000).

Eight main theoretical principles of effective restorative justice can be identified. First, those directly affected by a crime, the victims, are involved in the process of determining the outcome, including how best to repair the harm done. Second, consideration of the wishes and needs of the victim are perceived to be more important than in traditional criminal justice procedures. Third, young people have to take responsibility for their actions and acknowledge what they have done in accordance with the rational actor model of criminal behaviour before entering the restorative process. Fourth, young people are helped to see that their actions have negatively affected the lives of other real human beings. Fifth, restorative work should address the specific cultural, religious and language needs of all those involved. Sixth, all parties are entitled to express their feelings and contribute their views in a non-adversarial process. Seventh, all parties – including the perpetrator and the victim – can be helped to regain a sense of personal power and control over their lives. Eighth, positive outcomes for the victim and their community are valid objectives alongside change in the behaviour and attitudes of the offender (Marshall 1996; Graef 2000; McCold and Wachtel 2000; Youth Justice Board 2001b). Researchers have nevertheless emphasised a number of crucial tensions between the spirit of restorative justice and the practice of decision-making in the contemporary youth justice system. Haines and O'Mahoney (2006: 119) thus were to observe that:

> The growth in popularity and spread of restorative justice precisely at a time when attitudes towards young people find expression in generally more controlling and/or punitive measure (especially in England and Wales) both rest in, and at the same time expose, the crucial tension within restorative justice to be simultaneously both positive and punitive. In practice, the positive elements are more rhetorical whilst the punitive expressions are more materially apparent.

Research published by the Ministry of Justice shows that 85 per cent of victims and 80 per cent of offenders were satisfied with their experience of a restorative justice conference (Shapland et al. 2008). The report showed that: first, 78 per cent of victims who took part in restorative justice conferences said they would recommend it to other victims; second, 90 per cent of victims who took part in restorative justice received an apology from the offender in their case, as compared with only 19 per cent of victims in the control group; third, only six victims, and six offenders, out of 152 offenders and 216 victims interviewed, were dissatisfied with the restorative justice conference after taking part; fourth, around 80 per cent of offenders who took part thought it would lessen their likelihood of reoffending; fifth, victims who had been through a restorative justice conference were more likely to think the sentence the offender had received was fair than victims in the control group who did not participate. This research compares with just 33 per cent of victims who think the criminal justice system meets their needs; and 41 per cent of victims who think the system brought offenders to justice (Nicholas et al. 2005).

Intensive supervision and surveillance programmes

Intensive supervision and surveillance programmes (ISSPs) are targeted at that small minority of offenders we have previously identified in this book, who are responsible for a disproportionately large number of offences. The eligibility criteria require the young person to be appearing in court, charged with or convicted of an offence, to have previously been charged, warned or convicted of offences committed on four or more separate dates within the previous twelve months, and to have received at least one community or custodial penalty. A young person can also qualify for ISSP if they are at risk of custody, because the current charge or sentence relates to an offence which is so serious that an adult could be sentenced to fourteen years or more, or they have a history of repeat offending on bail and are at risk of a secure remand. There is some evidence nevertheless which suggests that the provision of intensive programmes to low-risk offenders can be counterproductive and they may actually lead to an increase in recidivism (Andrews et al. 1990). The accurate targeting of ISSP resources towards those who meet the eligibility criteria is thus considered essential (Stephenson et al. 2011).

The ISSP programme content should incorporate five core modules covering essential areas of youth justice effective practice intervention identified above – education and training, restorative justice, offender behaviour, interpersonal skills and family support – with ancillary options based on individual circumstances and local resources, including drug or alcohol work or 'constructive leisure/recreation' (Gray et al. 2005). In addition, those on ISSPs should also be subject to at least one form of surveillance. Smith (2007) observes that the framework and delivery requirements for the ISSP are highly prescriptive and this leaves little scope for the exercise of professional discretion by practitioners. The overall aim is nevertheless clearly to provide a demanding programme which reassures courts that it is an 'effective' alternative to custody.

Remand management

Remand and pre-trial services exist primarily to divert those considered to be appropriate young people from unnecessary custodial remands and to manage them while they are awaiting trial, or sentence, including preventing and/or reducing offending and ensuring attendance at court. It has become widely accepted that the use of custody for young people is undesirable and damaging, with periods spent in custody being disruptive to family life, employment and the education of the young person, particularly when they are detained a long way from home, while custodial remands may also be emotionally damaging and increase health risks (Cavadino and Gibson 1993; Moore and Smith 2001). Moreover, the Prison Service prioritises security and containment rather than welfare (Woolf 1991) and prison is not a safe or appropriate environment for young people where they may be vulnerable and lack the necessary coping strategies to deal with the conditions of incarceration (Her Majesty's Inspectorate of Prisons 2001). Problems of vulnerability are exacerbated by intimidation, violence and bullying, which are commonplace within the secure estate (Goldson 2002) and the incidence of self-harm and suicide is high among young people on remand (Liebling 1992).

Drug use is also widespread within penal establishments (Hucklesby and Wilkinson 2001); while the incidence of mental health problems is higher in prison establishments than in the population as a whole and young people with such difficulties may present a significant risk to themselves and others (Her Majesty's Inspectorate of Prisons 2000). Furthermore, there is evidence that custodial remands result in higher conviction rates, with a greater likelihood of incarceration on conviction (Cavadino and Gibson 1993). One factor which may explain this relationship is the difficulties of preparing a defence case when young people are in custody.

Safeguarding the rights of all unconvicted young people at every stage of the criminal justice process from arrest to final disposal is a key objective of remand management. This is an important component because research evidence suggests that young people are being remanded in custody unnecessarily (Goldson 2002) and this is a problem that has been exacerbated by heightened media interest in offending on bail and legislative change and consequently resulted in a rise in the number of young people subject to custodial remands (Home Office 2001). Other policy and legal changes, such as the introduction of electronic monitoring, have, however, increased the number, scope and restrictiveness of non-custodial remand options. This has increased the opportunities for diverting young people from custody but has, at the same time, increased the potential for 'net-widening' (Hucklesby 2001). This thus increases the importance of assessing the least intrusive remand option possible in the individual circumstances.

An important impetus behind legislative changes in the early twenty-first century relating to bail was the concern over the number of offences committed while on bail (Hucklesby and Marshall 2000). It was argued that offending on bail contributes to a large proportion of the total number of offences committed

(Avon and Somerset Constabulary 1991; Northumbria Police 1992; Hucklesby and Marshall 2000) and young people are believed to contribute to this problem disproportionately (Avon and Somerset Constabulary 1991; Northumbria Police 1992; Morgan and Henderson 1998). Several initiatives and changes to legislation were introduced to tackle the problem of offending on bail and these include the introduction of electronic monitoring (Criminal Justice and Police Act 2001) and increasing the powers of the court to impose a secure remand on young people it believes have offended on bail (Criminal Justice and Police Act 2001). These measures made the granting of bail more difficult and thus less likely. Reducing the incidence of offending on bail was to nevertheless remain a priority for the YJB and a key objective of remand management.

The youth remand provisions in the Legal Aid, Sentencing and Punishment of Offenders (LASPO) Act 2012 made significant changes to the remand framework for 10- to 17-year-olds in criminal proceedings. Where a child has been remanded on bail, they would continue to be dealt with under the Bail Act 1976, but where the court refuses bail, the new youth remand framework will permit the court to remand a child to local authority accommodation or to youth detention accommodation.

These changes to the youth remand framework were made following public concern that 17-year-olds were being remanded like adults and not on the same principles as younger children. That practice had attracted criticism from the UN Committee on the Rights of the Child with the placement of children in secure accommodation also seen to be discriminatory and unfair as it was predominantly determined by age and gender. Furthermore, many 15- to 17-year-olds whose alleged offences were not the most serious and whose behaviour does not pose a risk to the public were remanded securely. It was thus recognised that a better approach to youth remand that maintains community-led supervision, support, education and training was needed.

The changes to the youth remand framework that were introduced in December 2012 can be summarised as follows. First, 10- to 17-year-olds were now to be dealt with according to the same remand framework and conditions for custodial remand regardless of their age and gender. Second, the court must now first consider whether to remand a child on bail. Where bail is refused, the court should then consider whether to remand to local authority accommodation or whether, if the child is aged 12 to 17, the conditions for a remand to youth detention accommodation are met. Third, 17-year-olds who are remanded should now be dealt with in the same way as younger children. They may now be remanded to local authority accommodation. Fourth, a 12- to 17-year-old can now be remanded to youth detention accommodation if they meet one of two sets of conditions: the first is based on the type of offending, the second on the history of absconding or offending together with whether there is a real prospect of a custodial sentence. Fifth, every child remanded to youth detention accommodation will now be treated as 'looked after' by their designated local authority.

The new legislation also gives local authorities greater financial responsibility for remands to youth detention accommodation. YOTS will now have a financial interest in ensuring that they are adequately prepared for the remand hearing. Thus, for example, youth offending teams should, where appropriate, assist the court with information relating to: (i) available bail packages; (ii) available local authority accommodation; (iii) relevant conditions available that may be attached to a remand to local authority accommodation or bail; and (iv) which local authority should be designated by the court where a child has been remanded to local authority accommodation or youth detention accommodation.

Resettlement

Resettlement is formally defined as the effective reintegration of imprisoned offenders into the community after the sentence has been served (HM Inspectorates of Prisons and Probation 2001). Reoffending rates after custody are, as we have seen previously in this book, notoriously high, and the highest of all for young men in their teens leaving custody with a history of residential burglary convictions (Home Office 1998b) and those on short-term sentences (HM Inspectorates of Prisons and Probation 2001). These are among the most challenging people to reintegrate into the community and to set on a course that takes them away from their high-risk offending lifestyles. Research constantly demonstrates that many young offenders have dysfunctional families, very poor educational histories, mental health needs, and drug and alcohol problems (e.g., Hagell and Newburn 1994; Loeber and Farrington 1998; Rutter et al. 1998) and changing the way they behave and interact with their local communities is possibly the most difficult thing that youth justice practitioners can ever try to achieve.

In an ideal world, successful resettlement for these young people will include seven crucial elements. First, there will be a cessation of offending, or at least a significant reduction in their criminal involvement to encompass lower-level offences committed less frequently and with less risk to others. Second, there will be engagement in employment, education or training activities, in a way that will lead to a new life away from offending. Third, there will be a full realisation of any benefit entitlement and general support will be provided with financial planning. Fourth, the process of reintegration will include inclusion back into the health and dental services, including if necessary, engagement in substance misuse programmes. Fifth, there will be settlement into stable accommodation – in the parental home, if suitable, or in private, local authority or similar accommodation. Sixth, there will be crucial support in building new and better relationships with family – both existing family and a new young family they may be fathering. Seventh, there will be engagement in some way with people who can provide long-term mentoring or other kinds of social support during the short-term future when opportunities, pressures and temptations may conspire to push the young person back into offending (Stephenson et al. 2011).

HM Inspectors of Prison and Probation (2001) had pertinently observed that the term 'resettlement' is in reality a misnomer, as many of these young people will never have been in a position where these objectives could have been met, even before they went into custody. In many cases, a serious attempt at resettlement after the first custodial sentence may be the first time that anyone has ever really tried to engage these young people or attempt to socially include them. This consequentially makes the challenge even greater.

It is thus clear that unless the underlying causes of criminality are addressed, offending behaviour will continue after release. Among these underlying causes are the poor parenting, exclusion from education, unstable living conditions and mental health problems we have previously identified in this book. It is clear from this observation that successful resettlement and reintegration will play a crucial part in helping to prevent reoffending and, in addition, in order to reduce risks to the public from offenders, it is a highly significant way of ensuring a decline in the crime rate. The existing evidence for reducing the crime rate by increasing incarceration as proposed by proponents of the rational actor model is not strong, while statisticians have shown that we would have to imprison a significant and unrealistic proportion of the population to see a meaningful reduction in crime levels (Tarling 1993; Spelman 1994), so investment in more effective resettlement and reintegration into the community would appear to be the only real answer.

Conclusions

The key areas of effective practice which we have considered above have provided the basis of the multi-agency contemporary youth justice system. New Labour neo-communitarianism thus underpins an approach where the responsibilities of the individual are located in the context of a community with rights. The significance of the left realist intervention model with its dual emphasis on a balanced intervention that focuses not just on the crimes committed by young people but also very much on the social causes of that criminality is undeniably identified in the above interventions, which also have undoubted resonance with the concepts of risk and the audit society. Unquestionably the proclaimed aim of the Youth Justice Board to seriously reduce youth offending is an ambitious and extremely problematic project.

Stephenson et al. (2007) observe pertinently that if evidence-based youth justice is to be taken seriously by practitioners and key decision-makers in the contemporary system, then there has to be an accepted recognition of the limitations of the strategy. They observe quite correctly that:

> The basic contexts associated with offending such as poverty and childhood abuse may be very difficult to ameliorate. Devising interventions that are of an intensity, duration and sophistication that match the multiple challenges facing some young people, such as detachment from education and employment, homelessness, substance misuse, and poor mental health is often beyond the resources available to a YOT let alone an individual practitioner.
>
> (Stephenson et al. 2011: 255)

These issues are considered further in the fourth and final part of this book, which considers youth justice in the wider socio-economic context in a national and international context.

Summary of main points

1   The contemporary youth justice system was very much founded on the notion of effective evidence-based practice.
2   The identification and management of risk was to become central to the new system and the notion that young people who have one or more risk factors present in their lives are far more likely to be involved in criminal behaviour.
3   The youth justice system was very much influenced from the outset by the work of Utting and Vennard (2000), who identified four categories of risk factors (family, educational, community, individual/peer) and three categories of protective factors (social bonding; healthy beliefs and clear standards; opportunities, skills and recognition) in the research literature.
4   The key areas of effective practice that are considered here are not mutually exclusive but are closely interconnected and form part of a system for identifying and responding to youth offending.
5   Assessment, planning and supervision were considered to be essential elements of practice with young people at all stages of the contemporary youth justice system because they guide and shape all subsequent work which is conducted.
6   The key areas of effective practice for identifying and responding to these risk and protective factors are parenting; education, training and employment; substance misuse; and mental health.
7   Parsons and Howlett (2002) identified educational failure, permanent exclusion or non-attendance at school as the risk factors with the highest correlation to youth offending.
8   The following category more specifically addresses the lives of apprehended young offenders and the role of youth justice interventions in their lives: (1) offending behaviour programmes; (2) neighbourhood prevention; (3) mentoring; (4) restorative justice; (5) intensive supervision and surveillance programmes; (6) remand management; and (7) resettlement.
9   New Labour neo-communitarianism clearly underpinned an approach where the responsibilities of the individual are clearly located in the context of a community with rights.
10   The significance of the left realist intervention model with its dual emphasis on a balanced intervention that focuses not just on the crimes committed by young people but also very much on the social causes of that criminality is clearly identified.

Discussion questions

1   What is effective practice in the youth justice system?
2   What factors are identified as being important in the life of a child or young person at risk of offending?
3   What protective factors are identified in the life of a young person at risk of offending?

4 What is the particular impact of educational attainment or achievement in the life of a child or young person?
5 How can we identify the influence of communitarianism in the youth justice system?

Notes

1 Absolute poverty measures the number of people living below a certain income threshold or the number of households unable to afford certain basic goods and services. Relative poverty measures the extent to which a household's financial resources fall below an average income threshold for the economy. Although living standards and real incomes have grown because of higher employment and sustained economic growth over recent years, the gains in income and wealth have been unevenly distributed across the population.
2 The term 'parent' includes birth parents (whether married or unmarried) and guardians or other carers, including step-parents, adoptive parents, foster parents, grandparents, older siblings or other relatives.
3 The term 'mental' health encompasses varied disorders such as emotional disorders, depression, post-traumatic stress disorder, conduct disorders, hyperkinetic (hyperactivity) disorders, personality disorders, persuasive developmental disorders, mental retardation/learning difficulties and specific learning difficulties. For further information about specific disorders, the reader is referred to a child psychiatry text (Black and Cottrell 1993; Goodman and Scott 1997).
4 The term absolute poverty measures the number of people living below a certain income threshold or the number of households unable to afford certain basic goods. Relative poverty measures the extent to which the financial resources of a household fall below an average income threshold for the economy. Although living standards and real incomes have grown because of higher employment and sustained economic growth over recent years, the gains in income and wealth have been unevenly distributed across the population and services.

Part IV

Alternative youth justice systems and the contemporary world

14 Youth justice in wider context

Key issues

1 Risk-based contemporary youth justice revisited
2 Social exclusion and reintegrative tutelage reconsidered
3 Restorative justice revisited
4 Youth social exclusion in an era of austerity
5 Loïc Wacquant and the government of insecurity

In the third part of this book we considered the work of the youth justice system in the contemporary age of austerity. We thus reflected on the electoral coalition between the Conservatives and the Liberal Democrats, the 'Big Society', its underpinnings and implications and the nature of the contemporary youth justice system, while the final chapter in that section considered the work of youth offending teams in practice and involved an examination of the role and significance of identified key areas of effective practice. This fourth and final part of the book examines youth justice systems in the contemporary world or alternative ways of doing youth justice. This chapter starts that process by reflecting further on the effectiveness and structural limitations of the contemporary system in existence in England and Wales in the wiser socio-economic context.

Armstrong (2005) observes that the very idea of children and young people being involved in criminal behaviour is of considerable concern to most of us on different levels. Thus, first, it quite simply challenges any belief we may have in the notion of childhood innocence and, perhaps, some fundamental beliefs we may have about the possibility of a 'good society'. Second, it generates in us a fear of lawlessness and the effects of a breakdown in socialisation. We thus come to question the quality of our services for children, our support for parents and our investment in future generations; not least those of us who are ourselves parents. Yet it is also evident from the many self-report studies that have been undertaken over the years – and, indeed, in more recent years, the official crime statistics, even allowing for their widely acknowledged limitations – that most young people these days are *not* involved in crime at any level, illegal drug taking or even drinking alcohol.

For those who do get involved in offending behaviour, the evidence from both reconviction and self-report studies has consistently indicated that the great majority of young people continue to 'grow out' of it (MORI 2003) regardless of the virtually continuous 'moral panics' that suggest the very opposite. Moreover, of those who do report offending, a much smaller proportion than previously report coming into contact with the criminal justice system. Thus, a survey conducted for the YJB in 2003 had found that 21 per cent of children and young people in mainstream schools say that they have been caught by the police at least once (MORI 2003) but we should note that the converse of that finding: 80 per cent had not been apprehended.

The evidence we have of the relationship between children and young people and criminality in the contemporary world would thus seem to contradict popular widely held perceptions. Indeed, if we consider the 'fear of crime' from the perspective of the young person, what might be the most worrying, if perhaps ironic, observation about the crime statistics is that young people are the group more likely to be the victims of crime (Furlong and Cartmel 1997; Home Office 2002). Yet, as NACRO (2001b) observed, British public perceptions tend to overstate the extent of crime attributable to young people: thus, while 28 per cent believe that young people are responsible for more than half of all offences and a further 55 per cent believe that responsibility for crime is shared equally between adults and children, in reality, 76 per cent of detected crime was committed by persons over the age of 18, and those over 21 are responsible for almost 60 per cent. But it is as victims of crime that children and young people are significantly over-represented, although much of this victimisation – as much victimisation in general – is not represented in the crime statistics and does not come to the attention of the authorities.

Beckett and Warrington (2014) present the findings of an inquiry into the hidden victimisation of children and young people, undertaken on behalf of the All Party Parliamentary Group (APPG) for Victims and Witnesses of Crime, crucially finding that there are significant levels of crime and victimisation among children and young people in contemporary society. Approximately one-third of 11- to 17-year-olds, for example, reported that they had experienced physical violence within the previous year; while one-quarter of 11- to 24-year-olds said that they had experienced some form of abuse or neglect during their childhood (Radford et al. 2011). Evidence, moreover, indicates that children and young people are at higher risk than adults of experiencing certain forms of crime. Females aged 16 to 19 years thus are the age group at highest risk of being a victim of a sexual offence (Ministry of Justice et al. 2013); while existing vulnerabilities, such as a long-standing illness or disability, appear to significantly compound the vulnerability of children and young people to crime.

The majority of crimes against children and young people are not reported to the police and are invisible to the authorities. They simply do not officially exist. Only 13 per cent of violent offences and 15 per cent of thefts are reported by young victims to the authorities (ONS 2014). Similarly, retrospective accounts of childhood sexual abuse show that only 5–13 per cent of victims reported this to an adult at the time. Thus, whilst existing data offers pertinent insights, determining accurate prevalence levels of the victimisation of children and young people nevertheless remains a challenge because of variable approaches to collecting and categorising data.

Children and young people do not always know what constitutes crime and how to report it. Many simply do not realise that what they have experienced constitutes a crime or other form of victimisation requiring support and redress. This is particularly true where forms of criminal behaviour have been normalised within a peer group or a community, or when grooming by another individual is a factor. Moreover, they do not always know how to report experiences of victimisation even if they recognise these as such. Teachers are the professionals they are most likely to tell but they, and other practitioners, often lack confidence about how to recognise and respond to reports of child victimisation.

The circumstances in which victimisation occurs affects the likelihood of reporting. Thus, the fact that much of the victimisation of children occurs in contexts, such as school, where perpetrators are known to the victim, significantly reduces the likelihood of the latter choosing to report the crime. Children and young people identify a range of risks associated with reporting crime including reputational damage, implications for their family or fears of significant physical reprisal. Unwritten group 'rules' in certain social contexts de-legitimise the idea of reporting crime to the authorities and, in some instances, threats or blackmail by perpetrators exert a significant silencing power over the likelihood of reporting crime.

Moreover, children and young people may blame themselves for their victimisation, while many falsely assume responsibility for their experiences of harm. In such cases they are extremely unlikely to report these experiences or seek support. Practitioners can also be guilty of reinforcing damaging messages around responsibility to victims through their reactions to disclosure or use of language. At the same time, negative perceptions of the police can deter the reporting of crime. Thus, many children and young people have little confidence that the criminal justice system will deliver justice and protect victims, with attitudes towards the police often characterised by feelings of mistrust and fear. Many believe that the police treat them more negatively than they do adults and anticipate that their direct contact with the service is likely to be characterised by a lack of respect, suspicion or discrimination.

It is perhaps not surprising, in view of the extent of invisible victimisation of children and young people, that many of them do not appear to possess a tolerant 'let them grow out of it' attitude to criminality among their peers. In Chapter 6 of this book, we considered four diverse models which explain the development of the criminal justice system in different but nevertheless ultimately very compatible ways. We observed that the left realist hybrid model builds on the Foucauldian carceral society orthodoxy where it is readily accepted that disciplinary and tutelage strategies are often implemented by philanthropists, moral entrepreneurs, professional agents and practitioners who often have little or no idea how their often, but sometimes less, humble discourse contributes to the grand overall disciplinary control matrix. The left realist hybrid variation nonetheless recognises that there are further interests involved in the creation of that matrix and these significantly are ours. This hybrid perspective accepts the legitimacy of both radical conflict and social progress accounts because there were and are a multitude of motivations for both implementing and accepting the increasing surveillance and control of young people on the streets and elsewhere. But crucially among those who wish to see a rigorous intervention in the lives of those socially excluded young people – who are over-represented among the numbers of persistent offenders – are both ourselves as parents, who invariably go to great lengths to ensure that our children do not come into contact with this socially excluded underclass, an evasiveness perfectly epitomised by our careful choice of school for our offspring, and, perhaps more importantly, our children themselves. It is the latter who want protection from what they widely perceive to be the dangerous, threatening elements in their age group who are the most likely to make them victims of crime.

A survey conducted by IPO-Mori for the Youth Justice Board (Ipsos MORI 2006) showed that 60 per cent of young people between the ages of 10 and 17 years wanted to see more police on the beat as the best way to protect them from becoming a victim of crime at the hands of other young people. Moreover, 38 per cent called for harsher punishments for children and young people who offend. YJB Interim Chair Graham Robb said at the time:

> It's positive that young people believe the police have a major role to play in keeping them safe. However, the underlying issue is that many young people don't feel protected outside the home and, in particular, they are afraid of other youngsters.
>
> This type of situation can lead some children to carry weapons for self-protection and is something we must avoid at all costs. We all need to do more to make our children feel safe.

The apparent decline in youth crime observed in this book is a reflection of a similar apparent decrease in crime overall – the ubiquitous 'crime drop' that we have again questioned repeatedly throughout this text – both in the UK and in many other parts of the world. It could be argued that changes in the youth crime rate have been brought about, or at least influenced, by the policies and actions of the contemporary youth justice system. The evidence nevertheless shows that the trend of decline was clearly evident before the establishment of that system and it is extremely difficult to disentangle the possible causes that lie behind social trends and the impact of particular policies. Indeed, in practice it is likely that the causal relationship between different factors impacting upon the trend in youth crime is going to be extremely complex.

Armstrong (2005) observes that whatever the explanation for this downturn in offending behaviour by children and young people – and more than ten years has elapsed since she made that observation – there do appear to be fairly sound grounds for optimism, not least because there has been a huge reduction in the numbers of children and young people entering the youth justice system in recent years. The reasons for that decline are nevertheless vigorously contested. Thus, first, there is a serious possibility that increasing numbers of young people have simply desisted from involvement in offending behaviour in recent years because it is simply no longer a rational or 'cool' choice in a changed socio-economic context. It is a world where the only hope of legitimate material success is the adoption of an 'upward' strategy of educational attainment and we further critically explore this notion below. However, it might simply be the case that fewer children and young people are living their lives on 'the street' – that legendary 'place' identified in much criminological and sociological literature, plus contemporary popular culture – where young people have always met and 'hung out'. The virtual universal ownership of electronic communications gadgets has meant that more children and young people willingly spend their time in their bedrooms – either on their own or with others – engaged in social media or computer games online. Not on the street looking for some form of cheap entertainment, they do not come to the attention of the authorities and get in trouble. At the same time, significant reductions in resources has led to the inability of the police to maintain a visible presence on many of those streets.

We will now consider the increasing policing and surveillance of those groups who continue to pursue a 'downward strategy' which has seen them absorbed into the ranks of social exclusion. In particular, we are going to consider how a new industry of early intervention based upon an ideology of 'risk' has become a tool of governance in the lives of young people, their families and their schools, in some of our most deprived communities. For it is, in reality, these young people who are over-represented among the numbers of persistent young offenders with a multiplicity of risk factors that predispose them to crime – the 3 to 4 per cent identified in this book – from which the young people surveyed by the YJB seek protection.

Risk-based contemporary youth justice revisited

As we have seen, the contemporary youth justice system is very much founded on the notion of risk-focused prevention. From this perspective, it is argued that there is a strong correlation between the offending behaviour of young people and significant risk factors to be found in their life experiences; thus, dysfunction appears within or in relation to the family, school, community and the peer group of delinquent individuals (Hawkins et al. 1992), as well as in the personalities or genetic make-up of certain children (Farrington 1994b; Rutter et al. 1998). It has thus been proposed that early interventions which focus upon correcting these deficiences are likely to reduce the likelihood of involvement in offending behaviour.

The most influential study on the identification of risk factors related to criminal behaviour has been the Cambridge study in delinquent development, a longitudinal study of 411 working-class males born in London in 1953 (Farrington 1995) and this has been cited previously in the book. The original sample was followed up periodically from the age of 8 and a strong correlation was found between a number of risk factors – including low family income, large family size, poor housing, low intelligence, parental problems – and offending behaviour. This study has been extremely influential in reorienting thinking about youth crime in favour of a focus upon those psychogenic antecedents of criminal behaviour which are believed to lie in the immediate social environment of the child rather than in the structural characteristics of society itself. It has come to have a major influence on the policies of governments and has become integral to crime-reduction strategies in the UK, USA and elsewhere (see Graham and Bowling 1995; Utting 1996; Graham 1998), and in the former this approach has, as we have seen, found particular favour with the Youth Justice Board (2001a).

Pitts (2001b) has nevertheless alerted us to how the original findings of the 'Cambridge study' were processed and 'refined' by subsequent reports and have come to focus primarily on the family while ignoring wider structural issues. Indeed, this is seen as a good example of the ways in which governments employ social science creatively to support their positions. The original study actually discovered a multitude of risk factors – some in the immediate environment of the offender but others, such as a lack of employment opportunities, which can be located in the wider social structure – but, at the same time, had been unable to distinguish any 'cause' and 'effect' in what is, of course, a significantly complex reality. From that time onwards, the data from the original survey have come to be 'reinterpreted' and 'refined' in subsequent documents. Thus, the Conservative Party discussion document *Tackling the Causes of Crime* published in 1996 identified eight 'key risk factors': parenting, truancy, drug abuse, lack of facilities, homelessness, unemployment, low income and – interestingly and honestly – the effects of economic recession.

The influential Audit Commission report (1996) nevertheless refined these findings further into foreground familial and background factors, with those such as family income, employment and the socio-economic status of neighbourhood now relegated to the background factor category. Furthermore, a significant pamphlet, written by New Labour 'insiders' (Utting et al. 1993), had independently identified that 'the tangled roots of delinquency lie, to a considerable extent, inside the family'. Pitts (2001b) observes that this latter document came to significantly influence the prominent New Labour policy document *No More Excuses* published in 1997, which unequivocally reduced the multiplicity of risk factors in the original study to three main groupings of parenting, schooling and peer influence. The key risk factors were now identified as being male, poor parental discipline, criminal parents and poor school performance. Structural social exclusion factors such as unemployment and poverty had disappeared from the spectrum altogether, with the focus now clearly on the individual child and their parents.

Armstrong (2005) observes that the risk factor model appears to have provided a twofold legitimation of state intervention in the governance of children, families, schools and designated problematic communities. On the one hand, it provides a simplistic crime management system which – because it denies any social structural contribution to the construction and reproduction of offending behaviour – can focus its attention not on the causes of crime but rather on a policy of containment through the morality of 'blame'. On the other hand, the model is used to justify a whole paraphernalia of surveillance and intervention based on the assumption that youth crime is an outcome of dysfunctional individuals and communities and that these individuals can be identified through an assessment process determined by experts (see O'Malley 1992; Rose and Miller 1992; Stenson and Watt 1999; Kelly 2001; Stenson and Edwards 2003).

Armstrong (2005) observes that, significantly and problematically, such regulation has not been confined to the troublesome. Equally as important are the consequences of establishing criteria for 'normality' based upon a supposed scientific knowledge of the pathological or abnormal for maintaining the self-regulation of family life. These processes of governmentality, Armstrong argues, are embedded in the valuation of academic and professional judgements that masquerade as expertise. It is a masquerade because their science is decontextualised from the contested beliefs and values which give meaning and relevance to particular representations of normality and social order. Yet, the notion of 'risk' supports an anti-welfare rhetoric (Culpitt 1999) that legitimises the redistribution of social resources into a privatised world of individual responsibility and risk management. It is a language that has 'replac[ed] need as the core principle of social policy formation and welfare delivery' (Kemshall 2002: 1).

Armstrong (2005) further argues that what is lacking in these risk-analysis-based individualised accounts of criminal behaviour is: first, any sense of the significance of historically located, cultural and social forms in relation to the construction and negotiation of individual identities (as 'normal' or 'abnormal'); and, second, any discussion of the way in which social power is a factor, not only in the construction of 'risk' within society but also in the theorisation of 'risk' by social scientists themselves: thus, 'legitimacy is conferred almost exclusively on analysis at the individual level' (Susser 1998: 1). In this way, the representation of certain behaviours solely in terms of individual, or micro-social, dysfunction both hides from public view the social and cultural upheavals of the last thirty years while discouraging any attempt to understand the relationships between processes of social change and identity formation in young people.

Social exclusion and reintegrative tutelage reconsidered

We encountered earlier in the book the concept 'excluded tutelage', which was developed in order to make sense of an apparent – albeit relative, it was argued – success story in Conservative Party youth justice policy during the years 1979–97 (Hopkins Burke 1999a). Thus, for many young people this was an era characterised very much by 'the stick' of coercion and discipline but rather weak on 'the carrot' of socio-economic opportunity. Thus, a fundamental outcome of economic and social policy during that period was the creation of a socially excluded underclass. Youth justice policies, in particular, and welfare policies, in general, had, at best, done nothing to alleviate that situation, and, at worst, managed to exacerbate the problem.

It is the notion of reintegration into the community that enables us to both explain and contextualise the youth justice strategy of the New Labour government elected in 1997, and distinguish its policies from those of its populist Conservative predecessors. It is in this way a distinctive strategy which we observed at the outset of this third part of the book to be a significant component of a wider set of neo-communitarian strategies that have sought to reintegrate those sections of the population that have become increasingly socially and economically excluded during the past thirty years. This unwritten and unspoken government strategy, which has been termed 'reintegrative tutelage' (Hopkins Burke 1999a), nevertheless invites critical reconsideration in the context of recent recognition that prevailing discourses of transitions and social exclusion are no longer adequate to describe or explain the experiences of that substantial minority of young people who have become located in 'underclass locations' (Fergusson et al. 2000). Indeed, in this context, the whole notion of social reintegration came to be recognised as a fatally flawed strategy unlikely to be successful in society as it is currently structured.

The educational and employment prospects for all young people have clearly changed dramatically in the past forty years. Thus, in the early 1970s the majority left school at 16 and were able to secure full-time employment with seemingly relative ease. However, by the 1990s these young workers were replaced by full-time students, trainees, part-time workers and the unemployed working 'off the cards'.[1]

Since Income Support benefit was first abolished in 1988 for virtually all 16- and 17-year-olds, successive cohorts of that age group were faced with an apparently wide range of options but each with its own limitations: first, to continue with schooling or further education; second, accept a place on a government-sponsored training scheme; third, enter the labour market (often on a part-time or short-term basis); or, fourth, if unemployed, stay dependent on their families. As a result, it has been widely acknowledged that 'adolescence' has been formally extended in most social classes. At the same time, while most young people have been faced with extensive choices, they have been denied the possibility of full independence and the situation has not improved in the intervening years.

One of the most conspicuous consequences of a contracting and deregulated youth labour market has been the expansion of what Furlong and Cartmel (1997: 17) describe as 'an army of reluctant conscripts to post-compulsory education'. Thus, whereas in the mid-1970s a third of 16-year-olds stayed on at school, by the mid-1990s it was nearer 80 per cent. A range of vocational courses (BTEC, NVQ and GNVQ) have been introduced in schools and colleges of further education but with limited success. About a third of those starting a full-time post-16 course left early or failed the relevant examinations, while those entering youth training have fared little better. Despite government claims that various forms of youth training have been designed to improve skills and subsequent employability, these schemes have been consistently considered by young people themselves to be 'slave labour', with employers operating 'try-out schemes' in which the work performance of young people is assessed and only the best are retained (Coffield et al. 1986; Lee et al. 1990; Banks et al. 1992). Youth training schemes have thus been received by young people with a combination of resistance, denial and ambivalence (Mizen 1995: 197–202). The experience of training has also become fragmented and individualised but, at the same time, remains stratified by class, gender and 'race' (Furlong and Cartmel 1997: 32). Thus, the most disadvantaged and, in particular, those from minority ethnic groups tend to be concentrated in schemes with low rates of subsequent employment.

The promised new opportunities simply failed to materialise for many young people, with the vast majority of schemes reinforcing and reproducing gender stereotypes in their provision of 'suitable' work for young men and women (Griffin 1985; Cockburn 1987; Wallace 1987). Furthermore, the free-market logic of deregulation did not help young people get into work, despite them being cheaper to employ. Demand in industrialised economies for skilled workers has meant that the young – especially those without qualifications – have been left behind. Brinkley (1997) showed that in the previous year the unemployment rate for those under 25 was 14.8 per cent, which was almost twice the national average for all claimants. Unemployment has always hit the young hardest, particularly so those from ethnic minorities; thus while, in 1995, 15 per cent of white 16- to 25-year-olds were estimated to be unemployed, this compared quite favourably to the 51 per cent of African-Caribbean young men, 41 per cent of African-Caribbean young women, 34 per cent of Pakistani/Bangladeshi young men and 30 per cent of Indian young men (Runnymede 1996).

These estimates nevertheless ignore a sizeable percentage of the population. Wilkinson (1995) thus found, in his Sunderland-based study, that between 5 and 10 per cent of 16- and 17-year-olds were neither in education or training nor in employment and they did not have any access to income support or any form of legitimate income. Officially, they did not exist. This could amount to some 100,000 young people nationally who occupied what Williamson (1997) has, not without criticism, termed 'status-zero'.

In was in this context that the New Labour government in 1997 announced its Welfare-to-Work plans designed to take a quarter of a million under-25-year-olds 'off the dole'. Significantly, it was an extension of the former Conservative government's Job Seeker's Allowance and stipulated that if claimants refused to take up the proposed employment and training options, they would lose all right to claim welfare benefits. After a four-month induction period, designed to facilitate entry into the labour market, the young unemployed were now to take up a private-sector job for which the employer or training organisation was to be subsidised, work with a voluntary organisation or an environmental taskforce, or take up full-time education and training.

Fergusson et al. (2000) identified three interpretations of the collective experiences of 16- to 19-year-olds over the previous two decades. First, a transitions discourse was for many years the dominant discourse (Ashton and Field 1976) where this age range was seen as the critical period of transition, principally from student to employee, from adolescent to young adult and from a state of dependency to independence. From this perspective, post-16 activity is portrayed as a relatively rational process whereupon young people are matched to a range of possible places according to their preferences, their performance and the assessments of careers staff (Bates 1984). It is this effective matching that provides the foundations for careers which progress through further education, training and workplace experience. For the vast majority, it is argued, the period between 16 and 19 constitutes a relatively non-problematic linear transition from school to employment or further education/higher education.

Second, the markets and choice discourse is an outcome of the major restructuring of provision for 16- to 19-year-olds, from the late 1980s to the mid-1990s, in which providers were encouraged to open access and increase options in a competitive environment, and users were partially reconstructed as customers, with credit to spend and choices to exercise in pursuit of preferences and armed with information about the relative quality of institutions. This argument has impacted greatly on the first discourse by shifting responsibility for the transition away from careers guidance and towards the individual for mapping out their own education and training after the age of 16 (Hodkinson 1996).

Third, the social exclusion discourse is largely a product of the massive contraction of youth labour markets and has identified institutional arrangements as having failed to make adequate provision for those most vulnerable to market fluctuations. It is often combined with a discourse of disaffection where it is argued that they are cut off not only from traditional unilinear 'career' patterns, but also from finding a place in the market of studentships, jobs and training placements, either by structural factors such as inadequate provision and family poverty, or by individual factors, such as an anti-educational culture on the part of the individual young person. These patterns of experience tend to be interpreted through a discourse of exclusion when the factors are thought to be structural and through a discourse of disaffection when they are represented as personal shortcomings or as dysfunctional behaviour. Thus, much policy formulated following the election of New Labour in 1997 focused on making provision for this group as part of their reintegrative tutelage strategy.

Fergusson et al. (2000) proposed an alternative discourse where it was argued that the transitions discourse remained largely plausible for interpreting the careers of many entrants to higher education, and for a small proportion of young people who leave school at 16 and proceed through well-established training routes into a range of vocational openings. Moreover, a social exclusion/disaffection discourse might well be appropriate for explaining the experiences of those who opt out or become 'status zero'. Fergusson et al. nevertheless observe that neither of these discourses were appropriate for explaining the experiences of a growing number of young people who appeared to be neither 'in' nor 'out' and thus identified approximately a third of 16- to 18-year-olds who were seemingly engaged in a series of multiple trajectories. Such activities remain understandable in terms of a discourse of markets and choice, but the former is experienced in ways which not only fail to translate into 'transitions', but also do not permit exclusion or opting out. In the case of unsecured transitions, the processes of negotiating markets are, for some young people, resulting in dislocation from any hitherto identifiable mode of activity. For others, distinctive processes of marginalisation are being reproduced which cannot be attributed to structural exclusions or individualised disaffection alone. In contrast to social exclusion, which assumes a lack of means – or cultural capital – to take advantage of existing available opportunities, and to disaffection, which assumes an unwillingness to participate, a distinctive discourse of normalised dislocation identifies a partial lack of success at participation in a competitive environment, without any acknowledgement of structural or individual impediment.

Fergusson et al. (2000) argued that 'quasi-market' systems actively encourage instability in the trajectories of a substantial minority of young people. Through generating powerful pressures which force young people to make particular rational choices, markets draw into particular modes of participation young people who are either ill-informed about what they have committed themselves to, or are unable to identify or pursue a preferred option. The outcome is that options are found to be noticeably unsuitable, are pursued with little commitment and are short-lived. What is of particular interest is the nature of the pressures – and the complex mix of financial, social and cultural forces – which allows an apparently voluntary system of participation to result in unstable modes of activity.

Market-induced instability, it is argued, is experienced as a series of multiple relocations and unstable trajectories which occur within the context of a 'compulsory' market-driven inclusivity and which is characterised by default participation in education and resorting to part-time work. In short, there is a significant blurring of boundaries between those who have taken a conscious 'upward solution' of education and career pursuit progression and those who have taken a 'downward solution' of laissez-faire non-participation, albeit in the latter case invariably by default. There is thus a significant group in the middle sufficiently motivated to take an upward trajectory but are unable to acquire sufficient cultural capital[2] to obtain a stable successful economic location. Such young people with significantly weakened social bonds are very much at risk of being absorbed into the readily available offending subcultures we have encountered in this book even though they have few other risk factors present in their lives.

In short, the notion of reintegrative tutelage on which the whole New Labour neo-communitarian strategy was founded was evidently based on fragile socio-economic foundations, with the economy unable to provide accessible legitimate sustainable opportunities for increasingly large sections of young people. Thus, in these circumstances, the notion of restorative justice on which the whole neo-communitarian contemporary youth justice strategy was based was also equally problematic.

Restorative justice revisited

We have seen previously in this book that it is the purpose of restorative justice to bring together victims, offenders and communities to decide on a response to a particular crime. The intention is to put the needs of the victim at the centre of the criminal justice system and, to this end, finding positive solutions to crime by encouraging offenders to take responsibility for their actions. Victims may thus request a restorative justice approach to make an offender realise how the crime has affected their life, find out information to help put the crime behind them (e.g., why it was that the offender targeted them) and to openly forgive the offender.

Whereas 'traditional justice' is about punishing offenders for committing offences against the state, restorative justice is about offenders making amends directly to the people, organisations and communities they have harmed. The New Labour government thus supported restorative justice because it was seen as giving victims a greater voice in the criminal justice system, allowing victims to receive an explanation and more meaningful reparation from offenders, making offenders accountable by allowing them to take responsibility for their actions and, it was proposed, building community confidence that offenders are making amends for their wrongdoing. We saw in the third part of this book that restorative justice is still a significant key element of the contemporary youth justice system greatly endorsed by the Coalition and the later Conservative governments, who indeed seek its wider application. Research has clearly shown that this strategy has had some success in reducing reoffending by young people and it is certainly providing greater satisfaction for victims but there are nonetheless significant concerns about the legitimacy and efficacy of restorative justice in practice.

First, there have been concerns raised about the boundary between the negotiatory practices of restorative justice and the workings of the criminal justice system; thus, on the one hand, it is argued, the due-process safeguards for rights, equality and proportionality could all be lost, while, on the other hand, the power of judicial agencies can undermine and subvert the aims of restorative practices (Messmer and Otto 1992). Some have thus argued for completely separate and parallel systems, neither interfering with the other. Others have countered and argued that this would not lead to restorative justice at all, because all gains would be destroyed by the alienating and negative effects of adversarial justice. It is thus difficult to see how two independent systems can coexist for there is bound to be some influence each way and the problem cannot be avoided. Even though restorative justice involves a greater or lesser degree of devolution of control to individual citizens and communities, it is now generally accepted that it can and should be integrated as far as possible with legal justice as a complementary process that improves the quality, effectiveness and efficiency of a 'whole justice' (Marshall 1997). Restorative justice was thus to become an instrument of the neo-communitarian state-dominated contemporary youth justice system rather than having any significant independence from it.

A second limitation to any restorative justice practice which attempts to involve communities is the relative availability of resources and skills. Communities are not the integrated entities with high levels of mechanical solidarity that they once were in those Antipodean communities where restorative justice has been shown to be successful. In our contemporary post-industrial society, there is a greater emphasis on individual privacy and autonomy, and major social divides occur between cultures and age groups, without the interdependency of an ideal organic solidarity. Greater community involvement would thus inevitably mean increased education, training and practical resources, and more would need to be provided in some areas of significant deprivation than in others.

A third very closely related and highly significant limitation for restorative justice is the continuing existence of social injustice and inequality in and between communities. While problems such as these continue, the degree to which communities can be supportive, caring and controlling is seriously restricted. Social divisions also make voluntary participation less likely or less effective. If restorative justice involves the community as a major player, there simply needs to be a community with which the young person can identify and belong. The degree to which effective communities exist depends largely on other social policies apart from criminal justice and there are thus implications for education, housing, community development, employment opportunities, welfare, health and the environmental services on which the contemporary youth justice system is so dependent.

Gray (2005) has observed that responsibilisation through restorative justice interventions is one of the main technologies of risk management but the whole ethos, as we have observed above, envisages more than just holding young people responsible for their offending. It also professes a commitment to the restoration of victim–offender relations and the reintegration of young offenders into mainstream community life. Gray has nonetheless observed that the principles of restorative justice have been narrowly interpreted within the contemporary youth justice system and give undue weight to the responsibilisation of young offenders by challenging perceived deficits in their moral reasoning without any real attempt to legitimately challenge the exclusionary socio-economic constraints that severely limit their choices and ability to successfully reintegrate into mainstream society. The outcome has been that restorative justice has simply become bound to the interests of reinforcing 'moral discipline' rather than engaging with 'social justice' and the reinvigoration of community on which restorative justice and reintegrative tutelage are theoretically founded.

Proponents have argued that the reinvigoration of community through restorative justice mechanisms can facilitate strong bonds of social control: 'strong communities can speak to us in moral voices' and they allow 'the policing *by* communities rather than the policing *of* communities' (Strang 1995: 23). Nevertheless, as Crawford and Clear (2003) observe, alternative justice systems, through necessity, presuppose an existing degree of informal control upon which mutuality, reciprocity and commitment can be re-formed. Moreover, Braithwaite (1989: 100) observes that informal control processes, such as reintegrative shaming, which some community conferences seek to engender, are more conducive to – and more effective when drawing upon – communitarian cultures. The paradox is that in urban, individualistic and anonymous cultures, such as those that exist in most Western towns and cities, informal control mechanisms such as shaming lack potency. He observes that the appeal to revive or transform community has arisen at exactly the same time when it appears to be most absent, when

Durkheimian anomie or normlessness is rampant (Durkheim 1933). For some, this paradox provides the basis for the attraction of restorative and community justice.

The whole notion of community is nevertheless complex and extends beyond the more traditional definitions which are based on locality and embraces a multiplicity of groups and networks to which, it is believed, we all belong (Strang 1995: 28). This conception thus does not rely upon a fixed assumption of where a community will be found. Rather, it builds upon the notion of 'communities of care' – that is, the networks of obligation and respect between the individual and everyone who cares about the person the most – and these are significantly not bounded by geography (Braithwaite and Daly 1994: 195).

These communities of care are considered more relevant to contemporary modern living in urban societies because they provide a developed notion of 'community' where membership – or social identity – is personal and does not necessarily carry any fixed or external attributes of membership. Indeed, the fact that such communities do not carry any negative connotations of coercion or forced membership is one of the distinctive appeals of the concept (Crawford and Clear 2003) and from this perspective, there is an assumption that people can move freely between communities if they disagree with their practices and values and/or remain within a community but, at the same time, dissent from the dominant moral voice that exists. This is nonetheless a significantly problematic situation because, on the one hand, these contemporary 'light' communities are held up as examples of how they can allow sufficient space for individual or minority dissent, innovation and difference but, on the other hand, they are also seen as insufficient with regard to informal control.

Crawford and Clear (2003) observe that this all raises the question of exactly what is meant by the claim to 'restore' or 'reintegrate' communities as proposed by the proponents of both community and restorative justice (see Van Ness and Strong 1997; Braithwaite 1998; Clear and Karp 1999). For the very notion of restoring communities suggests a return to some pre-existing state and appears to involve a nostalgic urge to return to a mythical age of genuine human identity, connectedness and reciprocity. It certainly does seem questionable that the concept of community constitutes a dynamic force for democratic renewal that challenges existing inequalities of power and the differential distribution of life opportunities and pathways to crime that characterise our society.

Crawford and Clear (2003) argue that in order to consider the genuine potential of restorative and community justice, it is necessary to avoid the idealistic perceptions of many proponents and confront the empirical realities of most communities. The ideal of unrestricted entry to, and exit from, communities, needs to be reconciled with the existence of relations of dominance, exclusion and differential power. The reality is that many stable communities do, in fact, contain very high levels of mechanical solidarity but, at the same time, they tend to resist innovation, creation and experimentation, and shun diversity (Hopkins Burke and Pollock 2004). These communities may well be able to come together for informal social control but the way these processes play out lacks inclusive qualities and offender-sensitive styles. These communities can be, and often are, pockets of intolerance and prejudice. They can be coercive and tolerant of bigotry and discriminatory behaviour. Weaker individuals – and minority groups – within such communities often experience them not as a home of connectedness and mutuality but as the foundations of inequalities that sustain and reinforce relations of dependence (e.g., with regard to gender role and the tolerance of domestic violence or child abuse). Such communities are thus often hostile to minorities, dissenters and outsiders, and can tolerate and even encourage deviant and offending behaviour.

Communities are quite simply hierarchical formations which are structured upon lines of power, dominance and authority. They are intrinsically exclusive – as social exclusion presupposes processes of exclusion – and many solidify and define themselves around notions of 'otherness' that are potentially infused with racialised overtones. Challenging and disrupting established community order, its assumptions and power relations might thus be a more fundamental aspect of a progressive restorative justice programme and transforming communities may be a more appropriate strategy than the restoration of atavistic communities. The related question begged by this assertion is whether transforming communities is either feasible or an appropriate task of restorative justice in the contemporary youth justice system.

Furthermore, while the significant reduction in the number of children and young people in the youth justice system in recent years is clearly to be welcomed, this does return us again to the substantially unanswered question as to why this reduction has occurred. If one of the reasons for this reduction is that a resource-deficient police service is withdrawing from policing whole communities, then there is an issue of who might be 'policing' the locality and in what form. We might ask whether this space has been colonised by informal community policing mechanisms which, at one level, might be appealing – for example, the non-criminalisation of minor offending behaviour – but at another level, this appeal to self-policing can be rather scary for those caught up in these processes. Informal community policing has an appeal but it is very much a disputed concept in the literature (see Abel 1982; Cohen 1985; Findlay and Zvekic 1988; Matthews 1988; Merry and Milner 1993; Pavlich 1996) with some decidedly concerned at such developments. As Eugene McLaughlin (2013: 234) observes:

> Those who are wary of the whole idea of 'informal justice' continue to focus on the logical outcome of such a process – spontaneous or organized vigilantism where self-appointed 'guardians' will meet out justice. Lynchings in the southern states of the USA, 'burning tyre' justice in the townships of South Africa, and punishment beatings in Northern Ireland can all be cited as disturbing examples of informal justice.

> What is perhaps equally significant are ongoing examples of 'community justice' where specific types of dangerousness or threatening offenders are in the absence of decisive actions from the criminal justice system, hounded from their neighbourhoods.

At one level, the latter has remarkable similarities to state-sponsored anti-social behaviour strategies; at another level, it is an altogether more brutalised, privatised response where bullies and thugs are self-appointed police, judge, jury and punishment administrators.

Youth social exclusion in an era of austerity

It is clear from the discussion in this book – and in this chapter, in particular – that patterns of offending by children and young people and the nature of the response by the authorities are closely linked to significant socio-economic circumstances. Those circumstances have certainly not improved for the many young people experiencing – or at significant risk of – social exclusion since the great economic crash of 2008 and the introduction of rigorous austerity measures introduced by the Coalition in 2010. The rest of this chapter considers the socio-economic context of youth offending in the contemporary age of austerity before reconsidering these developments in a theoretical context.

Young people and (un)employment

Young people are invariably among the greatest victims of major economic recessions. At the beginning of 2015, young people were nearly three times more likely to be unemployed than the rest of the population and this was the largest gap in more than twenty years (Boffey 2015). The gap also appeared to be growing with all the implications for a parallel growth in the numbers experiencing social exclusion. The number of people aged 16–24 who were not in full-time education or employment had increased by 8,000 over the previous quarter with 498,000 in that age group without a job, a situation that was worse than at any point since 1992.

The youth unemployment rate is 14.4 per cent out of a total of 5.7 per cent of the working population, while Work and Pensions Secretary Iain Duncan Smith announced plans to deal with the problem by warning that unemployed teens under a future Tory government would be required to undertake community work such as picking up litter if they wanted to receive benefits. The Conservatives accused the Labour opposition of seeking to 'talk down the economy' by picking on the recent youth unemployment figures when the total number out of work in the UK had fallen by 97,000 to 1.86 million in the three months to December (albeit that many adults in work were on part-time or 'zero-hours'[3] contracts). Rachel Reeves, the shadow work and pensions secretary, responded by observing that youth unemployment had risen three months in a row – 3,000 that month and 30,000 the previous month – and consequently the country had German (low) levels of adult unemployment but levels of youth unemployment (high) that rivalled the poorer parts of Europe. Unemployment among people aged between 16 and 24 was now more than 16 per cent and it was increasing.

There was also an issue of low wages. Average wages for the population as a whole are now £1,600 lower than five years ago but if you are in your twenties then the average wage is now £1,800 lower. This is what contemporary austerity economics means for ordinary people because the burden of paying back the national debt is not equally distributed among the whole population, with younger people taking the brunt of the cuts.

Harrop and Reed (2015), in a report for the Labour Party 'think tank' the Fabian Society,[4] subsequently warned that over the next fifteen years rising prosperity will not be shared across society. Thus, high-income households are projected to see their incomes rise eleven times as quickly as low-income households, with family incomes for the rich projected to rise by £13,000 a year. Low-income households will be just £200 better off in relation to 2014 prices. Although GDP per person is assumed to grow by 32 per cent over the period, the living standards for low- and middle-income households are projected to stagnate with real disposable incomes growing by just 2 per cent and 9 per cent respectively.

The report proposes that social security and tax credit policies are the principle cause of rising poverty and inequality, so it warned against any major cuts to benefits after the forthcoming general election in May 2015. Andrew Harrop, co-author of the report and general secretary of the Fabian Society, observed in an interview with *The Observer* (Boffey 2015) that:

> The UK has endured a decade of falling living standards. Poverty and inequality are on the rise and our projections show they will continue to rise long into the future, unless politicians act.

> The gloomy prognosis we report is not inevitable. Political choices, not unstoppable economic forces, will determine the extent of inequality in 2030. We need to take a long view of this problem, but also have an immediate plan ready for after the election. The new government should make full employment and action on low pay its top two economic priorities. It should then establish a 'Prosperity Fund' to recycle to families the tax revenues generated from more people being in work and in better paid jobs. So-called 'predistribution' must pay for redistribution.

> Poverty and inequality could rise by even more than our projections if politicians introduce major benefit cuts after the election. Is that the Britain of the future we want?

This was not a warning that was to be heeded by the incoming Conservative government following their electoral success in May 2015. Unfettered now by the need to placate their coalition partners, they were now in a position to accelerate the offensive against the poor and in particular benefit claimants – especially young benefit claimants.

Homelessness and the benefit system

The homelessness charity Crisis[5] (2014) observes that homelessness is increasing and that it is younger male adults who are at particular risk. In the previous three years, the number of young people sleeping on the streets of London has more than doubled and new figures show that 8 per cent of 16- to 24-year-olds report recently being homeless. Between 2008/9 and 2011/12, living standards deteriorated faster for single under-35-year-olds than for any other group, with the percentage not reaching an acceptable standard of living rising from 29 per cent to 42 per cent. With almost a million young people unemployed, falling wages and deep benefit cuts, this age group is at particular risk of homelessness. Many cannot even find a room to rent, let alone thinking about buying a place of their own. One of the major reasons young people are facing homelessness is because single under-35-year-olds looking for private rented accommodation are only entitled to a lower rate of housing benefit, the Shared Accommodation Rate (SAR). This rate is based on the cost of a room in a shared house, rather than self-contained accommodation. In 2012, the SAR was extended to those under 35 (it previously applied only to under-25-year-olds), a change estimated to affect 62,500 people and in reality extending the social construction of childhood/adolescence to that age. The average age for young people finally leaving the parental home in London (i.e., excluding years at university etc.) is now 31. Crisis campaigned against this benefit cut, which has created greater pressure on the limited pool of shared accommodation available and believe that it is damaging and unfair to restrict young people to this lower rate.

Crisis (2014) are also concerned that flaws in the way that the SAR is calculated means that it fails even to cover the rent for rooms in cheap shared houses. They propose that the government should: 1) listen to the voices of people who are facing homelessness and focus on addressing the reasons why young people are struggling, such as falling wages and the housing shortage; 2) stop restricting young people to a lower rate of housing benefit, which is causing misery for many; 3) thoroughly review how housing benefit for single people under 35 (the 'shared accommodation rate') is calculated so that it covers the true cost of renting.

Crisis (2014) also argues that the government should also make sure those exemptions for people who have been homeless work effectively, which they currently do not. Ever since the Shared Accommodation Rate of Local Housing Allowance (housing benefit for private rented accommodation) was introduced it has caused problems both because there is a lack of shared accommodation available and because sharing is inappropriate for many vulnerable people. The extension of the SAR to those aged under 35 has also increased by 50 per cent the number of people in receipt of the rate and put further pressure on already limited supply.

Crisis observes that it is impossible to track where those people who are no longer in receipt of housing benefit end up and whilst some may be able to stay with their families many will not. There has thus been a particular increase in young people rough sleeping in London and it is likely that many will be in other insecure housing situations, such as living on the floors of friends, and the existing shortage of shared housing has been worsened by the fact more people are now restricted to the SAR. Government research on the impact of changes made to housing benefit since 2011 (including the extension of the SAR) observed a number of serious problems around the availability, affordability and appropriateness of shared accommodation for different groups in different areas of the country (DWP 2013).

Following their electoral success in May 2015, the new Conservative government continued the ongoing process of reforming benefit entitlement by deciding to withdraw housing benefit from all those aged 21 and under. Crisis (2015) are strongly opposed to these latest benefit cuts, observing that while the vast majority of young adults can either afford their own accommodation or live with their parents, for many housing benefit is all that stands between them and homelessness. Crisis observe that: (1) there were 19,031 18- to 21-year-olds claiming housing benefit and Jobseeker's Allowance; (2) three in five (11,834) live in social homes so will already have met strict eligibility criteria for housing; (3) those living in the private rented sector are already entitled to only the lowest rate of housing benefit, the SAR; (4) more than six in ten (4,498) receive less than £75 per week.

The government intention is clearly to ensure that young people live at home with their parents rather than becoming dependent on benefits. Many young people nevertheless cannot live at home with their parents. Of those accepted as homeless by their local authority in 2014, almost a third were under 25 and more than 8,000 said the reason for the loss of their last home was that their parents would not or could not house them. Some young people have very clear reasons why they cannot live in the family home, including being orphans, care leavers and those who have experienced violence or abuse from family members. Others may have experienced a relationship breakdown with their parents; for example, if they have been thrown out because they are gay, have an alcoholic parent or have never got on with a step-parent. Some parents may simply be unable to afford to house their adult children or may not have the space, particularly if they have downsized to reduce their housing costs. Even if young people in certain circumstances were exempted from rules limiting access to housing benefit, those whose parents cannot or will not house them may find this difficult to prove to the local housing department. There may be very little evidence to confirm their situation. Even those who have experienced abuse may find this difficult to demonstrate, since domestic abuse is significantly under-reported. Without housing benefit, many people in these sorts of situations are likely to be left without support.

Homelessness, including youth homelessness, is already on the rise. In four years the number of young people sleeping rough in London has more than doubled and 8 per cent of 16- to 24-year-olds report recently being homeless. Restricting access to housing benefit would put many more young people at serious risk of homelessness. This is especially true for those already living in homelessness accommodation projects, which are largely funded through housing benefit. Nearly half (49 per cent) of people using accommodation projects are aged under 25. Withdrawing housing benefit from young people would not only undermine the statutory homelessness safety net but also be expensive to the taxpayer. The annual cost of homelessness to the state is estimated to be up to £1 billion. This includes direct costs to local authorities, and also costs placed on the health service, justice system and in benefit payments. Recent research found that, once the costs of vital exemptions and knock-on costs to other public services have been taken into account, the policy would save a maximum of £3.3 million. This is a conservative estimate of the knock-on impacts; only an additional 140 young people would need to become homeless before the policy would end up costing more than it saves (Heriot Watt University 2015).

Crisis (2015) observe that young people who have left home to look for work – and those who have been working and renting independently prior to losing a job – may need housing benefit for a short period to help them stay near job opportunities. Currently 85 per cent of young people on Jobseeker's Allowance find a job within twelve months. Withholding support could easily transform a short period job hunting into long-term unemployment, putting young people at risk of homelessness, undermining their potential to contribute to the economy and putting them in a situation where criminality is for them a very rational choice not least because there are realistic alternatives available. Restoring adequate housing benefits would appear to be a very rational choice on the part of government but this does not fit with a long-term erosion of the welfare state that is far from irrational on the part of neoliberals.

Loïc Wacquant and the government of insecurity

Loïc Wacquant (2009) identifies a significant punitive trend in penal policies that has occurred in advanced societies over the past thirty years, which he argues cannot simply be explained in terms of traditional criminal justice discourse. In an analysis significantly compatible with the new modes of governance and risk society theses presented previously in this book, he argues persuasively that these changes have instigated the introduction of a new 'government of social insecurity' which is targeted at shaping the conduct of the men and women caught up in the turbulence of economic deregulation in advanced societies and the conversion of welfare into a mechanism which leads people towards precarious employment. Young people can be clearly identified as central to these contemporary disciplinary tutelage strategies.

Wacquant observes that within this apparently 'liberal-paternalist' apparatus, the prison has been restored to its original purpose (at the beginning of modernity) which is to discipline and control those populations and territories which are resistant to the emerging new economic and moral order, while, at the same time, ritually reasserting the resilience of the dominant groups. He recognises that it was in the USA that this new politics and policy of marginality, which brings together restrictive 'workfare' and expansive 'prison-fare', was invented, in the aftermath of the social and racial upheaval of the 1970s that was to instigate the neoliberal revolution, in a response that has transformed the socio-economic situation of the USA and which has subsequently spread to Europe, in general, and the UK, in particular.[6]

It is the USA which nonetheless provides the neoliberal template that is clearly being replicated in the UK and helps us explain the onslaught on welfare benefits as part of a major disciplinary tutelage project to reshape society in the interests of a low-cost (which means low wage), highly competitive neoliberal economy. Wacquant (2009a) thus argues that the social policy of transition from welfare to workfare that is incrementally taking place in advanced neoliberal societies needs to be analysed in conjunction with the rise of prisonfare, that is, the mass incarceration of certain categories of the population perceived to be problematic. Workfare and prisonfare are from this perspective simply two sides of the same coin: they are the areas where the neoliberal state can still assert its authority once depleted of its economic and social policy functions. The combination of workfare and prisonfare is seen to fulfil both economic and symbolic functions for the neoliberal punitive state (for workfare and prisonfare are both punishments) as it fights the crisis of legitimacy that pervades all developed democracies as the state progressively loses its capacity to establish successful economic policies in an increasingly competitive world and thus has little choice but to abandon social justice and redistribution strategies. Wacquant argues that with the assistance of the media, public attention is directed away from the massive transfer of wealth to the top of the social stratification structure and towards designated 'incorrigible' deviants who can be blamed for our lack of economic competiveness: welfare cheats and parasites, criminals and paedophiles against whom the ever-more intrusive mechanisms of the carceral surveillance society are rigorously applied.

The increasing regulation of the poor is the major outcome of these policies but there is not a large-scale conspiracy (as suggested by the radical conflict model of criminal justice development, for such an undertaking would require much more competent coordination and centralisation than is available in the USA and probably any other advanced liberal democratic society). The perceived outcome is in reality the logical conclusions and results of separately adopted neoliberal strategies: liberalisation/privatisation in the economic domain, the shrinking of the state in the name of efficiency, and the de-socialisation of waged labour (along with waves of outsourcing and off-shoring) and along with a moral cultural outlook on social deviance devised by politicians and 'experts' who may or may not be aware of their contribution to the pervasive socio-control matrix of the carceral surveillance society. Such economic policies are bound to be devastating for certain, usually poorer, segments of the population, who then need to be controlled for their individual moral failings, largely depicted in terms of a lack of self-control and responsibility.

The victims of neoliberal policies are thus targeted as irresponsible, unproductive individuals who need tutelage and discipline, and that is a job which is left to the state with recourse to partnerships with private sector agencies such as private welfare/child welfare administrations and private prisons. In this sense, in this punitive environment, structural conditions leave the most vulnerable members of society to fend for themselves even though their ghettoisation prevents them from improving their conditions. They are then blamed for their failure to get out of this situation. There is, of course, one form of economic activity which would lead to better material outcomes for the dispossessed poor and that is the illegal economy. Wacquant observes that is where the policies of the War on Drugs in the USA has worked to prevent those deprived of socialised wage labour from this one exit from poverty, leaving them, of course, in prison, serving large sentences for which there is no parole.

Wacquant (2009b) observes that this double regulation of poverty (through workfare and prisonfare) has been exported to Europe, starting with the liberalisation of the state through Thatcherism in the UK, the Kohl years in Germany and the Chirac years in France. Even the various left-of-centre parties, such as the socialist parties in Western Europe, are seen to have embraced the law-and-order view of the state and neoliberal economic 'reforms'. It is becoming increasingly apparent that the socio-control matrix of the carceral society continues to incrementally expand in close parallel with progressively more insurmountable economic pressures. The outcome is that more and more groups are being absorbed into the net of surveillance and tutelage as the inevitably failing liberal economies of advanced societies come under intense pressure to make significant cuts in services and the real incomes of it citizenry with young people in the frontline of this disciplinary tutelage project, to which we will return in the final chapter.

Summary of the main points

1 This chapter reflects further on the effectiveness and structural limitations of the contemporary system in existence in England and Wales in the wider socio-economic context.
2 Pitts (2001b) alerts us to how the original findings of the 'Cambridge study' were processed and 'refined' by subsequent reports and have come to focus primarily on the family while ignoring wider structural issues.
3 The influential Audit Commission report (1996) refined these findings further into foreground familial and background factors, with those such as family income, employment and the socio-economic status of neighbourhood now relegated to the background factor category.
4 The unwritten and unspoken government strategy, which has been termed 'reintegrative tutelage', invites critical reconsideration in the context of recent recognition that prevailing discourses of transitions and social exclusion are no longer adequate to describe or explain the experiences of that substantial minority of young people who have become located in 'underclass locations'.
5 The notion of reintegrative tutelage on which the whole New Labour neo-communitarian strategy was founded was evidently based on fragile socio-economic foundations, with the economy unable to provide accessible legitimate sustainable opportunities for increasingly large sections of young people.
6 In these circumstances, the notion of restorative justice on which the whole neo-communitarian contemporary youth justice strategy was based was also equally problematic.

7 Socio-economic circumstances have certainly not improved for the many young people experiencing – or at significant risk of – social exclusion since the great economic crash of 2008 and the introduction of rigorous austerity measures introduced by the Coalition in 2010.

8 Young people are invariably among the greatest victims of major economic recessions. Young people are currently nearly three times more likely to be unemployed than the rest of the population and this is the largest gap in more than twenty years.

9 The gap also appeared to be growing with all the implications for a parallel growth in the numbers experiencing social exclusion.

10 Average wages for the population as a whole are now £1,600 lower than five years ago but if you are in your twenties then the average wage is now £1,800 lower. Benefit levels for young people continue to be reduced or even withdrawn. This is what contemporary austerity economics means for ordinary people.

Discussion questions

1 Explain how research findings are not neutral but refined and manipulated with reference to the Cambridge Longitudinal Study.
2 Was the New Labour reintegrative tutelage project inevitably doomed to failure?
3 What were the implications of major economic recession for restorative justice?
4 How has the economic recession impacted on incomes for young people?
5 'Young, uneducated and homeless'. What are the prospects for young single males in contemporary society?

Notes

1 The term 'off the cards' was widely used among those working illegally while claiming welfare benefits and thus not having their National Insurance contributions paid by their employer.
2 Social capital can be defined as those resources inherent in social relations that facilitate collective action. Social capital resources include trust, norms and networks of association representing any group which gathers consistently for a common purpose.
3 Zero-hours contracts, or casual contracts, allow employers to hire staff with no guarantee of work. They mean employees work only when they are needed by employers, often at short notice. Their pay depends on how many hours they work.
4 The Fabian Society is a British socialist organisation whose purpose is to advance the principles of socialism via gradualist and reformist means. The society laid many of the foundations of the Labour Party and subsequently heavily influenced the policies of states emerging from the decolonisation of the British Empire, most notably India and Singapore. Originally, the Fabian Society was committed to the establishment of a socialist economy, alongside a commitment to British imperialism as a progressive and modernising force. Today, the society functions primarily as a think tank and is one of fifteen socialist societies affiliated with the Labour Party. Similar societies exist in

Australia (the Australian Fabian Society), in Canada (the Douglas-Coldwell Foundation and the now disbanded League for Social Reconstruction), in Sicily (Sicilian Fabian Society) and in New Zealand.

5 Crisis is the UK national charity for single homeless people. The charity offers year-round education, employment, housing and well-being services from centres in London, Newcastle, Oxford, Edinburgh and Merseyside, called Crisis Skylight Centres. As well as year-round services, Crisis runs Crisis at Christmas, which since 1972 has been offering food, warmth, companionship and vital services to homeless people over the Christmas period. In 2010 almost 3,000 homeless people visited Crisis at Christmas, which was run by about 8,000 volunteers. Since its inception Crisis has been a campaigning organisation, lobbying government for political change that prevents and mitigates homelessness based on research commissioned and undertaken by the organisation.

6 Crucial to this disciplinary-tutelage agenda in the USA has been the need to control an increasingly economically excluded but enduringly problematic and potentially dangerous black population.

15 Comparative youth justice

The gradual separation of systems of juvenile and youth justice from adult justice that was introduced in many Western jurisdictions from the mid- to late nineteenth century onwards tended to seek legitimation in terms of acting in the 'best interests' of the child. John Muncie (2013) nevertheless observes that the course of that enterprise has never been constant but has been victim to over-zealous paternalism, and invariably dominated by the 'best interests' of adults. Thus, what may have began as an attempt to prevent the 'contamination of young minds' by separating children and young people from adult offenders in prisons has evolved into a complex of powers and procedures that are both diverse and multifactorial. Typically, systems of youth justice are overwhelmed by the ambiguity, paradox and contradiction of whether children and young people in conflict with the law should be viewed as 'children first' and in need of help, guidance and support (welfare) or as 'offenders first' and thereby fully deserving their 'just deserts' (punishment). By the 1990s, the parameters of such debate were nevertheless significantly altered by various measures of 'adultification' whereby many young people have found that their special protected 'welfare' status (as in need of care and separate treatment) has been threatened. Indeed, in many Western jurisdictions it has become more common for the young to be held fully responsible for the consequences of any transgressions.

Such developments have nevertheless been far from universal, with numerous counter movements emerging which have been designed to further rather than diminish the rights of children and, indeed, as we shall see in the following chapter, the rights of adults. The restorative justice movement that we have encountered – and indeed critiqued – in this book, for example, raises the possibility of less formal crime control and more informal offender/victim participation and harm minimisation. The formulation of the United Nations Convention on the Rights of the Child in 1989 stresses the importance of incorporating a rights consciousness into all juvenile justice systems through, for example, the establishment of an age of criminal responsibility relative to developmental capacity; encouraging participation in decision-making; providing access to legal representation; protecting children from capital or degrading punishment; and ensuring that arrest, detention and imprisonment are measures of last resort. Above all, the Convention emphasises that the 'best interests' of all those aged under 18 should be a primary consideration. As a result, by the twenty-first century, juvenile justice in many (Western) jurisdictions has evolved into a significantly complex state of affairs. Many systems are apparently designed to punish 'young offenders' while simultaneously, and paradoxically – in keeping with international children's rights instruments – ensuring that their welfare is safeguarded and promoted as a primary objective, as in the case of the contemporary youth justice system established in England and Wales by new Labour. Discourses of child protection, restoration, punishment, public protection, responsibility, justice, rehabilitation, welfare, retribution, diversion, human rights and so on, intersect and circulate in a perpetually uneasy motion (Muncie and Goldson 2013).

Globalisation and youth justice

Muncie (2005, 2008) observes that globalisation has become a central concept in criminology but has tended to be used with uniformity in the discussion of transnational organised crime, international terrorism and policing rather than youth justice processes. Thus, its usefulness in understanding contemporary transformations in youth justice systems is relatively new, where it is now recognised that a combination of macro-socio-economic developments, initiatives in human rights and accelerations in processes of policy transfer are seen to be indicative of a rapid transition to uniformity.

Muncie (2005) observes that two quite different global narratives tend to characterise analytical discussions of international trends in youth justice. Thus, the first, and most dominant, narrative is fundamentally pessimistic where it is proposed that neoliberalism has largely eliminated welfarism and is increasingly bringing about diverse and intensifying 'cultures of control' where: (1) the special status previously afforded to childhood is significantly in decline; (2) the human rights of children are increasingly violated; and (3) the global population of child prisoners continues to grow. The second, but significantly less developed, narrative is inherently utopian and optimistic, where the unifying potential of international human rights standards, treaties, rules and conventions and the promise of progressive juvenile justice reform based on 'best interest' principles, 'child friendly' imperatives and 'last resort' rationales are observed.

Neoliberal penality

The concept of the 'neoliberal' – or the neoliberalism discussed widely in this book – has become a defining principle of much criminological discussion of globalisation and this is very much the case when addressing worldwide trends in youth justice. Thus, neoliberal visions of a globalising world imply that 'uncontrollable' economic forces have moved power and authority away from nation states and placed it in the hands of 'external' multinational capital and finance. Shifts in political economy, particularly those associated with international trade and capital mobility, it is argued, have severely constrained the range of political strategies and policy options that individual states can pursue (Bauman 1998b; Beck 2006; McGrew and Held 2002). The need to attract international capital has thus forced governments to adopt similar economic, social, welfare and criminal justice policies. Failure to do so would lead to major global companies moving their activities to more accommodating nation states, with the outcome being the loss of jobs and tax revenues. Muncie (2005) observes, in this context, a parallel withdrawal in commitments to social welfare, which is clearly going to have a significant impact on children and young people worldwide. This homogenisation, it is argued, has been brought about through a fundamental shift in the relations between the state and the market. Unregulated free market economics have become established as untouchable and the 'natural order', with critics of these developments widely ridiculed.

Castells (2008: 82) has observed that national governments are ill-equipped to deal with these global developments. Quite simply, contemporary major social problems such as global warming, worldwide financial collapse and terrorism are well beyond the capacity of individual nation states to control. Consequently, there is a crisis of legitimacy with: (1) a collapse in public faith in national politics and the ability of political parties to meet the expectations of its citizens; (2) a crisis of identity where state citizenship is subordinated to other community and religious affiliations; and (3) equity where economic competition is seen to significantly weaken redistributive welfarism while accentuating inequalities within and between populations. It is thus argued that the penal realm has expanded to monitor, control and punish increasing numbers in the population who have been rendered 'out of place' or 'undesirable'. Harcourt (2010: 81) pertinently observes that:

> This discourse of neoliberal penality—born in the eighteenth century, nurtured in the nineteenth century, and today in full fruition—facilitates the growth of the carceral sphere. Neoliberal penality makes it easier to resist government intervention in the marketplace and to embrace criminalizing any and all deviations from the market. It facilitates passing new criminal statutes and wielding the penal sanction more liberally because that is where administration is necessary, that is where the state can legitimately act, that is the proper sphere of governing. By marginalizing and pushing punishment to the outskirts of the market, neoliberal penality unleashes the state on the

carceral sphere . . . The logic of neoliberal penality facilitates contemporary punishment practices by encouraging the belief that the legitimate space for government intervention is in the penal sphere—there and there alone. The key to understanding our contemporary punishment practices, then, turns on the emergence in the eighteenth century of the idea of natural order and the eventual metamorphosis of this idea, over the course of the twentieth century, into the concept of market efficiency.

Wacquant (2008, 2009a) – as we saw in the previous chapter – views such punitiveness not simply as an unintended consequence but also as an integral part of the neoliberal state. His account of the 'punitive upsurge' notes six prominent features of the coming together of neoliberalism as a political project and the deployment of a proactive punitive penality. First, punitiveness is legitimated through a discourse of 'putting an end to leniency' by targeting not only crime but also all manner of disorders and nuisances through a zero-tolerance discourse. Second, there has been a proliferation of laws, surveillance strategies and technological quick fixes – from watch groups and partnerships to satellite tracking – that have significantly extended the reach of control agencies. Third, the necessity of this 'punitive turn' is everywhere conveyed by an alarmist, catastrophist discourse on 'insecurity' and 'perpetual risk'. Fourth, declining working-class neighbourhoods have become perpetually stigmatised targets for intervention – specifically, their ethnic minority, youth and immigrant populations. Fifth, any residual philosophy of 'rehabilitation' has been more or less supplanted by a managerialist approach centred on the cost-driven administration of carceral stocks and flows, paving the way for the privatisation of correctional services. Sixth, the implementation of these new punitive policies has invariably resulted in an extension of police powers, a hardening and speeding-up of judicial procedures and, ultimately, increases in the prison population (Wacquant 2008: 10–11). In this regard the personification of contemporary neoliberal penality is widely assumed to be the USA. Indeed, Wacquant (2008: 20) has maintained that the USA has been 'the theoretical and practical motor for the elaboration and planetary dissemination of a political project that aims to subordinate all human activities to the tutelage of the market':

> The United States has become a major exporter of punitive penal categories, discourses, and policies: with the help of a transnational network of pro-market think tanks, it spread its aggressive gospel of 'zero-tolerance' policing, the routine incarceration of low-level drug offenders, mandatory minimum sentences for recidivists, and boot camps for juveniles around the world as part of a neoliberal policy package, fuelling a global firestorm in law and order.
>
> (Wacquant 2012: x)

Policy transfers

Policy transfers are a core element in the processes of globalisation (Wacquant 1999; Christie 2000; Garland 2001; Jones and Newburn 2002; Newburn 2002a;

Newburn and Jones 2007). Wacquant details how various neo-conservative think tanks, foundations, policy entrepreneurs and commercial enterprises in the USA were able to rationalise the retreating social and welfare state – in the name of neoliberal economic competitiveness – and the expansion of a penal or punitive state as we saw above. Garland (2001) later supported this argument by identifying a new culture of control characterised by mass imprisonment, curfews, zero-tolerance strategies, naming and shaming, and 'three strikes' legislation which, he argued, had produced a punitive mentality. Much of this argument, moreover, resonated directly with the proliferation of law and order politics in the UK since the early 1990s and provided a valuable contextualisation for the response to youth offenders who were – as we have seen previously in this book – subjected to a 'new correctionalisation' of intensive pre-emptive intervention and dramatically rising penal populations.

Muncie (2015) observes that it does appear increasingly common for nation states to look 'worldwide' in efforts to discover 'what works' in preventing crime and reducing offending. Thus, characteristically, this has perhaps rather surprisingly meant looking towards the USA. He observes that, certainly, some aspects of zero-tolerance policing (in France, Australia, Germany, Brazil, Argentina, Ireland), curfews (Belgium, France, Scotland), scared-straight programmes (Italy), mandatory sentencing (Western Australia, Northern Territories) and pre-trial detention as a 'short, sharp, shock' (Germany, Holland, France), which all have their origins in the USA, have now been 'transported' to many Western jurisdictions. Moreover, they all have or have had a presence in the UK.

Muncie (2015) also observes that, not only does Anglo-US convergence tend to dominate the literature on policy transfer (Dolowitz 2000; Dolowitz and Marsh 2000; Garland 2001) but also at first sight it appears to be appropriate. In their early years of political opposition, Labour had nevertheless persistently challenged and condemned the overt transatlantic policy transfers in social and criminal justice matters pursued by the Conservatives. The situation was to change following Tony Blair's visit to the USA in 1993 and the incorporation of communitarian policies implemented by the Clinton Democratic Administration and the implementation of 'get tough' policies. Nevertheless, as various commentators have observed the implementation of strategies – such as zero-tolerance policing – tended not to survive short-term experiments (Jones and Newburn 2002; O'Donnell and O'Sullivan 2003) while those such as electronic tagging were very much adapted to the UK context. Muncie (2005) observes that these lines of enquiry suggest that policy transfer is rarely direct and complete but is partial and mediated through national and local cultures, which are themselves changing at the same time. Policy transfer can be viewed, on the one hand, as simply a pragmatic response where nothing is ruled in and nothing is ruled out, or, on the other hand, it can be seen as symptomatic of youth justice systems which have rather lost their way and no longer adhere to any fundamental values and principles, whether they have their foundations in welfare, punishment, protection or rights. Muncie (2015) observes that the logic of assuming we can learn 'what works' from others is certainly an attractive proposition. It implies rational planning and an uncontroversial reliance on a crime science which is free of any political interference. But there is an assumption that policies can be successfully transported from one jurisdiction to another without any consideration of local cultures and conditions – issues we will explore further later in this chapter.

The universal rights of children

In some contrast to the neoliberalism strategies discussed above, since the 1980s global human rights provisions with regard to youth justice have emerged and been devised via three key instruments.

First, the United Nations Standard Minimum Rules for the Administration of Juvenile Justice (the 'Beijing Rules') were adopted by the United Nations General Assembly in 1985. These provide guidance for the protection of the human rights of children in the development of separate and specialist juvenile justice systems and within a comprehensive framework of social justice for all juveniles (United Nations General Assembly 1985).

Second, the United Nations Guidelines on the Prevention of Delinquency (the 'Riyadh Guidelines') were adopted by the United Nations General Assembly in 1990. The guidelines are underpinned by diversionary and non-punitive imperatives: 'the successful prevention of juvenile delinquency requires efforts on the part of the entire society to ensure the harmonious development of adolescents' (para. 2); 'formal agencies of social control should only be utilised as a means of last resort' (para. 5); and 'no child or young person should be subjected to harsh or degrading correction or punishment measures at home, in schools or in any other institutions' (para. 54) (United Nations General Assembly 1990a).

Third, the United Nations Rules for the Protection of Juveniles Deprived of their Liberty (the 'Havana Rules') were adopted by the United Nations General Assembly in 1990. The Havana Rules centre on a number of core principles including: deprivation of liberty should be a disposition of 'last resort' and used only 'for the minimum necessary period' and, in cases where children are deprived of their liberty, the 'principles, procedures and safeguards provided by international human rights standards, treaties, rules and conventions must be seen to apply' (United Nations General Assembly 1990b). These core provisions were bolstered, in 1990, by the United Nations Convention on the Rights of the Child (UNCRC). The 'Articles' of the convention that have most direct bearing on juvenile justice state:

- In all actions concerning children . . . the best interests of the child shall be a primary consideration (Article 3).
- State parties should recognise the rights of the child to freedom of association and to freedom of peaceful assembly (Article 15).
- No child shall be subjected to arbitrary or unlawful interference with his or her privacy, family, home or correspondence (Article 16).
- No child shall be subjected to torture or other cruel, inhuman or degrading treatment or punishment (Article 37a).

- No child shall be deprived of his or her liberty unlawfully or arbitrarily. The arrest, detention or imprisonment of a child shall be in conformity with the law and shall be used only as a measure of last resort and for the shortest appropriate period of time (Article 37b).
- Every child deprived of liberty shall be treated with humanity and respect for the inherent dignity of the human person, and in a manner which takes into account the needs of persons of his or her age; and
- Every child deprived of liberty shall be separated from adults unless it is considered in the child's best interest not to do so (Article 37c).

(United Nations General Assembly 1989)

The United Nations/global human rights instruments have been reinforced, within the European context, by a movement towards 'child friendly justice' that is being driven by the Council of Europe. By extending the human rights principles that inform the 'European Rules for Juvenile Offenders Subject to Sanctions or Measures' (Council of Europe 2009), the Committee of Ministers has more recently formally adopted specific 'Guidelines for Child Friendly Justice' (Council of Europe 2010). The 'guidelines' echo the UNCRC in stating that 'a "child" means any person under the age of 18 years' (Council of Europe 2010: Section II (a)) and they apply 'to all ways in which children are likely to be, for whatever reason and in whatever capacity, brought into contact with . . . bodies and services involved in implementing criminal, civil or administrative law' (Council of Europe 2010: Section I para. 2).

Collectively the United Nations and the Council of Europe human rights standards, treaties, rules, conventions and guidelines provide what is now a well-established 'unifying framework' for modelling juvenile justice statute, formulating policy and developing practice in all nation states to which they apply (Goldson and Hughes 2010). As such – at face value at least – it might legitimately be argued that the same instruments provide the basis for 'globalised' human rights-compliant and 'child friendly' juvenile justice. After all, with the notable exceptions of the USA and Somalia, each of the United Nations member states – 193 'States Parties' in total – have formally ratified the UNCRC and committed themselves to its implementation (Goldson and Muncie 2012). Indeed, the UNCRC is the most ratified of all human rights conventions. Somalia has yet to ratify because, until 2012, it did not have an internationally recognised government. The failure to ratify in the USA is in the main the result of a long campaign by conservative parental rights groups to prevent its consideration (see, for example, ParentalRights.org) (although one also suspects that there is a general reluctance in the USA to cede any of its authority to the UN).

Muncie (2013) observes that, in many respects, the global narrative of the rights of children is the complete opposite of neoliberalism with: first, there is an emphasis on state protection rather than individual responsibility; second, there is a reduction rather than expansion of the penal sphere; and third, there is the promotion of child dignity rather than law and order as the core state response. Tomás (2009: 2) thus observes that: 'there is now an emergent transnational movement fighting for children's rights – childhood cosmopolitanism – which constitutes a form of counter-hegemonic globalisation'.

The complexities of youth justice reform

While both of these 'global narratives' – neoliberal penality and rights of children – provide plausible explanations, they are on their own insufficient in grasping the complexities and incoherence of youth justice reform. Significantly, juvenile justice laws, policies and practices appear formed, applied and fragmented through a complex of political, socio-economic, cultural, judicial, organisational and local filters; while it is also the case that the sovereignty of nation states continues to be vigorously defended and expressed through diverse national domestic law and order agendas. We will now consider some of the significant differences in youth justice outcomes worldwide.

Differential rates of custody

Rates of imprisonment are very different around the world. Using data collected by the International Centre for Prison Studies for sixteen industrialised (and what might be broadly considered 'neoliberal') nations in 2011/2012, the rate of imprisonment per 100,000 population varied from 730 in the USA to 55 in Japan. Comparing such figures across a twelve-year period (from the publication of the first of such lists in 1999) suggests a generalised increase in this rate in most countries but notably in the USA, New Zealand, Scotland, Australia, Greece, and England and Wales (Baker and Roberts 2005). Reductions are only notable in South Africa and Germany. But such statistics are arguably most significant in revealing national divergence. For example, they expose the USA imprisoning at a rate which is ten times that of Japan and the Scandinavian countries (see Table 15.1).

Indeed, such empirical 'evidence' seems to contradict any notion of neoliberal homogeneity or of any flattening of national or local political and cultural difference. It suggests that punitiveness (if indeed this can be reliably measured by incarceration rates) cannot simply be reduced to the effect of neoliberal market economies, even though the most advanced neoliberal society (USA) does appear the most punitive. Clearly the effect of neoliberal penality is also mediated by competing penalities and by specific national and cultural characteristics; while the picture is made more complex when we focus solely on custodial rates for under-18-year-olds (see Table 15.2).

Data collected through successive surveys carried out for the United Nations Office for Drugs and Crime records a similar diversity in rates of imprisonment, from 0.1 per 100,000 under-18-year-olds in Japan to 73.1 in Scotland. Over the five-year period 2005–10, juvenile prison populations also appear to have remained fairly static with the exception of Greece (26 point increase) and the Netherlands (46 point decrease). Indeed, it is difficult to observe any generalised international pattern.

Table 15.1 Prison populations in selected countries

Country	Total 2011/12	Rate per 100,000 of population	Increase/decrease in rate since 1999
USA	2,266,832	730	+85
South Africa	8,433	310	−10
New Zealand	8,433	190	+45
England and Wales	86,708	154	+29
Scotland	8,146	154	+34
Australia	29,106	129	+34
Canada	39,099	117	+2
Greece	12,586	111	+54
Italy	66,009	108	+23
France	67,373	102	+12
Netherlands	14,488	87	+2
Germany	67,671	83	−7
Norway	3,602	73	+18
Sweden	6,669	70	+10
Finland	3,189	59	+4
Japan	69,876	55	+15

Source: International Centre for Prison Studies (2013)

Table 15.2 Comparing juvenile prison populations

Country	Total 2009/10	Rate per 100,000 of population	Increase/decrease in rate since 2005
Scotland	866	73.1	−5.4
Greece	601	30.3	+26.2
Canada	1,898	27.2	−1.6
Netherlands	696	19.6	−46.6
Australia	835	16.3	+3.5
England and Wales	1,656	13.2	−5.9
USA	9,855	13.1	+09.9
Italy	1,157	11.3	=2.4
New Zealand	92	8.5	−1.4
Finland	73	6.7	−1.6
France	669	4.9	N/A
Norway	6	0.8	−0.3
Sweden	8	0.7	+0.1
Japan	17	0.1	+0.2
Germany	N/A	N/A	N/A
South Africa	N/A	N/A	N/A

Source: United Nations Office on Drugs and Crime (2011)

Cavadino and Dignan (2006) have located such patterns in international penality in terms of their relation to differing political economies. They classified these as the 'neoliberal' (such as USA, Australia, South Africa, England and Wales), conservative corporatist (such as Germany, Italy, France and the Netherlands), social democratic corporatist (such as Sweden, Finland) and oriental corporatist (such as Japan). Such typologies clearly suggest that societies which share a broadly similar social and economic organisation will 'also tend to resemble one another in terms of their penality' (Cavadino and Dignan 2006: 14). In short, those dependent on the free market and a minimalist welfare state (such as the USA) will have extreme income differentials, a tendency towards social exclusion, and high rates of imprisonment. Other advanced capitalist societies which have preserved a more generous welfare state (such as Norway, Sweden and Finland) will be more egalitarian and inclusionary, leading to relatively lower imprisonment rates (see also Pratt 2008a, 2008b).

There nevertheless remains a clear danger of falling into a trap of assuming that US neoliberal 'exceptionalism' is hegemonic and unchallengeable. Thus, even within the USA, whilst overall incarceration rates far exceed those known elsewhere, rates in particular states such as Maine and Minnesota are much closer to a European average than in other states such as Texas and Oklahoma. Similarly the National Conference of State Legislatures (2012) has argued that, in the first decades of the twenty-first century, US penal excess has been tempered (particularly for juveniles) not least by concerns for budgetary restraint and cost effectiveness. They note a state legislative trend to realign fiscal resources from state institutions towards more effective community-based services. This is reflected in an overall decline of juvenile penal populations but, even so, this movement is not shared by all USA states (see Table 15.3). A situation rather similar to the cost-effective approach apparently pursued in England and Wales post the 2010 General Election and identified earlier in the book. There is a suggestion that neoliberal criminal justice strategies are becoming too expensive and we will return to this crucial point in the following concluding chapter.

Local or inter-state differences in rates of juvenile imprisonment are also evident in Australia with incarceration rates varying from 1.55 per 1,000 relevant

Table 15.3 Youth confinement in US states 1997–2010

Increase in confinement rates %		*Decrease in confinement rates %*	
		USA Average: −37%	
Idaho	80	Tennessee	−66
West	0	Connecticut	−65
Arkansas	20	Arizona	−57
South Dakota	8	Louisiana	−56
Nebraska	8	New Jersey	−53
Pennsylvania	7	Georgia	−52

Source: Annie E. Casey Foundation (2013)

population in the Northern Territory to 0.12 in Victoria (see Table 15.4), which again suggests that the parameters of global neoliberal penality will always be subject to local translation and/or resistance. Questions also remain of how far a global vision of neoliberal penality resonates beyond the rich industrialised Western countries of North America and Western Europe. Criminological research has, like many disciplines, remained blind to experiences outside the countries of the 'core'. Newburn (2010), for example, maintains that the parameters of neoliberal penality are highly differentiated and will always be shaped and reworked through local cultures, histories and politics. There appears to be discrete and distinctive ways, for example, in which neoliberal modes of governance find expression in conservative and social democratic rationalities and in authoritarian, retributive, human rights or restorative technologies. The neoliberal penality thesis, then, not only tends to dismiss the continuance and co-existence of competing social democratic forms of penality (Brown 2013) but also risks imposing a framework shaped by one part of the world onto others to which it does not readily apply, either partially or fully (Lacey 2013).

Differential ages of criminal responsibility

Since the early nineteenth century, most young offender legislation worldwide has been formulated on the basis that young people should be protected from the full weight of the criminal law. It has been widely assumed that, under a certain age, young people are *doli incapax* (literally, incapable of evil) and cannot be held fully responsible for their actions. However, the age of criminal responsibility differs widely around the world (Cipriani 2009). In the USA, the minimum set age is 6 (in North Carolina) but most USA states have set no minimum age at all. This means that some offences committed by under-18-year-olds can attract a mandatory maximum sentence of life imprisonment without parole. In 2012, the Supreme Court ruled this to be a violation of the USA Constitution's prohibition of 'cruel and unusual punishment'. The sentence was thus made optional, rather

Table 15.4 Youth confinement in Australian states 2012

Australian state	Number of juveniles in detention	Rates per 1,000 relevant population
New South Wales	350	0.37
Victoria	167	0.12
Queensland	153	0.32
Western Australia	192	0.69
Northern Territory	41	1.55
Australian Capital Territory	24	0.65
South Australia	76	0.41
Tasmania	23	0.33

Source: AIHW (2013)

than mandatory. Even so, it is believed that the USA remains the only country in the world that is known to sentence children to die in prison without any hope of release (Ratledge 2012). In this context, it is also worth remembering that the death penalty for 16- and 17-year-old offenders in the USA was only abolished in 2005 (Amnesty International 2012).

In some Islamic societies, such as Iran, the age of criminal responsibility is linked to the age of maturity or puberty, which, according to Sharia law, is 9 years for girls and 15 years for boys (Alliance of Iranian Women 2010–13). Across the UK, it varies from 8 in Scotland (though as from 2010 those under 12 cannot be prosecuted in a criminal court) to 10 in England, Wales and Northern Ireland. These ages are the lowest in the EU (see Table 15.5). It differs even more markedly across Europe where children up to the age of 14, 16 or 18 are deemed to lack full criminal responsibility and, as a result, tend to be dealt with in civil tribunals rather than criminal courts. In England and Wales, whilst the under-10-year-olds cannot be found guilty of a criminal offence, for many years the law also presumed that those under 14 years of age were also incapable of criminal intent. To prosecute this age group, the prosecution had to show that offenders were aware that their actions were 'seriously wrong' and not merely mischievous. During the mid-1990s, however, the presumption of *doli incapax*, which had been enshrined in law since the fourteenth century, was abolished on the basis that 'children aged between

Table 15.5 Variance in ages of criminal responsibility

Country	Commencement age
USA	6+ (state variance)
Scotland	8 (but no criminal court prosecution before 12)
Australia	10
England and Wales	10 (*doli incapax* abolished 1998)
Northern Ireland	10
Canada	12 (established 1984)
Ireland	12 (raised from 7 in 2001)
Netherlands	12
Greece	12
France	13
New Zealand	14
Germany	14
Japan	14 (lowered from 16 in 2000)
Italy	14
Spain	14 (raised from 12 in 2001)
Denmark	14 (lowered from 15 in 2010)
Finland	15
Norway	15 (raised from 14 in 1990)
Sweden	15
Belgium	18

Source: Muncie 2009

10 and 13 were plainly capable of differentiating between right and wrong' (Muncie 2009: 239). Such a view was reiterated in 2012 by the Minister then responsible for youth justice who claimed that 'from the age of 10 children are able to recognise what they are doing is wrong' (Blunt 2012: para. 7). This was in direct contradiction to United Nations recommendations – first made in 1995 and repeated ever since – that the UK give serious consideration to raising the age of criminal responsibility and thus bring the UK in line with much of the rest of Europe.

Further doubt on the full responsibility of children (defined as under-18-year-olds by the UN Convention on the Rights of the Child) has been based on recent neuroscience research (Royal Society 2011), which has concluded that mature decision-making and impulse control is not fully formed until at least 20 years of age and we return to this significant issue in the concluding chapter. Nevertheless, the possibility of raising the age of criminal responsibility not only in England and Wales but also in Australia seems to be far from heading contemporary political agendas.

Continual disputes over the constitution of 'the child' and how those 'in conflict with the law' might be best treated further reveals not only international diversity but also how the meaning of justice is subject to ongoing revision not only between but also within nation state territories (Muncie 2011a).

Child well-being

An overview of twenty-nine developed countries, drawing on data for 2009/10, indicates that children in the Netherlands enjoy the highest level of well-being. The report, published by UNICEF (2013), measures well-being on the basis of twenty-six indicators grouped into five dimensions: (1) material well-being; (2) health and safety; (3) education; (4) behaviours and risks; and (5) housing and environment. Comparison with an earlier analysis of data from 2001/2002 (UNICEF 2007) shows that Finland and the Netherlands ranked in the top three countries for child well-being on both occasions; Austria, Greece, Hungary, the United Kingdom (UK) and the USA were all placed in the bottom third of the table in both 2001/2002 and 2009/2010. In the more recent period, child well-being in Romania, a country not included in the earlier assessment, was ranked lowest (see Table 15.6).

Welfare and inequality

Formulations of criminal and juvenile justice continue to operate in ways that are specific to local conditions and cultural contexts and reflective of the goals of particular policy-makers and agendas. Beckett and Western (2001) produced a correlation of welfare benefit and prison populations across the USA and discovered that 'punitive states' (such as Texas and Louisiana) had the lowest welfare provision, whilst 'non-punitive states' (such as Minnesota and Vermont) had the most generous. Similarly, in 2006 the Crime and Society Foundation published research exploring the relationship between the proportion of gross domestic product (GDP) devoted to welfare expenditure within eighteen Western countries and the local rate of imprisonment (Downes and Hansen 2006). The report concluded

Table 15.6 Child well-being ranking in twenty-nine 'rich' countries 2010

Order	Country	Child well-being ranking
1	Netherlands	2.4 (highest well-being)
2	Norway	4.6
3	Iceland	5.0
4	Finland	5.4
5	Sweden	6.2
13	France	12.8
14	Czech Republic	15.2
15	Portugal	15.6
16	UK	15.8
17	Canada	16.6
25	Greece	23.4
26	USA	24.8
27	Lithuania	25.2
28	Latvia	26.4
29	Romania	28.6 (lowest well-being)

Source: UNICEF 2013

that 'welfare aims' have become increasingly marginalised 'as key variables in criminal justice policy and practice' (Downes and Hansen 2006: 3), despite evidence that a generous welfare state might enhance perceptions of fairness, social cohesion and stability. But welfare and imprisonment appear inversely related, producing remarkable diversity rather than convergence. Countries with higher rates of welfare investment are likely to enjoy lower rates of custody, and vice versa. All those countries – including the UK – with the highest rates of imprisonment spend below average proportions of their GDP on welfare; those with the lowest levels of incarceration (such as Finland, Sweden, Denmark and Belgium – but not Japan) have above-average welfare expenditure (see Table 15.7).

Such diversity has also been explained with reference to income differentials and social inequality. The more stratified a society, the more likely the resort to imprisonment. Wilkinson and Pickett (2007, 2009) suggest that more unequal societies are 'socially dysfunctional' in many different ways. It is striking that a group of more egalitarian countries (usually including Japan, Sweden and Norway) perform well on a variety of outcomes (including resort to imprisonment), while more unequal countries (including the USA and the UK) tend to have poorer outcomes. Tonry (2009: 381) concludes that:

> moderate penal policies and low imprisonment rates are associated with low levels of income inequality, high levels of trust and legitimacy, strong welfare states, professionalised as opposed to politicised criminal justice systems and consensual rather than conflictual political cultures.

Table 15.7 The relationship between welfare expenditure and prison rates 1998

Country	Imprisonment rates per 100,000 populations (15+)	Percentage of GDP on welfare
USA	666	14.6
Portugal	146	18.2
New Zealand	144	21.0
UK	124	20.8
Canada	115	18.0
Spain	112	19.7
Australia	106	17.8
Germany	95	26.0
France	92	28.8
Luxembourg	92	22.1
Italy	86	25.1
Netherlands	85	24.5
Switzerland	79	28.1
Belgium	77	24.5
Denmark	63	29.8
Sweden	60	31.0
Finland	54	26.5
Japan	42	14.7

Source: Downes and Hansen 2006: 5

There are exceptions. Thus, the relatively low rate of imprisonment in Italy is probably due more to the peculiarities of its legal system in delaying outcomes than a sign of any enduring welfare tolerance; while, for many years, the Netherlands managed to combine a 'culture of tolerance' and a strong welfare state with rapidly expanding penal populations (Nelken 2011). Moreover, it has been argued that US 'exceptionalism' (particularly during the 1990s) is also only explicable in terms of its own specific cultural history and its particular configuration of Protestant fundamentalism, governmental structure and racialised ordering (Muncie 2011b). More refined analysis suggests that 'the best explanations for penal severity or leniency' will remain 'parochially national and cultural' rather than global or economic (Tonry 2001: 518). Thus, the specificities of juvenile justice continue to remain embedded in specific geo-political contexts.

Rights compliance

In order to monitor the translation of the UNCRC into the realm of law, policy and practice within the national borders of respective States parties, an international monitoring body has been established. The United Nations Committee on the Rights of the Child comprises eighteen democratically elected members drawn from the 193 States parties. The committee has two principal functions:

first, to issue 'General Comments' in order to elaborate the means by which the provisions and requirements of the UNCRC should be applied within specific subject-domains; second, to periodically investigate the degree to which each State party is implementing the Convention – and retaining compliance with it – within its corpus of law, policy and practice. On both counts the committee has identified institutionalised obstructions to the implementation of the UNCRC in general and, more specifically, serious breaches and violations of the human rights of children within particular juvenile justice systems (Goldson and Muncie 2012). The 'General Comments' in respect of juvenile justice (United Nations Committee on the Rights of the Child 2007) concludes that implementation of the UNCRC is often piecemeal and that the human rights obligations of States parties frequently appear as little more than afterthoughts:

> many States parties still have a long way to go in achieving full compliance with CRC, e.g. in the areas of procedural rights, the development and implementation of measures for dealing with children in conflict with the law without resorting to judicial proceedings, and the use of deprivation of liberty only as a measure of last resort . . . The Committee is equally concerned about the lack of information on the measures that States parties have taken to prevent children from coming into conflict with the law. This may be the result of a lack of a comprehensive policy for the field of juvenile justice. This may also explain why many States parties are providing only very limited statistical data on the treatment of children in conflict with the law.
>
> (United Nations Committee on
> the Rights of the Child 2007: para.1)

Concerns regarding piecemeal application or, worse still, regression in the implementation of international human rights standards stem – at least in part – from the fact that the UNCRC is ultimately permissive and breach attracts no formal sanction. In this sense, it may be the most ratified of all international human rights instruments but it also appears to be the most violated, particularly with regard to juvenile justice. Moreover, such violations occur within a context of relative impunity. Abramson (2006), for example, whilst presenting an otherwise positive assessment of the practical impact of the UNCRC in 'transforming the world of children and adolescents', argues that youth justice is essentially peripheralised and/or unduly disregarded, even to the point of being 'unwanted'.

Jurisdiction-specific non-compliance

With regard to the 'administration of juvenile justice', the United Nations Committee on the Rights of the Child has repeatedly reported violations of the human rights of children in both developed and developing societies. The recurring concerns raised by the committee particularly relate to issues of intolerance, over the use of custody, inhumane treatment, denial of freedom of movement and over-representation of ethnic minorities within the youth justice system (Kilkelly 2008; Goldson and Kilkelly 2013). Indeed, despite having had over twenty years to move towards full implementation, most states appear to have failed to integrate and embed the Convention within their own domestic juvenile justice law, policy and practice. Muncie (2008), for example, found that in Western Europe, Austria, Finland, Ireland, Germany, Portugal, Switzerland and the UK have each been specifically criticised for failing to separate children from adults in custody and/or for facilitating easier movement between adult and juvenile systems owing to diminishing distinctions between the two (as is characteristic of controversial processes of 'juvenile transfer' or 'juvenile waiver' that allow for the prosecution of children in adult courts in the USA). Similarly, the United Nations Committee report of 2004 (cited in Muncie 2008) on Germany condemned the increasing number of children placed in detention – especially children of foreign origin – including the custodial detention of children with persons up to the age of 25 years. The report on the Netherlands (2004) expressed concern that custody was no longer being used as a last resort whereas, in its report of the same year on France, the committee expressed concern over legislation and practice that tends to favour repressive over educational measures and increases the numbers of children in prison and the resulting worsening of conditions. The committee has long been critical of the low age of criminal responsibility adopted in the three UK jurisdictions and in Australia. For example, in its latest report on the UK (UN Committee on the Rights of the Child 2008), the committee condemned:

- negative public and media images;
- discrimination against minorities and asylum seekers;
- high levels of incarceration;
- proliferation of DNA testing and retention of samples (over 50,000 samples were taken from under-18-year-olds in 2012);
- gross invasions of privacy and age-specific restrictions on freedom of movement, such as the use of Mosquito devices.

The observations of the UN Committee on Australia from its report published in 2012 (UN Committee on the Rights of the Child 2012) includes critiques of:

- low age of criminal responsibility;
- over-representation of indigenous children;
- abuses in custody;
- mandatory sentencing in WA;
- failure to separate children from adults in Queensland.

Racialised (in)justice

The persistent recurrence of human rights violations – over time and across space – is intensified by an apparent racialisation of youth justice practice. Muncie (2008) reported that, of eighteen Western European jurisdictions studied, fifteen were explicitly exposed to critique by the United Nations Committee for negatively discriminating against children from minority ethnic communities and migrant children seeking asylum. The over-representation of such children is particularly conspicuous at the polar ends of the system – arrest and penal detention. This especially appears to be the case for the Roma and traveller communities in England and Wales, Finland, France, Germany, Greece, Ireland, Italy, Northern Ireland, Portugal, Scotland, Spain and Switzerland; for Moroccan and Surinamese children in the Netherlands; and for other North African children in Belgium and Denmark.

Trends across Europe, as elsewhere in the world, appear to indicate that the regulation and governance of 'urban marginality' and poverty is being increasingly prised away from the social welfare apparatus and redefined as 'crime problems' within burgeoning 'penal states' (Wacquant 2009). Moreover, within such shifts, minority ethnic communities and immigrant groups are bearing the brunt of a 'punitive upsurge'. In particular, eight million Roma – the largest minority ethnic group in the European Union – are widely reported as enduring systematic discrimination, harassment, ghettoisation, forced eviction, expulsion and detention. By collating data drawn from twenty-two country-specific reports, Gauci (2009: 6) notes: 'most . . . reports identify the Roma . . . as being particularly vulnerable to racism and discrimination . . . in virtually all areas of life'. Increased ghettoisation of 'foreigner' and Roma communities in various European countries, whether as a result of institutional decisions or practical realities such as chronic unemployment, is serving to consolidate structural exclusion and systematic marginalisation: 'the creation of spatial segregation and socially excluded localities where communities are effectively denied access to basic services such as water and electricity' (Gauci 2009: 10).

Of course, such phenomena are not restricted to Europe. Cunneen and White (2006) note similar processes of racialised justice in Australia, for example, in particular a persistent over-representation of indigenous young people held in juvenile justice detention, despite an apparent favouring of diversion and community-based sentences for other offenders. Research conducted for the AIHW (2013) noted that 'on an average night in the June quarter 2012, Indigenous young people aged 10–17 were 31 times as likely as non-Indigenous young people to be in detention, up from 27 times in the June quarter 2008'.

In the USA, African-American and Hispanic populations are markedly over-penalised (Miller 1996; Acoca 1999). For example, by 2010, black non-Hispanic males were incarcerated at the rate of 3,074 inmates per 100,000 USA residents of the same race and gender. White males were incarcerated at the rate of 459 inmates per 100,000 USA residents (US Department of Justice 2011).

Indeed, some of the most punitive elements of youth justice worldwide appear to be increasingly reserved for, and applied to, children from minority ethnic and/or immigrant populations.

Global (in)justices

Twenty years after the formulation of the UNCRC, UNICEF (2009) reported that:

- 2.2 billion children live in the world;
- 1 billion live in poverty;

- 8.8 million will die before their fifth birthday;
- 150 million 5- to 14-year-olds are exploited in child labour;
- 10.1 million have no access to primary education;
- 9 million are involved in child slavery;
- 1.2 million children are trafficked every year – two-thirds of these are girls under the age of 18;
- more than 300,000 children are involved in warfare as child soldiers.

In 2006, the United Nations Secretary-General's 'Study on Violence Against Children' (Pinheiro 2006: 16) concluded that:

> Millions of children, particularly boys, spend substantial periods of their lives under the control and supervision of care authorities or justice systems, and in institutions such as orphanages, children's homes, care homes, police lock-ups, prisons, juvenile detention facilities and reform schools. These children are at risk of violence from staff and officials responsible for their well-being. Corporal punishment in institutions is not explicitly prohibited in a majority of countries. Overcrowding and squalid conditions, societal stigmatization and discrimination, and poorly trained staff heighten the risk of violence. Effective complaints, monitoring and inspection mechanisms, and adequate government regulation and oversight are frequently absent. Not all perpetrators are held accountable, creating a culture of impunity and tolerance of violence against children.

The combination of universal human rights discourse and international recognition of state responsibilities to safeguard children, on the one hand, and the persistent abuse of children by the States parties themselves – particularly those in conflict with the law – on the other hand, is, to say the least, anomalous (Goldson 2009). Such anomalies echo the earlier research of Abramson (2000), who explored the implementation of the UNCRC within juvenile justice systems in 141 countries and argued that a complete overhaul of juvenile justice is required in many countries where a range of abuses are evident including: first, the inadequate or non-existent training of judges, police and prison authorities; second, no (or limited) access to legal assistance, advocacy and/or representation; third, delayed trials; fourth, disproportionate sentences; fifth, insufficient respect for the rule of law; sixth, incidence of police brutality; and seventh, improper use of the youth justice system to address other social problems. Particular concerns centre around penal detention including: first, failure to develop alternatives to incarceration; second, overcrowding and poor conditions in custodial facilities; third, limited prospects of rehabilitation; fourth, infrequent contact between child prisoners and their families; fifth, lack of separation between child and adult prisoners; sixth, inhumane treatment; and seventh, at the extremes, torture (Goldson and Kilkelly 2013).

Muncie (2013) observes that a focus on 'local translations' can also lose sight of the enduring function of juvenile justice and the extent of international indifference, whatever the jurisdiction or locality. Despite decades of reform, the historical role of youth justice to discipline the disadvantaged child has remained undisturbed. As Goldson (2004: 28) argued:

> Youth justice systems, however they are nuanced, characteristically process the children of the poor. No matter where we may care to look, the universal gaze of youth justice systems is routinely fixed upon children and young people who endure the miseries of poverty and inequality, alongside related forms of disadvantage including poor housing, educational deficits and both mental and physical ill-health.

A persistent and more serious problem is how human rights might be equally distributed within a world that is profoundly divided and polarised by social and economic inequalities. UNICEF (2010) has revealed that, even in rich nations, identifiable groups of children are unnecessarily 'left behind', subjected to poverty, denied access to 'well-being' and exposed to inequality. The UN Committee has also recently detected regressive movement in the form of:

- The continuation of the economic and financial crisis is causing drastic social cuts, reduced employment opportunities – especially for young people and women, reduced health services for the most needy, increased dropouts from school and reduced social protection to children and families.
- Climate change is increasingly affecting the lives of millions of children worldwide. Changes in rainfall patterns, greater weather extremes and increasing droughts and floods can have serious health consequences on children, including increases in rates of malnutrition and the wider spread of diseases.
- Discrimination and xenophobia are on the rise.
- Domestic violence and other forms of violence, including State violence, against children and women are on the rise in all regions of the world.
- A growing tendency to lower the age of criminal responsibility and increase penalties for children found guilty, in a misguided effort to reduce increasing public insecurity and, as a result, weakening the realization of children's rights.

(United Nations General Assembly 2012: paras 34–8)

Worldwide, more than one billion children lack proper nutrition, safe drinking water, decent sanitation, health-care services, shelter and/or education; and every day, 28,000 children die from poverty-related causes (Goldson and Muncie 2006). According to Save the Children UK (2007), children are treated as commodities across all continents in myriad ways including: child trafficking, child prostitution, bonded child labour, child slavery and child soldiers. It is difficult to conceive of what international justice for juveniles can actually mean in these contexts. Moreover, criminology has to date remained relatively silent on these global dimensions of child and juvenile harm.

Conclusion

The two rather obvious conclusions are that not only is compliance with rights frameworks piecemeal but also the neoliberal is highly differentiated and works alongside or within pre-existing social democratic forms of penality. This suggests that we need to go beyond global and binary analyses. The precise nature of any juvenile justice system is contingent on a variety of factors – not just global and international, but also national, regional and local layers of governance – such as cultural history; political commitment to expansionism or diversion; media toleration of children and young people; and the extent of autonomy afforded to professional initiative and discretion. These issues will seriously affect any possibility of whether any jurisdiction is actually moving toward a fully rights-compliant system of juvenile justice.

There is an ongoing theoretical challenge to articulate the dialectic between local and regional spaces of difference (the contingent relations) and national and international contexts (the determining relations) of juvenile justice reform. At an international level, attempts to adhere to rights directives and to satisfy the demands of a 'punitive upsurge' conjure up quite different future scenarios. At a local level, devolved powers, indigenous versioning, 're-branding' and local practice cultures can also be expected to continue to have a profound unsettling effect on all aspects of juvenile justice policy and practice. In many respects, it is clear that the specificities of youth justice continue to operate within differing national frameworks of penality and in ways that are specific to local conditions and cultural contexts, and reflective of the goals of particular policy-makers and political agendas. All such complexities once more reveal the limitations of 'doing comparative research' through a lens of either divergence and/or convergence. These traditional tools fail to acknowledge the continually shifting and contested terrain of contemporary juvenile justice. Rather, comparative analysis of juvenile justice draws attention to a succession of local encounters of complicity and resistance between and within national systems. Future comparative analysis must surely continue to focus on how the local, the sub-national, the national, the international and the global intersect differentially in particular contexts rather than assuming that any has an a priori determining effect.

Summary of main points

1 Muncie (2005) observes that two quite different global narratives tend to characterise analytical discussions of international trends in youth justice.
2 The first, and most dominant, narrative is fundamentally pessimistic where it is proposed that neoliberalism has largely eliminated welfarism and is increasingly bringing about diverse and intensifying 'cultures of control'.
3 The second, but significantly less developed, narrative is inherently utopian and optimistic, where the unifying potential of international human rights standards, treaties, rules and conventions and the promise of progressive juvenile justice reform based on 'best interest' principles, 'child friendly' imperatives and 'last resort' rationales are observed.

4   The concept of the 'neoliberal' – or the neoliberalism discussed widely in this book – has become a defining principle of much criminological discussion of globalisation and this is very much the case when addressing worldwide trends in youth justice.

5   Wacquant (2008, 2009) views a growing worldwide punitiveness not simply as an unintended consequence but as an integral component of the neoliberal state.

6   Policy transfers are a core element in the processes of globalisation and Wacquant details how various neo-conservative think tanks, foundations, policy entrepreneurs and commercial enterprises in the USA were able to rationalise the retreating social and welfare state – in the name of neoliberal economic competitiveness – and the expansion of a penal or punitive state.

7   Garland (2001) later supported this argument by identifying a new culture of control characterised by mass imprisonment, curfews, zero-tolerance strategies, naming and shaming, and 'three strikes' legislation which, he argued, had produced a punitive mentality.

8   Muncie (2015) observes that it does appear increasingly common for nation states to look 'worldwide' in efforts to discover 'what works' in preventing crime and reducing offending.

9   In contrast to these neoliberal strategies, since the 1980s, global human rights provisions with regard to youth justice have emerged and devised via three key instruments: (1) the United Nations Standard Minimum Rules for the Administration of Juvenile Justice (the 'Beijing Rules'); (2) the United Nations Guidelines on the Prevention of Delinquency (the 'Riyadh Guidelines'); and (3) the United Nations Rules for the Protection of Juveniles Deprived of their Liberty (the 'Havana Rules').

10   The United Nations/global human rights instruments have been reinforced, within the European context, by a movement towards 'child friendly justice' that is being driven by the Council of Europe.

Discussion questions

1   Explain the new punitiveness thesis with regard to the globalisation of youth justice strategies.

2   What is a policy transfer and how have they been used in the development of global youth justice strategies?

3   How effective have been the global/human rights instruments in the creation of a worldwide homogenous youth justice response?

4   Why do you think there are such huge discrepancies between prison populations in the USA (the richest nation on the planet) and the Scandinavian countries?

5   Do you think there are links between indicies of well-being and offending rates?

16 Conclusions

The future of youth justice

Key issues

1   The future of youth justice
2   New Labour and communitarianism revisited
3   The theoretical basis of radical moral communitarianism
4   The policy implications of radical moral communitarianism for young offenders
5   Neoliberalism revisited

It is clear from the discussion in this book that patterns of offending by children and young people and the nature of the response by the authorities are inextricably linked to significant socio-economic circumstances. As we have seen, the contemporary youth justice system was established by a New Labour government with a commitment to the philosophy of communitarianism via the Crime and Disorder Act 1998 and was subsequently superseded by a Conservative government (albeit in the first version with the Liberal Democrats as junior coalition partners) with their own version of communitarianism – the 'Big Society' – which while retained, more or less at a theoretical level, has been replaced in reality by a more cost-effective pragmatic approach compatible with contemporary neoliberal socio-economic orthodoxy we will explore further below. We will first consider some previous proposals for the future of youth justice in England and Wales.

The future of youth justice

The Youth Justice Board was at the outset given extensive powers, political access and a broad brief involving a degree of financial control and responsibility for the propagation of national standards and targets, service development, training, and inspection and audit. Pitts (2003b) observed, a few years later, that while at first sight the YJB appeared to have been given unprecedented autonomy and power, a closer examination revealed a rather different story. The YJB was, in fact, confronted by four closely interconnected problems from the outset. First, there was to be an unprecedented politicisation of youth crime under New Labour. Second, there was consequently an excessive link between the political and administrative spheres (Pitts 2001b). Third, there was a significant unwillingness of government to give the YJB a role in policy formation. Fourth, there was the tendency of the then Prime Minister (Tony Blair) to suddenly take control of a particular criminal justice issue at short notice and make it his own for short-term political gain. Pitts (2003b: 14) observed that:

> As a result, alongside the difficult task of transforming the youth justice system, the YJB constantly has to cobble together responses to whatever the issue of the week may be, while also serving as an apologist for these off-the-cuff initiatives, some of which appear to undermine the Board's key objectives. This attempt to 'run with the hare and the hounds' has led some Board members to threaten to resign, and others to publicly castigate the field for its failure to live in the 'real world of hard political choices'.

Pitts further noted that the youth justice specialists recruited to serve as a link between the Board and the YOTs were required to press practitioners to implement otherwise sound policies too hastily, or to meet politically driven – and hence frequently changing – priorities and targets. He argued that many of these problems could have been ameliorated, if not resolved, by the de-politicisation of the contemporary youth justice system, although it was accepted that this was unlikely to happen in the political climate. Pitts (2003b) proposed that such a depoliticised and autonomous supervising agency could become the champion and supporter of the youth justice system, its staff and its clients, from attempts by government to exploit them to political advantage. In such a scenario, he argued, the Board would gain the unequivocal support of the practitioners and managers who are precisely the people it needed to promote its agenda and realise its vision.

As we have seen, the Youth Justice Board came extremely close to being replaced in the aftermath of the electoral demise of New Labour and it replacement by the Coalition government in 2010 regardless of how unlikely that appeared seven years previously. Ultimately, the YJB gained the support of many of those practitioners, managers and commentators who previously had been less enthusiastic. In the end abolition was considered inappropriate and the YJB was retained in a rather emasculated form within the Ministry of Justice and was seen as a central component of a now pragmatic relatively depoliticised contemporary youth justice system.

Pitts (2003b: 17) provided us with an ideal-type template for an optimum Youth Justice Board or what he termed an autonomous supervising agency. First, it was proposed that there should be a powerful neutral autonomous element in youth justice policy-making which avoids short-term political imperatives and contingencies. Second, the supervising agency should be a robust, principled, non-political governmental policy adviser. Third, the agency should promote and champion the rights of children and young people. Fourth, the agency should challenge the political and media exploitation of youth crime and young offenders, and unrealistic political pressure for results. Fifth, the agency should be a perceptive strategic planner of youth justice services. Sixth, there should be an attentive, engaged and robust manager of the juvenile secure estate, committed to the realisation of relevant international rights conventions within its institutions and practice standards developed in residential child care (Warner 1992). Seventh, the agency should be a forum for debate and original thinking in the youth justice arena which would embrace the whole range of informed opinion, theory and research findings on relevant issues. Eighth, it should be an instigator and disseminator of apolitical evidence of good practice and the sponsor and defender of experimentation and innovation. Ninth, it should be a facilitator of dialogue within and between practice and the academy. Tenth, it should be the purveyor of coherent and consistent standards and priorities. Eleventh, it should be a facilitator of service development, training and support for the youth justice professions. Twelfth, the agency would need to be an innovative evaluator, devising data-collection methods relevant to local situations and ensuring that data held by partner agencies are compatible and accessible. Pitts (2003b) argued that such a revitalised Youth Justice Board, pursuing these goals – or something very much similar to them – would almost certainly gain greater respect, influence and support. The cost, which could well turn out to be a long-term benefit, would be a distancing from, and occasional conflict with, government. This template was of course produced in very different times – a period which can in many ways be seen as a highpoint in the history of the Youth Justice Board – before it was reduced to an emasculated subsidiary of the Ministry of Justice.

There is, moreover, an additional qualification that needs to be made if a properly independent contemporary youth justice system is to be introduced in the foreseeable future. It would simply need to deliver, to some measurable and widely acceptable extent, on its central aim of reducing youth offending, while, at the same time, it would need to be seen to deliver on an efficient, cost-effective basis. We live in a world where results are important and the customer expects value for money. In this case the customer is the general public, which clearly wants to see reductions in criminality and certainly among children and young people. Clearly – as we have seen in this book – the present Conservative government, another crucial customer, is very much driven by an essential cost-effective criteria, not least during this period of extended economic austerity and would very much need to be persuaded of the fiscal advantages of taking such a step.

Pitts (2003b) interestingly cites the Bank of England's monetary policy committee as an example of a key governmental function given to an independent agency in the interests of the state and one providing an appropriate model for the introduction of an autonomous contemporary youth justice system. That body clearly had significant public support – not least among key economic players – and there was a widespread, invariably unspoken expectation that it will do the right thing in the public interest without favour when called upon to make a tough decision. Moreover, the evidence, at least short term, suggests that it has not previously shirked that duty even when causing (at least) short-term political damage to the government, although there is probably much more public ambivalence following the banking crisis of 2008. It is nevertheless not clear that the public has that much confidence in a contemporary youth justice system which is clearly perceived to be a quasi-welfare agency. It thus seems indisputable that given proper independence of government it would need to visibly deliver on its key aims and provide value for money. Whatever negative observations we might make about quality assurance, accountability and the audit society, these systems are very much an inevitable part of the real non-negotiable contemporary world and for any foreseeable future. Quite simply, the public wants to see that its money is being well spent and this clear, understandable expectation needs to be acknowledged by those involved in youth justice, whether practitioners, researchers or commentators. This would be the basis of public trust and provide an independent youth justice system with the opportunity to serve children and young people well in a radical moral communitarian society that is discussed below. We start this discussion with a resume of the communitarian story outlined in this book so far.

New Labour and communitarianism revisited

As we have seen previously in this book, the contemporary youth justice system was established by the Crime and Disorder Act 1998 and introduced by a New Labour government strongly influenced by the political philosophy of communitarianism, which had emerged in the USA during the 1980s. This influential philosophy proposed that the individual rights, vigorously promoted by traditional liberals, need to be balanced with social responsibilities to the communities in which we live (Emanuel 1991; Glendon 1991; Etzioni 1993, 1995a, 1995b). Significantly, in terms of mainstream communitarianism, this was never intended as an argument for the restoration of traditional community with high levels of mechanical solidarity (Durkheim 1933), or a repressive dominance of the majority or the patriarchal family. In short, the intention was to restore an appropriate balance between the rights of the individual and their obligations and responsibility to the community. It was these ideas which were to become very influential with New Labour, while in opposition during the 1990s, and were carried on into government when they were elected in 1997.

Thus, in contrast to the traditional liberal idea that members of a society may be simply entitled to unconditional benefits or services, it was now argued that the primary responsibility to care for each individual should be seen as lying, first and foremost, with the individual and their families. This 'third way', emphasising the importance of civil society, was proposed as avoiding the full-on atomistic egotistical individualism which had unpinned the Thatcherite maxim that 'there is no such thing as society' and the traditional social-democratic recourse to a strong state as the tool by which to realise the aims of social justice (Giddens 1998). The state, it was argued, has a role to play, but as a facilitator, rather than a guarantor, of a flourishing community life.

Dissenters were nevertheless to observe from the outset that the subsequent New Labour agenda took a rather different, more authoritarian course, centred more on the use of a strong state apparatus to deliver particular outcomes, than is suggested by the rhetorical appeal to the relatively autonomous powers of civil society to deliver progress by itself (see Driver and Martell 1997; Jordan 1998). This outcome is perhaps not surprising when we consider that the concept of civil society has itself attracted considerable criticism.

Civil society is a social sphere which is separate from both the state and the market. The increasingly accepted understanding of the term defines civil society organisations as being non-state, not-for-profit, voluntary organisations, formed by people in that social sphere. It is a term used to describe a wide range of organisations, networks, associations, groups and movements that are independent from government and which sometimes come together to advance their common interests through collective action (Alagappa 2004). Civil society thus includes all organisations that occupy the 'social space' between the family and the state, excluding political parties and companies. Some definitions also include certain businesses, such as the media, private schools, and for-profit associations, while they are excluded by others (Edwards 2004).

This is of course all problematic, with state involvement in the funding and establishment of civil society and non-governmental organisations, which may well blur the boundaries between state and non-state bodies. Moreover, these institutions are not protected from the economic demands of market forces, nor wider society from the philosophical and material interests of moral entrepreneurs, who have a clear capacity to influence the agenda (Hopkins Burke 2012, 2013a, 2013b). The notion of the neutral civil society organisation is thus clearly contentious with democratically elected governments having both a legitimate right and definitely a responsibility to intervene in these processes ostensibly in the interests of the greater good.

It was thus New Labour *neo*-communitarian credentials that were clearly apparent in the establishment of a contemporary youth justice system epitomised by the central state control of youth offending teams by an autocratic Youth Justice Board. Their youth justice policies can be best explained as being part of a wider set of communitarian-driven government strategies introduced to help reintegrate those sections of the population that had become increasingly socially and economically excluded during the previous years of major economic re-structuring. These reintegrative strategies included: (1) measures to support families, including assistance for single parents to get off benefits and return to work; (2) policies to help children achieve at school, including steps to tackle truancy and prevent exclusions; (3) the provision of opportunities for jobs, training and leisure; and (4) action to tackle drug misuse (Hopkins Burke 1999a). This neo-communitarian youth justice strategy, located in the context of a wider multi-intervention strategy against social exclusion was summarised in Table 4.1 (Chapter 4).

It is thus this notion of reintegration back into the community that enables us to explain the approach to youth justice favoured by New Labour: a distinctive approach that was part of a wider set of government strategies that sought to reintegrate those sections of the population that had become socially and economically excluded during the previous twenty years of significant economic restructuring with the not totally unintended consequences of mass unemployment in many parts of the country. This unwritten and unspoken government strategy of 'reintegrative tutelage' (Hopkins Burke 1999a, 2005, 2008) was nevertheless fraught with difficulties in changing economic circumstances, not least the virtual impossibility of getting a large rump of uneducated, non-skilled youths into employment in a difficult, complex and highly competitive labour market. Thus, Fergusson et al. (2000) argued that the then dominant discourses of transitions – from school to employment – were no longer sufficient to explain the experiences of that substantial minority of young people who had become located in socially excluded 'underclass locations'. Indeed, it was becoming increasingly apparent that the whole notion of social reintegration was a fatally flawed strategy in society as it was currently structured.

In short, the whole notion of reintegrative tutelage on which the whole New Labour neo-communitarian strategy was founded appeared to be based on rather fragile socio-economic foundations, with the economy unable to provide accessible legitimate sustainable opportunities for increasingly large sections of young people, even in the credit-driven economic boom pre-2008. The situation was to become significantly worse from that date onwards when the worldwide 'credit crunch' brought to an end the long-run, worldwide economic boom of at least the previous ten years and heralded a global financial crisis unprecedented in recent times, a major economic recession with many business collapses, rising unemployment and, in many countries (such as the UK), a new austerity politics aimed at reducing high and unsustainable levels of national debt with little sign at the time of writing of an imminent improvement in the situation.

It was thus in this enduring economic context that those academics and commentators we have seen elsewhere in this book have argued that the last decades of the twentieth century saw the replacement of 'welfarism' as a regime of social regulation by neoliberalism in post-industrial Western societies (see Lacey 2013), with the latter often considered a monolith, itself solely responsible for the harsher penal regime of the last few decades (Cavadino and Dignan 2006), which has helped discipline and tutor a recalcitrant working-class population in the interests of a neoliberal economy (Wacquant 2009). Houdt and Schinkel (2013) have nevertheless gone further and pertinently observed that neoliberalism essentially operates in combination with elements from other rationalities, in particular, communitarianism. Thus, neoliberalism is not, as we might think at first sight, completely opposed to communitarianism; while a harsher penal climate cannot be solely attributable to neoliberalism, it is actually compatible with a communitarian governmental rationality. Thus, the emphasis on 'responsibility' in communitarianism is very compatible with the notion of 'responsibilisation' in neoliberalism; in other words, a neoliberal communitarianism.

Houdt and Schinkel (2013) thus argue that neoliberal communitarianism is a strategy of governmentality that combines the main features of neoliberal governmentality (Foucault 2004); with those of governmental communitarianism (Adams and Hess 2001; Delanty 2003; Ross 2003; Van Swaaningen 2008) and that this consists of a combination of the new public management and the outsourcing of responsibility. It combines scientific measurement and treatment of social problems with the stimulation of 'active citizenship' and the rational governing of community. The authors illustrate how neoliberal and communitarian elements have combined in crime policies over the last decades with reference to three crucial trends.

First, there has been 'the prioritisation of crime and the intensification and pluralisation of punishment', where we have seen increasing 'selective incapacitation' and 'selective rehabilitation' (Downes and Van Swaaningen 2007). This trend has involved a broader range of possible punishments, including restorative justice and a variety of tactics deployed to suppress 'risky' behaviour, while punishment has become plural in that it is executed and conceived by a broader circle of actors and agencies than is traditionally the case (not only the sovereign state but also local governments and administrations).

Second, there is the 'actuarialisation of crime' where there has been a transformation from the criminal subject as being causally determined towards one who is a bundle of risk factors, with a focus on choice and the discovery of culture as a risk factor. Thus, risk has become dominant in the field of crime regulation (O'Malley 1992), where a 'reinvented government' (Osborne and Gaebler 1993) uses measurable risks to increase the efficiency, effectiveness and legitimacy of public policy and interventions, and where this new penology and actuarial justice is based on (selective) incapacitation, preventive detention and profiling.

Third, there has been 'the institutional transformation of crime regulation' where penal welfarism came under attack for being 'inefficient' and 'ineffective' and which involved: (1) a disciplinarisation of the state through managerial principles (where a business model was introduced to make criminal justice both more 'effective' and 'efficient'); (2) an extension of state competencies and capacities, where the critique of penal welfarism was to involve a targeting of society as a whole from a criminal justice perspective (thus under the dual flag of prevention and repression the criminal justice system casts a wider net with a thinner mesh (cf. Cohen 1979)), with harsher punishment, new prisons, less tolerance and alternative punishments; (3) the incorporation of privatisation and facilitative and repressive responsibilisation, where governments came to recognise that they were unable to cope with crime alone and which was to lead to the mobilisation of individual citizens and civil society, including local government and the private sector, to take responsibility (responsibilisation) and to fight the control problem with special programmes targeted at the socially excluded underclass in particular. If you cannot reintegrate this new (at least potentially) dangerous social class, then control them in the most cost-effective way possible.

Hopkins Burke (2012, 2013a, 2013b), with the left realist hybrid model of criminal justice development (which we encountered in Chapter 6), argues that the practitioners, professionals and experts that have implemented these strategies contribute invariably unknowingly to the increasingly pervasive socio-control surveillance matrix of the carceral society, which is encouraged and legitimised by a depoliticised general public, ultimately but again usually unwittingly, in the interests of society and enhancement of the neoliberal market economy.

The theoretical basis of radical moral communitarianism

Hopkins Burke (2014, 2015) argues that it is the work of Emile Durkheim and his observations on the *moral* component of contract and the division of labour in society which provides the theoretical basis of a radical moral communitarianism, which challenges the orthodox articulation and its hybrid neoliberal variation. It is a formulation which actively promotes the rights and the responsibilities of both individuals and communities, but in the context of an equal division of labour; while, moreover, it is a communitarianism based on a particular conception of (French) individualism, which provides the basis of a rather different form of social organisation than those which emerge from rival conceptions (Anglo-Saxon and German) of individualism (Hopkins Burke 2014b, 2015a, 2015b).

It is a social policy agenda which provides us with the basis of a genuine moral communitarianism founded on notions of appropriate contributions to society (obligations and responsibilities), suitable fair rewards (rights), and consensual interdependency with others we all recognise, identify and respect as fellow citizens and social partners, not as people of no consequence to be ignored, avoided and, in criminological terms, identified as potential legitimate crime targets. Radical moral communitarianism promotes a fairer, more equal world, based on mutual respect between all citizens, but with commitment to and involvement in society being a central component of a new social contract.

Table 16.1 provides a brief summary of some of the fundamental closely linked rights which it is proposed should be available to citizens of all ages, alongside their simultaneous responsibilities, in a radical moral communitarian society built on mutual trust and respect in the context of an equal division of labour (Hopkins Burke 2013a, 2013b, 2015a, 2015b). From this perspective, it is argued that policies should be introduced on the basis that people and communities have both rights and responsibilities and that there is an essential need for a fine-balance between them. This balance will invariably require negotiation and renegotiation on a regular and reflective basis and it is beyond the parameters of this book to elaborate or indeed speculate on the political mechanisms that would need to be applied and implemented to bring about these very significant socio-economic changes (although we will reflect on the limitations of neoliberalism in the conclusion to this chapter and the book). This book nevertheless provides only a brief introduction to the suggested generic policy implications of radical moral communitarianism for all citizens, the emphasis below being on those suggested for young offenders. Hopkins Burke (2015) provides a comprehensive discussion of the generic policy proposals and their justifications.

The first policy proposal is that all citizens should have access to an acceptable level of income at all stages of their life. This is clearly commensurate with the provision of an adequate benefits system and a reinforcement of the basic right that all citizens enjoy in the appropriate circumstances. It should nevertheless be the responsibility of the individual to make an active contribution to society and the economy, wherever possible, in some form or another and they should certainly not refuse suitable work that becomes available but, at the same time, there should be no hounding of the sick and disabled who are unable to work.

Table 16.1 Rights and responsibilities in a moral communitarian society

Rights	Responsibilities
1 The provision of an adequate income on which to live at the appropriate stage of life.	1 To play an active role in the economy while fit and healthy and of working age.
2 The provision of good-quality affordable accommodation/housing of an acceptable size and proper rights of tenure.	2 To be a good neighbour and a responsible member of the community and not to engage in anti-social behaviour to the disadvantage of fellow citizens.
3 To be treated with fairness and respect by all agencies, institutions and individuals regardless of age, disability, ethnicity, gender and religion.	3 To treat others with fairness and respect regardless of age, disability, ethnicity, gender and religion.
4 The provision of good-quality health care.	4 To maintain a reasonable standard of natural health where possible.
5 The provision of a high-quality education and training.	5 To fully engage and participate in education and training and behave appropriately.
6 To be protected from crime and anti-social behaviour in our communities.	6 Not to engage in crime and criminal behaviour.

Based on: Hopkins Burke 2014a

Second, all citizens should have access to suitable, good-quality, affordable accommodation of an acceptable size and proper rights of tenure, with the rent paid linked to the ability to pay. There should also be an end to the stigmatisation of local authority and housing association estates referred to as 'social housing', with the provision of accommodation to a much wider section of the population as part of a process of community regeneration.

Third, all citizens should be entitled to respect and be treated fairly by all agencies, institutions and individuals regardless of their age, disability, ethnicity, gender, religion and sexuality. It will be the responsibility of all individuals to reciprocate this behaviour or face appropriate sanctions. Mutual respect should be central to any moral communitarian project, but will be difficult to achieve in a society epitomised by an excessively unequal division of labour. Conversely, a more equal division of labour with more equitable pay differentials will help provide a culture of respect for different occupational groups.

Fourth, there should be the provision of good-quality health care for all citizens, which means supporting the National Health Service. It will nevertheless be the responsibility of the citizen to actively pursue good health and the failure to do so will involve a state health and welfare (not criminal) intervention against, for example, those with alcohol, drugs and dietary (obesity) problems. The key to this strategy is the progressive decriminalisation, but not the legalisation, of drugs.

Fifth, all citizens should have access to good-quality education and every effort should be made to ensure that standards are maintained, improved and appropriate to the skills and aptitudes of individuals, with a close fit and links to employment opportunities. Nevertheless, not all people take advantage of these opportunities and it is their responsibility – and crucially that of the parents and carers – to ensure that they do so with appropriate sanctions taken against those who do not and/or are disruptive.

Sixth, all citizens should receive appropriate adequate public sector protection. It is thus the responsibility of citizens not to engage in criminality but it would be clearly overly utopian to suggest that everyone will abstain and desist from offending. Those who do not accept this responsibility to society should be targeted and dealt with efficiently and appropriately by the agencies of the criminal justice system but with the recognition that our prison system is full of people who could be dealt with without that sanction and for whom imprisonment is at best non-productive and at worst wholly destructive.

These six policy suggestions are all closely linked and appropriate for all citizens; those which follow are specifically proposed for young offenders, but should be considered in this wider generic context.

The policy implications of radical moral communitarianism for young offenders

Table 16.2 provides a summary of the additional basic rights and responsibilities to be afforded to young offenders who are clients of the contemporary youth justice system based on the values and principles of a radical moral communitarian society. The first three of these policy proposals can be located in the context of generic policy six (GP6), which focuses on crime and the criminal justice system.

The first proposed policy for young offenders is that the upper-age limit for the jurisdiction of the youth justice system should be increased to 21. There is a well-established movement involving professionals and predominantly influential charities – in particular the Barrow Cadbury Trust (2012) and T2A (Transitions to Adulthood) – who seek to establish transitional arrangements for young people involved in the criminal justice system between the ages of 18 and 25. The evidence they have gathered provides compelling arguments for raising the upper age limit in the youth justice system from 18 to 21 in the first instance. It is thus proposed that young people aged 21 and below should accept that they are part of this extended youth justice jurisdiction, accept their authority and behave accordingly as a part of being treated age appropriate. This policy would be a central component of a moral communitarian response to youth offending.

Second, the nature of the particular youth justice intervention should be appropriate to the level of maturity of the young person and the level of risk they pose to themselves and others, and is clearly very closely linked to the first policy proposal. Maturity is one of the most prominent themes in the literature about young adults, with many – if not most – considered to be youths rather than adults on a transitionary spectrum (T2A 2009). Prior et al. (2011) reviewed three key strands of empirical research (neurological, psychological and criminological) and supported this view, concluding that the current transition point to adulthood (18) in the criminal justice system is illogical.

The Barrow Cadbury Trust (2005) recommends that 'maturity' be taken into account when sanctioning young adults. The T2A (2009: 27) further advocates that 'youthfulness' should be a 'mitigating factor' when dealing with this age group, with assessments carried out by the probation service before young adults face a criminal trial. The concern is to divert young adults away from the criminal justice system, avoiding them getting a criminal record and the subsequent stigmatisation, and allowing them to 'learn from their mistakes' (T2A 2009: 25). This would seem a valid approach as the evidence shows that the peak ages for offending are between 19 and 24 (Von Hirsch and Ashworth 2005).

Undoubtedly, introducing a scheme where sentencers were required to consider the maturity of a young adult could provide benefits for individual young adults and improve their future prospects. Where the young adult is a first time offender who has committed minor crime, then this would seem a suitable and fair option, but it can be argued that for persistent offenders stuck in the 'revolving door' cycle, the issue of maturity – while it should be seen as a mitigating factor – cannot be the only consideration. It should also be borne in mind that, as

Table 16.2 Rights and responsibilities of young offenders in a moral communitarian society

Rights	Responsibilities
1 Young people age 21 and below should be dealt with as young offenders by the youth justice system not in the adult criminal justice system.	1 To accept that they are part of this extended youth justice jurisdiction, accept its authority and behave appropriately.
2 The youth justice intervention should be appropriate to the level of maturity of the young person and the level of risk they pose to themselves and others.	2 To accept responsibility for their actions, the need for reparation to their victims and cooperate with intervention plans.
3 Punishment in the community should be pursued in all but the most exceptional cases involving very serious crimes and offenders posing a high risk to the community.	3 Full cooperation with community sanctions and restorative justice interventions.
4 A comprehensive intervention in the welfare needs of the young person at an appropriate level.	4 Full cooperation with all proposed appropriate welfare interventions.
5 Appropriate training and education opportunities provided appropriate to the needs and skills of the individual and their employment prospects.	5 Full cooperation and involvement and educational opportunities.
6 Proper employment opportunities provided where appropriate as part of a macro-full employment strategy.	6 Full cooperation with all employment opportunities provided.

Prior et al. (2011) note, maturity is an elusive notion and not a 'wholly objective, measureable concept' by any means. This could raise difficulties for sentencers when attempting to determine how mature or immature an individual may be and leaves individuals subject to discretionary subjective opinion.

This approach is nevertheless used in Germany, which offers an interesting international comparison. In that country, the judge takes into account the personality of an individual and their maturity level and then a decision is made to either prosecute a young adult (in Germany 18–21) through adult or juvenile law. We should also note – as we saw in the previous chapter – that Germany has a 'lower crime rate, a lower incarceration rate, and lower reoffending rates than the UK' (T2A 2009: 25). Removing discretion and subjective interpretation would thus point to all young people 18–21 being treated as juveniles and logically in the extended youth justice system.

The third policy proposal for young offenders is that punishment in the community should be pursued in all but the most exceptional cases involving very serious crimes. Children and young people would be expected to offer full cooperation with community sanctions and restorative justice interventions. Again, as we have seen previously in this book, the most effective community supervision programmes have been shown to reduce offending 15 per cent more than a prison sentence and while there is still a lack of clear information (the Home Affairs Select Committee in 1998 had found 'the absence of rigorous assessment astonishing'), there is an increasing amount of evidence as to the effectiveness of community penalties. Moreover, they are considerably cheaper. It thus costs, according to estimates, £42,000 per year to lock up a young offender, but the costs of the most frequently used community sentences range between £2,000 and £4,000. The basic fact is that custody costs about twelve times more than a community sentence.

The use and experience of custody is itself problematic, and it is argued that short sentences cause particularly difficult disruption to the life of children, juveniles and young adults. Reoffending rates are high, making the supposed rehabilitative purpose of custody seem ineffective, despite the huge costs (Cavadino and Dignan 2007). Statistical evidence emphasises this with reconviction rates at 59.9 per cent. Incarceration, moreover, damages individuals and removes children and young people from having a 'normal life' (T2A 2009), appreciably affects their chances of getting a job and is regarded as a 'counterproductive tool' (Barrow Cadbury Trust 2005).

Organisations promoting reform for young adults advocate greater use of community orders because they can divert young adults from the harmful effects of custody and provide other benefits such as keeping them closer to their families (Howard League 2012). Research into community order schemes, used predominantly with young adults 18–24, is very limited, with results ambiguous (Make Justice Work 2011), but one thing is certain, community sanctions are significantly cheaper.

The use of custody can result in a 'revolving door' cycle effecting young adults who continuously go in and out of the justice system. There is a clear need for a specialist service for dealing with young adults when they leave custody, but currently the only one available is the adult probation service, which provides nowhere near the intensive support offered by youth offending teams for the younger age group. Young adults are invariably 'left out on their own' and require 'more attention than they currently get'. However, despite greater efforts being made to help those on probation, there are still many young adults failing and reoffending due to lack of support that could be provided by an enhanced youth justice system incorporating this age group.

The Transforming Rehabilitation proposals which are radically changing the way in which probation services are being delivered seem unlikely to help. The results from the payment by results pilots in Peterborough and Doncaster prisons in 2014 demonstrated that both projects were failures. Peterborough missed its target of reducing reoffending by 10 per cent and Doncaster did just enough not to lose any money, but not enough to make a profit (Crook 2014). Supervision and support for those released from Peterborough prison after short sentences was funded by substantial additional money through social impact bonds, which is extra investment from the lottery and charitable trusts that could have been allocated to good causes. The government, moreover, plans to take money from probation and to give it to private companies or consortia to manage people coming out of prison or on community sentences.

Under Transforming Rehabilitation, services will need to be provided to at least 50,000 people emerging from short prison sentences but no more money will be available (Crook 2014). In the Peterborough project, intensive and specialised services were provided by experienced charitable organisations, which still failed to make any significant impact on reoffending, because they were given the impossible task of undoing the damage done by the prison. The expansion of the scheme nationwide will simply be impossible to achieve without considerable expense with little likelihood of proper rehabilitation. Non-custodial sentences provide the most likelihood of successful rehabilitation and they will certainly be much cheaper.

The fourth policy proposal for young offenders is that there should be a comprehensive intervention in the welfare needs of the child or young person, at an appropriate level for the individual, with an expected full cooperation with such interventions. Appropriate accommodation (GP2) and income needs (GP1) are part of the generic moral communitarian intervention welfare strategies, but a significant issue for many young offenders – including young adults – which needs addressing is problematic involvement in drugs and alcohol (GP4). It is proposed that these issues should be addressed as a welfare, not criminal justice, intervention.

Drug and alcohol use are considered a significant causation factor for criminal behaviour among children, juveniles and young adults, while the misuse of illegal and legal substances is arguably more detrimental for those in these age groups than others (Devitt et al. 2009). These individuals have a larger amount of demographic variables when compared to other age groups, including in the case of young adults, homelessness (T2A 2009), and in the higher age range are more likely to be persistent users (Devitt et al. 2009). Many young adults are still in a difficult transitionary stage between childhood and fully formed adult status with many not having 'finished school, not been in any employment, usually have been excluded and previously been in youth offending' with 'acquisitive offending' linked closely to a drug- and alcohol-fuelled lifestyle (see Parker 1996). Statistical evidence suggests that drug and alcohol use is significantly more common among offenders than non-offenders (Devitt 2011).

The Barrow Cadbury Trust (2005) suggests that NOMS (National Offender Management Service), the National Treatment Agency and the Department of Health should all work together with the drug rehabilitation teams in prison to 'find the best way of working with young adults with drug problems in the CJS'. Although this is a sensible recommendation, there is also a drug and alcohol community order already in place which magistrates are free to use (Ashworth 2010), and this would perhaps provide a better starting point than attempting to bring in a multi-agency approach, which may be more difficult to achieve, and YOTs have considerable experience in dealing with such cases with the younger (under 18) cohort. It would again be eminently sensible that they have responsibility for this older age group.

The fifth policy proposal for young offenders is that they should be provided with suitable training and education opportunities appropriate to the needs and skills of the individual and their employment prospects, while the young person should fully cooperate with the educational and training opportunities provided is a mainstream policy proposal (GP5). The words 'suitable' and 'appropriate' are central to this strategy and closely linked to employment opportunities available in a moral communitarian society and a re-structured inclusive labour market. Central to this strategy is the recognition that not all worthwhile employment requires an expertise in differential calculus, nor is it necessary or sensible to keep all young people in education until they have mastered this. Education and training needs to be appropriate to the young person, their potential and aptitude, while recognising a potential problematic initiative that could exclude many able – but disadvantaged and excluded – young people from good-quality educational opportunities they might master with the appropriate educational input in their lives.

The sixth policy proposal for young people who offend is that proper employment opportunities should be provided where appropriate as part of a macro-full employment strategy pursued as part of a restructured economy in a moral communitarian society with full cooperation expected from the young people (GP1). Access to employment is seen as one of the most important ways of deterring young adults from crime, providing them with a stable job and lifestyle (T2A 2009).) Fifty per cent of young men are unemployed before they are sentenced to prison, so it is clear that half of this age group are affected by this problem (Howard League 2012). Moreover, following conviction they must disclose this to employers when seeking work, which can have an extremely negative impact on their job-seeking chances (see Parker 1996).

The Barrow Cadbury Trust (2005) has made a number of recommendations about improving standards and increasing the ability of young adults to gain employment. These include multi-agency responses and more learning programmes for young adults in custody, allowing them to gain better qualifications whilst in prison. The most interesting recommendation is to make it a legal requirement that young adults under 23 years of age do not have to disclose their convictions to employers, unless it is for a violent or sexual offence; 21 years of age and under could clearly be more politically acceptable, especially if these young people were to come under the jurisdiction of the youth justice system until that age.

It is the view taken in this book that the removal of youth justice support for young offenders when they reach the age of 18 is rather arbitrary, and given the relatively high level of investment in working with juveniles and the levels of expertise developed, this does suggest a poor use of resources. Extending the upper age limit to 21 thus seems to be eminently sensible and cost effective.

It is proposed that this new expanded youth justice system should intercede incrementally in the lives of children and young people who have offended in accordance with a realistic assessment of the level of risk they pose for reoffending. It is nevertheless important to remember that only 3–4 per cent of young offenders are persistent in their offending behaviour and thus in need of a more rigorous intervention in an appropriate setting. The system should thus be underpinned by an awareness of the dangers of 'net widening' and the incorporation of a large, relatively non-problematic group of young people, tangentially involved in 'offending', into a spiral of increased surveillance and intervention. The nettle must be grasped and a previously over-eager youth justice system, professionals and politicians must accept that increased intervention in the lives of young people, 'for their own good', is often far from their best interests.

Significantly, young offenders must be dealt with in a holistic way, in the context of a reformulated reintegrative tutelage strategy that fully addresses the social context of their behaviour. The youth justice system in a moral communitarian framework should be part of a rebalanced economy where all mentally and physically 'able' citizens are economically active. In this reformulated positive environment, *all* young people should be given legitimate opportunities which will enable a positive engagement, involvement and participation, in a society where they have appropriate rights and responsibilities based on their aptitude and potential. For too many young people, who have come to the attention of the youth justice system, their experience of (often multiple) factors of social exclusion and their paucity of legitimate life chances has made involvement in criminality as a long-term career option a rational choice. The task for a radical moral communitarian society is to make such choices far less rational.

Postscript: neoliberalism revisited

As we have seen, it is the central proposition of communitarianism that the individual rights promoted by traditional liberals need to be balanced with social responsibilities with a simultaneous commitment made by the individual to the community in which they live. We have nevertheless observed in this book how the balance between rights and responsibilities has shifted excessively and unhealthily towards the pole of community with a much greater emphasis on the responsibilities of individuals to the detriment of their rights. Communitarianism was thus to become a key component of the neoliberal project with the notion of responsibility in the former highly compatible with that of responsibilisation in the latter.

A highly significant element of the neoliberal disciplinary project in the UK from its instigation was the abandonment of full employment but in the long term this has been a hugely problematic economic strategy (Hopkins Burke 2015b). First, the major neoliberal economic restructuring of the 1980s destroyed traditional income-creating manufacturing jobs in huge numbers with the outcome being the emergence of a large non-productive workless sector with increasing associated social problems. Second, this situation was significantly intensified by the rapid expansion of a whole class of public sector employees paid increasingly good salaries to look after (health and social work) and control (the criminal justice system) the ever more problematic elements of the first non-productive workless sector. There was a clear recognised need to rebalance the economy, and the Coalition government (and subsequently a less restrained Conservative government) has sought to address this by the introduction of established neoliberal techniques of huge cuts in public expenditure and concerted assaults on the living standards of workers and the poor.

This author has previously argued that these various socio-economic problems seem to have reached a 'tipping point' where the social and economic costs of neoliberal fiscal policies have come to outweigh any benefits other than for a small group of powerful economic players. A radical moral communitarian response – as we have seen above – proposes an alternative approach founded on notions of appropriate contributions to society (obligations and responsibilities), suitable fair rewards (rights), and consensual interdependency in the context of a fairer, more equal world, based on mutual respect between all citizens.

These identified rights and responsibilities are – as we have seen – highly compatible and interconnected. Thus, the call for a return to full-employment policies will lead not only to a more productive and balanced economy but also provide the material and psychological preconditions of the other essential rights. The provision of good-quality (invariably rented public-sector) accommodation for all those who need it is also about rebuilding communities by providing a broad mix of interrelated interdependent people from different social backgrounds within a particular geographical neighbourhood. The right to be treated with respect by all public servants, with the parallel responsibility to treat each other with respect, is more achievable in a world of full-employment and good-quality accommodation in proper communities where people have self-respect. The provision of good-quality health care for all citizens with the parallel responsibility to pursue good health will be more achievable with sensible alcohol and drug policies which decriminalise and medicalise a significant social problem. The provision of good-quality education and the parallel responsibility to engage with this is also far more achievable in a society with full employment and citizens with good health and is also highly applicable to the right to live in a crime-free society. The provision of proper alternative rational choices to crime and criminality will lead to a significant reduction in the need to treat and punish miscreants and in this rebalanced economy provide more resources for highly skilled professionals and practitioners to concentrate their expertise on the very small groups of citizens with real medical or social problems who desperately need assistance.

Summary of main points

1 It is clear from the discussion in this book that patterns of offending by children and young people and the nature of the response by the authorities are inextricably linked to significant socio-economic circumstances.

2 Pitts (2003b) called for a depoliticised and autonomous supervising agency which could become the champion and supporter of the youth justice system, its staff and its clients, from attempts by government to exploit them to political advantage and provided a template for such a neutral agency.

3 As we have seen, the Youth Justice Board came extremely close to being replaced in the aftermath of the electoral demise of New Labour and its replacement by the Coalition government in 2010 regardless of how unlikely that appeared seven years previously.

4 As we have seen previously, the contemporary youth justice system was introduced by a New Labour government strongly influenced by the political philosophy of communitarianism.

5 Dissenters observed from the outset that the subsequent New Labour agenda took a rather more authoritarian course than suggested by the rhetorical appeal to the relatively autonomous powers of civil society to deliver progress by itself while the Conservative 'Big Society' variant has to date proved at best ineffective.

6 It was New Labour *neo*-communitarian credentials that were clearly apparent in the establishment of a contemporary youth justice system epitomised by the central state control of youth offending teams by an autocratic Youth Justice Board.

7 Houdt and Schinkel (2013) argue that neoliberal communitarianism is a strategy of governmentality that combines the main features of neoliberal governmentality with those of governmental communitarianism.

8 Hopkins Burke (2014, 2015) argues that it is the work of Emile Durkheim and his observations on the *moral* component of contract and the division of labour in society which provides the theoretical basis of a radical moral communitarianism and which challenges the orthodox articulation and its hybrid neoliberal variation.

9 It is a formulation which actively promotes both the rights and the responsibilities of both individuals and communities, but in the context of an equal division of labour.

10 It is proposed that youth justice strategies should be located in the context of radical moral communitarian socio-economic programme and this is not fanciful and idealistic because neoliberalism is reaching a 'tipping point' where its disadvantages (costs) are fast coming to outweigh its advantages (cost-effective production).

Discussion questions

1   What are the current possibilities for the establishment of a politically neutral independent agency for overseeing and supervising the youth justice system?
2   Should the Youth Justice Board be abolished, kept within the Ministry of Justice or made independent?
3   What were the identified problems with the neo-communitarian approach to youth justice pursued by New Labour?
4   Explain neoliberalism.
5   What would a radical moral communitarian youth justice look like?

References

Abel, R. (ed.) (1982) *The Politics of Informal Justice*, Vols 1 and 2. New York: Academic Press.

Abramson, B. (2000) *Juvenile Justice: The 'Unwanted Child' of State Responsibilities. An Analysis of the Concluding Observations of the UN Committee on the Rights of the Child, in Regard to Juvenile Justice from 1993 to 2000*. Brussels: International Network on Juvenile Justice/Defence for Children International.

Abramson, B. (2006) 'Juvenile Justice: The Unwanted Child', in E. Jensen and J. Jepsen (eds) *Juvenile Law Violators, Human Rights and the Development of New Juvenile Justice Systems*. Oxford: Hart.

Acoca, L. (1999) 'Investing in Girls: A 21st Century Strategy', *Journal of the Office of Juvenile Justice and Delinquency Prevention*, V1(1): 3–13.

Adams, D. and Hess, M. (2001) 'Community in Public Policy: Fad or Foundation', *Australian Journal of Public Administration*, 60(2): 13–23.

Aichhorn, A. (1925) *Wayward Youth*. New York: Viking Press.

Akers, R.L. (1985) *Deviant Behaviour: A Social Learning Approach*, 3rd edn. Belmont, CA: Wadsworth.

Akers, R.L. (1992) 'Linking Sociology and Its Specialities', *Social Forces*, 71: 1–16.

Akers, R.L. (1997) *Criminological Theories: Introduction and Evaluation*. Los Angeles, CA: Roxbury.

Akers, R.L., Krohn, M.D., Lanza-Kaduce, L. and Radosevich, M. (1979) 'Social Learning and Deviant Behaviour: A Specific Test of a General Theory', *American Sociological Review*, 44: 635–55.

Akester, K. (2000) 'The Changing Face of Youth Justice', *New Law Journal*, 21 April: 566.

Alagappa, M. (2004) *Civil Society and Political Change in Asia*. Stanford, CA: Stanford University Press.

Alexander, J., Barton, C., Schiavo, R. and Parsons, B. (1976) 'Systems-behavioural Interventions with Families of Delinquents: Therapists, Characteristics, Family Behaviour and Outcome', *Journal of Consulting and Clinical Psychology*, 44: 656–64.

Alliance of Iranian Women (2010–13) 'Under the Islamic Rule', *Alliance of Iranian Women*. http://allianceofiranianwomen.org/ (accessed 16 August 2013).

All-Party Group on Alcohol Misuse (1995) *Alcohol and Crime: Breaking the Link*. London: HMSO.

Allsopp, J.F. and Feldman, M.P. (1975) 'Extroversion, Neuroticism and Psychoticism and Antisocial Behaviour in Schoolgirls', *Social Behaviour and Personality*, 2: 184.

Allsopp, J.F. and Feldman, M.P. (1976) 'Personality and Antisocial Behaviour in Schoolboys', *British Journal of Criminology*, 16: 337–51.

Amnesty International (2012) *Executions of Juveniles Since 1990*. http://www.amnesty.org/en/death-penalty/executions-of-child-offenders-since-1990 (accessed 18 September 2015).

Anderson, E. (1990) *Street Wise*. Chicago: University of Chicago Press.

Anderson, S., Kinsey, R., Loader, I. and Smith, C. (1994) *Cautionary Tales: Young People, Crime and Policing in Edinburgh*. Aldershot: Avebury.

Andrews, D. (1995) 'The Psychology of Criminal Conduct and Effective Treatment', in J. McGuire (ed.) *What Works: Reducing Re-offending: Guidelines from Research and Practice*. Chichester: John Wiley.

Andrews, D. and Bonta, J. (2010) *The Psychology of Criminal Conduct*, 5th edn. New Providence, NJ: LexisNexis Matthew Bender.

Andrews, D., Bonta, J. and Wormith, J. (2011) 'The Risk-Need-Responsivity (RNR) Model: Does Adding the Good Lives Model Contribute to Effective Crime Prevention?', *Criminal Justice and Behavior*, 38: 735–55.

Andrews, D., Hollins, C., Raynor, P., Trotter, C. and Armstrong, B. (2001) *Sustaining Effectiveness in Working with Offenders*. Cardiff: The Cognitive Centre Foundation.

Andrews, D.A., Zinger, I., Hoge, R.D., Bonta, J., Gendreau, P. and Cullen, F.T. (1990) 'Does Correctional Treatment Work? A Clinically Relevant and Psychologically Informed Meta-analysis', *Criminology*, 28: 369–404.

Andry, R.G. (1957) 'Faulty Paternal and Maternal Child Relationships, Affection and Delinquency', *British Journal of Delinquency*, VIII: 34–48.

Annie E. Casey Foundation (2013) 'Reducing Youth Incarceration in the United States'. http://'.aecf.org/KnowledgeCenter/Publications.aspx?pubguid={DFAD838E-1C29-46B4-BE8A-4D8392BC25C9} (accessed 18 August 2015).

Aries, P. (1962) *Centuries of Childhood: A Social History of Family* (trans. Robert Baldick). New York: Alfred A. Knopf.

Armstrong, D. (1983) *The Political Anatomy of the Body*. Cambridge: Cambridge University Press.

Armstrong, D. (2005) 'A Risky Business? Research, Policy, Governmentality and Youth Offending', *Youth Justice*, 4(2): 100–16.

Ashford, M. (1998) 'Making Criminals out of Children: Abolishing the Presumption of Doli Incapax', *Criminal Justice*, 16(1): 16–17.

Ashford, M. and Chard, A. (2000) *Defending Young People in the Legal System*. London: Legal Action Group.

Ashton, D.N. and Field, D. (1976) *Young Workers*. London: Hutchinson.

Ashworth, A. (2010) *Sentencing and Criminal Justice*, 5th edn. Cambridge: Cambridge University Press.

Ashworth, A., Gardner, J., Morgan, R., Smith, A.T.H., Von Hirsch, A. and Wasik, M. (1998) 'Neighbouring on the Oppressive: The Government's "Anti-social Behaviour Order" Proposals', *Criminal Justice*, 16(1): 7–14.

Audit Commission (1996) *Misspent Youth: Young People and Crime*. London: Audit Commission.

Audit Commission (2004) *Youth Justice 2004: A Review of the Reformed Youth Justice System*. London: Audit Commission.

Audit Commission (2006) *Strategic Plan*. London: HMSO.

Australian Institute of Health and Welfare (AIHW) (2013) *Juvenile Detention Population in Australia 2012*. Juvenile Justice Series Number 11. Canberra: Australian Institute of Health and Welfare.

Avon and Somerset Constabulary (1991) *The Effect of 'Re-Offending' on Bail on Crime in Avon and Somerset*. Bristol: Avon and Somerset Constabulary.

Ayers, C. (1999) 'Assessing Correlates of Onset, Escalation, De-escalation and Desistance of Delinquent Behaviour', *Journal of Quantitative Criminology*, 15(3): 277–306.

Bailey, V. (1987) *Delinquency and Citizenship: Reclaiming the Young Offender 1914–48*. Oxford: Clarendon Press.

Baker, E. and Roberts, J. (2005) 'Globalisation and the New Punitiveness', in J. Pratt, D. Brown, M. Brown, S. Hallsworth and W. Morrison (eds) *The New Punitiveness*. Cullompton: Willan.

Baker, K., Jones, S., Merrington, S. and Roberts, C. (2005) *Further Development of ASSET*. London: Youth Justice Board.

Baker, K., Jones, S., Roberts, C. and Merrington, S. (2002) *Validity and Reliability of ASSET*. London: Youth Justice Board.

Baker, K., Kelly, G. and Wilkinson, B. (2011) *Assessment in Youth Justice*. Bristol: Policy Press.

Balding, J. and Shelley, C. (1993) *Very Young Children in 1991/2*. Exeter: University of Exeter Schools Health Education Unit.

Baldwin, J.D. (1990) 'The Role of Sensory Stimulation in Criminal Behaviour, with Special Attention to the Age Peak in Crime', in L. Ellis and H. Hoffman (eds) *Crime in Biological, Social, and Moral Contexts*. New York: Praeger.

Ball, C. (1998) 'R v B (Young Offender: Sentencing Powers): Paying Due Regard to the Welfare of the Child in Criminal Proceedings', *Child and Family Law Quarterly*, 10(4): 417–24.

Ball, C. (2000) 'The Youth Justice and Criminal Evidence Act 1999 Part I: A Significant Move Towards Restorative Justice, or a Recipe for Unintended Consequences?', *Criminal Law Review*, April: 211–22.

Bandura, A. and Walters, R.H. (1959) *Adolescent Aggression*. New York: Ronald Press.

Banks, M., Bates, I., Breakwell, G., Bynner, J., Emler, N., Jamieson, L. and Roberts, K. (1992) *Careers and Identities*. Buckingham: Open University Press.

Barclay, G.C. (1995) *The Criminal Justice System in England and Wales 1995*. London: Home Office, Research and Statistics Department.

Baron, S.W. and Kennedy, L.W. (1998) 'Deterrence and Homeless Male Street Youths', *Canadian Journal of Criminology*, 40: 27–60.

Barrow Cadbury Trust (2005) *Lost in Transition: A Report of the Barrow Cadbury Commission on the Young Adults and the Criminal Justice System*. London: Barrow Cadbury.

Barrow Cadbury Trust (2012) *Why Prioritise Young Adults? Four Key Messages for Police and Crime Commissioners*. London: Barrow Cadbury.

Barry, A., Osborne, T. and Rose, N. (1996) *Foucault and Political Reason: Liberalism, Neo-Liberalism and Rationalities of Government*. London: UCL Press.

Basic Skills Agency (2002) *Basic Skills and Social Exclusion: Findings from a Study of Adults Born in 1970*. London: Centre for Longitudinal Studies, Institute of Education.

Bateman, T. (2005) 'Reducing Child Imprisonment: A Systemic Challenge', *Youth Justice*, 5(2): 91–104.

Bateman, T. (2006) 'Youth Crime and Justice: Statistical "Evidence", Recent Trends and Responses', in B. Goldson and J. Muncie (eds) *Youth Crime and Justice*. London: Sage.

Bateman, T. and Pitts, J. (2005) 'Conclusion: What the Evidence Tells Us', in T. Bateman and J. Pitts (eds) *The RHP Companion to Youth Justice*. Lyme Regis: Russell House.

Bates, I. (1984) 'From Vocational Guidance to Life Skills: Historical Perspectives on Careers Education', in I. Bates, J. Clarke, P. Cohen, D. Finn, R. Moore and P. Willis (eds) *Schooling for the Dole?* Basingstoke: Macmillan.

Bauman, Z. (1998a) *Work, Consumerism and the New Poor*. Buckingham: Open University Press.

Bauman, Z. (1998b) *Globalisation: The Human Consequences*. Cambridge: Polity.

Bauman, Z. (2000) 'Social Uses of Law and Order', in D. Garland and R. Sparks (eds) *Criminology and Social Theory*. Oxford: Oxford University Press.

BBC (2001) England's Failing Prisons. http://news.bbc.co.uk/1/hi/uk/1222271.stm (accessed 1 July 2015).

BBC News (2012) ASBOS to Be Replaced in New Government Proposals. http://www.bbc.co.uk/news/uk-18155579 (accessed 18 August 2015).

BBC News (2013) Austerity 'May Last Until 2020'. http://www.bbc.co.uk/news/business-22819843.

Beck, U. (1992) *Risk Society: Towards a New Modernity*. New Delhi: Sage.

Beck, U. (2006) *Power in the Global Age*. Cambridge: Polity.

Becker, G.S. (1968) 'Crime and Punishment: An Economic Approach', *Journal of Political Economy*, 76(2): 169–217.

Becker, H. (1963) *Outsiders: Studies in the Sociology of Deviance*. New York: Free Press.

Becker, H. (1967) 'Whose Side Are We On?', *Social Problems*, 14(3): 239–47.

Beckett, H. and Warrington, C. (2014) *Suffering in Silence: Children and Unreported Crime*. London: Victim Support and the University of Bedfordshire.

Beckett, K. and Western, B. (2001) 'Governing Social Marginality: Welfare, Incarceration and the Transformation of State Policy', *Punishment and Society*, 3(1): 43–59.

Behlmer, J.K. (1998) *Friends of the Family: The English Home and Its Guardians*. Stanford: Stanford University Press.

Beinart, S., Anderson, B., Lee, S. and Utting, D. (2002) *Youth at Risk? A National Survey of Risk Factors and Problem Behaviour among Young People in England, Scotland and Wales*. London: Communities that Care.

Bell, C. (1999) 'Appealing for Justice for Children and Young People: A Critical Analysis of the Crime and Disorder Bill 1998', in B. Goldson (ed.) *Youth Justice: Contemporary Policy and Practice*. Aldershot: Ashgate.

Belson, W.A. (1975) *Juvenile Theft: The Causal Factors*. London: Harper and Row.

Bennett, T. (2000) *Drugs and Crime: The Results of the Second Developmental Stage of the New-Adam Programme*. Home Office Research Study 2005. London: Home Office.

Bennett, T., Holloway, K. and Williams, T. (2001) *Drug Use and Offending: Summary Results from the First Year of the NEW-ADAM Research Programme, Findings 148*. London: Home Office.

Black, D. and Cottrell, D. (eds) (1993) *Child and Adolescent Psychiatry*. London: Royal College of Psychiatrists.

Blair, T. (1998) *The Third Way: New Politics for the New Century*. London: The Fabian Society.

Blanch, M. (1979) 'Imperialism, Nationalism and Organized Youth', in J. Clarke et al. (eds) *Working Class Culture*. London: Hutchinson.

Blond, P. (2010) *Red Tory: How Left and Right Have Broken Britain and How We Can Fix It*. London: Faber and Faber.

Blunt, C. (2012) Speech to Centre for Social Justice Launch of Report into Youth Justice System, 16 January. http://www.justice.gov.uk/news/speeches/previous-ministers-speeches/crispin-blunt/centre-for-social-justice-160112 (accessed 18 September 2015).

Blyth, D.A., Hill, J.P. and Thiel, K.S. (1982) 'Early Adolescents, Significant Others: Grade and Gender Differences in Perceived Relationships with Familial and Nonfamilial Adults and Young People', *Journal of Youth and Adolescence*, 11: 425–50.

Boeck, T. and Fleming, J. (2011) 'The Role of Social Capital and Resources in Resilience to Risk', in H. Kemshall and B. Wilkinson (eds) *Good Practice in Assessing Risk: Current Knowledge, Issues and Approaches.* London: Jessica Kingsley.

Boffey, D. (2015) 'Youth Unemployment Rate Is Worst for 20 Years, Compared with Overall figure', *The Observer*, Sunday 22 February.

Borduin, C., Mann, B., Cone, L., Henggeler, S., Fucci, B., Blaske, D. and Williams, R. (1995) 'Multisystemic Treatment of Serious Juvenile Offenders: Long Term Prevention of Criminality and Violence', *Journal of Consulting and Clinical Psychology*, 34: 105–13.

Boswell, G. (1995) *Violent Victims: The Prevalence of Abuse and Loss in the Lives of Section 53 Offenders.* London: The Prince's Trust.

Bottomley, K. and Pease, K. (1986) *Crime and Punishment: Interpreting the Data.* Milton Keynes: Open University Press.

Bottoms, A. (1974) 'On the Decriminalization of the Juvenile Court', in R. Hood (ed.) *Crime, Criminology and Public Policy.* London: Heinemann.

Bottoms, A. (1977) 'Reflections on the Renaissance of Dangerousness', *The Howard Journal*, 16(2): 70–96.

Bottoms, A. (2005) 'Methodology Matters', *Safer Society*, Summer: 10–12.

Bowlby, J. (1952) *Maternal Care and Mental Health.* New York: World Health Organisation.

Box, S. (1981) *Deviance, Reality and Society*, 2nd edn. London: Rinehart and Winston.

Box, S. (1987) *Recession, Crime and Punishment.* London: Macmillan.

Bradley, K.M. (2008) 'Juvenile Delinquency, the Juvenile Courts and the Settlement Movement 1908–50: Basil Henriques and Toynbee Hall', *20th Century British History*, 19: 133–55.

Bradley, K.M. (2009a) *Poverty, Philanthropy and the State: Charities and the Working Classes in London 1918–79.* Manchester: Manchester University.

Bradley, K.M. (2009b) 'Cesare Lombroso', in K. Hayward, S. Maruna and J. Mooney (eds) *50 Key Thinkers in Criminology.* London: Routledge.

Braithwaite, J. (1989) *Crime, Shame and Reintegration.* Cambridge: Cambridge University Press.

Braithwaite, J. (1998) 'Restorative Justice', in M. Tonry (ed.) *Handbook of Crime and Punishment.* New York: Oxford University Press.

Braithwaite, J. and Daly, K. (1994) 'Masculinities, Violence and Communitarian Control', in T. Newburn and E.A. Stanko (eds) *Just Boys Doing Business? Men, Masculinities and Crime.* London: Routledge.

Brake, M. (1980) *The Sociology of Youth Cultures and Youth Sub-cultures.* London: Routledge and Kegan Paul.

Brake, M. (1985) *Comparative Youth Culture.* London: Routledge.

Brand, S. and Price, R. (2000) *The Economic and Social Costs of Crime*, Research Study 217. London: Home Office.

Brewer, D.D., Hawkins, J.D., Catalano, R.F. and Neckerman, H.J. (1995) 'Preventing Serious, Violent and Chronic Juvenile Offending: A Review of Evaluations of Selected Strategies in Childhood, Adolescence, and the Community', in J.C. Howell, B. Krisberg, J.D. Hawkins and J.J. Wilson (eds) *Serious, Violent and Chronic Juvenile Offenders: A Sourcebook.* Thousand Oaks, CA: Sage.

Brinkley, I. (1997) 'Underworked and Underpaid', *Soundings*, 6: 161–71.

Brown, D. (2013) 'Prison Rates, Social Democracy, Neoliberalism and Justice Reinvestment', in K. Carrington, M. Ball, E. O'Brien and J. Tauri (eds) *Crime, Justice and Social Democracy*. London: Palgrave Macmillan.

Brown, S. (1998) *Understanding Youth and Crime*. Buckingham: Open University Press.

Buckland, G. and Stevens, A. (2001) *Review of Effective Practice with Young Offenders in Mainland Europe*. European Institute of Social Services, University of Kent at Canterbury.

Burgess, E.W. (1928) 'The Growth of the City', in R. Park, E.W. Burgess and R.D. McKenzie (eds) *The City*. Chicago: University of Chicago Press.

Burgess, R.L. and Akers, R.L. (1968) 'A Differential Association-Reinforcement Theory of Criminal Behaviour', *Social Problems*, 14: 128–47.

Burney, E. (2005) *Making People Behave: Anti-social Behaviour, Politics and Policy*. Cullompton: Willan.

Burt, C. (1945) *The Young Delinquent*. London: University of London Press.

Butler, I. and Drakeford, M. (1997) 'Tough Guise: The Politics of Youth Justice', *Probation Journal*, 44: 216–19.

Campbell, B. (1993) *Goliath: Britain's Dangerous Places*. London: Methuen.

Campbell, B. (1999) 'Criminalising Children', *Community Care*, 29 July: 14.

Campbell, S. (2002) *A Review of Anti-social Behaviour Orders*, Home Office Research Series 236. London: Home Office.

Campbell, S. and Harrington, V. (2000) *Youth Crime: Findings from the 1998/99 Youth Lifestyles Survey*, Home Office Research Findings 126. London: Home Office.

Carew, R. (1979) 'The Place of Knowledge in Social Work Activity', *British Journal of Social Work*, 19(3): 349–64.

Carpenter, M. (1853) *Juvenile Delinquents: Their Condition and Treatment*. London: Cash.

Carrabine, E. (2010) 'Youth Justice in the United Kingdom', *Essex Human Rights Review*, 7(1): 12–24.

Carson, D. and Bain, A. (2008) *Professional Risk and Working with People*. London: Jessica Kingsley.

Case, S. (2007) 'Questioning the "Evidence" of Risk that Underpins Evidence-led Youth Justice Interventions', *Youth Justice*, 7: 91–105.

Castells, M. (2008) 'The New Public Sphere: The Global Civil Society, Communication Networks and Global Governance', *The Annals of the American Academy of Political and Social Science*, 616: 78–93.

Cavadino, M. and Dignan, J. (1997) *The Penal System: An Introduction*. London: Sage.

Cavadino, M. and Dignan, J. (2006) *Penal Systems: A Comparative Approach*. London: Sage.

Cavadino, M., Dignan, J. and Mair, G. (2013) *The Penal System: An Introduction*, 5th edn. London: Sage.

Cavadino, P. (1997a) 'Government Plans for Youth Justice', *Childright*, 141: 4–5.

Cavadino, P. (1997b) 'Goodbye Doli, Must We Leave You?' *Child and Family Law Quarterly*, 9(2): 165–71.

Cavadino, P. and Gibson, B. (1993) *Bail: The Law, Best Practice and the Debate*. Winchester: Waterside Press.

CDCU (Central Drugs Co-ordination Unit) (1995) *Tackling Drugs Together: A Strategy for England 1995–1998*. London: HMSO.

Chapman, T. and Hough, M. (1998) *Evidence Based Practice: A Guide to Effective Practice*. London: H.M. Inspectorate of Probation/Home Office.

Charlesworth, L. (2010) 'England's Early "Big Society": Parish Welfare under the Old Poor Law'. *History and Policy*. www.historyandpolicy.org/papers/policy-paper-108.html.

Charlton, B.G. (1999) 'The Ideology of "Accountability"', *Journal of the Royal College of Physicians of London*, 33: 33–5.

Charlton, B.G. (2001) 'Clinical Governance: A Quality Assurance Audit System for Regulating Clinical Practice', in A. Miles (ed.) *Clinical Governance: Encouraging Excellence or Imposing Control?* London: Aesculaepius Medical Press.

Childright (1998) 'The Crime and Disorder Bill: Will It Really Curb Youth Crime?', *Childright*, 143: 8–9.

Chilton, R.J. and Markle, G.E. (1972) 'Family Disruption, Delinquent Conduct, and the Effect of Subclassification', *American Sociological Review*, 37: 93–108.

Christiansen, K.O. (1968) 'Threshold of Tolerance in Various Population Groups Illustrated by Results from the Danish Criminologic Twin Study', in A.V.S. de Reuck and R. Porter (eds) *The Mentally Abnormal Offender*. Boston: Little, Brown.

Christie, N. (2000) *Crime Control as Industry*, 3rd edn. London: Routledge.

Cipriani, D. (2009) *Children's Rights and the Minimum Age of Criminal Responsibility: A Global Perspective*. Aldershot: Ashgate.

Clapham, B. (1989) 'A Case of Hypoglycaemia', *The Criminologist*, 13: 2–15.

Clapp, E.J. (1998) *Mothers of All Children: Women Reformers and the Rise of Juvenile Courts in Progressive Era America*. University Park, PA: Pennsylvania State University Press.

Clarke, J. (1975) *Ideologies of Control of Working Class Youth*. Birmingham: University of Birmingham, Centre for Contemporary Cultural Studies.

Clarke, J. and Cochrane, A. (1998) 'The Social Construction of Social Problems', in E. Saraga (ed.) *Embodying the Social Construction of Difference*. London: Routledge/Open University.

Clarke, R.V.G. (1987) 'Rational Choice Theory and Prison Psychology', in B.J. McGurk et al. (eds) *Applying Psychology to Imprisonment: Theory and Practice*. London: HMSO.

Clayden, J. and Stein, M. (2002) *Mentoring for Care Leavers*. London: The Prince's Trust.

Clear, T.R. and Karp, D.R. (1999) *The Community Justice Ideal: Preventing Crime and Achieving Justice*. Boulder, CO: Westview.

Cloward, R.A. and Ohlin, L.E. (1960) *Delinquency and Opportunity: A Theory of Delinquent Gangs*. New York: Free Press.

Cmnd. 7227 (1946–7) *Summary of Statistics Relating to Crime and Criminal Proceedings for the Years 1939–1945*. London: HMSO.

Cockburn, C. (1987) *Two-Track Training: Sex Inequalities and YTS*. London: Macmillan.

Coffield, F., Borrill, C. and Marshall, S. (1986) *Growing Up at the Margins*. Milton Keynes: Open University Press.

Cohen, A.K. (1955) *Delinquent Boys: The Culture of the Gang*. New York: Free Press.

Cohen, L.E. and Felson, M. (1979) 'Social Inequality and Predatory Criminal Victimization: An Exposition and Test of a Formal Theory', *American Sociological Review*, 44: 588–608.

Cohen, L.E., Kluegel, J. and Land, K. (1981) 'Social Inequality and Predatory Criminal Victimisation: An Exposition and Test of a Formal Theory', *American Sociological Review*, 46: 505–24.

Cohen, M. (1998) 'The Monetary Value of Saving a High-risk Youth', *Journal of Quantitative Criminology*, 14: 5–33.

Cohen, P. (1972) 'Sub-Cultural Conflict and Working Class Community', Working Papers in Cultural Studies, No. 2. Birmingham: CCCS, University of Birmingham.

Cohen, S. (1973) *Folk Devils and Moral Panics*. Oxford: Martin Robertson.

Cohen, S. (1980) *Folk Devils and Moral Panics*, 2nd edn. Oxford: Martin Robertson.

Cohen, S. (1985) *Visions of Social Control*. Cambridge: Polity Press.

Coid, J., Carvell, A., Kittler, Z., Healey, A. and Henderson, J. (2000) 'Opiates, Criminal Behaviour and Methadone Treatment', RDS Occasional Paper. London: Home Office.

Coleman, C. and Moynihan, J. (1996) *Understanding Crime Data*. Buckingham: Open University Press.

Coleman, J. and Roker, D. (2001) 'Setting the Scene: Parenting and Public Policy', in J. Coleman and D. Roker (eds) *Supporting Parents of Teenagers: A Handbook for Professionals*. London: Jessica Kingsley.

Coleman, J.C. and Warren-Adamson, C. (1992) *Youth Policy in the 1990s: The Way Forward*. London: Routledge.

Collins, J.J. (1988) 'Alcohol and Interpersonal Violence: Less than Meets the Eye', in A. Weiner and M.E. Wolfgang (eds) *Pathways to Criminal Violence*. Newbury Park, CA: Sage.

Communities that Care (2001) *The Risk and Protective Factors for Youth Crime – Prevalence, Salience, and Reduction*. London: Youth Justice Board.

Conklin, J.E. (1977) *Illegal but Not Criminal*. River Vale, NJ: Spectrum.

Connexions. (2002) *Transforming Youth Work Resourcing Excellent Youth Services*. Nottingham: Department for Education and Skills.

Corrigan, P. (1979) *The Smash Street Kids*. London: Paladin.

Cortes, J.B. and Gatti, F.M. (1972) *Delinquency and Crime: A Biopsychological Approach*. New York: Seminar Press.

Coulshed, V. and Orme, J. (1998) *Social Work Practice: An Introduction*, 3rd edn. Basingstoke: Macmillan Press.

Council of Europe (2009) *European Rules for Juvenile Offenders Subject to Sanctions or Measures*. Strasbourg: Council of Europe Publishing.

Council of Europe (2010) *Guidelines of the Committee of Ministers of the Council of Europe on Child Friendly Justice* (adopted by the Committee of Ministers on 17 November 2010 at the 1098th meeting of the Ministers' Deputies). Strasbourg: Council of Europe.

Coupland, D. (1992) *Generation X: Tales for an Accelerated Culture*. London: Abacus.

Cox, P. (2003) *Gender, Justice and Welfare: Bad Girls in Britain 1900–50*. Basingstoke: Routledge.

Crawford, A. and Clear, T.R. (2003) 'Community Justice: Transforming Communities through Restorative Justice?' in E. McLaughlin, R. Fergusson, G. Hughes and L. Westmarland (eds) *Restorative Justice: Critical Issues*. London: Sage/Open University.

Crawford, A. and Newburn, T. (2003) *Youth Offending and Restorative Justice*. Cullompton: Willan.

Crewe, I. (1989) 'Values: The Crusade That Failed' in D. Kavanagh and A. Seldon (eds) *The Thatcher Effect*. Oxford: Oxford University Press.

Crimmens, D. and Pitts, J. (2000) *Positive Residential Practice: Learning the Lessons of the 1990s*. Lyme Regis: Russell House.

Crisis (2014) *Nations Apart? Experiences of Single Homeless People across Great Britain*. London: Crisis.

Crisis (2015) *Access to Housing Benefit for 18- to 21-Year-Olds*. London: Crisis.

Croall, H. (1992) *White-collar Crime*. Buckingham: Open University Press.

Croall, H. (2001) *Understanding White-collar Crime*, Crime and Justice Series. Buckingham: Open University Press.

Crook, F. (2014) *Payments by Results Have Failed and What Is Coming Is Worse*. London: Howard League of Penal Reform.

Crowther, C. (2000a) *Policing Urban Poverty*. Basingstoke: Macmillan.

Crowther, C. (2000b) 'Thinking about the "Underclass": Towards a Political Economy of Policing', *Theoretical Criminology*, 4(2): 149–67.

Crowther, C. (1998) 'Policing the Excluded Society', in R.D. Hopkins Burke (ed.) *Zero Tolerance Policing*. Leicester: Perpetuity Press.

Culpitt, I. (1999) *Social Policy and Risk*. London: Sage.

Cunneen, C. and White, R. (2006) 'Australia: Containment or Empowerment?' in J. Muncie and B. Goldson (eds) *Comparative Youth Justice*. London: Sage.

Cunningham, H. (1980) *Leisure in the Industrial Revolution*. London: Croom Helm.

Curtis, L.A. (1975) *Violence, Race and Culture*. Lexington, MA: Heath.

Dahrendorf, R. (1985) *Law and Order*. London: Stevens.

Dale, D. (1984) 'The Politics of Crime', *Salisbury Review*, October.

Darlington, Y. and Osmond, J.L. (2001) *Using Knowledge in Practice*. Brisbane: University of Queensland.

Davidson, N. (2006) 'Chernobyl's "Nuclear Nightmares"', *Horizon*, BBC. http://news.bbc.co.uk/1/hi/sci/tech/5173310.stm.

Davies, B. (1982) 'Juvenile Justice in Confusion', *Youth and Policy*, 1(2): 3–6.

Davis, J. (1990) *Youth and the Condition of Britain*. London: Athlone Press.

Dawes, F. (1975) *A Cry from the Streets: The Boys' Club Movement in Britain*. Hove: Wayland.

Day-Sclater, S. and Piper, C. (2000) 'Re-moralising the Family? Family Policy, Family Law and Youth Justice', *Child and Family Law Quarterly*, 12(2): 135–51.

Delanty, G. (2003) *Community*. London: Routledge.

De Luca, J.R. (ed.) (1981) *Fourth Special Report to the US Congress on Alcohol and Health*. Rockville, MD: National Institute on Alcohol Abuse and Alcoholism.

Dencik, L. (1989) 'Growing Up in the Post-Modern Age: On the Child's Situation in the Modern Family, and on the Position of the Family in the Modern Welfare State', *Acta Sociologica*, 32(2): 155–80.

Dennis, N. and Erdos, G. (1992) *Families without Fatherhood*. London: Institute of Economic Affairs.

Dennis, N., Henriques, F. and Slaughter, C. (1956) *Coal Is Our Life*. London: Eyre & Spottiswoode.

Department of Health (2005) *Smoking, Drinking and Drug Use among Young People in England in 2004*. London: Department of Health.

DHSS (1981) *Offending by Young People: A Survey of Recent Trends*. London: DHSS.

Desforges, C. and Abouchaar, A. (2003) 'The Impact of Parental Involvement, Parental Support and Family Education on Pupil Achievement and Adjustment: A Literature Review', Research Report 433. Nottingham: Department for Education and Skills.

Devitt, K. (2011) *Substance Misuse and Young Adults in the Criminal Justice System*. Brighton: Young People in Focus.

Devitt, K., Knighton, L. and Lowe, K. (2009) *Young Adults Today*. Brighton: Young People in Focus.

Diduck, A. (1999) 'Justice and Childhood: Reflections on Refashioned Boundaries', in M. King (ed.) *Moral Agendas for Children's Welfare*. London: Routledge.

Dignan, J. (1999) 'The Crime and Disorder Act and the Prospects for Restorative Justice', *Criminal Law Review*, 48–60.

Dignan, J. (2000) 'Victims, Reparation and the Pilot YOTs', *Justice of the Peace*, 164: 296–7.

Dolowitz, D. (ed.) (2000) *Policy Transfer and British Social Policy: Learning from the USA?* Buckingham: Open University Press.

Dolowitz, D. and Marsh, D. (2000) 'Learning from Abroad: The Role of Policy Transfers in Contemporary Policy Making', *Governance*, 13(1): 5–24.

Donajgrodzki, A. (1977) *Social Control in Nineteenth Century Britain*. London: Croom Helm.

Donald, J. (1985) 'Beacons of the Future', in V. Beechey and J. Donald (eds) *Subjectivity and Social Relations*. Milton Keynes: Open University Press.

Donzelot, J. (1980) *The Policing of Families: Welfare versus the State*. London: Hutchinson University Library.

Douglas, M. (1966) *Purity and Danger: An Analysis of Concepts of Pollution and Taboo*. London: Routledge and Kegan Paul.

Dowden, C. and Andrews, D.A. (1999) 'What Works in Young Offender Treatment: A Meta-analysis', *Forum on Corrections Research*, 11: 21–4.

Downes, D. (1966) *The Delinquent Solution*. London: Routledge & Kegan Paul.

Downes, D. and Hansen, K. (2006) *Welfare and Punishment: The Relationship between Welfare Spending and Imprisonment, Briefing No.2*. London: Crime and Society Foundation.

Downes, D. and Rock, P. (1998) *Understanding Deviance*, 3rd edn. Oxford: Oxford University Press.

Downes, D. and Van Swaaningen, R. (2007) 'The Road to Dystopia: Changes in the Penal Climate in the Netherlands', in M. Tonry and C. Bijleveld (eds) *Crime and Justice in the Netherlands*. Chicago: Chicago University Press.

DPAS and SCODA (2000) *Drugs and Young Teams and Youth Offending Teams*. London: DPAS and SCODA.

Drakeford, M. and McCarthy, K. (2000) 'Parents, Responsibility and the New Youth Justice', in B. Goldson (ed.) *The New Youth Justice*. Lyme Regis: Russell House.

Driver, S. and Martell, L. (1997) 'New Labour's Communitarianisms', *Critical Social Policy*, 52: 27–46.

Dugdale, R.L. (1877) *The Jukes*. New York: Putnam.

Dunkel, F. (1996) 'Juvenile Delinquents', in W. Carney (ed.) *Juvenile Delinquents and Young People in Danger in an Open Environment*. Winchester: Waterside Press.

Durkheim, E. (1933; orig. pub. 1893) *The Division of Labour in Society*. Glencoe: Free Press.

Durkheim, E. (1964; orig. pub. 1915) *The Elementary Forms of Religious Life*. Glencoe: Free Press.

DWP (2013) Monitoring the Impact of Changes to the Local Housing Allowance. https://www.gov.uk/government/uploads/system/uploads/attachment_data/file/203107/rrep838_pt6.pd (accessed 9 September 2015).

Dyer, F. and Gregory, L. (2014) 'Mental Health Difficulties in the Youth Justice Population: Learning from the First Six Months of the Ivy Project, Centre for Youth and Criminal Justice', Briefing Paper 05. Strathclyde.

Dyhouse, C. (1981) *Girls Growing Up in Late Victorian and Edwardian England*. London: Routledge and Kegan Paul.

Edmunds, M., Hough, M. and Turnbull, P.J. (1999) 'Doing Justice to Treatment: Referring Offenders to Drug Treatment Services', Drugs Prevention Initiative Paper No. 2. London: Home Office.

Edwards, M. (2004) *Civil Society*. Cambridge: Polity Press.

Ehrenkranz, J., Bliss, E. and Sheard, M.H. (1974) 'Plasma Testosterone: Correlation with Aggressive Behaviour and Social Dominance in Man', *Psychosomatic Medicine*, 36: 469–83.

Elias, N. (1978) *The Civilising Process, Vol. 1: The History of Manners*. Oxford: Blackwell.

Elias, N. (1982) *The Civilising Process, Vol. 2: State-Formation and Civilisation*. Oxford: Blackwell.

Elliot, D., Ageton, S. and Canter, J. (1979) 'An Integrated Theoretical Perspective on Delinquent Behaviour', *Journal of Research in Crime and Delinquency*, 16: 126–49.

Elliot, P.S. and Voss, H.L. (1974) *Delinquency and Drop-out*. Toronto: Lexington.

Ellis, L. and Coontz, P.D. (1990) 'Androgens, Brain Functioning, and Criminality: The Neurohormonal Foundations of Antisociality', in L. Ellis and H. Hoffman (eds) *Crime in Biological, Social, and Moral Contexts*. New York: Praeger.

Emanuel, E. (1991) *The Ends of Human Life: Medical Ethics in a Liberal Polity*. Cambridge, MA: Harvard University Press.

Emsley, C. (1996) *The English Police: A Political and Social History*. Harlow: Longman.

Emsley, C. (2001) 'The Origins and Development of the Police', in E. McLaughlin and J. Muncie (eds) *Controlling Crime*. London: Sage with the Open University.

Ericson, R.V. and Haggerty, D. (1997) *Policing the Risk Society*. Oxford: Clarendon Press.

Etzioni, A. (1993) *The Spirit of Community: The Reinvention of American Society*. New York: Touchstone.

Etzioni, A. (ed.) (1995a) *New Communitarian Thinking: Persons, Virtues, Institutions and Communities*. Charlottesville: University of Virginia Press.

Etzioni, A. (1995b) *The Parenting Deficit*. London: Demos.

Eysenck, H.J. (1959) *Manual of the Maudsley Personality Inventory*. London: University of London Press.

Eysenck, H.J. (1970) *Crime and Personality*. London: Granada.

Eysenck, H.J. (1977) *Crime and Personality*, 3rd edn, London: Routledge & Kegan Paul.

Fagan, J. (1990) 'Intoxication and Aggression', in M. Tonry and J.Q. Wilson (eds) *Crime and Justice: A Review of Research*. Chicago: University of Chicago Press.

Family Policy Studies Centre (1998) *The Crime and Disorder Bill and the Family*. London: Family Policy Studies Centre.

Farrington, D.P. (1992a) 'Juvenile Delinquency', in J.C. Coleman (ed.) *The School Years*, 2nd edn. London: Routledge.

Farrington, D.P. (1992b) 'Explaining the Beginning, Progress and Ending of Anti-social Behaviour from Birth to Adulthood', in J. McCord (ed.) *Facts, Frameworks and Forecasts: Advances in Criminological Theory*, Vol. 3. New Brunswick, NJ: Transaction.

Farrington, D.P. (1994a) 'Human Development and Criminal Careers', in M. Maguire, R. Morgan and R. Reiner (eds) *The Oxford Handbook of Criminology*. Oxford: Clarendon.

Farrington, D.P. (1994b) 'Introduction', in D.P. Farrington (ed.) *Psychological Explanations of Crime*. Aldershot: Dartmouth.

Farrington, D.P. (1995) 'The Twelfth Jack Tizard Memorial Lecture: The Development of Offending and Antisocial Behaviour from Childhood: Key Findings from the Cambridge Study in Delinquent Development', *Journal of Child Psychology and Psychiatry*, 36: 929–64.

Farrington, D.P. (1996) *Understanding and Preventing Youth Crime*. York: Joseph Rowntree Foundation.

Feeley, M. and Simon, J. (1996) 'Actuarial Justice: The Emerging New Criminal Law', in D. Nelkin (ed.) *The Future of Criminology*. Thousand Oaks, CA: Sage.

Feest, J. (1990) *New Social Strategies and the Criminal Justice System*. Brussels: Council of Europe.

Felson, M. (1998) *Crime and Everyday Life*, 2nd edn. Thousand Oaks, CA: Pine Forge.

Fergusson, R., Pye, D., Esland, G., McLaughlin, E. and Muncie, J. (2000) 'Normalised Dislocation and the New Subjectivities in Post-16 Markets for Education and Work', *Critical Social Policy*, 20(3): 283–305.

Ferri, E. (1895) *Criminal Sociology*. London: Unwin.

Field, F. (1989) *Losing Out: The Emergence of Britain's Underclass*. Oxford: Blackwell.

Findlay, M. and Zvekic, U. (1988) *Analysing Informal Mechanisms of Crime Control: A Cross-Cultural Perspective*. Rome: UNSDRI

Fionda, J. (1999) 'New Labour, Old Hat: Youth Justice and the Crime and Disorder Act 1998', *Criminal Law Review*, 36–47.

Fishbein, D.H. and Pease, S.E. (1990) 'Neurological Links between Substance Abuse and Crime', in L. Ellis and H. Hoffman (eds) *Crime in Biological, Social, and Moral Contexts*. New York: Praeger.

Flanzer, J. (1981) 'The Vicious Circle of Alcoholism and Family Violence', *Alcoholism*, 1(3): 30–45.

Fletcher, H. (2005) *ASBOs: An Analysis of the First 6 Years*. London: ASBO Concern/ Napo.

Flood-Page C., Campbell, S., Harington, V. and Miller, J. (2000) *Youth Crime Findings from the 1998/99 Youth Lifestyles Survey*, Home Office Research Study 209. London: Home Office.

Fo, W.S.O. and O'Donnell, C.R. (1974) 'The Buddy System: Relationship and Contingency Conditioning in a Community Intervention Program for Youth with Nonprofessionals as Behaviour Change Agents', *Journal of Consulting and Clinical Psychology*, 42: 163–9.

Forrester-Jones, R. (2006) 'Reflections on a Young Offenders Institution Communication: A Need, a Want, a Right', *International Journal of Offender Therapy and Comparative Criminology*, 50(2): 218–31.

Foucault, M. (1971) *Madness and Civilisation: A History of Insanity in the Age of Reason*. London: Tavistock.

Foucault, M. (1976) *The History of Sexuality*. London: Allen Lane.

Foucault, M. (1980) *Power/Knowledge: Selected Interviews and Other Writings 1972–77* (ed. C. Gordon). Brighton: Harvester Press.

Fraser, D. (1973) *The Evolution of the British Welfare State*. London: Macmillan.

Freud, S. (1927) *The Ego and the Id*. London: Hogarth.

Friedlander, K. (1947) *The Psychoanalytic Approach to Juvenile Delinquency*. London: Kegan Paul.

Friedlander, K. (1949) 'Latent Delinquency and Ego Development', in K.R. Eissler (ed.) *Searchlights on Delinquency*. New York: International University Press.

Furlong, A. and Cartmel, F. (1997) *Young People and Social Change*. Buckingham: Open University Press.

Fyfe, N.R. (1995) 'Law and Order Policy and the Spaces of Citizenship in Contemporary Britain', *Political Geography*, 14(2): 177–89.

Gardner, H. (1993) *Frames of Mind: The Theory of Multiple Intelligences*. New York: Basic Books.

Garland, D. (1996) 'The Limits of the Sovereign State: Strategies of Crime Control in Contemporary Society', *British Journal of Criminology*, 34(4): 445–71.

Garland, D. (2001) *The Culture of Control*. Oxford: Oxford University Press.

Garofalo, R. (1914) *Criminology*. Boston: Little, Brown.

Garside, R. and McMahon, W. (2006) *Does Criminal Justice Work? The 'Right for the Wrong Reasons' Debate*. London: CCJS, King's College.

Gatrell, V. (1980) 'The Decline of Theft and Violence in Victorian and Edwardian England', in V. Gatrell, B. Lenman and G. Parker (eds) *Crime and the Law: The Social History of Crime in Europe Since 1500*. London: Europa.

Gauci, J.-P. (2009) *Racism in Europe*. Brussels: European Network Against Racism.

Gelsthorpe, L. (1999) 'Parents and Criminal Children', in A. Bainham, S. Day Sclater and M. Richards (eds) *What Is a Parent? A Socio-legal Analysis*. Oxford: Hart.

Gelsthorpe, L. and Morris, A. (1994) 'Juvenile Justice 1945–1992', in M. Maguire, R. Morgan and R. Reiner (eds), *The Oxford Handbook of Criminology*. Oxford: Clarendon Press.

Gelsthorpe, L. and Morris, A. (1999) 'Much Ado about Nothing: A Critical Comment on Key Provisions Relating to Children in The Crime and Disorder Act 1998', *Child and Family Law Quarterly*, 11(3): 209–21.

Gendreau, P., Paparozzi, M., Little, T. and Goddard, M. (1993). 'Does "Punishing Smarter" Work? An Assessment of the New Generation of Alternative Sanctions in Probation', *Forum on Corrections Research*, 5: 31–4.

Ghate, D. and Ramella, M. (2002) *Positive Parenting*. London: Youth Justice Board.

Gibbens, T.C.N. (1963) *Psychiatric Studies of Borstal Lads*. Oxford: Oxford University Press.

Gibbons, D.C. (1970) *Delinquent Behaviour*. Englewood Cliffs, NJ: Prentice-Hall.

Gibbs, J. (1975) *Crime, Punishment, and Deterrence*. New York: Elsevier.

Gibson, B. (1994) *The Youth Court: One Year Onwards*. London: Waterside Press.

Giddens, A. (1990) *Consequences of Modernity*. Cambridge: Polity Press.

Giddens, A. (1994) *Beyond Left and Right: The Future of Radical Politics*. Cambridge: Polity Press.

Giddens, A. (1998) *The Third Way*. Cambridge: Polity Press.

Giddens, A. (1999) 'Risk and Responsibility', *Modern Law Review*, 62(1): 1–10.

Gilliom, J. (1994) *Surveillance, Privacy and the Law: Employee Drug Testing and the Politics of Social Control*. Michigan: University of Michigan Press.

Gillis, G.R. (1974) *Youth and History*. London: Academic Press.

Gillis, G.R. (1981) *Youth and History*, 2nd edn. London: Academic Press.

Gittins, D. (1985) *The Family in Question: Changing Households and Familiar Ideologies*. London: Macmillan.

Glendon, M.A. (1991) *Rights Talk: The Impoverishment of Political Discourse*. New York: Free Press.

Glueck, S. and Glueck, E. (1950) *Unravelling Juvenile Delinquency*. Oxford: Oxford University Press.

Goddard, H.H. (1914) *Feeblemindedness: Its Causes and Consequences*. New York: Macmillan.

Godfrey, C., Eaton, G., McDougall, C. and Culyer, A. (2002) *The Economic and Social Costs of Class A Drug Use in England and Wales, 2000*. London: Home Office.

Goldson, B. (1999) 'Re-visiting First Principles and Re-stating Opposition to Child Incarceration', *Ajjust*, 44: 4–9.

Goldson, B. (2000a) '"Children in Need" or "Young Offenders"? Hardening Ideology, Organisational Change and New Challenges for Social Work with Children in Trouble', *Child and Family Social Work*, 5(3): 255–65.

Goldson, B. (2000b) 'Youth Justice and Criminal Evidence Bill Part I: Referrals to Youth Offender Panels', in L. Payne (ed.) *Child Impact Statements 1998/99*. London: National Children's Bureau and UNICEF.

Goldson, B. (2002) *Vulnerable Inside: Children in Secure and Penal Settings*. London: The Children's Society.

Goldson, B. (2004) 'Differential Justice? A Critical Introduction to Youth Justice Policy in UK Jurisdictions', in J. McGhee, M. Mellon and B. Whyte (eds) *Meeting Needs, Addressing Deeds: Working with Young People Who Offend*. Glasgow: NCH Scotland.

Goldson, B. (2005) Youth Policy: Bullying the New Labour Way, *Socialist Review*. http://www.socialistreview.org.uk/article.php?articlenumber=9543 (accessed 29 June 2015).

Goldson, B. (2006) 'Penal Custody: Intolerance, Irrationality and Indifference', in B. Goldson and J. Muncie (eds) *Youth Crime and Justice*. London: Sage.

Goldson, B. (2008) *Dictionary of Youth Justice*. Devon: Willan.

Goldson, B. (2009) 'Child Incarceration: Institutional Abuse, the Violent State and the Politics of Impunity', in P. Scraton and J. McCulloch (eds) *The Violence of Incarceration*. London: Routledge.

Goldson, B. and Hughes, G. (2010) 'Sociological Criminology and Youth Justice: Comparative Policy Analysis and Academic Intervention', *Criminology and Criminal Justice*, 10(2): 211–30.

Goldson, B. and Jamieson, J. (2002) 'Youth Crime, the "Parenting Deficit" and State Intervention: A Contextual Critique', *Youth Justice*, 2(2): 82–99.

Goldson, B. and Kilkelly, U. (2013) 'International Human Rights Standards and Child Imprisonment: Potentialities and Limitations', *International Journal of Children's Rights*, 21(2): 345–71.

Goldson, B. and Muncie, J. (2006) 'Rethinking Youth Justice: Comparative Analysis, International Human Rights and Research Evidence', *Youth Justice: An International Journal*, 6(2): 91–106.

Goldson, B. and Muncie, J. (eds) (2006) *Youth Crime and Justice*. London: Sage.

Goldson, B. and Muncie, J. (2012) 'Towards a Global "Child Friendly" Juvenile Justice?', *International Journal of Law, Crime and Justice*, 40(1): 47–64.

Goldthorpe, J.H. (1968–9) *The Affluent Worker in the Class Structure*, 3 Vols. Cambridge: Cambridge University Press.

Goodman, R. and Scott, S. (1997) *Child Psychiatry*. Oxford: Blackwell.

Gordon, D. and Kacir, C. (1998) 'Effectiveness of an Interactive Parent Training Program for Changing Adolescent Behavior for Court-Referred Parents', unpublished manuscript. University of Ohio, Athens.

Goring, C. (1913) *The English Convict: A Statistical Study*. London: HMSO.

Gottfredson, M.R. and Hirschi, T. (1990) *A General Theory of Crime*. Stanford, CA: Stanford University Press.

Graef, R. (2000) *Why Restorative Justice?* London: Calouste Gulbenkian Foundation.

Graham, J. (1998) 'What Works in Preventing Criminality', in P. Goldblatt and C. Lewis (eds) *Reducing Offending*, Home Office Research Study No 187. London: HMSO.

Graham, J. and Bowling, B. (1995) *Young People and Crime*, Home Office Research Study No. 145. London: HMSO.

Gray, E., Taylor, E., Roberts, C., Merrington, S., Fernandez, R. and Moore, R. (2005) *Intensive Supervision and Surveillance Programme: The Final Report*. London: Youth Justice Board.

Gray, P. (2005) 'The Politics of Risk and Young Offenders' Experiences of Social Exclusion and Restorative Justice', *British Journal of Criminology*, 45: 938–57.

Gregory, L. and Joseph, R. (2015) 'Big Society or Welfare Failure: How Does Food Insecurity Reflect Future Welfare Trends?' in L. Foster, A. Brunton, C. Deeming and T. Haux (eds) *In Defence of Welfare II*. Bristol: Policy Press.

Griffin, C. (1985) *Typical Girls?* London: Routledge.

Griffin, C. (1997) 'Representations of the Young', in J. Roache and S. Tucker (eds) *Youth in Society*. London: Sage.

Grimwood, G.G. and Strickland, P. (2013) Young Offenders: What Next? House of Commons, Home Affairs Section: Standard Note: SN/HA/5896.

Grygier, T. (1969) 'Parental Deprivation: A Study of Delinquent Children', *British Journal of Criminology*, 9: 209.

Guardian Online, The (2015) UK GDP since 1955. http://www.theguardian.com/news/datablog/2009/nov/25/gdp-uk-1948-growth-economy (accessed 3 June 2015).

Guerra, N.G., Tolan, P.H. and Hammond, W.R. (1994) 'Prevention and Treatment of Adolescent Violence', in L.D. Eron, J.H. Gentry and P. Schlegel (eds) *Reason to Hope: A Psychosocial Perspective on Violence and Youth*. Washington, DC: American Psychological Association.

Habermas, J. (1989) *The New Conservatism*. Cambridge: Polity Press.

Hagedorn, J. (1992) 'Gangs, Neighbourhoods, and Public Policy', *Social Problems*, 38(4): 529–42.

Hagell, A. (2002) *The Mental Health of Young Offenders*. London: The Mental Health Foundation.

Hagell, A. and Newburn, T. (1994) *Persistent Young Offenders*. London: Policy Studies Institute.

Haines, K. (2000) 'Referral Orders and Youth Offender Panels: Restorative Approaches and the New Youth Justice', in B. Goldson (ed.) *The New Youth Justice*. Lyme Regis: Russell House.

Haines, K. and O'Mahony, D. (2006) 'Restorative Approaches, Young People and Youth Justice', in B. Goldson and J. Muncie (eds) *Youth Crime and Justice*. London: Sage.

Hall, G.S. (1905) *Adolescence, Its Psychology and Its Relations to Physiology, Anthropology, Sociology, Sex, Crime, Religion and Education*. New York: Appleton.

Hallden, O. (1988) 'The Evolution of the Species: Pupil Perspectives and School Perspective', *International Journal of Science Education*, 10(5): 541–52.

Hallet, C. and Hazel, N. (1998) *The Evaluation of the Children's Hearings in Scotland, Volume 2: The International Context*. Edinburgh: Scottish Office.

Hammersley, R., Marsland, L. and Reid, M. (2003) *Home Office Research Study 261: Substance Use by Young Offenders: The Impact of the Normalisation of Drugs Use in the Early Years of the 21st Century*. London: Home Office Research, Development and Statistics Directorate.

Harcourt, B. (2010) 'Neoliberal Penality: A Brief Genealogy', *Theoretical Criminology*, 14: 74–92.

Hare, D.R. (1982) 'Psychopathy and Physiological Activity during Anticipation of an Aversive Stimulus in a Distraction Paradigm', *Psychophysiology*, 19: 266–80.

Harris, R. and Webb, D. (1987) *Welfare, Power and Juvenile Justice*. London: Tavistock.

Harrop, A. and Reed, H. (2015) *Inequality 2030: Britain's Choice for Living Standards and Poverty*. London: Fabian Society.

Hart, J. (1978) 'Police', in W. Cornish (ed.) *Crime and Law*. Dublin: Irish University Press.

Harvey, D. (1989) *The Condition of Postmodernity: An Enquiry into the Origins of Cultural Change*. Oxford: Blackwell.

Harvey, I. (2000) 'Youth Culture, Drugs and Criminality', in J. Pickford (ed.) *Youth Justice: Theory and Practice*. London: Cavendish.

Hawkins, J.D. and Catalano, R.F. (1992) *Communities That Care: Action for Drug Abuse Prevention*. San Francisco: Josey Bass.

Hawkins, J.D., Catalano, R.F. and Miller, J.Y. (1992) 'Risk and Protective Factors for Alcohol and Other Drug Problems in Adolescence and Early Adulthood: Implications for Substance Abuse Prevention', *Psychological Bulletin*, 112: 64–105.

Haydon, D. and Scraton, P. (2000) 'Condemn a Little More, Understand a Little Less: The Political Context and Rights Implications of the Domestic and European Rulings in the Venables-Thompson Case', *Journal of Law and Society*, 27(3): 416–48.

Hayes, M. and Williams, C. (1999) '"Offending" Behaviour and Children Under 10', *Family Law*, May: 317–20.

Healy, W. and Bronner, A.F. (1936) *New Light on Delinquency and Its Treatment*. New Haven, CT: Yale University Press.

Hebdige, D. (1976) 'The Meaning of Mod', in S. Hall and T. Jefferson (eds.) *Resistance through Rituals: Youth Sub-cultures in Post-war Britain*. London: Hutchinson.

Hebdige, D. (1979) *Subculture: The Meaning of Style*. London: Methuen.

Hendrick, H. (1986) 'Personality and Psychology: Defining Edwardian Boys', *Youth and Policy*, 18: 33–56.

Hendrick, H. (1990a) 'Constructions and Reconstructions of British Childhood: An Interpretive Study 1800 to the Present', in A. James and A. Prout (eds) *Constructing and Reconstructing Childhood*. London: Falmer Press.

Hendrick, H. (1990b) *Images of Youth: Age, Class and the Male Youth Problem 1880–1920*. Oxford: Clarendon.

Hendrick, H. (1994) *Child Welfare: England 1872–1989*. London: Routledge

Henggeler, S., Melton, G., Brondino, M., Scherer, D. and Hanley, J. (1997) 'Multisystemic Therapy with Violent and Chronic Juvenile Offenders and Their Families: The Role of Treatment Fidelity in Successful Dissemination', *Journal of Consulting and Clinical Psychology*, 65: 821–33.

Henle, M. (1985) 'Rediscovering Gestalt Psychology', in S. Koch and D.E. Leary (eds) *A Century of Psychology as a Science*. New York: McGraw-Hill.

Heriot Watt University (2015) *Lifeline Not Lifestyle: An Economic Analysis of the Impacts of Cutting Housing Benefit for Young People*. Edinburgh: Heriot Watt University.

Henriques, B. (1950) *Indiscretions of a Magistrate: Thoughts on the Work of the Juvenile Court*. London: Harrap.

Her Majesty's Inspectorate of Prisons for England and Wales (2000) *Unjust Desserts: A Thematic Review by HM Chief Inspector of Prisons for the Treatment and Conditions for Unsentenced Prisoners in England and Wales*. London: Home Office.

HM Inspectorate of Prisons and Probation (2001) *Through the Prison Gate: A Joint Thematic Review*. London: HM Prison Service.

HM Treasury (2010) *Spending Review 2010*. London: HMSO.

Herrnstein, R.J. and Murray, C. (1994) *The Bell Curve*. New York: Basic Books.

Hine, J. and Celnick, A. (2001) *A One Year Reconviction Study of Final Warnings*. Sheffield: University of Sheffield.

Hirschi, T. (1969) *Causes of Delinquency*. Berkeley, CA: University of California Press.

Hirschi, T. (1995) 'The Family', in J.Q. Wilson and J. Petersilia (eds) *Crime*. San Francisco: ICS Press.

Hirschi, T. and Hindelang, M.J. (1977) 'Intelligence and Delinquency: A Revisionist Review', *American Sociological Review*, 42: 572–87.

Hodgson, P. and Webb, D. (2005) 'Young People, Crime and School Exclusions: A Case of Some Surprises', *The Howard Journal*, 44(1): 12–28.

Hodkinson, P. (1996) 'Careership: The Individual, Choices and Markets in the Transition to Work', in J. Avis, M. Bloomer, G. Esland, D. Gleeson and P. Hodkinson (eds) *Knowledge and Nationhood*. London: Cassell.

Hoffman, M.L. and Saltzstein, H.D. (1967) 'Parent Discipline and the Child's Moral Development', *Journal of Personality and Social Psychology*, 5: 45.

Hogg, E. (2000) 'The New Approach to Parental Responsibility: Practical Application', *Justice of the Peace*, 164: 735–8.

Hogg, J.G. (1999) 'Crime and Disorder Act: First Crack in the Threshold', *Family Law*, August: 574–7.

Hoghughi, M.S. and Forrest, A.R. (1970) 'Eysenck's Theory of Criminality: An Examination with Approved Schoolboys', *British Journal of Criminology*, 10: 240.

Holdaway, S., Davidson, N., Dignan, J., Hammersley, R., Hine, J. and Marsh, P. (2001) *New Strategies to Address Youth Offending: The National Evaluation of the Youth Justice Board's Final Warning Projects*. London: Youth Justice Board.

Hollin, C.R. (1990a) 'Social Skills Training with Delinquents: A Look at the Evidence and Some Recommendations for Practice', *British Journal of Social Work*, 20: 483–93.

Hollin, C.R. (1990b) *Cognitive-Behavioural Interventions with Young Offenders*. Elmsford, NY: Pergamon Press.

Hollin, C.R. (1995) 'The Meaning and Implications of Programme Integrity', in J. McGuire (ed.) *What Works: Reducing Re-offending: Guidelines from Research and Practice*. Chichester: John Wiley.

Home Office (1980) *Young Offenders*, Cmnd 8045. London: HMSO.

Home Office (1997) *No More Excuses: A New Approach to Tackling Youth Crime in England and Wales*. London: HMSO.

Home Office (1998a) *The Crime and Disorder Act 1998*. London: Home Office.

Home Office (1998b) *Criminal Statistics*. London: Home Office

Home Office (2000) *British Crime Survey*. London: HMSO.

Home Office (2001) 'Criminal Careers of Those Born Between 1953 and 1978', Home Office Statistical Bulletin, 4/2001.

Home Office (2002) *British Crime Survey*. London: HMSO.

Home Office (2004) *Finding and Measuring Anti-Social Behaviour*. London: Home Office.

Home Office (2005a) *Criminal Statistics*. London: Stationery Office.

Home Office (2005b) 'Children, Risk and Crime: The On Track Youth Lifestyles Surveys', Home Office Research Study 278. London: Home Office.

Home Office (2012) *Putting Victims First: More Effective Responses to Anti-Social Behaviour*. London: Home Office.

Honey, P. and Mumford, A. (1986) *The Manual of Learning Styles*. Maidenhead: Peter Honey.

Hood, R. (1965) *Borstal Re-Assessed*. London: Heinemann.

Hooton, E.A. (1939) *The American Criminal: An Anthropological Study*. Cambridge, MA: Harvard University Press.

Hope, T. (2001) 'Community Crime Prevention in Britain: A Strategic Overview', *Criminal Justice*, 1: 421–39.

Hopkins Burke, R.D. (ed.) (1998a) *Zero Tolerance Policing*. Leicester: Perpetuity Press.

Hopkins Burke, R.D. (1998b) 'A Contextualisation of Zero Tolerance Policing Strategies' in R.D. Hopkins Burke (ed.) *Zero Tolerance Policing*. Leicester: Perpetuity Press.

Hopkins Burke, R.D. (1998c) 'Begging, Vagrancy and Disorder', in R.D. Hopkins Burke (ed.) *Zero Tolerance Policing*. Leicester: Perpetuity Press.

Hopkins Burke, R.D. (1999a) 'Youth Justice and the Fragmentation of Modernity', Scarman Centre for the Study of Public Order Occasional Paper Series. Leicester: University of Leicester.

Hopkins Burke, R.D. (1999b) 'The Socio-Political Context of Zero Tolerance Policing Strategies', *Policing: An International Journal of Police Strategies & Management*, 21(4): 666–82.

Hopkins Burke, R.D. (2000) 'The Regulation of Begging and Vagrancy: A Critical Discussion', *Crime Prevention and Community Safety: An International Journal*, 2(2): 43–52.

Hopkins Burke, R.D. (2001) *An Introduction to Criminological Theory*. Cullompton: Willan.

Hopkins Burke, R.D. (2002) 'Zero Tolerance Policing: New Authoritarianism or New Liberalism?' *The Nottingham Law Journal*, 2(1): 20–35.

Hopkins Burke, R.D. (ed.) (2004a) *'Hard Cop/Soft Cop': Dilemmas and Debates in Contemporary Policing*. Cullompton: Willan.

Hopkins Burke, R.D. (2004b) 'Policing Contemporary Society', in R.D. Hopkins Burke, *'Hard Cop/Soft Cop': Dilemmas and Debates in Contemporary Policing*. Cullompton: Willan.

Hopkins Burke, R.D. (2004c) 'Policing Contemporary Society Revisited' in R.D. Hopkins Burke, *'Hard Cop/Soft Cop': Dilemmas and Debates in Contemporary Policing*. Cullompton: Willan.

Hopkins Burke, R.D. (2005) *An Introduction to Criminological Theory*, 2nd edn. Cullompton: Willan.

Hopkins Burke, R.D. (2007) 'Moral Ambiguity, the Schizophrenia of Crime and Community Justice', *British Journal of Community Justice*, 5(1): 43–64.

Hopkins Burke, R.D. (2009) *An Introduction to Criminological Theory*, 3rd edn. Cullompton: Willan.

Hopkins Burke, R.D. (2012) *Criminal Justice Theory: An Introduction*. London: Routledge.

Hopkins Burke, R.D. (2013a) 'Theorising the Criminal Justice System: Four Models of Criminal Justice Development', *Criminal Justice Review*, 38(3): 277–90.

Hopkins Burke, R.D. (2013b) *Criminal Justice Theory: An Introduction*. London: Routledge.

Hopkins Burke, R.D. (2014a) *An Introduction to Criminological Theory*, 4th edn. Oxford: Routledge.

Hopkins Burke, R.D. (2014b) 'Theorising Radical Moral Communitarianism', *British Journal of Community Justice*, 12(3): 5–18.

Hopkins Burke, R.D. (2015a) 'Theorising the Radical Moral Communitarian Agenda', *British Journal of Community Justice*, 13(1): 7–24.

Hopkins Burke, R.D. (2015b) 'Theorizing Moral Communitarianism in an Age of Austerity', *The International Journal of Interdisciplinary Civic and Political Studies*, 10(4): 1–12.

Hopkins Burke, R.D. and Hodgson, P. (2015) 'Anti-social Behaviour, Community and Radical Moral Communitarianism', *Cogent Social Sciences*, 1(1): 1033369 http://dx.doi.org/10.1080/23311886.2015.1033369. Published online: 15 May 2015.

Hopkins Burke, R.D. and Hopkins Burke, K.J. (1995) 'The Differential Needs of Young People in Local Authority Care', paper given to conference organised by Susie Lamplaugh Trust on Child Victims, British Telcom Centre, London (January).

Hopkins Burke, R.D. and Morrill, R. (2002) 'Anti-social Behaviour Orders: An Infringement of the Human Rights Act 1998?' *The Nottingham Law Journal*, 2(2): 1–16.

Hopkins Burke, R.D. and Morrill, R. (2004) 'Human Rights v. Community Rights: The Case of the Anti-Social Behaviour Order', in R.D. Hopkins Burke (ed.) *'Hard Cop/Soft Cop': Dilemmas and Debates in Contemporary Policing*. Cullompton: Willan.

Hopkins Burke, R. and Orrock, E. (2003) *Youth Crime: A Base Audit of Youth Work Interventions in England That Impact on Young People as Perpetrators or as Victims of Crime*. Leicester: National Youth Association.

Hopkins Burke, R.D. and Pollock, E. (2004) 'A Tale of Two Anomies: Some Observations on the Contribution of (Sociological) Criminological Theory to Explaining Hate Crime Motivation', *Internet Journal of Criminology*. http://www.flashmousepublishing.com/Hopkins%20Burke%20&%20Pollock%20-%20A%20Tale%20of%20Two%20Anomies.pdf: 18.

Hopkins Burke, R.D. and Sunley, R. (1996) '"Hanging Out" in the 1990s: Young People and the Postmodern Condition', Occasional Paper II, Scarman Centre of the Study of Public Order, University of Leicester.

Hopkins Burke, R.D. and Sunley, R. (1998) 'Youth Subcultures in Contemporary Britain', in K. Hazelhurst and C. Hazelhurst (eds) *Gangs and Youth Subcultures: International Explorations*. New Brunswick, NJ: Transaction Publishers.

Houdt, J.F. van and Schinkel, W. (2013) 'A Genealogy of Neoliberal Communitarianism', *Theoretical Criminology*, 17: 493–515.

Howard League for Penal Reform, The (2005) Abolish ASBOs for Children. www.howard league.org/index.php?id=222&0

Howard League (2012) *Mentors Won't Repair Damage Caused by Short Jail Sentences*. London: Howard League for Penal Reform.

Hoyles, M. and Evans, P. (1989) *The Politics of Childhood*. London: Journeyman Press.

Hucklesby, A. (2001) 'Police Bail and the Use of Conditions', *Criminal Justice*, 1(4): 441.

Hucklesby, A. and Marshall, E. (2000) 'Tackling Offending on Bail', *Howard Journal of Criminology*, 29(2): 150–70.

Hucklesby, A. and Wilkinson, C. (2001) 'Drug Misuse in Prisons: Some Comments on the Prison Service Drug Strategy', *Howard Journal of Criminology*, 40(3): 347–63.

Hughes, G. (1998) *Understanding Crime Prevention: Social Control, Risk and Late Modernity*. Buckingham: Open University Press.

Humphries, S. (1981) *Hooligans or Rebels?* Oxford: Blackwell.

Hutchings, B. and Mednick, S.A. (1977) 'Criminality in Adoptees and Their Adoptive and Biological Parents: A Pilot Study', in S.A. Mednick and K.O. Christiansen (eds) *Biosocial Bases of Criminal Behaviour*. New York: Gardner.

Idriss, M.M. (2001) 'The Power to Impose Curfew Orders', *Justice of the Peace*, 165: 58–62.

Ignatieff, M. (1978) *A Just Measure of Pain: The Penitentiary in the Industrial Revolution 1750–1850*. London and Basingstoke: Macmillan.

Institute of Alcohol Studies (2005a) *Adolescents and Alcohol*. St Ives, Cambridge: IAS.

Institute of Alcohol Studies (2005b) *Alcohol and Crime*. St Ives, Cambridge: IAS.

International Centre for Prison Studies (2013) World Prison Brief. http://www.prisonstudies. org/info/worldbrief/ (accessed 3 August 2015).

Ipsos MORI (2006) *Five Year Report: An Analysis of Youth Survey Data*. London: Ipsos MORI/Youth Justice Board.

Jackson, S.E. (1999) 'Family Group Conferences and Youth Justice: The New Panacea?', in B. Goldson (ed.) *Youth Justice: Contemporary Policy and Practice*. Aldershot: Ashgate.

Jefferis, B.J.M.H., Power, C. and Manor, O. (2005) 'Adolescent Drinking Level and Adult Binge Drinking in a National Cohort', *Addiction*, 100(4): 543–9.

Jeffery, C.R. (1979) *Biology and Crime*. Beverly Hills, CA: Sage.

Jeffs, T. (1979) *Young People and the Youth Service*. London: Routledge & Kegan Paul.

Jeffs, T. and Smith, M. (eds) (1988) *Welfare and Youth Work Practice*. London: Macmillan.

Jenks, C. (1996) *Childhood*. London: Routledge.

Jessor, R. and Jessor, S. (1997) *Problem Behaviour and Psychosocial Development: A Longitudinal Study of Youth*. New York: Academic Press.

Johnstone, L., (2013) 'Mental Disorder and Violence', in C. Logan and L. Johnstone (eds) *Managing Clinical Risk: A Guide to Effective Practice*. London: Wiley.

Jones, D.W. (2001) '"Misjudges Youth" a Critique of the Audit Commission's Reports on Youth Justice', *British Journal of Criminology*, 41(2): 362–80.

Jones, J. and Newburn, T. (2002) 'Policy Convergence and Crime Control in the USA and the UK', *Criminal Justice*, 2(2): 173–203.

Jones, S. (1993) *The Language of the Genes*. London: Harper Collins.

Jones, S. (2001) *Criminology*, 2nd edn. London: Butterworths.

Jordan, B. (1998) 'New Labour, New Community?' *Imprints*, 3(2): 113–31.

Justice (2000) *Restoring Youth Justice: New Directions in Domestic and International Law and Practice*. London: Justice.

Katz, J. (1988) *Seductions of Crime: Moral and Sensual Attractions in Doing Evil*. New York: Basic Books.

Kavanagh, D. (1987) *Thatcherism and British Politics: The End of Consensus?* Oxford: Oxford University Press.

Kelly, P. (2001) 'The Post Welfare State and the Government of Youth at Risk', *Social Justice Special Issue: Aftermath of Welfare Reform*, 28(4): 96–113.

Kemshall, H. (2002) *Risk, Social Policy and Welfare*. Buckingham: Open University Press.

Kemshall, H. (2008) 'Risks, Rights and Justice: Understanding and Responding to Youth Risk', *Youth Justice*, 8(1): 21–37.

Kemshall, H., Marsland, L., Boeck, T. and Dunkerton, L. (2006) 'Young People, Pathways and Crime: Beyond Risk Factors', *The Australian and New Zealand Journal of Criminology*, 39: 354–70.

Kendler, H.H. (1985) 'Behaviourism and Psychology: An Uneasy Alliance', in S. Koch and D.E. Leary (eds) *A Century of Psychology as Science*. New York: McGraw-Hill.

Keverne, E.B., Meller, R.E. and Eberhart, J.A. (1982) 'Social Influences on Behaviour and Neuroendocrine Responsiveness in Talapoin Monkeys', *Scandinavian Journal of Psychology*, 1: 37–54.

Kilkelly, U. (2008) 'Youth Justice and Children's Rights: Measuring Compliance with International Standards', *Youth Justice: An International Journal*, 8(3): 187–92.

Klinefelter, H.F., Reifenstein, E.C. and Albright, F. (1942) 'Syndrome Characterized by Gynecomastia, Aspermatogenesis without Aleydigism and Increased Excretion of Follicle-Stimulating Hormone', *Journal of Clinical Endocrinology*, 2: 615–27.

Kolvin, I., Miller, F.J.W., Scott, D.M., Gatzanis, S.R.M. and Fleeting, M. (1990) *Continuities of Deprivation?* Aldershot: Avebury.

Kreuz, L.E. and Rose, R.M. (1972) 'Assessment of Aggressive Behaviour and Plasma Testosterone in a Young Criminal Population', *Psychosomatic Medicine*, 34: 321–33.

Krisberg, B. (1974) 'Gang Youth and Hustling: The Psychology of Survival', *Issues in Criminology*, 9 (Spring 1): 115–31.

Kulik, J.A. and Kulik, C.-L.C. (1989) 'Meta-analysis in Education', *International Journal of Educational Research*, 13: 221–340.

Kumpfer, K. and Alvarado, R. (1998) 'Effective Family Strengthening Interventions', Juvenile Justice Bulletin, November, Office of Juvenile Justice Delinquency Prevention, Office of Justice Programmes, US Department of Justice.

Kumpfer, K., Molgaard, V. and Spoth, R. (1996) 'The Strengthening Families Program: The Prevention of Delinquency and Drug Use', in R.D.V. Peters and R.J. McMahon (eds) *Preventing Childhood Disorders, Substance Abuse and Delinquency*. Thousand Oaks, CA: Sage.

Labour Party (1996) *New Labour, New Life for Britain*. London: The Labour Party.

Labour Party (2006) *Labour: The Future for Britain*. London: The Labour Party. http://www.labour.org.uk/home.

Lacey, N. (2013) 'Punishment, (Neo)Liberalism and Social Democracy', in J. Simon and R. Sparks (eds) *The Sage Handbook of Punishment and Society*. London: Sage.

Lange, J. (1930) *Crime as Destiny*. London: Allen and Unwin.

Lasch, C. (1977) *Haven in a Heartless World: The Family Besieged*. New York: Basic Books.

Lea, J. (1999) 'Social Crime Revisited', *Theoretical Criminology*, 3(5): 169–82.

Lea, J. and Young, J. (1984) *What Is to Be Done about Law and Order?* London: Penguin.

Lee, D., Marsden, D., Rickman, P. and Duncombe, J. (1990) *Scheming for Youth: A Study of YTS in the Enterprise Culture*. Milton Keynes: Open University Press.

Lemert, E. (1951) *Social Pathology: A Systematic Approach to the Theory of Sociopathic Behavior*. New York: McGraw-Hill.

Lerman, P. (1984) 'Policing Juveniles in London, Shifts in Guiding Discretion, 1893–1968', *British Journal of Criminology*, 24: 168–84; 175–6.

Lesser, M. (1980) *Nutrition and Vitamin Therapy*. New York: Bantam.

Levitas, R. (1996) 'The Concept of Social Exclusion and the New Durkheimian Hegemony', *Critical Social Policy*, 16(1): 5–20.

Lewis, J. (1995) *The Voluntary Sector, the State and Social Work in Britain: The Charity Organisation Society/Family Welfare Association Since 1869*. Aldershot: Edward Elgar.

Liazos, A. (1972) 'The Poverty of the Sociology of Deviance: Nuts, Sluts and Perverts', *Social Problems*, 20: 103–20.

Liebling, A. (1992) *Suicides in Prison*. Routledge: London.

Lipsey, M.W. (1992) 'Juvenile Delinquency Treatment: A Meta-analytic Inquiry into the Viability of Effects', in T. Cook, H. Cooper, D.S. Cordray, H. Hartmann, L.V. Hedges, R.J. Light, T.A. Louis and F. Mosteller (eds), *Meta-analysis for Explanation*. New York: Sage.

Lipsey, M. (1995) 'What Do We Learn from 400 Research Studies on the Effectiveness of Treatment with Juvenile Delinquents?', in J. McGuire (ed.) *What Works: Reducing Re-offending – Guidelines from Research*. London: John Wiley.

Lipsey, M.W. (1999) 'Can Rehabilitative Programs Reduce the Recidivism of Juvenile Offenders? An Inquiry into the Effectiveness of Practical Programs', *Virginia Journal of Social Policy and the Law*, 6: 611–41.

Lipsey, M.W. and Wilson, D.B. (1998) 'Effective Intervention for Serious Juvenile Offenders: A Synthesis of Research', in R. Loeber and D.P. Farrington (eds) *Serious and Violent Offenders: Risk Factors and Successful Interventions*. Thousand Oaks, CA: Sage

Lister, R. (2011) 'The Age of Responsibility: Social Policy and Citizenship in the Early 21st Century', in C. Holden, M. Kilkey and G. Ramia (eds) *Analysis and Debate in Social Policy*. Bristol: Policy Press.

Literacy Working Group (1999) *A Fresh Start: Improving Literacy and Numeracy*. London: The Literacy Working Group.

Little, A. (1963) 'Professor Eysenck's Theory of Crime: An Empirical Test on Adolescent Offenders', *British Journal of Criminology*, 4: 152.

Loeber, R. and Farrington, D. (1998) *Serious and Violent Juvenile Offenders: Risk Factors and Successful Interventions*. Thousand Oaks, CA: Sage.

Loeber, R. and Stouthamer-Loeber, M. (1986) 'Family Factors as Correlates and Predictors of Antisocial Conduct Problems and Delinquency', in N. Morris and M. Tonry (eds) *Crime and Justice*, Vol. 7. Chicago: University of Chicago Press.

Logan, A. (2005) 'A Suitable Person for Suitable Cases': The Gendering of Juvenile Courts in England c.1910–39', *20th Century British History*, 16: 129–45.

Lombroso, C. (1876) *L'uomo delinquente (The Criminal Man)*. Milan: Hoepli.

Long, M. and Hopkins Burke, R.D. (2015) *Vandalism and Anti-Social Behaviour*. Basingstoke: Palgrave Macmillan.

Lyon, J. (2014) 'Putting Children in Custody Punishes Disadvantage', Prison Reform Trust. http://www.prisonreformtrust.org.uk/PressPolicy/Comment/Puttingchildrenin custodypunishesdisadvantage (accessed 2 July 2015).

Lyotard, J.D.F. (1984) *The Postmodern Condition: A Report on Knowledge*. Manchester: Manchester University Press.

McCold, P. and Wachtel, T. (2000) 'Restorative Justice Theory Validation', paper presented at the Fourth International Conference on Restorative Justice for Juveniles, Tübingen, Germany, 1–4 October.

McCord, J. (1982) 'A Longitudinal Review of the Relationship between Paternal Absence and Crime', in J. Gunn and D.P. Farrington (eds) *Abnormal Offenders, Delinquency, and the Criminal Justice System*. Chichester: Wiley.

McCord, W., McCord, J. and Zola, I.K. (1959) *Origins of Crime: A New Evaluation of the Cambridge-Somerville Youth Study*. New York: Columbia University Press.

MacDonald, G. (1998) 'Promoting Evidence-based Practice in Child Protection', *Clinical Child Psychology and Psychiatry*, 3(1): 123–36.

McEwan, A.W. (1983) 'Eysenck's Theory of Criminality and the Personality Types and Offences of Young Delinquents', *Personality and Individual Differences*, 4: 201–4.

McGrew, A. and Held, D. (eds) (2002) *Governing Global Transformations*. Cambridge: Polity Press.

McGuire, J. (2000) *Cognitive-Behavioural Approaches: An Introduction to Theory and Research*. London: Home Office.

McGurk, B.J. and McDougall, C. (1981) 'A New Approach to Eysenck's Theory of Criminality', *Personality and Individual Differences*, 13: 338–40.

McLaughlin, E. (2013) 'Informal Justice', in E. McLaughlin and J. Muncie (eds) *The Sage Dictionary of Criminology*, 3rd edn. London: Sage.

McLauglin, E. and Muncie, J. (1994) 'Managing the Criminal Justice System', in J. Clarke et al. (eds) *Managing Social Policy*. London: Sage.

McNeill, F. (2009) 'Young People, Serious Offending and Managing Risk: A Scottish Perspective', in K. Baker and A. Sutherland (eds) *Multi-Agency Public Protection Arrangements and Youth Justice*. Bristol: Policy Press.

Make Justice Work (2011) *Community or Custody? A National Enquiry*. London: Make Justice Work.

Malthus, T.R. (1959) *Population*. Ann Arbor, MI: Michigan University Press.

Mannheim, H. (1948) *Juvenile Delinquency in an English Middletown*. London: Kegan Paul, Turner, Trubner and Co. Ltd.

Manning, M. (2005) 'The New Public Management and Its Legacy', Administrative and Civil Service Reform. http://www1. worldbank.org/public-sector/civilservice/debate1.htm.

Marshall, G., Roberts, S. and Burgoyne, C. (1996) 'Social Class and the Underclass in Britain and the USA', *British Journal of Sociology*, 47(10): 22–44.

Marshall, T.F. (1996) 'The Evolution of Restorative Justice in Britain', *European Journal on Criminal Policy and Research*, 4: 21–43.

Marshall, T.F. (1997) 'Seeking the Whole Justice', in S. Hayman (ed.) *Repairing the Damage: Restorative Justice in Action*. London: ISTD.

Marshall, T.F. (1998) *Standards for Restorative Justice*. London: Restorative Justice Consortium.

Marshall, T.F. (1999) 'Restorative Justice: An Overview', Occasional Paper. London: Home Office.

Martin, G. and Pear, J. (1992) *Behaviour Modification: What It Is and How to Do It*, 4th edn. Englewood Cliffs, NJ: Prentice-Hall.

Martinson, R. (1974) 'What Works? – Questions and Answers about Prison Reform', *The Public Interest*, 35: 22–54.

Matthews, R. (1988) *Informal Justice*. London: Sage.

Matthews, R. and Young, J. (eds) (1986) *Confronting Crime*. London: Sage.

Matthews, R. and Young, J. (eds) (1992) *Issues in Realist Criminology*. London: Sage.

Matza, D. (1964) *Delinquency and Drift*. New York: Wiley.

May, M. (1973) 'Innocence and Experience: The Evolution of the Concept of Juvenile Delinquency in the Mid-nineteenth Century', in J. Muncie, G. Hughes and E. McLaughlin (eds) (2002) *Youth Justice: Critical Readings*. London: Sage.

Mays, J.B. (1954) *Growing Up in the City: A Study of Juvenile Delinquency in an Urban Neighbourhood*. Liverpool: Liverpool University Press.

Mazur, A. (1998) *A Hazardous Inquiry: The Rashemon Effect at Love Canal*. Cambridge, MA: Harvard University Press.

Mears, D. and Kelly, W. (1998) 'Assessment and Intake Processes in Juvenile Justice Processing: Emerging Policy Considerations', *Crime and Delinquency*, 45(4): 508–29.

Mednick, S.A. (1977) 'A Biosocial Theory of the Learning of Law-Abiding Behavior', in S.A. Mednick and K.O Christiansen (eds) *Biosocial Bases of Criminal Behavior*. New York: Gardner.

Mednick, S.A., Gabrielli, T., William, F. and Hutchings, B. (1984) 'Genetic Influences on Criminal Convictions: Evidence from an Adoption Cohort', *Science*, 224: 891–4.

Mednick, S.A., Pollock, V., Volavka, J. and Gabrielli, W.F. (1982) 'Biology and Violence', in M.E. Wolfgang and N.A. Weiner (eds) *Criminal Violence*. Beverly Hills, CA: Sage.

Mednick, S.A., Moffit, T.E. and Stack, S. (eds) (1987) *The Causes of Crime: New Biological Approaches*. Cambridge: Cambridge University Press.

Melossi, D. and Pavarini, M. (1981) *The Prison and the Factory: Origins of the Penitentiary System* (trans. G. Cousin). London and Basingstoke: Macmillan.

Menard, S. and Morse, B. (1984) 'A Structuralist Critique of the IQ – Delinquency Hypothesis: Theory and Evidence', *American Journal of Sociology*, 89: 1347–78.

Merry, S.E. and Milner, N. (1993) *The Possibility of Popular Justice: A Case Study of Community Mediation in the United States*. New Brunswick, NJ: Rutgers University Press.

Merton, R. (1938) 'Social Structure and Anomie', *American Sociological Review*, 3(5): 321–37.

Messmer, H. and Otto, H. (1992) *Restorative Justice on Trial: Pitfalls and Potentials of Victim Offender Mediation*. Norwell, MA: Kluwer.

Miller, J. (1996) *Search and Destroy: African-American Males in the Criminal Justice System*. Cambridge: Cambridge University Press.

Miller, W.B. (1958) 'Lower Class Culture as a Generalising Milieu of Gang Delinquency', *Journal of Social Issues*, 14: 5–19.

Miller, W.R. (1990) 'When the United States Has Failed to Solve Its Youth Gang Problem', in C.R. Huff (ed.) *Gangs in America*. Newbury Park, CA: Sage.

Miller, W.R. (1999) *Cops and Bobbies*, 2nd edn. Columbus, OH: Ohio State University Press.

Ministry of Justice (2013) *Compendium of Re-offending Statistics and Analysis*. London: Ministry of Justice.

Ministry of Justice (2014) 'Proven Re-offending, Statistics Quarterly Bulletin, April 2011 to March 2012, England and Wales', Ministry of Justice Statistics Bulletin, London.

Ministry of Justice (2015) *Youth Custody Data Report: December*. London: Ministry of Justice.

Mizen, P. (1995) *The State, Young People and Youth Training*. London: Mansell.

Monaghan, G. (2000) 'The Courts and the New Youth Justice', in B. Goldson (ed.) *The New Youth Justice*. Lyme Regis: Russell House.

Monahan, T.P. (1957) 'Family Status and the Delinquent Child: A Reappraisal and Some New Findings', *New Forces*, 35: 250–66.

Moore, J.W. (1991) *Going Down to the Barrio*. Philadelphia, PA: Temple University Press.

Moore, S. and Smith, R. (2001) *The Pre-Trial Guide: Working with Young People from Arrest to Trial*. London: The Children's Society.

Morash, M. and Rucker, L. (1989) 'An Exploratory Study of the Connection of Mother's Age at Childbearing to Her Children's Delinquency in Four Data Sets', *Crime and Delinquency*, 35: 45–58.

Morgan, P. (1975) *Child Care: Sense and Fable*. London: Temple Smith.

Morgan, P. (1978) *Delinquent Fantasies*. London: Temple Smith.

Morgan, P.M. and Henderson, P.F. (1998) *Remand Decisions and Offending on Bail: Evaluation of the Bail Process Project*. London: Home Office.

Morgan, R. (2010) 'Axing the Youth Justice Board Could Be a Bold Step', *The Guardian*, 26 October.

MORI (2003) *Youth Survey 2003*. London: Youth Justice Board.

Morris, A. and Gelsthorpe, L. (2000) 'Something Old, Something Borrowed, Something Blue but Something New? A Comment on the Prospects for Restorative Justice under the Crime and Disorder Act 1998', *Criminal Law Review*, 18–30.

Morris, A. and Giller, H. (1987) *Understanding Juvenile Justice*. London: Croom Helm.

Morris, A., Giller, H., Szwed, E. and Geach, H. (1980) *Justice for Children*. London: Heinemann.

Morris, T.P. (1957) *The Criminal Area: A Study in Social Ecology*. London: Routledge & Kegan Paul.

Morrison, W. (1995) *Theoretical Criminology: From Modernity to Post-modernity*. London: Cavendish.

Morse, S.M. (1997a) 'Immaturity and Irresponsibility', *Journal of Criminal Law and Criminology*, 88: 68–136.

Morse, S.M. (1997b) 'Delinquency and Desert', *The ANNALS of the American Academy of Political and Social Science*, 564(1): 56–80.

Muller, P. (1973) 'Childhood's Changing Status over the Centuries', in L.M. Brockman, J.H. Whiteley, and J.P. Zubak (eds) *Child Development: Selected Readings*. Toronto: McClelland and Stewart.

Muncie, J. (1984) *The Trouble with Kids Today: Youth and Crime in Postwar Britain*. London: Hutchinson.

Muncie, J. (1990) '"Failure Never Matters": Detention Centres and the Politics of Deterrence', *Critical Social Policy*, 28: 53–66.

Muncie, J. (1999a) *Youth and Crime*. London: Sage.

Muncie, J. (1999b) 'Auditing Youth Justice', *Prison Service Journal*, 126: 55–9.

Muncie, J. (1999c) 'Institutionalized Intolerance: Youth Justice and the 1998 Crime and Disorder Act', *Critical Social Policy*, 19(2): 147–75.

Muncie, J. (2004) *Youth and Crime*, 2nd edn. London: Sage.

Muncie, J. (2005) 'The Globalisation of Crime Control: The Case of Youth and Juvenile Justice', *Theoretical Criminology*, 9(1): 35–64.

Muncie, J. (2006) 'Governing Young People: Coherence and Contradiction in Contemporary Youth Justice', *Critical Social Policy*, 26: 770–93.

Muncie, J. (2008) 'The Punitive Turn in Juvenile Justice: Cultures of Control and Rights Compliance in Western Europe and the USA', *Youth Justice: An International Journal*, 8(2): 107–121.

Muncie, J. (2009) *Youth and Crime*, 3rd edn. London: Sage.

Muncie, J. (2011a) 'Illusions of Difference: Comparative Youth Justice in the Devolved UK', *British Journal of Criminology*, 51(1): 40–57.

Muncie, J. (2011b) 'On Globalisation and Exceptionalism', in D. Nelken (ed.) *Comparative Criminal Justice and Globalisation*. Farnham: Ashgate.

Muncie, J. (2013) 'International Juvenile (In)justice: Penal Severity and Rights Compliance', *International Journal for Crime, Justice and Social Democracy*, 2(2): 43–62.

Muncie, J. (2015) *Youth and Crime*, 4th edn. London: Sage.

Muncie, J. and Goldson, B. (2013) 'Youth Justice: In a Child's Best Interests?', in J. Simon and R. Sparks (eds) *The Sage Handbook of Punishment and Society*. London: Sage.

Munro, E. (2011) *The Munro Review of Child Protection Final Report: A Child Centred System*. London: Department for Education.

Murray, C. (1990) *The Emerging British Underclass*. London: Institute of Economic Affairs: Health and Welfare Unit.

Murray, C. (1994) *Underclass: The Crisis Deepens*. London: Institute of Economic Affairs.

NACRO (1998) *Wasted Lives: Counting the Cost of Juvenile Offending*. London: Nacro/ Prince's Trust.

NACRO (2000) *Young People, Drug Use, and Offending*. London: Nacro.

NACRO (2001a) *Directory of Offending Behaviour Programmes*. London: Youth Justice Board.

NACRO (2001b) *Some Facts about Young People Who Offend*. London: NACRO.

Naess, S. (1959) 'Mother–Child Separation and Delinquency', *British Journal of Delinquency*, 10: 22.

Naess, S. (1962) 'Mother-Child Separation and Delinquency: Further Evidence', *British Journal of Criminology*, 2: 361.

NAPO (National Association of Probation Officers) (1998) *Briefing on the Crime and Disorder Bill*. London: NAPO.

National Audit Office (2004) *Youth Offending: The Delivery of Community and Custodial Sentences*. London: NAO.

National Conference of State Legislatures (2012) Trends in Juvenile Justice State Legislation 2001–2011. http://www.ncsl.org/issues-research/justice/juvenile-justice-trends-report.aspx (accessed 5 August 2015).

Nava, M. (1984) 'Youth Service Provision, Social Order and the Question of Girls', in A. McRobbie and M. Nava (eds), *Gender and Generation*. London: Macmillan.

Nelken, D. (1994) 'Reflexive Criminology?' in D. Nelken (ed.) *The Futures of Criminology*. London: Sage.

Nelken, D. (ed.) (2011) *Comparative Criminal Justice and Globalisation*. Farnham: Ashgate.

Nelken, D. and Andrews, L. (1999) 'DNA Identification and Surveillance Creep', *Sociology of Health and Illness*, 21(5): 689–706.

Neubacher, F., Walker, M., Valkova, H. and Krajewski, K. (1999) 'Juvenile Delinquency in Central European Cities: A Comparison of Registration and Processing Structures in the 1990s', *European Journal on Criminal Policy and Research*, 7: 533–58.

Newburn, T. (1995) *Crime and Criminal Justice Policy*. London: Longman.

Newburn, T. (1996) 'Back to the Future? Youth Crime, Youth Justice and the Rediscovery of "Authoritarian Populism"', in J. Pilcher and S. Wagg (eds) *Thatcher's Children? Politics, Childhood and Society in the 1980s and 1990s*. London: Routledge.

Newburn, T. (1998) 'Tackling Youth Crime and Reforming Youth Justice: The Origins and Nature of "New Labour" Policy', *Policy Studies*, 19(3): 199–213.

Newburn, T. (2002a) 'Atlantic Crossings: Policy Transfer and Crime Control in the USA and Britain', *Punishment and Society*, 4(2): 165–98.

Newburn, T. (2002b) 'Young People, Crime, and Youth Justice', in M. Maguire, R. Morgan and R. Reiner (eds) *The Oxford Handbook of Youth Justice*. Oxford: Oxford University Press.

Newburn, T. (2010) 'Diffusion, Differentiation and Resistance in Comparative Penality', *Criminology and Criminal Justice*, 10(4): 341–52.

Newburn, T. and Jones, T. (2007) 'Symbolising Crime Control: Reflections on Zero Tolerance', *Theoretical Criminology*, 11(2): 221–43.

Nicholas, S., Povey, D., Walker, A. and Kershaw, C. (2005) 'Crime in England and Wales 2004/2005', Home Office Statistical Bulletin. London: Home Office.

Norman, J. (2010) *The Big Society: The Anatomy of the New Politics.* Buckingham: University of Buckingham.

Norris, C. and Armstrong, G. (1999) *The Maximum Surveillance Society: The Rise of CCTV.* Oxford: Berg.

Northumbria Police (1992) *Bail and Multiple Offending.* Newcastle: Northumbria Police.

Nugent, W., Umbreit, M., Winnamaki, L. and Paddock, J. (1999) 'Participation in Victim Offender Mediation Reduces Recidivism', *Connections* (VOM Association), 3, Summer.

Nutre, S.M., Davies, H.T.O. and Tille, N. (2000) 'Editorial: Getting Research into Practice', *Public Money and Management*, 20(4): 3–6.

Nye, F.I. (1958) *Family Relationships and Delinquent Behaviour.* New York: Wiley.

O'Donnell, I. and O'Sullivan, E. (2003) 'The Politics of Intolerance – Irish Style', *British Journal of Criminology*, 43(1): 41–62.

Office for National Statistics (2001) *Psychiatric Morbidity among Adults Living in Private Households, 2000.* London: ONS.

Olwens, D. (1987) 'Testosterone and Adrenaline: Aggressive and Antisocial Behaviour in Normal Adolescent Males', in S.A. Mednick, T.E. Moffit and S. Stack (eds) *The Causes of Crime: New Biological Approaches.* Cambridge: Cambridge University Press.

O'Malley, P. (1992) 'Risk, Power and Crime Prevention', *Economy and Society*, 21(3): 252–75.

O'Malley, P. (2008) 'Experiments in Risk and Criminal Justice', *Theoretical Criminology*, 12: 451–69.

ONS (2014) Chapter 3: Experiences of Crime among 10- to 15-Year-Olds. http://www.ons. gov.uk/ons/dcp171776_365203.pdf.

Osborne, D. and Gaebler, T. (1993) *Reinventing Government: How the Entrepreneurial Spirit Is Transforming the Public Sector.* New York: Penguin.

Padfield, N. (1998) 'No More Excuses', *New Law Journal*, April 17: 561–3.

Parenti, C. (2000) *Lockdown America.* London: Verso.

Parker, H.J. (1974) *View from the Boys.* Newton Abbot: David and Charles.

Parker, H.J. (1996) *Methadone Maintenance and Crime Reduction on Merseyside*, Crime Detection and Prevention Series. London: Home Office, Police Research Group.

Parsons, C. and Howlett, K. (2002) *A Review of the Relationship between Non-attendance at School and Youth Offending.* London: Youth Justice Board.

Parsons, T. (1951) *The Social System.* London: Routledge & Kegan Paul.

Parry Jones, W.L. (1989) 'The History of Child and Adolescent Psychiatry: Its Present Day Relevance,' *Journal of Child Psychology and Psychiatry*, 30: 3–11.

Patterson, G.R. and Yoerger, K. (1997) 'A Developmental Model for Late-onset Delinquency', in D.W. Osgood (ed.) *Motivation and Delinquency: Nebraska Symposium on Motivation.* Lincoln, NE: University of Nebraska Press.

Pavlich, G.C. (1996) *Justice Fragmented: Mediating Community Disputes Under Postmodern Conditions.* London: Routledge.

Pearson, G. (1983) *Hooligan: A History of Respectable Fears.* London: Macmillan.

Peled, D. (2013) 'Labour's Legacy: Six Years of What Exactly', *The Conversation.* http://the conversation.com/labors-legacy-six-years-of-what-exactly-17526 (accessed: 2 July 2015).

Persky, H., Smith, K.D. and Basu, G.K. (1971) 'Relation of Psychological Measures of Aggression and Hostility to Testosterone Production in Man', *Psychosomatic Medicine*, 33: 265–75.

Petrosino, A., Turpin-Petrosino, C. and Finckenauer, J.O. (2000) 'Well-meaning Programs Can Have Harmful Effects! Lessons from Experiments of Programs Such as Scared Straight', *Crime and Delinquency*, 46: 354–79.

Philip, K. (1997) 'New Perspectives on Mentoring: Young People, Youth Work and Mentoring', unpublished PhD thesis, University of Aberdeen.

Philips, D. and Storch, R. (1999) *Policing Provincial England, 1829–1856*. Leicester: Leicester University Press.

Piaget, J. (1977) *The Department of Thought*. New York: Viking Press.

Pickford, J. (ed.) (2000) *Youth Justice: Theory and Practice*. London, Cavendish.

Pihl, R.O. (1982) 'Hair Element Levels of Violent Criminals', *Canadian Journal of Psychiatry*, 27: 533–45.

Pihl, R.O. and Peterson, J.B. (1993) 'Alcohol/Drug Use and Aggressive Behaviour', in S. Hodgins (ed.) *Moral Disorder and Crime*. Newbury Park, CA: Sage.

Pinchbeck, I. and Hewitt, M. (1973) *Children in English Society*, Vol. 2. London: Routledge & Kegan Paul.

Pinchbeck, I. and Hewitt, M. (1981) 'Vagrancy and Delinquency in an Urban Setting', in M. Fitzgerald, G. McLennan and J. Pawson (eds) *Crime and Society: Readings in History and Theory*. London: Routledge and Kegan Paul/Open University Press.

Pinheiro, P.S. (2006) *World Report on Violence against Children*. Geneva: United Nations.

Pitts, J. (1982) 'Policy, Delinquency and the Practice of Youth Control 1964–81', *Youth and Policy*, 1(1): 25–48.

Pitts, J. (1986) 'Black Young People and Juvenile Crime: Some Unanswered Questions', in R. Matthews and J. Young (eds) *Confronting Crime*. London: Sage.

Pitts, J. (1988) *The Politics of Juvenile Crime*. London: Sage.

Pitts, J. (1996) 'The Politics and Practice of Youth Crime', in E. McLaughlin and J. Muncie (eds) *Controlling Crime*. London: Sage in Association with the Open University.

Pitts, J. (2000) 'The New Youth Justice and the Politics of Electoral Anxiety', in B. Goldson (ed.) *The New Youth Justice*. Lyme Regis: Russell House.

Pitts, J. (2001a) *The New Politics of Youth Crime: Discipline or Solidarity*. Basingstoke: Macmillan/Palgrave.

Pitts, J. (2001b) 'The New Correctionalism: Young People, Youth Justice and New Labour', in R. Matthews and J. Pitts, *Crime, Disorder and Community Safety: A New Agenda?* London: Routledge.

Pitts, J. (2003a) 'Youth Justice in England and Wales', in R. Matthews and J. Young, *The New Politics of Crime and Punishment*. Cullompton: Willan.

Pitts, J. (2003b) 'Changing Justice', *Youth Justice*, 3(1): 5–20.

Pitts, J. (2005) Bedfordshire: Action for Children.

Platt, A. (1969) 'The Rise of the Child-Saving Movement', *The Annals*, 381: 21–38.

Pollock, L.A. (1983) *Forgotten Children: Parent Child Relations from 1500–1900*. Cambridge: Cambridge University Press.

Power, M. (1997) *The Audit Society: Rituals of Verification*. Oxford: Oxford University Press.

Pratt, J. (1989) 'Corporatism: The Third Model of Juvenile Justice', *British Journal of Criminology*, 29: 236–54.

Pratt, J. (2008a) 'Scandinavian Exceptionalism in an Era of Penal Excess – Part I: The Nature and Roots of Scandinavian Exceptionalism', *British Journal of Criminology*, 48(2): 119–37.

Pratt, J. (2008b) 'Scandinavian Exceptionalism in an Era of Penal Excess – Part II: Does Scandinavian Exceptionalism Have a Future?', *British Journal of Criminology*, 48(3): 275–92.

Presdee, M. (2000) *Cultural Criminology and the Carnival of Crime*. London: Routledge.

Price, W.H. and Whatmore, P.B. (1967) 'Behaviour Disorders and Patterns of Crime among XYY Males Identified at a Maximum Security Hospital', *British Medical Journal*, 1: 533.

Prinz, R.J., Roberts, W.A. and Hantman, E. (1980) 'Dietary Correlates of Hyperactive Behaviour in Children', *Journal of Consulting and Clinical Psychology*, 48: 760–85.

Prior, D., Farrow, K., Hughes, N., Kelly, G., Manders, G., White, S. and Wilkinson, B. (2011) Maturity, Young Adults and Criminal Justice: A Literature Review. University of Birmingham. http://www.t2a.org.uk/wp-content/uploads/2011/09/Birmingham University-Maturity-final-literature-review-report.pdf.

Prison Reform Trust. (2008) Criminal Damage: Why We Should Lock Up Fewer Children. http://www.prisonreformtrust.org.uk/Portals/0/Documents/CriminalDamage.pdf (accessed 2 July 2015).

Prison Service (1989) *The 1998/99 Prison Service Annual Report*. London: The Prison Service.

Pryce, K. (1979) *Endless Pressure: A Study of West Indian Life-styles in Bristol*. Harmondsworth: Penguin.

Radford, L., Corral, S., Bradley, C., Fisher, H. and Bassett, C. (2011) *Child Abuse and Neglect in the UK Today*. London: NSPCC.

Raloff, J. (1983) 'Locks – A Key to Violence', *Science News*, 124: 122–36.

Ramdin, R. (1987) *The Making of the Black Working Class in Britain*. Aldershot: Wildwood House.

Ratledge, L. (2012) Inhuman, Sentencing: Life Imprisonment of Children in the Commonwealth, *Child Rights Information Network*. http://www.crin.org/violence/search/closeup.asp?infoID=29148 (accessed 4 August 2015).

Reckless, W.C. (1967) *The Crime Problem*. New York: Apple-Century-Crofts.

Redl, F. and Wineman, D. (1951) *Children Who Hate*. New York: Free Press.

Redondo, S., Sánchez-Meca, J. and Garrido, V. (1999) 'The Influence of Treatment Programmes on the Recidivism of Juvenile and Adult Offenders: A European Meta-analytic Review', *Psychology, Crime and Law*, 5: 251–78.

Reid, K. (1997) 'The Abolition of Cautioning? Juveniles in the "Last Chance" Saloon', *The Criminal Lawyer*, December: 4–8.

Reiner, R. (2000) *The Politics of the Police*, 3rd edn. Oxford: Oxford University Press.

Reiss, A.J. (1951) 'Delinquency as the Failure of Personal and Social Controls', *American Sociological Review*, 16: 213–39.

Reith, C. (1956) *A New Study of Police History*. London: Oliver and Boyd.

Rhodes, J., Contreras, J.M. and Mangelsdorf, S.C. (1995) 'Natural Mentor Relationships among Latina Adolescent Mothers, Psychological Adjustment, Moderating Processes and the Role of Early Parental Acceptance', *American Journal of Community Psychology*, (22): 211–28.

Rhodes, J., Ebert, L. and Fischer, K. (1992) 'Natural Mentors: An Overlooked Resource in the Social Networks of Adolescent Mothers', *American Journal of Community Psychology*, 20(4): 445–61.

Robins, L.N. and Hills, S.Y. (1966) 'Assessing the Contribution of Family Structure, Class and Peer Groups to Juvenile Delinquency', *Journal of Criminal Law, Criminology and Police Science*, 578: 325–34.

Rohrer, R. (1982) 'Lost in the Myths of Crime', *New Statesman*, 22 January.

Rose, N. (1999) *Powers of Freedom: Reframing Political Thought*. Cambridge: Cambridge University Press.

Rose, N. and Miller, P. (1992) 'Political Power Beyond the State: Problematics of Government', *British Journal of Sociology*, 43(2): 173–205.

Rose, R.M., Bernstein, I.S., Gorden, T.P. and Catlin, S.E. (1974) 'Androgens and Aggression: A Review and Recent Findings in Primates', in R.L. Holloway (ed.) *Primate Aggression: Territoriality and Xenophobia*. New York: Academia Press.

Rosen, Q. (1994) 'Knowledge Use in Direct Practice', *Social Service Review*, 68(4): 561–77.

Rosenthal, M. (1986) *The Character Factory. Baden Powell and the Origins of the Boy Scout Movement*. London: Collins.

Ross, P. (2003) 'Marxism and Communitarianism', *Imprints*, 6(3): 215–43.

Rowe, D.C. (1990) 'Inherited Dispositions toward Learning Delinquent and Criminal Behaviour: New Evidence', in L. Ellis and H. Hoffman (eds) *Crime in Biological, Social and Moral Contexts*. New York: Praeger.

Rowe, D.C. and Rogers, J.L. (1989) 'Behaviour Genetics, Adolescent Deviance, and "d": Contributions and Issues', in G.R. Adams, R. Montemayor and T.P. Gullotta (eds) *Advances in Adolescent Development*. Newbury Park, CA: Sage.

Joseph Rowntree Foundation (1995) *Income and Wealth: Report of the JRF Inquiry Group, Summary*. York: Joseph Rowntree.

Rothman, D. (1971) *The Discovery of the Asylum: Social Order and Disorder in the New Republic*. Boston, MA: Routledge and Kegan Paul.

Rothman, D. (1980) *Conscience and Convenience: The Asylum and Its Alternatives in Progressive America*. Boston: Little Brown.

Royal Society (2011) *Brain Waves 4: Neuroscience and the Law*. London: Science Policy Centre, Royal Society.

Runnymede (1996) *Runnymede Bulletin*, No. 292, February: 6–7.

Rusche, G. and Kirchheimer, O. (1968; orig. pub. 1938) *Punishment and Social Structure*. New York: Russell and Russell.

Rutherford, A. (1978) 'Decarceration of Young Offenders in Massachusetts', in N. Tutt (ed.) *Alternative Strategies for Coping with Crime*. Oxford: Blackwell/ Martin Robertson.

Rutherford, A. (1992) *Growing Out of Crime*, 2nd edn. London: Waterside Press.

Rutter, M. (1981) *Maternal Deprivation Reassessed*. Harmondsworth: Penguin.

Rutter, M. and Giller, H. (1983) *Juvenile Delinquency: Trends and Perspectives*. Harmondsworth: Penguin.

Rutter, M., Giller, H. and Hagell, A. (1998) *Anti-social Behaviour by Young People*. Cambridge: Cambridge University Press.

Sampson, R. and Laub, J. (1993) *Crime in the Making: Pathways and Turning Points through Life*. Cambridge, MA: Harvard University Press.

Sandin, B. (1986) 'Home, Street, Factory or Schools. Popular Education and Childcare in Swedish Cities 1600–1850', dissertation, Linköping University.

Saunders, W. (1984) *Alcohol Use in Britain: How Much Is Too Much?* Edinburgh: Scottish Health Education Unit.

Save the Children UK (2007) *The Small Hands of Slavery*. London: Save the Children UK.

Scales, M. and Gibbons, R. (1996) 'Extended Family Members and Unrelated Adults in the Lives of Young Adolescents: A Research Agenda', *Journal of Early Adolescence*, 16(4): 365–89.

Scarmella, T.J. and Brown, W.A. (1978) 'Serum Testosterone and Aggressiveness in Hockey Players', *Psychosomatic Medicine*, 40: 262–75.

Schaffer, H.R. (1990) *Making Decisions about Children: Psychological Questions and Answers*. Oxford: Blackwell.

Schalling, D. (1987) 'Personality Correlates of Plasma Testosterone Levels in Young Delinquents: An Example of Person-Situation Interaction', in S.A. Mednick, T.E. Moffit and S.A. Stack (eds) *The Causes of Crime: New Biological Approaches*. Cambridge: Cambridge University Press.

Sclater, S.D. and Piper, C. (2000) 'Remoralising the Family? Family Policy, Family Law and Youth Justice', *Child and Family Law Quarterly*, 12(3): 135–51.

Scraton, P. and Chadwick, K. (1996; orig. pub. 1992) 'The Theoretical Priorities of Critical Criminology', in J. Muncie, E. McLaughlin and M. Langan (eds) *Criminological Perspectives: A Reader*. London: Sage.

Scruton, R. (1980) *The Meaning of Conservatism*. Harmondsworth: Pelican.

Scruton, R. (1985) *Thinkers of the New Left*. London: Longman.

Scruton, R. (2001) *The Meaning of Conservatism*, 3rd edn. Houndmills: Palgrave.

Shah, S.A. and Roth, L.H. (1974) 'Biological and Psychophysiological Factors in Criminality', in D. Glaser (ed.) *Handbook of Criminology*. London: Rand McNally.

Shapland, J., Atkinson, A., Atkinson, J., Dignan, J., Edwards, L., Hibbert, J., Howes, M., Johnstone, J., Robinson, G. and Sorsby, A. (2008) 'Does Restorative Justice Affect Reconviction? The Fourth Report from the Evaluation of Three Schemes', Ministry of Justice Research Series, 10/08.

Sharland, E. (2006) 'Young People, Risk Taking and Risk Making: Some Thoughts for Social Work', *British Journal of Work*, 36: 247–65.

Shaw, C. and McKay, H.D. (1972; orig. pub. 1931) *Juvenile Delinquency and Urban Areas*. Chicago: University of Chicago Press.

Shea, G.F. (1992) *Mentoring: A Guide to the Basics*. London: Kogan Page.

Sheldon, B. (1995) *Cognitive-Behavioural Therapy: Research, Practice and Philosophy*. London: Routledge.

Sheldon, W.H. (1949) *Varieties of Delinquent Youth*. London: Harper.

Sherman, L. and Strang, H. (1997) 'Restorative Justice and Deterring Crime', RISE Working Papers. Canberra: Australian National University.

Shoenthaler, S.J. (1982) 'The Effects of Blood Sugar on the Treatment and Control of Antisocial Behaviour: A Double-Blind Study of an Incarcerated Juvenile Population', *International Journal for Biosocial Research*, 3: 1–15.

Simon, B. (1965) *Education and the Labour Movement 1870–1920*. London: Lawrence and Wishart.

Skinner, B.F. (1984) 'The Evolution of Behavior', *Journal of Experimental Behavior*, 41(2): 217–21.

Smith, D.E. and Smith, D.D. (1977) 'Eysenck's Psychoticism Scale and Reconviction', *British Journal of Criminology*, 17: 387.

Smith, R. (2003) *Youth Justice: Ideas, Policy, Practice*. Cullompton: Willan.

Smith, R. (2006) 'Actuarialism and Early Intervention in Contemporary Youth Justice', in B. Goldson and J. Muncie (eds) *Youth Crime & Justice: Critical Issues*. London: Sage.

Smith, R. (2007) *Youth Justice: Ideas, Policy, Practice*, 2nd edn. Cullompton: Willan.

Solomon, E. and Garside, R. (2008) *Ten Years of Labour's Youth Justice Reforms: An Independent Audit*. London: Centre for Crime and Justice Studies.

Spelman, W. (1994) *Criminal Incapacitation*. New York: Plenum.

Spergel, I.A. (1964) *Racketsville, Slumtown, Haulburg*. Chicago: University of Chicago Press.

Spergel, I.A. (1995) *The Youth Gang Problem: A Community Approach*. Oxford: Oxford University Press.

Springhall, J. (1977) *Youth, Empire and Society: British Youth Movements 1883–1940*. London: Croom Helm.

Springhall, J. (1986) *Coming of Age: Adolescence in Britain 1860–1960*. Dublin: Gill and Macmillan.

Squires, P. (2006) *Understanding Community Safety*. Bristol: Policy Press.

Squires, P. and Stephen, D.E. (2005) *Rougher Justice: Anti-social Behaviour and Young People*. Cullompton: Willan.

Stedman Jones, G. (1984) *Outcast London: A Study in Relationships between Classes in Victorian Society*, 2nd edn. Harmondsworth: Penguin.

Stenson, K. and Edwards, A. (2003) 'Crime Control and Local Governance: The Struggle for Sovereignty in Advanced Liberal Polities', *Contemporary Politics*, 9(2): 203–17.

Stenson, K. and Watt, P. (1999) 'Governmentality and the Death of the Social? A Discourse Analysis of Local Government Texts in the South-east of England', *Urban Studies*, 36(1): 189–201.

Stephenson, M., Giller, H. and Brown, S. (2007) *Effective Practice in Youth Justice*, 2nd edn. Cullompton: Willan Publishing.

Stern, V. (1998) *A Sin against the Future: Imprisonment in the World*. London: Penguin.

Stewart, D., Gossop, M., Marsden, J. and Rolfe, A. (2000) 'Drug Misuse and Acquisitive Crime among Clients Recruited to the National Treatment Outcome Research (NTORS)', *Criminal Behaviour and Mental Health*, 10: 13–24.

St James Roberts, I. and Samlal Singh, C. (2001) *Can Mentors Help Primary School Children with Behaviour Problems?* Home Office Research Study No. 233. London: Home Office.

St James Roberts, I., Greenlaw, G., Simon, A. and Hurry, J. (2004) *National Evaluation of Youth Justice Board Mentoring Schemes 2001 to 2004*. London: Youth Justice Board.

Storch, R. (1975) 'The Plague of the Blue Locusts: Police Reform and Popular Resistance in Northern England 1840–57', *International Review of Social History*, 20: 61–90.

Storch, R. (1989) 'Policing Rural Southern England before the Police: Opinion and Practice 1830–1856', in D. Hay and F. Snyder (eds) *Policing and Prosecution*. Oxford: Clarendon Press.

Strachan, R. and Tallant, C. (1997) 'Improving Judgement and Appreciating Biases within the Risk Assessment Process', in H. Kemshall and J. Pritchard (eds) *Good Practice in Risk Assessment and Risk Management 2*. London: Jessica Kingsley.

Strang, H. (1995) 'Replacing Courts with Conferences', *Policing*, 11(3): 21–30.

Strang, H. (2000) 'Victim Participation in a Restorative Justice Process: The Canberra Reintegrative Shaming Experiments', PhD dissertation, Law Program, Research School of Social Sciences. Canberra: Australian National University.

Strang, H. (2001) *Repair or Revenge: Victim Participation in Restorative Justice*. Oxford: Oxford University Press.

Steedman, C. (1984) *Policing the Victorian Community*. London: Routledge & Kegan Paul.

Street, R. (2000) *Restorative Justice Steering Group, Review of Existing Research*. London: Home Office (unpublished).

Street, S. (2010) *Safeguarding the Future: A review of the Youth Justice Board's Governance and Operating Arrangements*. London: The Stationary Office.

Styles, M. and Morrow, K. (1992) *Understanding How Elders and Youth Form Relationships: A Study of Four Linking Lifetimes Projects*. Philadelphia, PA: Public/Private Ventures.

Susser, M. (1998) 'Does Risk Factor Epidemiology Put Epidemiology at Risk? Peering into the Future', *Journal of Epidemiology and Community Health*. http://proquest.umi.com/pqdlink?

Sutherland, E.H. (1939) *Principle of Criminology*. Chicago: Lippincott.

Sykes, G. and Matza, D. (1957) 'Techniques of Neutralization: A Theory of Delinquency', *American Sociological Review*, 22: 664–70.

Szapocznik, J., Rio, A., Murray, E., Cohen, R., Scopetta, M.A., Rivas-Vasquz, A., Hervis, O.E. and Poseda, V. (1989) 'Structural Family versus Psychodynamic Child Therapy for Problematic Hispanic Boys', *Journal of Consulting and Clinical Psychology*, 57(5): 571–8.

Szreter, S. and Ishkanian, A. (2012) 'Introduction: What Is a Big Society?: Contemporary Social Policy in a Historical and Comparative Perspective', in A. Ishkanian and S. Szreter (eds), *The Big Society Debate: A Brand New Agenda for Social Policy?* Cheltenham: Edward Elgar.

TA2 (2009) *Young Adult Manifesto*. London: Barrow Cadbury.

Tappan, P.W. (1960) *Crime, Justice and Correction*. New York: McGraw-Hill.

Tarde, G. (1969) 'On Communication and Social Influence', in T. Clark (ed.) *Gabriel Tarde on Communication and Social Influence*. Chicago: University of Chicago Press.

Tarling, R. (1993) *Analysing Offending: Data, Models and Interpretations*. London: HMSO.

Tarling, R. and Adams, M. (2013) *Summer Arts Colleges Evaluation Report 2007–12*. London: Unitas.

Taylor, C.S. (1990) *Dangerous Society*. East Lansing, MI: Michigan State University Press.

Taylor, I. (1997) 'The Political Economy of Crime', in M. Maguire, R. Morgan and R. Reiner (eds) *The Oxford Handbook of Criminology*, 2nd edn. Oxford: Clarendon Press.

Taylor, I., Walton, P. and Young, J. (1973) *The New Criminology: For a Social Theory of Deviance*. London: Routledge & Kegan Paul.

Taylor, L., Lacey, R. and Bracken, D. (1979) *In Whose Best Interests: The Unjust Treatment of Children in Courts and Institutions*. London: Cobden Trust/Mind.

Thane, P. (1981) 'Childhood in History', in M. King, (ed.) *Childhood, Welfare and Justice*. London: Batsford.

Thane, P. (1982) *The Foundations of the Welfare State*. Harlow: Longman.

Thom, D. (2003) 'The Healthy Citizen of Empire or Juvenile Delinquent? Beating and Mental Health in the UK', in M. Gijswijt-Hofstra and H. Marland (eds) *Cultures of Child Health in Britain and the Netherlands in the 20th Century*. Amsterdam: Editions Rodopi.

Thomas, D.W. and Hyman, J.M. (1978) 'Compliance, Theory, Control Theory and Juvenile Delinquency', in M. Krohn and R.L. Acker (eds) *Crime, Law and Sanctions*. London: Sage.

Thomas, T. (2005) 'The Continuing Story of the ASBO', *Youth and Policy*, 87: 1–14.

Thompson, W.E., Mitchell, J. and Doddler, R.A. (1984) 'An Empirical Test of Hirschi's Control Theory of Delinquency', *Deviant Behavior*, 5: 11–22.

Thornberry, T. (2005) 'Explaining Multiple Patters of Offending across the Life Course and across Generations', *Annals of the American Academy of Political and Social Science*, 602: 296–302.

Thorpe, D., Green, C.J. and Smith, D. (1980) 'Punishment and Welfare', Occasional Papers in Social Administration, No. 4, University of Lancaster.

Tierney, J.P. and Grossman, J.B., with Resch, N.L. (1995) *Making a Difference: An Impact Study of Big Brothers/Big Sisters*. Philadelphia, PA: Public/Private Ventures.

Tolman, E.C. (1959) 'Principles of Purposive Behaviour ', in S. Koch and D.E. Leary (eds) *A Century of Psychology as a Science*. New York: McGraw-Hill.

Tomás, C. (2009) Childhood and Rights: Reflections on the UN Convention on the Rights of the Child. http://www.childhoodstoday.org/download.php?id=19 (accessed 10 August 2015).

Tonry, M. (2001) 'Symbol, Substance and Severity in Western Penal Policies', *Punishment and Society*, 3(4): 517–36.

Tonry, M. (2009) 'Explanations of American Punishment Policies', *Punishment and Society*, 11(3): 377–94.

Trasler, G. (1967) *The Explanation of Criminality*. Routledge & Kegan Paul.

Trasler, G. (1986) 'Situational Crime Control and Rational Choice: A Critique', in K. Heal and G. Laycock (eds) *Situational Crime Prevention: From Theory into Practice*. London: HMSO.

Trinder, L. and Reynolds, S. (eds) (2000) *Evidence-based Practice: A Critical Appraisal*. Oxford: Blackwell Science.

Trotter, C. (1999) *Working with Involuntary Clients: A Guide to Practice*. London: Sage.

Tutt, N. (1981) 'A Decade of Policy', *British Journal of Criminology*, 21(4): 246–56.

Tzannetakis, T. (2001) 'Neo-Conservative Criminology', in McLaughlin and J. Muncie (eds) *The Sage Dictionary of Criminology*. London: Sage.

UKADCU (United Kingdom Anti-Drugs Co-ordinating Unit) (1998) *Tackling Drugs to Build a Better Britain: The Government's 10-year Strategy for Tackling Drug Misuse*. London: The Stationery Office.

Umbreit, M. and Roberts, A. (1996). *Mediation of Criminal Conflict in England: An Assessment of Services in Coventry and Leeds*. Rochester, MN: Center for Restorative Justice and Mediation, University of Minnesota.

UNICEF (2007) *Child Poverty in Perspective: An Overview of Child Well-being in Rich Countries*, Innocenti Report Card 7. Florence: UNICEF Innocenti Research Centre.

UNICEF (2009) *The State of the World's Children*. Florence: UNICEF.

UNICEF (2010) *The Children Left Behind: A League Table of Inequality in Child Well-being in the World's Rich Countries*, Innocenti Report Card 9. Florence: UNICEF Innocenti Research Centre.

UNICEF (2013) *Child Well Being in Rich Countries: A Comparative Overview*, Innocenti Report Card 11. Florence: UNICEF, Innocenti Research Centre.

United Nations Committee on the Rights of the Child (2007) General Comment No. 10: Children's Rights in Juvenile Justice, Forty-fourth session, 15 January–2 February. Geneva: Office of the High Commissioner for Human Rights.

United Nations Committee on the Rights of the Child (2008) Consideration of Reports Submitted by States Parties Under Article 44 of the Convention: United Kingdom of Great Britain and Northern Ireland, CRC/C/GBR/CO/4. Geneva: Office of the High Commissioner for Human Rights.

United Nations Committee on the Rights of the Child (2012) Consideration of Reports Submitted by States Parties Under Article 44 of the Convention: Concluding Observations Australia, CRC/C/AUS/CO/4. Geneva: Office of the High Commissioner for Human Rights.

United Nations General Assembly (1985) *United Nations Standard Minimum Rules for the Administration of Juvenile Justice*. New York: United Nations.

United Nations General Assembly (1989) *United Nations Convention on the Rights of the Child*. New York: United Nations.

United Nations General Assembly (1990a) *United Nations Guidelines for the Prevention of Juvenile Delinquency*. New York: United Nations.

United Nations General Assembly (1990b) *United Nations Rules for the Protection of Juveniles Deprived of Their Liberty*. New York: United Nations.

United Nations General Assembly (2012) Report of the Committee on the Rights of the Child. New York: United Nations.

United Nations Office on Drugs and Crime (2011) Juveniles Held in Prisons, Penal Institutions or Correctional Institutions, Table CTS 2011. http://www.unodc.org/unodc/en/data-and-analysis/statistics/data.html (accessed 13 August 2015).

US Department of Justice (2011) *Prisoners in 2010*. Washington, DC: Bureau of Justice Statistics, NCJ 236096.

Utting, D. (1996) *Reducing Criminality among Young People: A Sample of Relevant Programmes in the UK*, Home Office Research Study No. 161. London: HMSO.

Utting, D. and Vennard, J. (2000) *What Works with Young Offenders in the Community?* Ilford: Barnado's.

Utting, W., Bright, J. and Hendrickson, P. (1993) 'Crime and the Family, Improving Child Rearing and Preventing Delinquency', Paper No. 16. London: Family Policy Studies Centre.

Van Ness, D. and Strong, K.H. (1997) *Restoring Justice*. Cincinnati, OH: Anderson.

Van Swaaningen, R. (2008) 'Sweeping the Street: Civil Society and Community Safety in Rotterdam', in J. Shapland (ed.) *Justice, Community and Civil Society: A Contested Terrain*. Cullompton: Willan.

Virkkunen, M. (1987) 'Metabolic Dysfunctions amongst Habitually Violent Offenders: Reactive Hypoglycaemia and Cholesterol Levels', in S.A. Mednick, T.E. Moffit and S.A. Stack (eds) *The Causes of Crime: New Biological Approaches*. Cambridge: Cambridge University Press.

Vizard, E., Hickey, N., French, L. and McCory, E. (2011) 'Children and Adolescents Who Present with Sexually Abusive Behaviour: A UK Descriptive Study', *Journal of Forensic Psychiatry and Psychology*, 18(1): 59–73.

Vold, G.B., Bernard, T.J. and Snipes, J.B. (1998) *Theoretical Criminology*, 4th edn. Oxford: Oxford University Press.

Von Hirsch, A. and Ashworth, A. (2005) *Proportionate Sentencing: Exploring the Principles*. Oxford: Oxford University Press.

Wacquant, L. (1999) 'How Penal Common Sense Comes to Europeans', *European Societies*, 1(3): 319–52.

Wacquant, L. (2008) 'Ordering Insecurity: Social Polarisation and the Punitive Upsurge', *Radical Philosophy Review*, 11(1): 9–27.

Wacquant, L. (2009a) *Prisons of Poverty*. Minneapolis, MN: University of Minnesota Press.

Wacquant, L. (2009b) *Urban Outcasts: A Comparative Sociology of Advanced Marginality*. Cambridge: Polity Press.

Wacquant, L. (2012) 'Probing the Meta-Prison', in J.I. Ross (ed.) *The Globalisation of Supermax Prisons*. New Brunswick: Rutgers University Press.

Wadham, J. and Modi, K. (2003) 'National Security and Open Government in the United Kingdom', in *National Security and Open Government: Striking the Right Balance*. Syracuse, NY: Campbell Public Affairs Institute.

Walker, M. (1983) 'Some Problems in Interpreting Statistics Relating to Crime', *Journal of the Royal Statistical Society Series A*, 146, part 3: 282–93.

Walklate, S. (1998) '"No More Excuses!" Young People, Victims and Making Amends', *Policy Studies*, 19(3): 213–22.

Wallace, C. (1987) *For Richer, For Poorer: Growing Up In and Out of Work*. London: Tavistock.

Walsh, C. (1999) 'Imposing Order: Child Safety Orders and Local Child Curfew Schemes', *Journal of Social Welfare and Family Law*, 21(2): 135–49.

Walvin, J. (1982) *A Child's World: A Social History of Childhood 1800–1914*. Harmondsworth: Penguin.

Ward, J. and Bayley, M. (2007) 'Young People's Perceptions of "Risk"', in B. Thom, R. Sales and J. Pearce (eds) *Growing Up With Risk*. Bristol: Policy Press.

Ward, T. and Maruna, S. (2007) *Rehabilitation: Beyond the Risk Paradigm*. London: Routledge.

Warner, N. (1992) *Choosing with Care – The Report of the Committee of Inquiry into the Selection: Development and Management of Staff in Children's Homes*. London: HMSO.

Warner, N. (1999) 'Implementing the Youth Justice Reforms', Youth Justice: A Conference for the Bedfordshire & Hertfordshire, & Kent, East & West Sussex Area Committees: Conference Report, para 5–37.

Wasik, M. (1999) Reparation: Sentencing and the Victim', *Criminal Law Review*, 470–9.

Wasserman, G., Miller, L., Pinner, E. and Jaramillo, B. (1996) 'Parenting Predictors of the Development of Conduct Problems in High-risk Boys', *Journal of the American Academy of Child and Adolescent Psychiatry*, 35: 1227–36.

Wedd, S. (2000) 'The Criminal Lawyers Reaction to Youth Court Referral Orders', *Criminal Practitioners Newsletter (Law Society)*, October 1–2.

Weiner, M.J. (1990) *Reconstructing the Criminal Culture, Law and Policy in England, 1830–1914*. Cambridge: Cambridge University Press.

West, D.J. (1967) *The Young Offender*. New York: International Universities Press.

West, D.J. (1969) *Present Conduct and Future Delinquency*. London: Heinemann.

West, D.J. and Farrington, D.P. (1973) *Who Becomes Delinquent?* London: Heinemann.

Westergaard, J. (1995) *Who Gets What? The Hardening of Class Inequality in the Late Twentieth Century*. Cambridge: Polity Press.

White, J. (1980) *Rothschild Buildings: Life in an East End Tenement Block 1887–1920*. London: Routledge and Kegan Paul.

Whyte, B. (2009) *Youth Justice in Practice: Making a Difference*. Bristol: Policy Press.

Wikström, P.-O. and Sampson, R. (eds) (2009) *The Explanation of Crime: Context, Mechanisms and Development*. Cambridge: Cambridge University Press.

Wilcox, A. (2003) 'Evidence-based Youth Justice? Some Valuable Lessons from and Evaluation for the Youth Justice Board', *Youth Justice*, 3(1): 21–35.

Wilkins, L. (1964) *Social Deviance*. London: Tavistock.

Wilkinson, C. (1995) *The Drop-Out Society: Young People on the Margin*. Leicester: Youth Work Press.

Wilkinson, R.G. and Pickett, K.E. (2007) 'The Problems of Relative Deprivation: Why Some Societies Do Better than Others', *Social Science & Medicine*, 65(9): 1965–78.

Wilkinson, R.G. and Pickett, K.E. (2009) *The Spirit Level*. London: Allen Lane.

Willets, D. (1995) *Civic Conservatism*. London: The Social Market Foundation.

Williams, T. (1989) *The Cocaine Kids: The Inside Story of a Teenage Drug Ring*. Reading, MA: Addison-Wesley

Williamson, H. (1997) 'Status Zero Youth and the Underclass', in R. MacDonald (ed.) *Youth the 'Underclass' and Social Exclusion*. London: Routledge.

Willis, P. (1977) *Learning to Labour*. London: Saxon House.

Wills, T.A., Vaccaro, D., McNamara, G. and Hirky, E.A. (1996) 'Escalated Substance Use: A Longitudinal Grouping Analysis from Early to Middle Adolescence', *Journal of Abnormal Psychology*, April: 166–80.

Wilmott, P. (1966) *Adolescent Boys in East London*. London: Routledge & Kegan Paul.

Wilson, H. (1980) 'Parental Supervision: A Neglected Aspect of Delinquency', *British Journal of Criminology*, 20: 315–27.

Wilson, J.Q. and Herrnstein, R.J. (1985) *Crime and Human Nature*. New York: Simon and Schuster.

Wilson, S.J. and Lipsey, M.W. (2000) 'Wilderness Challenge Programs for Delinquent Youth: A Meta-analysis of Outcome Evaluations', *Evaluation and Program Planning*, 23: 1–12.

Wilson, W.J. (1987) *The Truly Disadvantaged*. Chicago: University of Chicago Press.

Wilson, W.J. (1991) 'Public Policy Research and the Truly Disadvantaged', in C. Jencks and P.E. Peterson (eds) *The Urban Underclass*. Washington, DC: The Brookings Institution.

Windlesham, Lord (1993) *Responses to Crime (Vol 2): Penal Policy in the Making*. Oxford: Oxford University Press.

Winlow, S. and Hall, S. (2013) *Rethinking Social Exclusion: The End of the Social?* London: Sage.

Witkin, H.A., Mednick, S.A. and Schulsinger, F. (1977) 'XYY and XXY Men: Criminality and Aggression', in S.A. Mednick and K.O. Christiansen (eds) *Biosocial Bases of Criminal Behaviour*. New York: Gardner Press.

Wolfgang, M.E. and Ferracuti, F. (1967) *The Sub-Culture of Violence: Towards an Integrated Theory in Criminology*. Beverly Hills: Sage.

Wolfgang, M.E., Figlio, R.M. and Sellin, T. (1972) *Delinquency in a Birth Cohort*. Chicago: University of Chicago Press.

Wonnacott, C. (1999) 'The Counterfeit Contract: Reform, Pretence and Muddled Principles in the New Referral Order', *Child and Family Law Quarterly*, 11(3): 271–87.

Woolf, Lord Justice (1991) *Prison Disturbances April 1990: A Report of an Inquiry*, Cmnd 1456. London: Home Office.

Wootton, B. (1959) *Social Science and Social Pathology*. London: Allen & Unwin.

Wootton, B. (1962) 'A Social Scientist's Approach to Maternal Deprivation', in M.D. Ainsworth (ed.) *Deprivation of Maternal Care: A Reassessment of Its Effects*. Geneva: World Health Organisation.

World Health Organisation (2011) Youth Violence, Factsheet No. 356. http://www.who.int/mediacentre/factsheets/fs356/en/ (accessed 31 August 2015).

Wright, R.A. (1993) 'A Socially Sensitive Criminal Justice System', in J.W. Murphy and D.L. Peck (eds) *Open Institutions: The Hope for Democracy*. Westport, CT: Praeger.

Wynne, J. and Brown, I. (1998) 'Can Mediation Cut Re-offending?' *Probation Journal*, 46(1): 21–6.

Young, J. (1971) *The Drug Takers: The Social Meaning of Drugtaking*. London: Paladin.

Young, J. (1994) '"Incessant Chatter": Recent Paradigms in Criminology', in M. Maguire, R. Morgan and R. Reiner (eds) *The Oxford Handbook of Criminology*. Oxford: Clarendon Press.

Young, J. (1997) 'Left Realist Criminology: Radical in Its Analysis, Realist in Its Policy', in M. Maguire, R. Morgan and R. Reiner (eds) *Oxford Handbook of Criminology*, 2nd edn. Oxford: Oxford University Press.

Young, J. (1999) *The Exclusive Society: Social Exclusion, Crime and Difference in Late Modernity*. London: Sage.

Youth Justice Board (2001a) *Risk and Protective Factors Associated with Youth Crime and Effective Interventions to Prevent It*. London: Youth Justice Board.

Youth Justice Board (2001b) *Good Practice Guidelines for Restorative Work with Victims and Young Offenders*. London: Youth Justice Board.

Youth Justice Board (2002) *Youth Justice Board Review 2000/2002: Delivering Change*. London: Youth Justice Board.

Youth Justice Board (2008) *Assessment, Intervention Planning and Supervision* (Source Document). London: Youth Justice Board.

Youth Justice Board/Ministry of Justice (2015) *Youth Justice Statistics: 2013/14 England and Wales*. London: Youth Justice Board Ministry of Justice.

Zelizer, V. (1985) *Pricing the Priceless Child: The Changing Social Value of Children*. Princeton: University of Princeton Press.

Zimring, F. and Hawkins, G. (1973) *Deterrence*. Chicago: University of Chicago.

Author index

Subject index